TRIPLE JEOPARDY

TRIPLE JEOPARDY

A Story of Law

at Its Best — and Worst

ROGER PARLOFF

The American Lawyer/Little, Brown and Company

LITTLE BROWN AND COMPANY
Boston   New York   Toronto   London

FIRST EDITION

Library of Congress Cataloging-in-Publication Data
Parloff, Roger.
Triple jeopardy : how determined lawyers fought to save one man's life / Roger Parloff. — 1st ed.
p. cm.
"An American Lawyer / Little, Brown and Company title"
Includes index.
ISBN 0-316-69261-1
1. Knapp, John Henry — Trials, litigation, etc.   2. Trials (Arson) — Arizona.   3. Trials (Murder) — Arizona.   4. Capital punishment — Arizona.   5. Criminal justice, Administration of — Arizona.
I. Title.
KF224.K63P37   1996
364.1'523'09791 — dc20   95-53721

10 9 8 7 6 5 4 3 2 1

HAD

Published simultaneously in Canada by Little, Brown & Company (Canada) Limited

Printed in the United States of America

FOR MY PARENTS

Great moral issues . . . often cannot be fully understood without images. The death penalty is such an issue. . . .

On the evening of November 16, 1973, John Knapp entered the room of his two infant daughters. By pouring Coleman fuel throughout and lighting a match, he turned their sleeping place into a crematory. He then returned to lie down while his children burned. . . .

. . . [T]he failure to execute can be itself barbaric and brutal because with that failure society announces that it attaches a higher regard for depraved life than innocent life. . . . As George Will recently noted, [the death-penalty abolitionists'] only success has been in 'making people feel ashamed of sentiments essential for a decent society—sentiments such as anger about crime, and the desire for vengeance against criminals. Those are virtuous sentiments when grounded in a sense that the important laws express more than calculations of social utility. Those laws express a natural, life-enhancing moral order.'

We need cite no greater authority for the truth of this proposition than our visceral reaction to [such] images [as that of] Knapp—images by which we know the morality of executing deadly criminals.

—*Chief Assistant Arizona Attorney General Steven Twist,*
in PHOENIX MAGAZINE, *May 1981*

He's innocent. He's innocent.

—*Charles Diettrich, John Knapp's lawyer, on*
November 19, 1974, immediately after Knapp's
conviction

Contents

AUTHOR'S NOTE

In fairness to the lawyers depicted in the book, I should sound a note of caution to readers, especially readers who are themselves lawyers.

To reduce this book to readable length, I have omitted mention of many legal maneuvers and skirmishes that I considered minor in the grand scheme of things.

If a reader wonders at any stage in the book why a prosecutor or defense lawyer did not pursue a certain strategy, the answer may well be that the lawyer in question *did* pursue it and that it came to naught for complex reasons, or that the lawyer decided not to pursue it after careful consideration of a multitude of factors.

PART 1.

Get the S.O.B.

One

Witnesses said they first saw smoke sometime between 8:00 and 8:15 on Friday morning, November 16, 1973.

It was coming from a tract house in East Mesa, Arizona. John Henry Knapp, twenty-seven, lived there, along with his wife Linda, twenty-two, and their two little girls, Linda Louise, three and a half, and Iona Marie, two and a half. The older child was known as Little Linda, and the younger one they called Noni.

The Knapps' one-story, three-bedroom home — just 1,040 square feet in all — sat in the desert about twenty-five miles east of Phoenix. It was part of a new, federally subsidized development a few miles east of Mesa, then a town of about 63,000.

No freeways yet stretched that far east from Phoenix, and the nearest road from Mesa turned to gravel a block before reaching the cross street that led to the development.

The house at 7435 East Capri had just been built in January. In April, the Knapps had moved in. Like some of their neighbors, they did not yet have a grass lawn — an expensive undertaking in the desert.

The sun had risen at exactly 7:00 A.M. on November 16. Though the temperature had gotten up to 78 degrees the day before, it was a chilly 44 when the fire started.

A tall, Mexican-American neighbor of Knapp's, Dave Contreras, was probably the first to get to the scene. He ran half-dressed the fifty yards or so to the Knapps', entering the house through a back door.

"When I entered, John Knapp was coming in the house with the garden hose," he later testified, "and he was by the hallway. There was quite a bit of smoke, and there was a full blaze in the hallway. That's when I asked him if there was anyone in there. He turned around and very sarcastically said, 'Who do you think? My daughters are in there, and they're burned to death.' At some point another neighbor, Jim Garrison, came in the house. We were all trying to pour water into the hallway and get to the bedroom, but there was no way. The flames were over the hallway and the smoke was too great to even try."*

Shirley Grenko had just finished breakfast when she looked out the window and noticed smoke pouring out of the Knapps' cooler. (Houses in the development were equipped with large, box-shaped evaporative coolers on their shingle roofs. Coolers, which are less expensive to operate than air-conditioners, work well as long as the humidity is very low.) She shouted to her husband and son to bring a hose, and then ran over to the Knapps'. When she got there, Knapp was outside the burning bedroom window with a garden hose.

"He broke the window with the end of the hose — the nozzle," Grenko later testified. "Well, he had to jump back because the flames shot out about four feet. There was just a blast of black smoke. Mr. Knapp tried to get the hose up to the fire, but the flames were shooting out. The heat was intense."

Three other neighbors also said they saw Knapp break out the window with the hose.

Jim Garrison, who lived across the street from the Knapps, remembered learning about the fire when a neighbor came hammering at his door at what the neighbor said was 8:10 A.M. When Garrison looked outside, John and Linda Knapp were standing "toward the end of the driveway off on the grass," as he remembered it. Linda was "frantic . . . upset, and screaming, 'My babies are in there,'" while John Knapp appeared "calm and collected." While at least one other witness remembered Linda as "hysterical," at least six others said she showed suspiciously little emotion.

---

* Quotations in this chapter, which are drawn from court testimony, have been edited for brevity, clarity, and to convert question-and-answer colloquy into a narrative.

Garrison ran in the front door of the Knapp house and tried to crawl through the living room toward the fire on his belly, but there was too much smoke and heat. He came back out and got a hose from his house. He hooked it up to the spigot in the back of the Knapp house, since someone had already attached a hose to the spigot in front. He brought his own hose around to the front and tried to pour water in the window of the burning bedroom.

Garrison remembered the fire engines arriving some time shortly after that.

About five minutes after John broke the window out, as Shirley Grenko remembered it, John noticed her standing there.

John did not seem upset, according to Grenko. He was wearing a blue shirt, blue pants, and white shoes, she said.

Most neighbors who saw Knapp that morning remembered him as having worn white shoes. Two neighbors, however, said he was carrying his shoes in his hands when they first saw him and put them on only later. Days afterward, John and Linda would say that John had been wearing white socks at first and that after the firefighters put out the flames he returned to the house and got his shoes.

John asked Shirley Grenko if she would go across the street and console his wife, which she did. Linda, who was wearing a blue, flower-patterned terry-cloth robe, told Grenko she wanted to talk to her mother.

"We went over to a neighbor's house to use her phone," Grenko recalled. "After John broke the window, it seemed like it took the fire trucks fifteen to twenty minutes to come. It seemed like a long time."

At 8:28 A.M. the firefighters at Station 20 in Scottsdale got an alarm for a house fire, with children trapped inside, at 7435 East Capri. Eight firefighters set out for the fire in three trucks and a car.

Even before they left the station the firemen could see the thick, black smoke rising to the south less than two miles away.

Chief Geary Roberts's car and the attack truck arrived together at about 8:30. Heavy flames and smoke were rolling out the front middle bedroom window. Two half-dressed men were ineffectually pointing garden hoses at that window, which was already broken out.

A firefighter jumped from the attack truck and put on his air pack while his partner, a lieutenant, dragged a fire hose toward the front window.

The second truck pulled onto the vacant lot next door, and its men brought a second hose in through the back door.

5

— Is there anyone in there? — a fireman shouted to the two men with garden hoses.*

— There's two little girls trapped inside, — one screamed.

A tall, thin, awkward young man with black hair approached the firefighter.

— My two daughters are in there, and they're dead, — he said. — Forget about the house. —

John Knapp was fully dressed, according to the firemen, and not dirty or smoky.

Later, most neighbors remembered Knapp as having been very clean, with no smoke or soot on him. One neighbor, however, who said he saw Knapp at about the time the fire engines were arriving, remembered him being "all smoked over and dirty" and looking "like he had been fighting the fire." That neighbor, and one other, also remembered seeing Knapp wash his face at water spigots in front of other houses.

Two firefighters with air packs took up the line from the second truck and pulled it down the hall toward the flames that were pulsating from the open door leading to the children's bedroom. They attacked the fire from the inside while the lieutenant poured water in the window from the outside.

The fire kept flaring back, but after three or four minutes they knocked it down. Then they searched the rest of the house, looking for hot spots or survivors.

Although the whole house had suffered smoke damage, the fire had not spread to any other area except the hallway outside the bedroom.

In the living room the lieutenant found a large, unharmed tomcat. He picked him up and took him out of the house. Seeing Knapp, the lieutenant began to hand the cat to him.

— Throw the damn cat in the garbage, — Knapp told him. — I don't want it. Go back in there and find my kids. —

Another firefighter got a ladder and checked the attic for fire extension, looking through a scuttle hole in the carport.

— They're not in the attic, damn it, — Knapp told him.

---

* In this book, quotation marks are used only for words that were recorded by audiotape, videotape, stenographer, or by the author's notes. All other conversations are marked with dashes. The essential content of such conversations is undisputed, unless otherwise noted, and is drawn from accounts of the conversations provided by participants or witnesses to them, either in their testimony, interviews with police or lawyers, or, in later chapters, in interviews with the author.

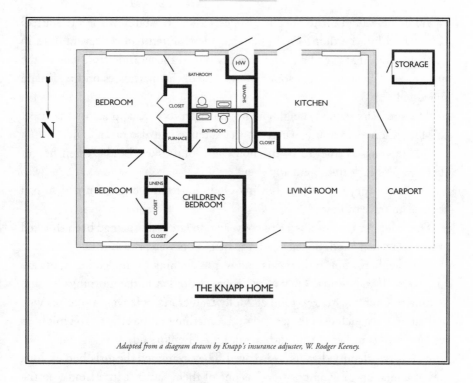

THE KNAPP HOME

Adapted from a diagram drawn by Knapp's insurance adjuster, W. Rodger Keeney.

When the children's room had cooled, Chief Roberts and a firefighter began removing the larger pieces of debris. A portion of the ceiling had come down, further obscuring the contents. But within a minute or two they found two charred objects with bones protruding from them.

"You couldn't really tell if they were human or animal," one fireman later wrote in his report. The smaller object, Iona, was found lying under the window on the north side of the room. Little Linda's body was found under the remains of a mattress near the west wall of the room.

Moments later John Knapp walked into the hallway.

— Can I help you? — asked Chief Roberts.

— I'm the father, — said Knapp, pushing past him and entering the bedroom.

Roberts pulled him back and then, not wanting him to see his children like this, said, — They're not in here. Are you sure they're in here? —

— I know they're in here, — Knapp responded, — and if you don't do something I'll knock your damn head off. —

Roberts asked a fireman to get a deputy sheriff to take Knapp out of the house.

While he waited for the deputy, Roberts asked Knapp how the fire started. Knapp told him he didn't know, but that the children had set several fires in the house and that they had once recently pulled the stuffing from one of the mattresses. Maybe they had somehow set one of the mattresses on fire, Knapp suggested.

At a fireman's request, neighbor Jim Garrison took Knapp across the street to Molly Cameron's house, where Shirley Grenko had also taken Linda.

— Are you sure they're in the house? — John asked Linda, when he got there. — We can't find them anywhere. —

— I know they're in there. Oh my God, don't tell me they burned so bad there is no trace of them. —

The neighbor who recalled this conversation later said she had been shocked at how detached Linda seemed. All the neighbors were, she said.

Two neighbors got in their cars and went searching for the children, in case they were off wandering. They were known to do that in the mornings.

Shirley Grenko also saw John at Molly Cameron's. "He went up to his wife and sat on the couch next to her and said something to the effect, 'You might as well get it in your head. Your kids are dead,' " Grenko said.

By 8:55 two deputy sheriffs had arrived. They examined the girls' bodies. Iona was in a fetal or "praying position," as one of them saw it. Little Linda, on the other hand, had apparently "crawled under the bed to escape the fire," he wrote in his report.

The deputies asked Chief Roberts how the fire started. Chief Roberts told them, according to each deputy's notes, that it looked to him as if the fire started when a mattress caught fire, and that he saw no indications of arson, flammable liquids, or foul play. Roberts later denied ever making such statements.

The higher-ranking deputy decided there was no need to call any detectives. But he also wrote down that the father "appeared very calm and composed as he carried a cup of coffee around with him."

At various points that morning Knapp made remarks that his neighbors considered inappropriate. Molly Cameron remembered that when she urged a fireman to get into the house because the children were in there, John Knapp turned to her and said, — You might as well forget it. They're among the dead. —

Cameron also remembered him saying to someone else, — If that don't kill them, I don't know what will. —

Almost everyone found Knapp's demeanor odd.

"It's hard to explain exactly how John acted," Garrison later said. "He didn't

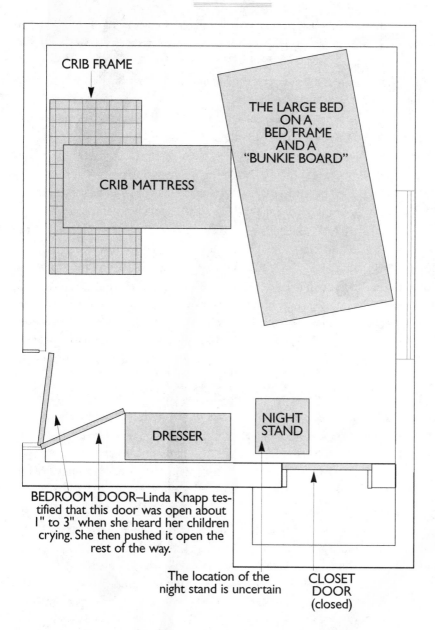

CRIB FRAME

THE LARGE BED
ON A
BED FRAME
AND A
"BUNKIE BOARD"

CRIB MATTRESS

DRESSER

NIGHT
STAND

BEDROOM DOOR–Linda Knapp testified that this door was open about
1" to 3" when she heard her children
crying. She then pushed it open the
rest of the way.

The location of the
night stand is uncertain

CLOSET
DOOR
(closed)

THE CHILDREN'S BEDROOM: MAJOR KNOWN FURNISHINGS

Adapted from a diagram drafted by the Weyerhaeuser Fire Technology Laboratory act like really anything happened, like. Just like there was a lot of things he had to do, and he was hurrying here and there. He just acted very active."

As the smoke cleared, the firemen began to appreciate that the Knapp house was the filthiest they had ever seen. Two firemen, making assumptions that reflected the mores of the time and place, observed in their notebooks that no woman could have lived there for months. In the entire home, only two pieces of clothing were actually hanging in the closet — two men's shirts. Everything else was piled or strewn at random on the floor or on any available piece of furniture.

Throughout the house there were toys, cardboard boxes, garbage, broken debris, open jars and cans of rotting food, dirty dishes, cat feces, newspapers, magazines, and dirty clothes. In the master bedroom, in the southeast corner of the house, there was a mattress and a broken box spring with a torn cover; mattress stuffing was scattered all about the room. In the far east bedroom, which had also not been involved in the fire, there were broken pieces of a crib and a small chest that had all its drawers pulled out and strewn about the room.

The kitchen counters were filled with dirty dishes and rotting food. Two firefighters almost vomited, they later wrote in their reports, when they opened the refrigerator. It contained only spoiled food and a pool of unidentifiable, molding pink liquid.

The living room, where the Knapps had apparently been sleeping on the folded-down sofa, was littered with delinquency notices from utility services and other creditors. The firemen determined that the gas in the house had, in fact, been shut off at the time of the fire, apparently due to nonpayment.

Aside from chaos, the salient feature of the Knapp home was flammable liquid. As the firemen entered the house through the front door, there was a red can of Coleman fuel sitting on a low homemade bookcase to the left and a second can of Coleman fuel sitting on the floor to the right. The one on the bookcase was standing open and had a funnel sitting in the spout. That can was about half full, the firemen found, while the one on the floor was full.

Yet another Coleman fuel can — an empty one — was lying outside the house in the carport, while an empty gasoline can lay in the mud of the lawn.

On top of the conventional kitchen stove was a two-burner, camping-style Coleman stove, and a few feet away on a kitchen counter there was a small container of charcoal lighter fluid. A Coleman lantern stood on the back of the toilet in the bathroom in the hallway, across from the fire-involved room.

The house also showed damage from several very small fires, apparently unrelated to the fatal fire. At the north end of the living room, between the sofa and a front window, there were four burn spots on the thick gold carpet, and in the hallway bathroom there was another series of burn spots on the carpet. The lower exterior of the toilet bowl had a large burn discoloration, as did the underside of the toilet seat.

Throughout the house there were implements to start fires. There were at least ten books of matches in the house, all but one of which were lying on the floor or on low items of furniture. One or two lighters also lay on the floor. Individual paper matches — some struck, but most unstruck — were strewn about. Inside the oven in the kitchen was a roaster pan filled with burned paper. There was more burned paper in an ashtray in the living room. When the firemen folded up the back of the sofa, turning it from a bed back into a couch, they found partially burned pages of magazines lying under it, some of them rolled like torches.

Linda's mother, Louise Ramsey (a pseudonym), was working at the Motorola factory in Tempe when a supervisor told her that her daughter had a problem with her little girls. Louise drove to the house and, when she saw the fire engines, was so unnerved that she ran over a neighbor's rose garden in her car.

Five neighbors later remembered that Linda was not crying and showed no emotion until her mother arrived. Two remembered Louise and Linda having the following conversation:

— Oh, my God! What have you done to these children now? — Louise asked.

— Both my children are dead. —

— Both of them? —

— Yes, both of them. —

Linda then began to cry.

Linda's sobs seemed forced, according to one neighbor. Her emotion didn't look genuine, said another.

Linda's mother, Louise, later told a state investigator that Linda came running up to her and said, "Momma, my babies are dead." Louise had asked, "Are you sure it's both of them?" and Linda answered, "Yes, it's both of them, I'm sure."

A fire department photographer, officer-trainee Stephen Hermann, arrived at 9:35, and a sheriff's department photographer came about ten minutes later.

While they were taking pictures, John Knapp went to a neighbor's and telephoned the bishop of the 12th ward of the Church of Jesus Christ of Latter-Day Saints, who also ran a tire store in East Mesa. The bishop's wife, Carolyn Goodman, answered.

— I want to talk to the bishop, — he said.

— Well, he isn't here right now. Can I take a message for him? —

— I need to talk to the bishop. —

— He's out of town, is there anything I can do? —

— My children have just been burnt to death and my wife needs someone here with her. —

— Well, I'll be right there. —

Goodman arrived at Knapp's house about fifteen minutes later.

"I said, 'I'm sister Goodman,' " she later testified. "And John came at me like a bear, and he said, 'If the bishop would have paid the utility bill the children wouldn't have been trying to light a fire to keep warm!' "

After photographs had been taken of the bodies in the debris, a deputy attached red tags to the remains of the girls' feet. He wrote on the back of one, "no suspicious surroundings," and on the other, "no foul play."

At 10:15 two firemen removed the bodies on stretchers and put them in an ambulance. A local television news crew captured the moment on videotape. Knapp, shown from the waist up, is wearing a blue, polo-style pullover shirt. He appears somber and is looking down at the ground. A neighbor later remarked that this was the only moment Knapp showed grief. People later speculated that maybe he was playing for the camera.

Once the children's bodies were removed, firemen cleaned out the rest of the room. A large mound of undifferentiated fire debris was piled outside the window, and no written inventory of the contents of the fire-involved room was ever made.

While this was going on Jim Garrison, the neighbor who had fought the fire, chatted with Chief Roberts. The children were probably better off now, Garrison commented, given the way the parents took care of them. Garrison said they were locked out of the house nearly all day every day and that the neighbors probably fed them more than their parents did. Garrison also mentioned that Knapp had lost his job recently and that the family had had its utilities shut off. They were using a Coleman stove and lantern for cooking and lighting.

— Was the house burglarized? — fire inspector James McDaniel asked the firemen when he first set foot in the house at about 10:35. Because of the disarray, McDaniel assumed that the house had been ransacked by intruders.

McDaniel, thirty-two, was the son of a fire chief. He had first started fighting fires with his father when he was eleven. He later testified that he had seen about 9,000 fires by the time he inspected the Knapp home, including about 1,000 flammable liquid fires. (For that estimate to be true, McDaniel would have to have seen about 427 fires a year from age eleven forward.)

While McDaniel began inspecting the house, the photographer Hermann discovered yet another Coleman fuel can, this one in the living room closet, which stood open. The can was covered up with about a foot and a half of newspapers and other debris. This can was empty.

As the firefighters continued clearing debris from the children's room, portions of the floor were becoming visible. McDaniel pulled a rubber squeegee across a section of wet, bare floor. As he did, he noticed an oily film on the water. The film smelled like Coleman fuel, he thought.

Several other firemen dipped their fingers in the film, smelled them, and agreed that it smelled like a flammable liquid. One of them then sifted through the pile of debris outside the window to see if any flammable liquid container had been in the room, but found none.

Once the oily film was discovered, the whole complexion of the investigation changed, according to officer-trainee Hermann.

"Everybody out of the water," he later remembered thinking to himself.

Hermann radioed the assistant chief, who was already on his way back to headquarters in Scottsdale.

— I think we've got something here, — Hermann told him.

A few minutes later the assistant chief called the state fire marshal to report a possible arson.

McDaniel scooped up a sample of the oily film with a jar and then placed in the same jar pieces of carpet and pad that were saturated with the same film. He sealed the jar and labeled it.

He then had the rest of the debris from the floor removed. The carpet had been consumed in a very erratic manner, he noticed. In a few places the fire had burned all the way through the carpet, pad, and vinyl floor tile down to the concrete, yet in other spots the carpet was intact. McDaniel believed that the heavily charred areas were areas where flammable liquid had been poured.

When all the carpet and padding was removed, there were irregular char patterns on the floor, like large inkblots. McDaniel believed these were flammable liquid runs, showing where an accelerant had been poured.

He had the firefighters clean the floor with squeegees and dry it with rags from the Knapps' home before he took more samples. (A dispute later arose over how carefully the firefighters inspected these rags before using them. Were they clean? Could the rags have been soaked with anything?)

The firemen then took two "extract" samples of the floor using the solvent methylene chloride. A piece of gauze was soaked with the solvent, rubbed on the floor with a stainless steel spatula, and then placed in a jar and sealed. The solvent was supposed to soak up any residue of flammable liquid still present on the floor.

At one point as the firemen worked, Knapp came back to the house and asked if he could get some personal items.

— My wife's the world's worst housekeeper, — Knapp said under his breath as the fireman escorted him to the master bedroom. — She's mentally disturbed. I should have had her committed a long time ago. —

Edward Beyer arrived at the scene at about 10:30 A.M., not long after the children's bodies had been driven away to the mortuary in ambulances.

Beyer had a strange job. He had radios in his car and home that were tuned to the emergency frequencies used by the fire department. Whenever he heard about a fire or some other calamity that might involve an insurance claim, he headed to the scene. He would find the victim of the tragedy and offer to act as his or her agent in dealing with the victim's insurance company, taking 10 percent of anything the insurer paid. Beyer was called a public insurance adjuster and was licensed by the state to do what he did.

Upon arriving at 7435 East Capri, Beyer made his pitch to John Knapp, whom he later described as having been in a state of confusion. Beyer discovered that Knapp did not know what sort of insurance he had on the house or how much it was going to cover.

Since Linda's mother, Louise, was about to drive John and Linda to her home in Tempe, John invited Beyer to meet him there and talk further.

At some point — it could have been either before or after Beyer's arrival — Shirley Grenko invited the Knapps and Louise into her house and gave them coffee and cookies. Grenko later remembered John Knapp having remarked that "he guessed he'd still have to pay for his carpet. And I told him if he was making payments on it, maybe he had insurance on it, and to check into it."

Neighbor Jim Garrison later also remembered Knapp having mentioned the carpet to him.

"He seemed more concerned about the house and about the carpet that was not paid for than worrying about his children," according to Garrison.

Louise and Kenneth Ramsey (pseudonyms), Linda's mother and stepfather, lived in a small one-story house at 1708 South Hardy Drive in Tempe, about fifteen miles west of the Knapp home in East Mesa. They lived there with their three teenage daughters — Linda's half-sisters.

At the Ramseys', John and Linda signed a contract appointing public insurance adjuster Beyer as their agent. Beyer then advised John to go with him to the insurance company.

Beyer drove Knapp to Kenneth Templeton's office in Tempe, arriving in the late morning. Knapp explained to Templeton, who had sold him the policy, that he'd had a fire in his home and that his daughters had burned to death.

Templeton was dumbfounded at Knapp's callousness in coming to the insurer so rapidly after such an event. "The emotion and concern John Knapp showed," he later told a state investigator, "was no more than if his cat had burned to death."

Templeton looked up Knapp's policy. Knapp had dwelling insurance, which covered the house but not the furnishings. Templeton wasn't sure if it covered the wall-to-wall carpeting. Knapp would have to check with the claims adjuster, who worked at a different office to the north.

Beyer took Knapp back to the Ramseys'.

Chief deputy state fire marshal David Dale arrived at the fire scene at 12:55 P.M. Dale, forty-two, was a tall, robust, angular, balding man. By his estimates, he had investigated about 500 fires, of which about 100 had involved flammable liquids.

As Dale examined the house he noticed that the smoke and heat damage to the rest of the house were minor, suggesting that the fire had not lasted very long.

Inside the children's bedroom, Dale saw from the charring of the baseboards that there had been significant floor-level burning. The charring was on all four baseboards, and the damage to all four Sheetrock walls and the ceiling had been about equal. Dale concluded that there had been no single, localized "point of origin" for the fire. Instead, a flammable liquid must have been poured throughout the room, so that the fire effectively started everywhere at once.

The inkblot char patterns on the floor were flammable liquid runs, Dale thought. The heavy floor-level burning in two of the corners was another sign of flammable liquid, since corners were, according to his training, "dead air spaces" that didn't burn readily in ordinary fires.

At about 1:30 P.M. a neighbor came to the Knapp house and called Chief Roberts to come look at the Knapps' cat, which a neighbor was holding. He found that much of the gray cat's fur was matted and soaked in something that smelled like Coleman fuel. Roberts carried the cat back to the Knapp house so McDaniel could smell it, but the cat broke free and fled before he could take a fur sample.

In the afternoon Dale examined the larger items of fire debris that were lying out on the lawn. There had been two beds in the room. One was a small crib mattress. Virtually all that remained of it were the metal springs. The frame had a crease in it, and some springs had collapsed while others had not. Dale inferred that flammable liquid must have been poured underneath the portion where the springs had collapsed. Only where the flammable liquid had been poured had the temperatures been hot enough to anneal — or deform — the metal springs, he reasoned.

All in all, Dale concluded, so much of the damage in the room could only have been caused by flammable liquids that he estimated that the arsonist must have used at least a half-gallon to a gallon of flammable liquid — presumably Coleman fuel.

By midday, Melba Burr, a friend of Louise, had come by the Ramseys'. Burr was an outspoken, garrulous woman who worked as a cocktail waitress and lived within walking distance of the Ramseys'.

At about 2:00 Melba drove John, Linda, and Louise to the doctor, who gave them each a shot of the sedative Vistaril, according to the doctor's records. Melba then drove Linda and Louise back to the Ramseys', where they went to sleep, and drove John on to do some errands.

First, John asked to stop at his dentist's, who had just won a small-claims judgment against Knapp three days earlier for an unpaid bill; Knapp owed an installment on the judgment in a few days.

Since the dentist wasn't in, Burr drove Knapp to the insurance claims office in Scottsdale.

There, claims representative Edward Moore explained to Knapp that his insurance was not going to cover the carpeting after all. Counting interest, John still owed more than $1,800 on that carpet.

— What's the sense of having insurance if you're not protected by it, — Knapp snapped at Moore.

Moore considered Knapp very callous to be fretting about such things after such a calamity. Melba Burr also noticed how angry Knapp was when he came back to the car. Here he had lost his two children, and all he could think of was his carpeting, she thought.

At 5:45 P.M., as the firemen and detectives were locking and sealing the fire scene at 7435 East Capri, Chief Roberts saw the gray cat he had seen earlier that day. He and a detective caught him and snipped off a fur sample where the smell of flammable liquid was strongest. They sealed it in a jar for testing.

Before leaving, inspector McDaniel took into evidence the half-full Coleman can that had been sitting on the bookcase to the left of the front door.

That evening, between 7:00 and 7:30, Lila Johnson, another friend of Linda's mother, came by the Ramseys' to pay her respects.

John's mother, Mary Knapp, arrived from California at about 8:00. Lila later said she was shocked by John and Mary's conversation.

They just "exchanged pleasantries," Lila later told a state investigator. She asked John whether he had insurance, and John told her all about it. Not once were the children mentioned. Well, maybe once. Mary Knapp saw the girls' pictures on top of the TV, and she remarked that she hadn't seen them in such a long time. But otherwise neither of them spoke one word about the babies — just about material things.

They watched some television and, at 10:00, the news came on. The national news every night during this period revolved around the then unfolding Watergate scandal. In fact, it was on the following night, Saturday, November 17, that President Richard Nixon told the nation, "I'm not a crook."

But the local news on November 16, 1973, focused on the tragic fire at 7435 East Capri. Lila got up and asked if she should turn it off, she later recalled, but John told her not to.

Lila considered John's attitude inappropriate.

John and Mary just showed "no emotion" all evening, she later told police. She was "falling apart," but John and his mother were just carrying on a normal conversation.

Later that evening, John borrowed a car from the Ramseys and went into Mesa. On his way back, at about 12:30 A.M., Knapp was in an accident, which was the other driver's fault. Knapp sat in the car and read a newspaper while a police officer did the paperwork.

— Did you see this? — John asked the officer, pointing to an article about the fire.

— Yeah, I did. Terrible thing. —

— Those were my two children. —

— You're kidding. —

— No, — John said, and he pointed out to the officer that the name and address on his driver's license were the same as those mentioned in the story.

Knapp showed no emotion, the officer thought.

The officer later became a witness against John.

So did Shirley Grenko, Jim Garrison, Molly Cameron, battalion chief Geary Roberts, Carolyn Goodman, James McDaniel, David Dale, Melba Burr, and Kenneth Templeton.

Two

The next morning, Dr. Heinz Karnitschnig, the Maricopa County medical examiner in Phoenix, performed an autopsy on the corpses of Iona and Linda Louise Knapp.

The children were "well nourished," he wrote in his report, and normally developed. Both children's throats and lungs contained "large amounts of aspirated soot," which showed that they were still breathing when the fire started. He found no evidence that either child had been injured in any way before the fire.

Karnitschnig also evaluated the laboratory tests that the toxicologist had performed the previous day on the children's blood. They showed relatively low levels of carbon monoxide. Little Linda's carboxyhemoglobin level — the amount of hemoglobin in her blood that had bonded with carbon monoxide instead of oxygen — was only 8 percent, while Iona's was 23 percent. Neither level was fatal in itself. People who died from inhaling carbon monoxide from a long-smoldering fire might show levels as high as 60 to 90 percent.

Apparently the Knapp fire had progressed rapidly, and the children had died fairly quickly. On the other hand, they had not died instantly. Each had had time to inhale carbon monoxide, and Iona had inhaled a substantial amount.

That afternoon, detectives returned to the scene of the fire on East Capri to interview neighbors.

They heard more horror stories. The children had always been dirty, poorly dressed, barefoot, and hungry, and they had roamed untended all hours of the day and night. One neighbor said she'd seen one of the girls take a piece of fly-covered chicken away from a cat and eat it without any restraint from Linda, who was present.

The neighbors knew less about John, however, whom they rarely saw around.

At about 10:30 on Monday morning, Leon Stratton, a tall, strapping, veteran detective, went to the fire scene with fire marshal Dale and the man who would be heading the investigation, detective Sergeant Robert Malone. Malone, who had been with the Maricopa County Sheriff's Office for about eight years, was a shorter, muscular man with a crew cut and a bluff demeanor.

At about noon, detective Stratton took into evidence a second Coleman fuel can — the full one that had been sitting on the floor to the right of the door.

That afternoon, Stratton and Dale drove to the Ramseys' to pick up the Knapps for questioning. John Knapp agreed to talk to them, but since Linda was at the beauty parlor, getting ready for the funeral the next day, they arranged to have her brought to the station when she was done. John got in the back seat of the unmarked car, where the Coleman fuel can stood on the floor, and the detectives drove him to the sheriff's substation in Mesa, arriving at about 2:00 P.M.

They led John into the district commander's office — a nine-by-nine-foot room in the back of the substation — and closed the door. In those cramped quarters Stratton and Dale — periodically joined by Sergeant Malone — questioned Knapp. They had him go through, at least twice, everything he had done on the day of the fire and the couple days leading up to it.

Knapp believed that the entire interview was being tape-recorded, and later thought he remembered a detective occasionally turning the tape over or replacing it. Stratton later testified, however, that while he started to tape the interview, the batteries gave out after about fifteen minutes, and none of the tape was usable. Sergeant Malone later testified that part of the interview may have been taped, but that he did not know where the tape was.

Accordingly, the only documentation of what was said is what Stratton and Dale later wrote in their investigative reports, which are not completely consistent with each other.

Those reports are largely — though not completely — consistent with the more detailed account that follows, which is an amalgam of John Knapp's later court testimony about the same subjects and comments recorded in Stratton's police report.

"Earlier that week," John Knapp explained, "I had called my mother long distance collect and I informed her that our utilities were off, and we were having financial difficulties, and if she would be able to help us, and I asked her if she would come out and take care of the two children for me. And on Wednesday the fourteenth I received a letter from her with a money order for $120 for the utilities, and also a check for two house payments. She said she'd be out the first of January to take care of the house and the kids.

"On November 14, I went into Mesa, cashed the check, and then went to work the night shift at the cab company. I got there around 4:00 in the afternoon, waited around until about 5:00 till a cab became available, and started working then.

"I finished at around 4:00 A.M. Thursday morning [November 15, the day before the fire]. I turned my cab in and went up to the office, got my trip tickets made out, and I sat around the cab office until, roughly, close to ten o'clock, waiting till the utility offices opened. So I went to the electric company and paid that bill. Then I went over and talked to the water company, and made arrangements to pay them on the twentieth. The gas company I could not get to, because it was out past my place."

While the electricity company's office was in Mesa near the cab company — several miles west of Knapp's home on East Capri — the gas company was in the other direction from Knapp's home, several miles to the east.

"After that, I did some window shopping, went and got a haircut, and then eventually I took a cab and went home.

"I went into the house, and my wife told me the electricity was already on. She was actually watching TV when I walked in. It was about 4:30. Then I went around and checked with neighbors to see if I could find somebody to run me up to the gas and get it turned on. But I couldn't [before the office closed at 5:00].

"I informed my wife that I would have the gas turned on the next day. And she said that would be okay.

"And then I went back in the house and kicked my shoes off, and I emptied my pockets, took my glasses off, and I laid down on the couch to go to sleep. We were sleeping on the couch in the living room.

"I had been up for about thirty hours by then, since I had worked all night. So I went to bed at about five thirty or six in the evening. I slept in my clothes, which I often do. I was wearing my white socks, a pair of light blue pants, and I think it was an Orlon pullover shirt with an open collar. It was blue in color also.

"The next thing I remember is waking up early in the morning, the sixteenth. I had to go to the bathroom, so I got up and crawled over my wife, and she had woke up and looked at me, asked me what time it was. And I walked over to the bookcase, and I looked at the clock, and I told her it was six fifteen.

"I went to the bathroom, and I came back out, and I looked toward the kids' bedroom. The door was closed, and there was nothing — I heard no noise coming out of the bedroom at all, so I went back in and went back to bed.

"The next thing I recall is — well, I woke up, and I saw my wife walking toward the hallway, and I heard the children crying, and since she was up — well, I closed my eyes and started to go back to sleep.

"Then I heard my wife, she screamed my name, and I got up, and she was standing in front of the door to the children's bedroom, and I went down the hall to see what was wrong, and I looked in the room, and the room was on fire.

"The fire was between the two beds. The small baby mattress was not where it should have been on the frame. One end of it was on the floor, against the large bed, and the other end was standing up in the air, propped up against the frame. And it was on fire. A pile of clothing between the two beds was also on fire, and so was the rug. The dresser [along the east wall and to the right of the entry door] was also on fire. The whole doorway was blocked by flames, and there was no way I could get in there.

"My wife had tried to go into the bedroom by crawling on her stomach, and when she did so her hair caught on fire. I grabbed her by the seat of the pants and pulled her back out.

"I turned and ran down the hallway out the front door to get the garden hose. It was not in the front yard. So I went around the driveway into the backyard and found it there. I disconnected the garden hose and brought it back around to the front of the house, reconnected it there, turned the water on and went back into the house. The house was full of heavy, dense, black smoke. I tried to get down the hallway, but the heat was extreme. It was unbearable. Flames were coming out of the kids' bedroom door. I started spraying water down the hallway, but the heat got too intense.

"So I went back out the front door to the kids' bedroom window, and I used the end of the garden hose, and I swung it and smashed the kids' bedroom window in with it, and I swung it about two or three times to break the glass. Then I used my fist and hit the glass a glancing blow. It shattered, and the flames were coming, and they were leaping all over the room, and I jumped back. After the flames receded again back into the room, I went back up towards the front of the house to get the hose in the window and start spraying the water in.

"And at that time the flame had shot out of the house and singed my hair. And I used the garden hose to wet my hair down, and when I was doing this, someone came up from behind me and grabbed the garden hose and went into the house, and I went in behind him. Later on I found out it was Jim Garrison. He could not make it, so we both come back out of the house.

"I picked up a piece of cloth, told Jim to wet it, pulled it across my face, and went back in to see if I could get down the hallway. I wasn't able to, due to the fact the smoke had started burning my eyes, and I came back out of the house.

"I stumbled out, and I fell down by the driveway, and I sat there for a little bit to clear my head, and I got back up and I went back to the window, and at this time Mr. Grenko had arrived with his hose. They were putting water in. Mr. Garrison had my hose and Mr. Grenko had his, and I had asked one of the neighbors to go over and stay with my wife. And, more or less, I was just going around in circles, I guess.

"It appeared to me to be quite some time before the fire department got there, I would have to say at least fifteen, twenty minutes.

"I had almost fourteen hours sleep and I was more or less in a daze. I never actually saw the children, but I heard them crying. One of the firemen told me they could not find the children. And I became upset, more or less, and I went into the house and into the kids' bedroom, and I could not see them either. And one of the firemen asked Mr. Garrison to take me out. I was getting in their road, and I was very upset about the firemen — I told them if they don't do something I was going to, you know, more or less, start to punch them. I had already almost punched one fireman when he come carrying the cat out of the house instead of my two children.

"Mr. Garrison took me out of the house and took me over to Molly Cameron's house, and told me he would get me some coffee. I went over, talked to my wife. I told her they could not find the children. I would be going back and forth, talking to her off and on.

"We made some phone calls. My wife had been calling her father in Nebraska and her mother in Tempe. I called my mother in California. We also called the church, too."

Knapp told Stratton and Dale that he did not know how the fire started. The only thing he could think of, he told them, was that the children were playing with matches, maybe trying to keep warm. He mentioned that a little while back the kids had pulled some stuffing out of the crib mattress and that Linda had taped it back up. Maybe they pulled the stuffing out again and lit it.

He said he had caught Little Linda playing with matches once, and had spanked her for it, but had never actually seen her light one. The reason there were individual matches all over the house, Knapp explained, was that Little Linda used to pull them out of the matchbooks and drop them.

"We once had an incident where the kids got hold of a lit candle," Knapp also told them. "This was after the electricity was shut off and before I bought the lantern. I had fallen asleep. They were dropping pieces of paper on the candle, and then they knocked over the candle and burned the rug in the living room.

"The children also once got hold of the lantern. This is what my wife told me. I had fallen asleep on the couch again. She said she had woke me up and told me to baby-sit, and I had fallen back to sleep. I couldn't remember it. But if I am not up off the couch I will automatically go back to sleep. It is my nature. And when she come home, she found the children in the hall dragging the Coleman lantern and trying to light it with a match."

Knapp also explained that the burned letter in the ashtray was his doing. His wife, Linda, wrote "love letters," Knapp said, to "pen pals," who were mainly prisoners. She got their names from the backs of his detective magazines and other sources. When she got angry with Knapp, she would write these letters and leave them around the house for him to find. When he did, he would burn them.

As for the burned, rolled-up magazine pages that were found under the living room couch, Knapp said he had no idea how they got there.

At about 3:00 P.M., the Ramseys drove Linda over to the substation from the beauty parlor. She was led into the same room as John. Then, in John's presence, Stratton and Dale questioned her.

"We were sleeping on the sofa in the living room, which was folded down to make a bed.* John slept between me and the wall.

"I woke up one time before the fire, maybe about four o'clock in the morn-

---

* This account is an amalgam of Linda Knapp's later testimony about the same events, supplemented with Stratton's notes of her comments, and edited to form a narrative. Like John's, her later testimony was largely, but not completely, consistent with the versions recorded in Stratton's and Dale's notes.

ing. I got my daughter a drink of water and covered them up. They were both sleeping on the big bed.

"At that time the room was pretty messed up. At least one or two of the dresser drawers — maybe all of them — had been pulled out of the chest and dragged into the middle of the room. The mattresses were in their ordinary places. Then I went back to sleep.

"The next thing I recall is waking up and having to go to the bathroom. I got halfway across the living room. I could hear the children crying so I went back to their room. The door was open about one to three inches. I opened it the rest of the way.

"I seen the room was on fire. The whole baby mattress, to the left of the door, was on fire. The flames were going clear up to the ceiling, and arching back down to the dresser on the right. The rug was also on fire. The baby mattress was off — it wasn't where it was supposed to be. It was on the floor between the two beds and leaning up against the baby bed frame at an angle, about like that.

"I could see my youngest daughter, Iona, standing in the [northeast] corner by the closet door.

"I screamed for John. John jumped off the couch and came to the door. Thinking about it later, that surprised me, because it's usually so hard to wake him.

"I asked Little Linda where she was, and then I heard her say, 'I'm right here, Mommy.' I couldn't see her.

"I started into the room after Iona. I came within a few inches of having Iona's hand. That's when my hair caught fire and John reached in and pulled me out.

"John ran out to get a garden hose. He said he would go out and get 'em through the window.

"Next thing I knew the window broke, and the room exploded."

Linda told Stratton and Dale that she had once caught Little Linda playing with matches before, but had never seen her light one. Like John, she said she had no idea how the fire started, but she said the girls could have been playing with matches.

Toward the end of her statement, the officers asked Linda if she had ever had any emotional problems.

— Well, I've always been a very emotional person, — she said. — I did see a social worker at Tri-City Mental Health about a year ago, but just twice. That was mainly because I'm not a very good housekeeper sometimes. —

At about 3:45 Stratton took Linda out of the room and asked her to wait. He returned with Sergeant Malone. Stratton then read Knapp his Miranda warnings from a printed card, and Knapp agreed to speak without a lawyer present.

Malone then came to the point.

— John, what would you say if I told you there was Coleman fuel in the children's bedroom. —

— Was there? —

— It looks that way. —

Knapp said he had no idea how it could have gotten there. There weren't any Coleman fuel cans or containers in the children's bedroom, he said.

Then Dale explained what he had learned from the fire damage. He laid out his theory of the case and explained to Knapp that all signs indicated that a good bit of flammable liquid propellant — maybe as much as a gallon — had been spread all over the room. And he explained that the fire inspector and the firemen had even found some remnants of what seemed to be Coleman fuel in the room.

Having been told all this, "Mr. Knapp stuck to his original story," detective Stratton wrote in his report, "and denied setting it or any knowledge who could have set it other than he admitted that it was possible his wife could have started the fire because of her emotional problems."

Knapp then mentioned that they had had a kitchen fire when they were living in Pomona, California, in late 1971 or early 1972. That fire had puzzled him a little, he said.

— My wife left some grease in a pan on the stove, for making French fries, and it caught fire, — Knapp said. — The fire department came, but a neighbor and I put it out before they got there. My wife said that Little Linda must have turned the gas on under the grease, but I don't think she could have. It was kind of hard to turn the knob, and she was less than two at the time. —

The investigators had Knapp go through his whole story again, at least three more times by their later estimates. He stuck to his original account.

After an hour and a quarter, Knapp was asked to leave the room, and Linda was summoned back in. Stratton read Linda her Miranda warnings and told her, too, that the investigators now knew that the fire had been started with liquid accelerants, probably Coleman fuel, and Dale explained how they knew that.

Malone asked her if she had somehow set the fire, accidentally or otherwise. She denied having done so.

— Did you smell any type of fuel when you opened the door of the room? — one investigator asked her.

— No. —

— Can you think of anything in that room that could have caused such a fast fire? —

— No, — she said. — The only thing I can think of is maybe the baby mattress. —

— What was it made of? —

— It had a vinyl cover, and it was stuffed with excelsior. —

At about 5:40 P.M., the officers finished their questioning and allowed Linda and John to go back to the Ramseys'. But Malone told them that there was going to be a coroner's inquest a week from Tuesday, on November 27, and that they should stay in town in case they were needed as witnesses.

Funeral services were held at 2:00 on a warm fall afternoon at Meldrum's Mortuary, a small funeral parlor at the center of Mesa. The Mormon Church paid for the services, while Mary Knapp paid for the casket, which served for both girls. Those relatives and friends present at the small gathering later disagreed about whether John or Linda cried at the funeral.

After the burial, Linda did not get into her mother's car, but got into that of her mother's friend Melba Burr, instead.

— I'm just taking Linda to pick up twelve yards of material that the church set aside for her, — Melba told John. — Why don't you go on home with Ken and Louise? —

— Well, I'll go along for the ride. —

— No, it's okay, — Burr said. — There's no need for you to bother. —

— Go ahead, — Louise Ramsey told John, — get in the LTD and we'll run you home. They'll just be a little while. —

The Ramseys took John back to their house. In the evening, they left to visit friends, leaving John alone.

Linda didn't come home. As it got late John tried to walk over to Melba Burr's to look for Linda, but he couldn't find the right house. He returned to the Ramseys'.

Then he called a cab and went searching for Melba's house again. This time he found it.

Melba did not explain the whole thing to him right then. But when he returned to the Ramseys', Louise filled in the gaps.

Melba hadn't taken Linda to the church. She took her to a rendezvous point near a restaurant. Linda's natural father, Arthur Holiday (a pseudonym), who had come for the funeral, was waiting there in his car. It was already packed with Linda's clothes. Not even Linda knew until then that the Ramseys and the

Holidays had decided to get Linda out of town. Holiday drove her back to his home in Leshara, Nebraska, a rural hamlet near Fremont.

On the evening after the funeral, a Wednesday, a deputy came by the Ramseys' to subpoena John and Linda to the inquest on November 27. Knapp told the officer that Linda had gone to Nebraska.

About an hour later, detective Sergeant Malone showed up, along with a heavyset young detective, Donald Ashford.

— Why'd Linda leave the state? — Malone demanded.

— I don't know. I didn't even know she was going anywhere till she was gone. I've got her address and phone number, though. —

— You let her know, — Malone told him, — that if she doesn't show up for the inquest, I'll issue a warrant for her arrest. —

Though Malone was threatening to arrest her for fleeing, Knapp later said that he thought Malone was threatening to arrest her for murder.

Malone was, in any event, bluffing. Since Linda had left before they served the subpoena, she probably had not violated any law. Since she wasn't charged with a crime, they had no power to bring her back from Nebraska. They could go to Nebraska and interrogate her there, but there were administrative hurdles to doing even that. Since Malone knew where Linda was, he took no immediate action to follow her.

The next day it turned chilly and began to rain. It continued raining intermittently for the next five days — a long stretch for the Salt River Valley.

Meanwhile, deputy fire marshal Dale was concluding his investigation.

"It is my opinion," he wrote in a report dated November 25, "that this fire was deliberately set, [and] that a minimum of one-half to one gallon of flammable liquid was used to assure the destruction of property and claim the lives of [Little] Linda and Iona Knapp with malicious intent."

That same morning, at the state crime lab in Phoenix, forensic chemist Jack Strong completed gas chromatographic testing of the samples McDaniel had taken of fire residue. Strong wrote up a very brief typed report, stating only his conclusions.

Strong found that the oily film that the firemen had found on the water in the children's bedroom, as well as the two "extract" samples taken from the floor with a piece of gauze soaked in solvent, contained "vapors similar in composition to those in" the Coleman fuel can seized from the bookcase of the house, which he had also tested.

At the same time, Strong performed analyses on the fur sample that had been clipped from the Knapps' cat — the cat that reeked of Coleman fuel according to the neighbors, Inspector McDaniel, and Chief Roberts. The results were puzzling. Strong found that this sample did *not* show the presence of any combustible vapors.

That afternoon inspector McDaniel, Chief Roberts, and officer-trainee Hermann paid their last visit to the fire scene before Roberts and McDaniel issued their own reports. This time they took into evidence the third Coleman fuel can that had been found inside the house — the empty one that Hermann had found in the hall closet on the day of the fire.

The investigators had begun to focus attention on this can. It was clear that the other two cans had probably not been used to set the fire. The can that had been found on the floor by the door, for instance, had been full or almost full when recovered; so it clearly could not have been used. And since Dale believed that a lot of fuel had been poured, perhaps as much as a gallon, it was even questionable whether the can on the bookcase — which was still half full — could have been the one used.

As the fire investigators made their last inspection of the house, one of them found a torn-up letter in the living room. Detective Ashford later took it into evidence and then pieced it back together:

November 9, 1973

Dear Daddy,

Could you lend me enuf money to get to Nebraska? . . . I tell you, I can't take it any more. We are so far in det that they truned the gas off 3-1/2 week ago. They truned the electric off last week. It's cold and the kids are sick but I can't even get John to go to work. He would rather sleep than spend time with his family.

I want to come to Nebraska and get a job so at least the kids will be warm. I also plan to get a devorce. I have had all I can take. My nerves are so bad that I find myself shakeing all over. I have to go for walks just to keep from realy beating the hell out of John with a broom or something.

Please see if eather you or Grandma can lend me enuf money to get me and the kid back there with you where they might have a chance to get warm.

Love always,
Linda

On Sunday evening, November 25, Louise and her friend Melba found Knapp sitting at the Ramseys' kitchen table, weeping. John was looking at portraits of Iona and Little Linda that he and Linda had had made at a shopping plaza a couple weeks earlier. The photography studio had learned about the fire and had sent over the photos without charge. There was one photo of each beautiful, smiling, blue-eyed, blond-haired child. Little Linda wore a purple dress with a white collar, while Iona wore a blue pinafore over a white top patterned with baby-blue hearts.

"He fell apart," Melba later recounted. "He went to pieces. He started shaking all over and crying."

The next morning when Louise came down to make breakfast she found Knapp still there at the table, crying. He had apparently been there all night.

About an hour later, detective Ashford came to pick John up, as previously arranged, to give him a polygraph test. (Later, they planned to give Linda one as well.) Under an overcast sky — perhaps, through a drizzling rain — Ashford drove John back to the Mesa substation.

Knapp seemed extremely nervous to Sergeant Charles Fuchs, the polygrapher. Knapp complained about not having slept and about a borderline diabetic condition,* murmured something about a history of migraine headaches, and seemed to be constantly thirsty. During the pretest interview Knapp left the room three times to get a drink of water and once to go to the bathroom. Finally, Fuchs just brought a pitcher of water and a glass into the examining room. Fuchs thought Knapp was exaggerating his stress and lack of sleep in hopes that Fuchs would cancel the test.

Fuchs noticed Knapp's strange emotionlessness and mentioned it in his report: "During the entire interview, the subject failed to show any emotion concerning this incident with one exception; that is, he related that he had been awake all night thinking about his two children and looking at their pictures, and at that point appeared to be on the verge of tears. Afterward he showed no emotion and, in fact, acted in a nonchalant manner."

Fuchs gave Knapp the polygraph, during which Knapp denied any wrongdoing or knowledge of wrongdoing.

"The results of this examination are considered inconclusive," Fuchs wrote in his report, "because of the subject's real or pretended condition."

---

* Knapp had a hypoglycemic condition, according to other witnesses.

The transcript (and polygraph chart) from the polygraph interview has been lost.

After the interview, Fuchs told Ashford that he believed John had used the Coleman fuel can from the living room closet, according to Ashford's later testimony.

According to Knapp, Ashford then drove him back to the Ramseys'. Along the way, Knapp later testified, Ashford told him he had flunked the polygraph. (Such deceit is a permissible police technique.) Knapp says he told Ashford that he wanted a lawyer, and Ashford told him to ask the judge at the inquest the next day to appoint him one.

Ashford later testified that he had no recollection of whether he drove Knapp home, and he denied that Knapp had asked him for an attorney at that time.

Three

The inquest began on Tuesday, November 27, at 8:30 A.M. at the East Mesa Justice Court, which was not far from the sheriff's substation. Having been subpoenaed, Knapp put on his black suit and went to court. When he got there, though, the prosecutor, deputy county attorney Hugo Zettler, told him to leave.

Knapp walked next door to a Circle K convenience store to get a cup of coffee. He made small talk with the clerk there, who thought he seemed a little nervous. Knapp mentioned that he wasn't supposed to take sugar because of diabetes — though he promptly took two lumps — and he noted that he didn't like the Cremora the store had because it didn't dissolve well. Then he griped about having been subpoenaed to appear at an inquest only to be told to get lost. In passing he told her the subject of the inquest.

The clerk was shocked at his apparent nonchalance. She became another witness against him.

At the inquest — which determined only the cause of death, but did not initiate a criminal proceeding — deputy county attorney Zettler presented evidence to a jury of six citizens. The presiding judge was Leo Coombs, a nonlawyer justice of the peace, who was also the coroner. The justice courts are authorized to handle certain minor matters, like misdemeanors, and to start proceedings in more serious matters that must later be transferred to higher courts.

In a brisk proceeding that was over by midday, Zettler presented the testimony of the fire experts, two deputy sheriffs, and the medical examiner, Heinz Karnitschnig.

Karnitschnig, speaking with a distinguished, Austrian accent, testified that, judging from the low levels of carbon monoxide in Little Linda's blood, she had probably died "within a matter of seconds" and after "maybe one or two breaths." John Knapp's claim, that he had heard the children crying, and Linda Knapp's claim that she had heard Little Linda say, "I'm right here, Mommy," were evidently impossible.

"This child," Karnitschnig testified, "could not have communicated with anybody."

Iona had died after "maybe four or five breaths of the carbon monoxide–laden atmosphere," Karnitschnig said. Linda Knapp had claimed that she saw Iona in the corner crying and had spoken to her. Was that possible?

"[Iona] could conceivably have said something," Karnitschnig opined, "but I doubt it."

The coroner's jury swiftly found that Iona Marie and Linda Louise died from a fire "set by person unknown by criminal means."

John Knapp spent most of the morning near the justice court, awaiting the result. When the sheriffs, firemen, and prosecutor filed out, one of them told him the verdict.

Knapp rushed up to prosecutor Zettler and may have asked him for a lawyer.

"I recall just telling him that I couldn't talk to him," Zettler later testified. "That if he wanted to get a lawyer — I don't remember if he used those words — but . . . I was not the one who should tell him what to do."

At that point Knapp went to the justice of the peace to ask for a lawyer. But now American constitutional law played a prank on John Knapp, one that reached its culmination later that evening.

"Mr. Knapp asked me to appoint a public defender to represent him," justice of the peace Coombs later testified, "and I informed him that at that point I could not appoint a public defender, because he had not been charged with anything."

Knapp was confused. A week earlier, at his interrogation on the Monday after the fire, detective Stratton had read him his Miranda rights, telling him that he had a right to an appointed attorney. Now that he wanted one, the judge was telling him he couldn't have one until he was formally charged.

The problem, which no one explained to Knapp, was that there are two different rights to counsel. There is a Fifth Amendment right that applies when a citizen is being questioned by police officers while in custody or under certain other intimidating circumstances and a Sixth Amendment right that comes into play when someone is formally charged with a crime.

Knapp was falling through the cracks. He hadn't asked for counsel when the Fifth Amendment protections were in effect — while he was being interrogated a week earlier — but now that he was asking for it, it had vanished. Meanwhile, the Sixth Amendment's protections hadn't yet kicked in.

If Knapp had had money, he could have simply hired a lawyer at this point. That lawyer, if competent, would have told him not to speak to the police any more. In that event, Knapp would probably never have been arrested.

Ever.

Even with all the evidence of arson the police now had, they still had no way to prove, beyond a reasonable doubt, whether John did it or Linda did it, or — as most people then suspected — both of them did it.

That evening at about 6:30, Sergeant Malone and detective Ashford came by the Ramseys'. Knapp agreed to go with them to answer more questions.

The detectives drove him back to the fire scene at East Capri, picking up a third detective on the way. It was dark when the four men arrived.

The detectives took out their flashlights and led Knapp back into the pitch-dark house. (The firefighters had turned off the electricity.) It was almost as damp and cold inside as it was outside, and the stench of the fire, rotting garbage, and mildew had only gotten worse.

Inside the house, Malone gave John his Miranda warnings again, telling him of his right to have a lawyer appointed if he wanted. Now, unbeknownst to Knapp, his evanescent Fifth Amendment right to counsel was once again coalescing, since the officers were about to question him under intimidating circumstances.

— But Judge Coombs told me I couldn't have a lawyer until there were charges against me, — Knapp told Malone (according to both Malone and Knapp).

Malone stuck to the script he had been taught to read, simply repeating the Miranda warning without explanation, — If you want an attorney, one will immediately be appointed for you. —

— Well, I'll answer questions, — Knapp said, — but only those questions I have direct knowledge of. —

With that odd response, the detectives were home free. They had shot the perilous right-to-counsel rapids. Knapp hadn't asked for a lawyer at the magic moment when he had a right to one. And why would he have? A judge had just told him a few hours earlier that he couldn't have one!

Malone wanted Knapp to reenact his motions on the morning of the fire while he timed him.

He asked Knapp to lie down on the living room sofa and start from there. Knapp declined to do that, since the sofa was damp, but he otherwise did as the officers requested. Malone determined that for John to get up, walk down the hall to the children's room, look in the door, and then leave the house to get the garden hose, took thirty-eight seconds.

Malone considered this reenactment relevant to Karnitschnig's statement that morning at the inquest — that Little Linda had lived "a matter of seconds" while Iona had lived only a couple breaths longer. Though his reasoning is not crystal clear, Malone appears to have believed that he was proving that Linda could not have seen or talked to the children and that Knapp could not have heard them crying.

After the reenactment, Knapp stood in front of the house with detective Ashford while Sergeant Malone and the other detective interviewed neighbors.

At this point memories diverge again. According to Knapp, Knapp told Ashford that he was cold and was getting a headache, and asked if they could hurry up so he could get back to the Ramseys' where he had his prescription headache medicine.

According to Ashford, Knapp said nothing about a headache, only that he wanted them to hurry up because he was cold. Both agree that they got in the car and turned on the heater.

About a half hour later, the four men drove back to the Mesa substation, arriving between 8:00 and 9:00. The detectives got some hamburgers from a Jack-in-the-Box on the way. Knapp turned down a hamburger, but did have a Coke when they got back to the substation.

Then Malone and Ashford took Knapp back to the tiny room at the back of the station and closed the door.

Little is known about precisely what happened during the next two to four hours.

All that is certain is that at some point — and without the use of force or threats — John Knapp admitted that he had set the fire in just the way Dale thought it had been set.

Then Knapp retracted the confession about fifteen minutes to an hour after making it.

Though there were tape recorders available in the substation, Malone did not tape the confession. He later testified that he had never taped any of the roughly 1,000 interrogations he estimated he had conducted up to that point in his career — because he just did not feel that it was necessary to do so.

Only Malone heard the whole confession. Since detective Ashford, as he later testified, left the room "to get a pad or something" shortly before it began and returned about five minutes later, Ashford missed almost all of it.

There are not merely two competing accounts of the confession, but rather four. There is one defense version, and there are three prosecution versions: the version in the police report, the version presented at a pretrial hearing nine months later, and the version presented at trial after that.

What follows is the first prosecution version, the one in the police report. That summary of the interrogation, which, according to the report itself, lasted about three hours, is one and a half pages long. Malone did not take notes during the confession itself, so he wrote down his recollections sometime later that night, and had it typed the next day.

Mr. Knapp was further advised that [the] undersigned officers' investigation had eliminated the two children spilling the Coleman fuel due to the fact that there were no children's fingerprints found on these containers. . . . He was advised that since the children had been eliminated, that there were only two other people [that] had access to the Coleman fuel and the matches — Mr. Knapp or his wife Linda.

Mr. Knapp was then asked, "Was his wife capable of starting the fire?" . . . Mr. Knapp advised that knowing her as he did, she was not capable of perpetrating this act.

At this point Mr. Knapp was advised that all parties involved . . . had been eliminated, . . . that the expert witnesses had substantiated . . . [that] Coleman fuel was poured throughout the children's room and . . . that it was the feeling of [the] undersigned officer that he had started the fire. Mr. Knapp first advised that if he did, he did not recall. However, after further questioning, Mr. Knapp did break down and cry, pulled his hair and stated, "Oh my god I killed them, please forgive me."

After making this statement Mr. Knapp was asked why he had killed his children. At this time he appeared emotionally upset and crying. He stated that he had gotten up in the morning . . . proceeded down the hall, checked the girls' bedroom and observed spots all over the floor. He proceeded back to the hall closet, removing a can of Coleman fuel, which he stated he believed to be water. Took it into the room and poured it throughout the carpet. He then returned the Coleman can to the hall closet where he left it. He proceeded back to the children's room, observed [that] the spots were still there, and attempted to destroy them with fire.

Although he appeared to be very emotional at this time, undersigned officer attempted to light a cigarette with Mr. Knapp's lighter and it did not work. Mr. Knapp's emotions ceased and [he] told undersigned officer, "That damn thing doesn't work half the time," and [then he] appeared to be emotional once again.

After [a brief discussion of other matters] Mr. Knapp changed his story and advised, in essence, that he did not attempt to wash away the spots, but did in fact remove a can of Coleman fuel from the hall closet, which was almost full, proceeded to the children's bedroom where they were both sleeping, poured it throughout the carpet, the entire container contents of the can, consisting of approximately one gallon, and returned the can to the hall closet. Once he had done this he proceeded back to the bedroom and struck a match. At this time Mr. Knapp advised a large pool of fire came out the door and singed his hair. At this point he shut the door, went back into the living room, laid down on the couch. A very short period of time elapsed when he heard his wife calling him and observed her standing in the hallway. . . .

Mr. Knapp advised that he started the fire due to the fact that he knew his wife was going to leave him and he loved her very much. He stated that he had read a letter that she had written to her father from Nebraska, requesting money for the purpose of going to Nebraska and getting away from John. He further advised that he was physically sick, that he was tired of seeing his children go hungry, seeing them living in a filthy house, observing them eating cat and dog food and drinking the milk from the cat's dish. John stated that his children were always cold and that they had only had one blanket on their bed and no sheets. John said, "They won't be cold any more."

Knapp's account of how and why he confessed, which remained relatively static over time, follows.*

"We started going back over things I had done the day of the fire. And they started asking questions. We went over the story about three times at the station.

"My headache was still there [that is, the headache Knapp says he had begun to feel at the East Capri house] and I asked Sergeant Malone to send a squad car to the Ramsey residence to inform them where I was and to send my medicine down to me. He said they would look into it.

"And sometime later on Sergeant Malone had told me that they had eliminated the kids as having set the fire, because they could find no children's fingerprints on the Coleman cans. He asked me if I thought my wife might have set the fire, and I told him that, 'As well as I know her, I don't think she could have.'

"Sergeant Malone said they had eliminated the children, they had eliminated my wife, and that left me, and I knew very well I did not have anything to do with the fire.

"He asked me, 'Well, did you set the fire?' I got belligerent and said, 'If I did, I don't remember.' I was getting fed up. I had gone through it with the officers on the nineteenth. I had conversations with the police officers the day after the subpoena was served, had conversations with police officers on the same subjects on the twenty-sixth, and again on the twenty-seventh. I mean, you know, I can see answering a question maybe once or twice, maybe even three times, but when they keep it up I don't go for that.

"I was getting emotional, and the headache got worse.

"I've had trouble with headaches for many years, but never to the severity that I have had since moving out west in 1969. They start with the pain coming up the back of my neck and up to the back of my skull and around the sides into the front. The pain was very intense, and it affects my vision. It gets to the point where I pull my hair out.

"The worst one I had was back in August 1973 [three months before the fire]. My wife took me to the hospital, and I passed out in the emergency room. I was in the hospital for a week.

"They put me on some prescription medicine. The first was called Percodan. Then they switched me to — I don't know what it was [Darvon Compound].

"Well, as we sat there, the tile floor in the office is a green with white spots on it — more or less a polka dot.

---

* This account is an amalgam of his testimony at three different court proceedings, edited to form a narrative, as opposed to answers to an attorney's questions.

"The spots started having an effect on my eyes. I do have a little bit of double vision, and it does affect my sight, and the headache got severe, and at one point I was actually pulling my hair out of my head again.

"Sergeant Malone stuck a solid-colored green chair in front of me and told me to look at it.

"I remember bits and pieces of that night, but as to put it in a time continual sequence, I don't think I could do it.

"I was emotional and very upset. I was thinking about my wife. Up until about then, I was of the opinion that the fire had been an accident, and there had been no arson involved. And I would be told, by Mr. Dale and Sergeant Malone and them, what some of their findings were about, and I thought about my wife, the fact she was awake prior to myself, that she did leave the state the day after we were questioned. Also my wife is very emotional. On two occasions she has attempted suicide. The second time, I think she swallowed seventy-two A.P.C. tablets, and I had gotten home from work in time enough to get her to a hospital to have her stomach pumped. She sometimes gets to the point where she would go into hysterics, to the point where she was actually shaking and bawling and screaming and couldn't do much about it.

"I was thinking about possible consequences if she had been arrested. And from what I was told by Mr. Dale and Sergeant Malone and detective Ashford, there was a very good possibility my wife might have had something to do with the fire. And because of her emotional state, if she had, I don't think — the best place for her would have been in a mental institution and not in the county jail.

"I mentioned spots, and Malone started asking me questions about the spots, and I just started answering, Yes, yes, yes, yes. I think I answered yes to about every question that he asked, and it's confusing. I know at one time we stopped for a little bit, and he come back, and he asked me, he said, 'You didn't see no spots on the day of the fire, did you John?' And I knew right then and there he wasn't willing to believe the story just given him about seeing the spots on the day of the fire.

"The only thing I was trying to do was protect my wife, because I did not want her arrested, because she is very suicidal, and she does things — some of the dumbest things I have ever seen a woman do — but she does them. So I started — I believe I more or less — the basis of the information they gave me I went along with their theory and just told them a story that I felt they might believe. The headache was getting worse, I was getting sick and tired of being questioned, I don't like somebody on my back constantly. I can't take it. And he was on my back. And I felt there was an extreme threat to my wife, and I would not permit that."

Knapp's account was, of course, greatly at odds with Malone's. The police report mentioned nothing about headaches. It said nothing about any information having ever been suggested to Knapp, and certainly nothing about him ever answering yes to a series of leading questions. It read, instead, as if Knapp had volunteered everything in a spontaneous narrative.

When John hadn't returned home by about 12:10 A.M., the Ramseys drove to the substation to find out what was going on.

When they arrived, Malone told them that Knapp had just admitted setting the fire and that he wanted to speak to them.

"You might as well have hit me with a Mack truck," Louise later recounted. She refused to see him.

Malone led Ken to the district commander's office, and let him speak to John alone. Louise told a deputy to keep an eye on Ken, though, to make sure he didn't physically attack John. The deputy stayed just outside the door.

Ken had never liked John, whom he considered a lazy, ambitionless dullard.

— Well, you really tore your ass now, — Ken told Knapp, according to an account Ramsey gave a state investigator in April 1974.

— Well, I got tired of them being on my back so I confessed to the crime, — Knapp had responded, according to the same account.

— Well, you're a stupid son-of-a-bitch if you confessed to a crime you didn't commit, and you're one of the sickest persons I've ever met if you did it. —

Seven months later, during trial testimony, Ken Ramsey recollected the conversation this way: "I made some statement to the effect, 'Well, you really messed up this time,' and he said, well, you know, he wanted to talk to Mom too. I said, 'Well, she doesn't want to talk to you.' He said, 'Well, I want you to believe that I didn't do it.' I said, 'Well, if you didn't do it, why did you tell them that you did?' And he said, 'Well, I want to talk to you and Mom.'

"John seemed obviously tired, a little cranky. He was a little defiant like. He was angry.

"Before we left he asked my wife and I if we could bring his prescription headache medicine over to him, and Sergeant Malone told us, even if we did, they wouldn't allow him to have it. He would be checked by a doctor when he got to the jail, and if he needed medication they would provide it."

"I can't actually say what exactly I told Mr. Ramsey," Knapp later testified. "I believe I made the statement that Sergeant Malone was all over my back and I wanted him off my back, and they were going after my wife, Linda, and I would have none of it. I would prevent it at all costs."

At about 1:10 A.M. on November 28, John was charged with two counts of first-degree murder.

He was now entitled to a lawyer.

Four

On Wednesday afternoon, November 28, Judge Coombs ordered Knapp held without bond and appointed the public defender's office to represent him.

Meanwhile, the investigation continued. Detectives found out that Knapp had no criminal record in Arizona, California, or in Pennsylvania, where he grew up. All they could find was that on September 4, 1967, while in the U.S. Army, Knapp had had his pay docked $25 when he overslept and missed reveille.

That same Wednesday, the detectives interviewed people at the cab company where Knapp had worked. The employer gave the officers a letter Knapp had brought to the cab company, which had been lying around the office ever since the fire.

It was another letter from Linda to her father, Holiday, written on November 13, just four days after the letter in which she had asked for money to go to Nebraska — the one John had torn up and later mentioned in his confession. But all the desperation of the earlier letter was gone from this one, a chatty letter mentioning nothing about divorce or money problems:

Dear Daddy,
   Just thought I would write and say "Hi." I hope everyone is fine.
   Well tomorow I'll be 22 years old. I'm realy getting old. . . .
   Tell Brenda Happy Birthday for me. . . .

Well, I going to bed now so I will close for now. . . . There realy isn't much to say. . . .

Love Always,
Linda & Family

By Friday, Sergeant Malone had made the necessary arrangements to go to Nebraska to interrogate Linda. Before leaving, he spoke on the phone with deputy fire marshal Dale, who asked if they were bringing Linda back to the Valley. When Malone said he wasn't, Dale protested that the story she had given them on the Monday after the fire was impossible. She could never have stood in the doorway, let alone crawled inside the room and reached for Iona. She would have been burned to a crisp. But Malone explained that prosecutor Zettler didn't think they had enough evidence to arrest her.

Upset, Dale called Zettler himself to explain why Linda had to be lying. But Zettler told him they just didn't have the evidence to arrest her at this point.

— Here's a little case I think would be good for you, — David Basham's supervisor said to him, as he passed him the John Henry Knapp file.

Deputy public defender Basham, twenty-seven, was one year out of law school and had never tried a felony matter. He had just inherited his first felony docket about two weeks earlier from a senior trial attorney who was leaving the office, and Basham was still staggering under the weight of that burden. Many years later Basham actually wondered if his supervisor assigned him the Knapp case maliciously — to take him down a peg or two. Basham had had a very good trial record in the misdemeanor section and had let some of his superiors know about those successes in an impolitic way.

Basham was tall and thin, and unusually introspective for a trial lawyer. While in law school at Arizona State University in Tempe, Basham had been drawn to criminal defense. As a boy he had had a few run-ins with the police — underage drinking and the like — and had been pushed around a bit. When he was nineteen and going to summer school in Hawaii, police had raided the group home where he was living and had thrown him in jail for six days for possession of two marijuana cigarettes. (Though Basham was no stranger to marijuana, to this day he maintains that he didn't have any at the time of the raid.) The case was thrown out, but Basham and his friends had been roughly handled. As an upper-middle-class white kid thrown into a Hawaiian jail, he had had a mild but memorable glimpse of what it was like to be a minority defendant charged with a crime.

Now that he was a lawyer, Basham was comfortable representing guilty people and fond of shocking others with that fact.

"I felt kind of religious about my obligations as a defense attorney," Basham later recalled. If his client was guilty of a vicious crime, by God he would "make a good record — miles of it — cause a lot of trouble, and make it as expensive as possible to prosecute him." Less provocatively, he saw himself as enforcing the constitutional restraints that protect all citizens from police abuse. He liked teaching police a lesson.

When the file was passed to him it probably contained the formal complaint against Knapp, a number of police and fire reports, and the chemist Strong's two-sentence report stating that something "similar to" Coleman fuel had been found in the fire debris. At some point early on, Basham also learned that the fingerprints on the three Coleman fuel cans, though smudged, were obviously those of adults. The cans had not, apparently, been handled by the children.

It was amply clear to Basham that Knapp was facing the possibility of execution. The Arizona legislature had just reestablished capital punishment as of August 8, 1973 — three months before the fire.

Arizona's law permitting the death penalty to be imposed for murder — like almost every other such law in the country — had been struck down by the U.S. Supreme Court in *Furman v. Georgia* in June 1972. But while two justices had considered the death penalty unconstitutional in all circumstances, the majority had invalidated those laws only on narrower grounds. The Court had ruled that the existing statutes gave the sentencing authority — the judge or the jury, depending on the state — too much discretion in choosing between a life sentence or a death sentence. As a result, the death penalty was being imposed erratically, with no relationship to the severity of the crime. Worse, the penalty was being imposed disproportionately on ethnic minorities and almost exclusively on the poor.

Arizona's new law attempted to meet the Court's concerns by providing lists of certain aggravating factors, which would justify imposition of death, and certain mitigating circumstances, which would counsel a show of mercy. In theory these lists would channel the judge's discretion in choosing whether to impose life or death. (In Arizona, the judge imposes the sentence in a capital case.)

Basham and the chief investigator for the public defender's office paid Knapp a brief visit at the jail the same day Basham got the case. The jail was a four-story reinforced concrete building adjoining the courthouse in Phoenix. Each of the top three floors contained thirty-nine old-fashioned, steel-barred cells, arranged in rows and separated by narrow corridors. The stench of toilets pervaded the stale, close air.

Knapp was "very soft-spoken and polite" at that first visit, Basham later remembered. "Calm. Nonchalant. Maybe even to the point of almost an inappropriate way."

Knapp told Basham that he was innocent, though the claim had little impact on Basham at that stage, either emotionally or strategically.

"I think I felt pretty much that he probably was involved in it in some way," Basham recounted. But it made no difference. "If I could have got him off, I would've done it and enjoyed my work. Even if he would've told me, 'Yes, I did it, I enjoyed it, and I can't wait to get married again so I can have two more kids to burn.' "

Basham's job at this stage was the same whether Knapp was innocent or guilty. He would investigate the facts and see what scenarios, if any, were consistent with a claim of innocence.

If John was innocent, there seemed to be two other ways the fire could have started, and the defense would have to investigate them both: either Linda set it, or the children set it.

But, in pursuing the second possibility, there was a very important secondary issue that had to be investigated. Was either Knapp child — the older of whom was just three and a half years old — even capable of lighting a match?

Linda's natural father, Art Holiday, was a short, stocky truck driver. Holiday took Linda to the Fremont sheriff's office at about 10:00 A.M. on December 1, 1973. Holiday had contacted a lawyer before doing so, and the lawyer had assured him that, without papers, the detectives couldn't force Linda to go back to Arizona. If they tried, Holiday was to have the officers call the lawyer.

They never tried. Holiday stayed in a waiting room while Sergeant Malone and detective Ashford interviewed Linda in a closed, windowed room. The interview, which was taped, lasted roughly six hours; the officers questioned her all morning, took an hour break, and then questioned her again until about 5:00. After about two hours, they gave her her Miranda warnings. She never asked for a lawyer, although when Malone told her he wanted her to take a polygraph, she told him he should speak to her father's lawyer about that. (Linda never took a polygraph.)

Only about three hours of tapes of this interrogation survive, and they are of very poor quality. The remaining tapes have been inexplicably lost or destroyed. The account of Linda's interrogation is based on transcripts of the surviving tapes, where they exist, and otherwise on the police reports. From those sections of tape that do survive, however, it is apparent that the police report is a very selective and adversarial summary of the interrogation.

Malone's questions suggest that he had at least three objectives in this interview. First, he sought background information about John Knapp that might confirm that he was a man evil enough to burn his infant daughters alive. Second, he hoped to see if Linda could corroborate John's confession in any way, and if she would abandon those portions of her own statements that deputy fire marshal Dale and medical examiner Karnitschnig had pronounced impossible. Third, he would try to get a confession from her.

While his first mission bore some fruit, the second two were dismal failures. Linda was certainly willing to say terrible things about her estranged husband. Yet everything she said about the fire itself ran counter to the state's case. And she steadfastly denied having set it herself.

The most useful statements Malone got from Linda — all of these would be admissible if Linda testified — were those in which she deflected onto John all blame for the neglect of the children. She blamed him for the disgusting condition of the house, for the unpaid bills, and for not feeding the children properly. She admitted she had stopped housekeeping, but said that she gave up because John refused to help and was always dropping cigarette ashes and tracking in dirt and grease and making her efforts futile. (John smoked at the time of the fire. Linda began smoking shortly after the fire, although at least two witnesses remembered her having occasional cigarettes before then.) John wouldn't buy her a washer or dryer, or take her to the laundromat, Linda complained. He would eat out at restaurants and then not provide enough money for her to feed the kids. She would have to wait till he was asleep and sneak money out of his wallet, she told Malone. She couldn't get him to wake up and go to work. She couldn't imagine what he was doing with the money he was earning.

Of more questionable admissibility — some of these accusations might be allowed in court, others wouldn't — were Linda's assertions about John's violent temper. Even the inadmissible accusations were important, however, because they affected the way prosecutors viewed John Knapp, and they handicapped Knapp's defense as well; defense lawyers would have to refrain from demonstrating good aspects of John's character, lest they open the door to the state to rebut that claim by inquiring about Linda's accusations — even though most of these accusations could never be verified in any way.

John had on many occasions, Linda claimed, threatened to kill her if she ever left him. He had once said something like, "If I can't have you and the kids, nobody will." John had also once threatened to kill Bobby Vinson (a pseudonym), her extramarital boyfriend.

In their police report, Ashford and Malone wrote that Linda had suddenly left Arizona after the funeral *because* of Knapp's threats. But the surviving tape transcripts confirm only that this was the *detectives' theory*, not that Linda ever *voiced* that theory.*

Linda also told the detectives of John's violent conduct toward her. He had thrown things at her; he had fired a BB gun in her direction; and he had choked her once. The choking had happened when they had been "playing," she said, but the incident had given her a scare.

"He never really liked kids," Linda remarked about her husband. But she also said, somewhat inconsistently, that Iona was John's favorite and that he doted on her, while he often became irritated with Little Linda.

While it was true that Linda had attempted suicide twice, one of those attempts had been triggered, she said, when she caught John trying to molest a teenager. John had met two young hitchhikers or runaways, she said, and had brought them back to the house. Linda left the room to take care of one of her children, and when she returned John was down on the rug with one of the girls, and her pants were down to the knees.

"He denied it, but I'd seen him," Linda told Malone.

While Malone had unearthed a treasure of malicious and unverifiable accusations against John, he got nowhere when it came to actually implicating John in setting the fire.

In fact, early in the interrogation Linda told Malone that, despite the confession, she had a hard time believing Knapp could have done it. As violent as she said he was, he had never really hurt or threatened the children, and she had a hard time believing he could do such a thing. In addition, she didn't see how he could have done it *as a simple matter of mechanics.*

---

* Referring to Knapp's threats when she started up a romantic relationship with Vinson in February 1973, Linda said, "That's why I had to leave." In context, however, it is apparent that she was referring to the time she left Knapp in February 1973 and returned to the Ramseys' for a period. The detectives may have misunderstood her to be saying that she left Arizona after the funeral because of such threats.

They had been sleeping on the sofa, Linda explained to Malone, with John lying on the side nearest the wall, and her on the outside. To get out of bed he either had to crawl over her or over the end of the sofa, neither of which was easy to do. Linda was a very light sleeper, she said. To commit the crime he had to have gotten out of bed to set the fire, and to have gotten back into it afterward, all without waking her.

Linda told Malone: "I can't see how he could have did this — gotten back to the couch, and have been laying down before I knew it. This has been bothering me."

In his police report, Malone mentioned nothing about Linda's qualms in this regard.

In addition, Linda mentioned in passing — without even knowing, of course, the significance of what she was saying — that the can in the hall closet had been empty *before* the fire.

"That was an empty or full one?" Malone asked, to make sure he had heard right.

"An empty one," she repeated. "The only full one was sitting by the living room door," she said. (She was right; the one by the living room door had, in fact, been full.)

If the hall can was empty, of course, then John's confession was false. John said he had poured one full gallon of fuel from that can to set the fire. Malone didn't mention this remark of Linda's in his police report either. (In fairness, Linda later told Malone that the can on the bookcase was empty — which it *wasn't*. It was about half full. Malone may have convinced himself that Linda simply couldn't recall the condition of the various cans.)

Linda also confirmed most of John's key recollections about the fire. She said he hadn't slept for almost thirty-nine hours before he went to sleep on the afternoon of the fifteenth; that he slept in his clothes; and that when he got up, he was wearing only socks on his feet until after the fire department came and put out the fire. In fact, she told Malone, he had gotten the insides of his shoes all muddy when he put them on.

She mentioned that John generally didn't show his emotions and that she had very rarely ever seen him cry. She said he *had* cried briefly when they had gone to pick out a casket for the girls. Malone did not mention that incident in his police report.

Linda was particularly adamant about having seen Iona and heard Little Linda, though Malone questioned her pointedly, explaining to her that the medical examiner had declared those observations improbable and impossible, respectively.

But these were obviously the most vivid memories that Linda had of the fire. Iona "had on a yellow nylon top with white diamonds, and her blue shorts," Linda told Malone. "She had a ponytail in her hair."

And even after the fire, when the rest of the world — at least in hindsight — was finding John's behavior outrageous and suspicious, Linda, who knew him best, had noticed nothing out of the ordinary.

"Linda, after you was over to the office and talked to us [on Monday the nineteenth], did you ever think that John had anything to do with this fire?"

"No."

"You never suspected him?"

"No. I didn't know he had anything to do with the fire until Ken Ramsey called my father [after the confession] and he told me that John did start it."

In fact, surviving tape transcripts suggest that the main reason Linda was happy to leave Arizona after the fire was not that John had *threatened* her but rather that John had deeply offended her *because he suspected her of having set the fire.* After their first interrogation session on November 19, Linda told the officers, Knapp had seriously asked her whether, given her mental state, she possibly could have had something to do with the fire. That he could ask such a question had hurt her terribly, she told Malone. "I just wanted to go away. I wanted to get away from him."

Linda's memories and perspectives on all these issues were out of synch with the state's theory. And given that all her other comments about John's character were so malign, it was hard to believe that she was trying to protect him.

Finally, Malone began to probe the possibility that Linda had participated in the crime. About a half hour into the interview, Malone asked her why she fled the state after he told her to stay for the inquest. Linda denied he ever told her to stay, and the two argued about that issue.

Then Malone asked her about the burn marks throughout the house. Linda said that the children had caused the burn marks in the living room, by knocking over a candle, but she admitted that she had caused the ones in the bathroom.

"I knocked the candle off the sink," she said. "It caught a very thin nylon shirt. That's what caught on fire, and it burned real fast."

After about two hours, and after giving Linda her Miranda warnings, Malone began pressing for a confession.

"Linda, is it at all possible that in a confused state of mind that maybe you could have set the fire?" he asked.

"No. . . ."

"Listen, listen," Malone pressed. "I'm trying to unblock something. . . . I think that, when the fire was started, it was started with, believe it or not, good intentions. . . . It may have been started to relieve the kids from their suffering."

Malone suggested that maybe the person who set the fire thought, "I'm going to help them. . . . They're not going to ever be hungry and they're not going to ever be cold."*

But Linda never confessed.

Without a confession from Linda, only the case against John was provable in court. While the physical evidence suggested that John *or* Linda *or* both may have set the fire, without a confession the state could not prove beyond a reasonable doubt either's involvement. Without a confession from John, the evidence would have been consistent with Linda's having set the fire (without John's involvement); and without a confession from Linda, the evidence was consistent with John's having set the fire (without Linda's involvement). Since the detectives had a confession from John and only John — and, in fact, that confession exonerated Linda — they could proceed only against John.

But if John killed the children, what had his motive been? Though the state doesn't need to prove motive to win a criminal conviction, jurors often need to see one to believe, beyond a reasonable doubt, that someone has committed a crime — especially one as unspeakable as this one.

Insurance did not provide a convincing motive. John had no insurance on the children. John's concerns about whether his carpeting was insured — as callous as they may have been — showed only that he correctly feared that it wasn't. In any event, insurance on the carpeting, had he had it, would have provided reimbursement only for the damage caused by the fire. That didn't even provide much of a motive for setting a fire in an empty room. What kind of motive was it for killing the girls?

---

* The language was startlingly close, of course, to the language that Malone had attributed to John Knapp in his police report recording the confession: "[Knapp] further advised . . . that he was tired of seeing his children go hungry. . . . John said, 'They won't be cold any more.'"

The defense lawyers later wondered: Could Malone have asked similar questions of John, and thereby supplied, through leading questions, these details of Knapp's confession?

Just as Basham was trying on different theories of innocence, to see if any would fit the known facts, the prosecutors were trying on different theories of guilt. The insurance-motivated arson theory didn't fit.

That left the investigators with the motive John had mentioned in his confession: that after Linda showed* him her letter to her father of November 9, he grew desperate about Linda's plans to divorce him, and that he thought that killing the children might somehow bring them together again.

But there were some problems with that theory as well. First, there was the letter Linda had written just four days later — after John's mother had agreed to send them some money — in which she seemed to have dropped all thoughts of divorce. In that letter Linda had sounded chatty and content. But, under the rules of criminal procedure, it wasn't clear that a prosecutor would have to tell the defense about that second letter. So perhaps that wasn't a problem.

The more serious flaw with the theory that John killed the children to save his marriage was that the children seemed to be the only thing holding the marriage together. But, then, to commit a crime this irrational, the perpetrator might well have had an irrational motive.

As it developed, the state eventually *took the position* that John thought he could save his marriage by killing the children. Perhaps he believed that caring for the children was what was putting him in debt, and if he got rid of them he could reduce his overhead and resume a happy marriage.

Did any prosecutor ever really *believe* that John had this motive?

No lawyer — either for the state or for the defense — needs to believe in the merit of every contention he makes in court. While, as a matter of professional ethics, a prosecutor *should* believe that a defendant is guilty if he is trying to convict him of a capital crime, he need *not* believe every secondary argument that he makes along the way while seeking a conviction — whether he is arguing to the jury about how best to interpret the evidence or arguing to the judge about how best to interpret the law. Certainly the prosecutor can imply to both

---

* Prosecutors later invariably took the position that John "found" this letter. That word implied that Linda tried to keep the letter secret, understanding that such a letter would provoke John to violence. But Linda told Malone during her interrogation in Nebraska that she *gave* John the letter. "He knew I wrote it," she told Malone. "I told him I wrote it." She also later testified, "I gave it to him to mail," while John testified, "She gave it to me to mail." But since there were also instances in the record in which Linda meekly answered "yes" to detectives' or prosecutors' questions that incorporated the statement that Knapp "found the letter," prosecutors argued that Knapp had "found" the letter.

judge and jury, through confident intonation and body language, that he regards the interpretations that are most useful to his case to be virtually unassailable, when, in fact, he recognizes them to be merely hypotheses at best.

Lawyers are not sworn, and what they say in court is not evidence. They merely argue about what the evidence shows. Lawyers never say in court, "I believe"; they say, "the state *takes the position*," or "the defense *argues*," or, in the most famous phrase of all, since only lawyers ever use it, "*I submit to you that* . . ." It is, in fact, unethical for a lawyer to tell the jury what he believes, because then he would be vouching for the credibility of his witnesses and the strength of his case, which would turn the lawyer into an unsworn witness in the case.

Lawyers can even be sanctimonious about making arguments they do not personally believe should be accepted: "It's not my role to decide what happened," a lawyer may accurately say. "That's the jury's function."

Nor is it necessary for the state to be consistent over time about the positions it takes. As the Knapp case wended its way through the courts over the years, there would be few propositions advanced by the state that it would adhere to consistently other than the claim that Knapp was somehow involved in setting the fire and that he should be executed as a result.

But did any prosecutor ever *believe* that John killed his children in order to save his marriage? It is doubtful that any prosecutor believed it very strongly, since the prosecutors and investigators still suspected that Linda may have been involved in the murders. If Linda was involved, then John's alleged motive made no sense. If he did it because he feared she was about to leave him, then why had she helped him?

But nothing prevented the state from *taking the position* that John's motive for killing his children was to save his marriage. So that is what it did.

In early December 1973, the case was transferred to the Superior Court of Arizona for Maricopa County, in Phoenix, where a new judge and prosecutor would be assigned to handle it. Just before its transfer, the prosecutor at the justice court, Hugo Zettler, made some notes on the case log for his successor prosecutor to consider: "I believe we should shoot for death penalty!!! Case must be assigned to experienced [prosecutor] as I believe it to be the most emotional and serious case I've seen since I have been in office . . . Get the S.O.B."

Five

In the superior court in Phoenix, Knapp's case was assigned to Judge Charles Hardy. The conventional wisdom among defense lawyers was that Hardy was a very good draw. Though not considered a brilliant scholar, he was fair and compassionate. He would "let you try your case," lawyers would say, meaning that he did not police lawyers very closely. On the other hand, his relatively loose rein on his courtroom meant that forceful lawyers could run a little wild.

And if Judge Hardy had a flaw, it was that he was indecisive. One lawyer who practiced before him at the time later joked that, with Judge Hardy, the lawyer who argues last, wins.

Once the case reached the superior court, the county attorney's office assigned it to a much more experienced prosecutor, deputy county attorney Charles Hyder. Hyder, thirty-four, had a reputation as an extremely dogged and well-prepared lawyer. He was a heavyset man with a large, pear-shaped head and black swept-back hair. He was not handsome, but he had a deep, beautiful baritone voice that was a valuable asset for a trial lawyer.

He was not showy or quick on his feet, but he was thorough. He sometimes even typed out in advance the questions he planned to ask his witnesses — and the answers he expected them to give.

Some defense lawyers complained that Hyder was overly aggressive and suffered from tunnel vision, but those were common complaints for adversaries to make about any formidable opponent. Hyder's colleagues thought highly of him. Not much of a socializer outside the office, he had a good sense of humor and took time to help and teach the younger lawyers.

Hyder had overcome some adversity in his life. An outstanding third baseman in high school, Hyder had lost his foot in an on-the-job accident during college and now used an artificial foot. Far worse, his ten-year-old boy had died of cancer just three years earlier.

Later, people would speculate about whether the horror of the Knapp case — a father allegedly burning his own children to death — could have incited a degree of revulsion and passion in Hyder that clouded his judgment. Hyder would strenuously deny the accusation.

By mid-December David Basham realized he needed help on the John Knapp case. The long docket of cases Basham had inherited from the departing senior attorney, Charles Diettrich, needed a lot of attention, since Diettrich had placed them all on the back burner while he tried a highly publicized murder case in late 1973. Beyond that, both the county attorney's office and the public defender's office had extremely heavy case loads at that time; it was not unusual for attorneys to try twenty to twenty-five cases in a single year.

Basham, who had learned that Knapp's mother, Mary, had a little money, suggested that she try to hire Diettrich, who was now in private practice, to assist Basham. Diettrich was a first-rate, experienced trial lawyer. Perhaps he would take such a high-profile case for a reduced fee, especially if Basham would take on the brunt of the preparation, leaving the more glorious courtroom work for Diettrich. It would be a good advertisement for Diettrich's new practice.

Mary and John liked the idea, and Diettrich was flattered by it.

"Somebody coming to me saying, 'We need your help,' I mean that appealed to me," Diettrich later recounted. On December 28, Diettrich's thirty-fourth birthday, Mary signed a $5,000 retainer agreement with him, paying $1,200 up front.

As much as Basham admired Diettrich's trial skills — as did many in the criminal law community — Diettrich's recent departure from the public defender's office had not been motivated solely by his desire to hang up his shingle. Diettrich had been fired.

Charles Conrad Diettrich looked a little like a miniature version of his hero, Mickey Mantle. He was about five feet eleven inches tall, blond, green-eyed, athletic, and good-looking. He grew up in eastern Washington State, the son of a housewife and a grocer — though his father's heart was in his moonlighting career as the conductor of a local orchestra.

Though Chuck Diettrich was quick-witted, as a young man he excelled as a sportsman, not a student. He became an Eagle Scout and then a Silver Explorer, and he wrestled and ran track in high school and college.

In 1962 he transferred from the University of Washington in Seattle to Brigham Young University in Provo, Utah, to be near his fiancée. He also switched from a criminology major to English literature — he especially loved American poetry — and improved as a student.

He returned to the Pacific Northwest in 1964 to enter law school at Willamette University in Salem, Oregon. He wanted to be a criminal trial lawyer. Though he didn't get the grades to qualify for law review, he was an outstanding student in the practical courses requiring courtroom skills, and he was elected president of his second-year class.

Diettrich seemed to be hitting his stride. But in law school he was also, for the first time, drinking. As a competitive wrestler he had never allowed himself that sort of indulgence. In law school he could, and did.

In 1967, a few days after graduating, Diettrich and his wife moved to Phoenix.

"I'd never been to Arizona before," Diettrich recounted in 1993. "We just picked it out as a place with a good climate and [where I knew] there'd be plenty of opportunity to practice criminal law. . . . Instead of going back home and doing the hometown-type thing, we came here, out of the clear blue, so to speak."

He spent his first three and a half years as a county prosecutor, trying scores of major felony cases, winning eight to ten murder convictions and becoming a supervisor of one of the felony trial groups.

Diettrich's style was very different from Charles Hyder's. Diettrich was flamboyant, quick, and charismatic. But he was also less meticulous.

After work, Diettrich liked to hang out at the Flame Rooster, where prosecutors, judges, and defense lawyers sometimes went to trade war stories over a few drinks. If Diettrich was lucky, he might get a chance to rub shoulders there with titans of the Arizona bar like John Flynn or John Frank — the lawyers who had represented Ernesto Miranda before the U.S. Supreme Court in 1966.

By the time he left the office in 1970 to become a federal prosecutor, Diettrich had earned a reputation for being able to hold his liquor. He seemed to be able to stay out late, drink heavily, and yet appear in court the next day with no adverse consequences. Friends nicknamed him the "Iron Man."

After nine months Diettrich took a position with a prestigious new body called the Arizona Organized Crime Strike Force, under the control of the Arizona attorney general.

But frictions developed between Diettrich and his supervisors there. Diettrich voiced impatience with the fact that the task force wasn't tackling the big-time mob cases he had envisioned. In addition, some of Diettrich's supervisors were becoming less convinced that the Iron Man was as impervious to human frailty as Diettrich and his friends believed. They feared that his drinking might be affecting his job performance. As the time neared to extend Diettrich's contract, Diettrich and his supervisors agreed that he should move on.

He landed on his feet at the public defender's office. Returning to his strength — trying cases — he once again excelled, this time as a senior trial attorney. He was much admired by younger attorneys, like Basham, who would have drinks with him after work at the Under Three, a basement-level defense lawyer hangout near the courts. Unlike the Flame Rooster, though, the Under Three was déclassé. Diettrich wouldn't rub shoulders with the likes of John Frank at the Under Three. —

In late 1973 Diettrich defended Shawn Jensen in a high-profile murder case, where the defense was insanity. The night before he planned to put on his key psychiatric expert, Diettrich took the expert out to dinner.

"We just had this great evening," Diettrich recalled twenty years later. "He was playing the piano, I was reciting poetry. And I'd already drank maybe two carafes of wine. The club was closing, and I had just ordered another one, and it was practically full. We got in the car and I put the carafe of wine between my legs. I dropped him off [at his hotel], and I had just come out to an intersection — this was about one in the morning now — and I was sitting there waiting for the light to change, and I fell asleep. A cop car happened to come along and when the light changed two circuits he came over and knocked on the window and I looked up and the first thing he sees is the wine. So I got arrested for DUI, went to jail, was bailed out about three in the morning, and was in court the next day presenting the defense case. No one even knew about it until they heard about it on the noon news at lunchtime."

Diettrich, representing himself, eventually beat the driving-under-the-influence charge. (Jensen, his client, was eventually convicted of murder and sentenced to life imprisonment.)

Shortly after Diettrich's arrest the county board of supervisors decided that Diettrich — who had been driving a county vehicle when he was stopped — should resign as soon as he finished the Jensen case.

That was how Diettrich came to enter private practice.

The weekend after the Knapp case was first assigned to the public defender's office, the office's chief investigator, Jack Richmond, fifty-seven, drove to the East Capri house and began canvassing the neighborhood, talking to whoever would speak to him. Over the next several months he or a younger colleague returned about half a dozen times, day and night, leaving business cards in the doors of those who weren't home. Basham and Diettrich made several trips themselves, although the fifty-minute ride each way from downtown Phoenix was a major imposition on a lawyer's schedule.

Investigating for the defense is more challenging than investigating for the state. People feel freer refusing to talk, as is their right.

Those who did speak to the defense had little good to say about John Knapp. Now that John had been arrested they had no trouble believing he had set the fire, given the horrible way the children had been neglected and John's cold demeanor on the morning of the fire. The only thing some neighbors couldn't understand was why Linda hadn't been arrested, too. They had seen firsthand the way she treated her children.

The most important thing the investigators were looking for was evidence that either child was capable of lighting a match. But no neighbor had actually seen either do so.

An early police report contained a reference suggesting that a neighbor named Tony Rosales had seen one of the girls playing with matches. But when the investigators located Rosales and his wife, Sandra, the Rosaleses did not confirm the police report. On the other hand, they did provide intriguing information.

— One time we saw the little girls throwing pieces of paper and trash into a small fire that was burning in the Knapps' backyard, — Sandra told them. — It was early in the morning, about 7:30, and Linda and John Knapp were nowhere to be seen. We just assumed that the mother or father must have started the fire and then gone back into the house, leaving the children to play with the fire. —

One other neighbor also offered an interesting tidbit. Ernest Paredes said the girls had dragged a gasoline or Coleman fuel can into his yard a few days before the fire. He had stopped them and made them take it back home. The can seemed to be empty, from the way they were swinging it.

Richmond also had an interesting interview with Louise Ramsey, Linda's mother, on the Sunday after he first got involved in the case. To Richmond, Louise seemed very concerned about her own possible indirect culpability in the children's deaths. Louise admitted to Richmond that when the California child welfare authorities had taken the children away from Linda in 1972 — when John was temporarily out of town — they had refused to return them directly to Linda and John. They had given the children to the Ramseys to care for, instead, until Linda could get counseling — which she never did. But the Ramseys had allowed Linda and John to take the children back shortly thereafter anyway.

In addition, Louise and Ken had gone to visit Linda on her birthday on November 14, just two days before the fire, Louise told Richmond. They had seen the miserable circumstances in which the children were living. They had told Linda to "get off her butt" and clean the house, as Louise put it, but they had not tried to take the children out of that environment.

And Linda had also told her at that time, Louise remembered, about a nightmare Linda had had the previous night — just three nights before the fire. Linda had dreamed she saw the two girls totally engulfed in flames and one of the girls was swinging a Coleman lantern. Linda had been hysterical when she woke up, and John had had a hard time calming her down. Linda had regarded it as a vision.*

Though Knapp continued to write to Linda, and told psychiatrists that he still loved her and hoped to reunite with her, her letters to him indicated that such prospects were exceedingly dim.† In her letters she expressed anger toward him, although the cause of that anger ranged greatly and inconsistently from sentence to sentence. In one sentence she seemed to hate him for having murdered their children; in the next, she expressed humiliation that he had actually believed that she might have murdered them; and in a third, she expressed conventional spousal anger over his having let his mother dominate their lives.

December 14, 1973

Dear John:

I got your letter today. I thought I would answer it and get it over with.

I really don't know what to belive any more. . . . I don't care how bad of

---

* There is a dispute about whether Linda first told Louise about the dream on the fourteenth, before the fire, or on the sixteenth, immediately after it. On different occasions, both Linda and Louise have remembered it different ways. Ken Ramsey always said it was on the sixteenth.

† Within days of his assignment to the case, Basham, pursuing every possible defense, including insanity, had asked for a standard psychiatric evaluation of Knapp. All three psychiatrists who examined him found him competent.

a head ache I had I would never have said I did it. I wouldn't have said it to protect you eather because even if I didn't love you I believed you couldn't have done it. . . .

Don't expect any harts and flowers from me. I think your getting just what you deserve. I have to go now. May God forgive, because I can't.

Merry Christmas,
Linda

January 12, 1974:

Dear John,

I got your letter today. I thought I would write and ask you what you would say if I said I was in love. Well, that is presisly what I am going to tell you. I am not going to tell you who. . . . I just thought you might like to know.

I'm realy not trying to be mean. I don't know what you expect from me. You have known for a long time that I don't love you. Now I don't even have my children to love. . . .

I don't hate you. Lord knows I should but I don't. I just hope you get the help you need, so that some day you will be able to [illegible]. If you do find someone don't let your mother run your lives like she did ours. If you do you will lose her to.

Well, I have to go now. Try to understand that I need some[one] to love. I hope that some day you will have someone too.

Your wife,
Peanuts
(Thats my nickname)

P.S. If what you say is the truth, God will help you. Trust him. He is your only hope now.

On January 30, defense attorneys Basham and Diettrich won the court's permission to inspect the sealed house. But the next day, when Diettrich went to see Hyder about scheduling that inspection, Hyder learned, for the first time, that Diettrich was involved in the case. Hyder was incensed. Six days later he moved to have either Basham or Diettrich thrown off the case.

If a defendant has money, of course, he can have as many attorneys as he can afford. But Knapp didn't have money. Accordingly, Hyder had a plausible, legitimate argument that Knapp should have been getting worse representation than he was in fact getting.

Hyder's argument turned on the definition of "indigence." Deputy public defender Basham was assigned to the case because Knapp was indigent. But was Knapp still indigent once a relative donated enough money to his defense that he could also hire Diettrich?

Hyder framed his argument in lofty terms. What the defense lawyers were trying to do was "procedurally, morally, and ethically improper," he argued. Hyder sought to protect the interests of all the other truly indigent defendants, who had a right to the undivided attention of the public defender's office without competition from pseudo-indigents like Knapp.

At a hearing on February 6, Judge E. B. McBride, temporarily substituting for Judge Hardy, could not understand Hyder's furor. Hyder was demanding an evidentiary hearing, and he wanted to subpoena the public defender himself, members of his staff, private defense attorneys, members of the county board of supervisors, and members of the state legislature.

"Is it this big a problem, really?" Judge McBride asked.

"I think it is," Hyder replied. Judge McBride set a hearing at which Judge Hardy could consider the question.

Then the judge turned to a matter he thought had already been resolved — the house inspection. The enmity between Hyder and the defense lawyers was already so great that they had been unable to arrange a mutually agreeable time for the defense to inspect the house, even though the court had already granted permission for the defense to do so. Hyder was insisting that he did not have time to monitor such an inspection for at least another month, and he was refusing to permit any other sheriff or prosecutor to stand in for him while the defense lawyers performed the inspection.

Judge McBride ordered the inspection for the morning of February 16, a Saturday, ten days away.

"There are two ways to try a lawsuit," Judge McBride commented toward the end of the hearing. "The easy way and the hard way. You two guys are sure trying it the hard way."

Basham needed a fire expert of his own — someone who could go with them to inspect the premises and who could critique the state fire investigators' reports.

A lawyer friend suggested a mechanical engineer in Tucson, Marshall Smyth. Smyth, fifty-one, had conducted several major fire investigations, including one involving a catastrophic fire at the Pioneer International Hotel in Tucson, which had killed twenty-eight people in December 1970. An insurance company had hired Smyth to investigate that fire, and he had later ended up testifying in a criminal matter arising out of it as well.

Basham drove down to meet with Smyth in early February 1974. Smyth seemed very capable, had a dry sense of humor, and was willing to help, but he was also very understated and cautious. Smyth listened carefully and answered only the precise questions Basham asked.

From the start, he explained to Basham that the case presented some questions that were outside his area of expertise. He could look at the fire damage and devise tests to see whether such damage could be caused without flammable liquids. But the question would still remain whether a three-and-a-half-year-old child could light matches. As a mechanical engineer, he had no insights into child behavior. And as a father, he had his doubts.

Before setting up his consulting practice in 1968, Smyth had worked for twenty-four years as an airplane maintenance engineer, including several years as a failure analyst at a missile testing facility, looking at wreckage and trying to figure out what had gone wrong. He would come up with alternative hypotheses, construct different physical models, and then test the varying hypotheses by experiment.

Smyth was, therefore, a very different type of expert than deputy fire marshal Dale. Smyth had less training in fire investigation, but his method was far more empirical. Dale's approach was almost entirely oracular. He inspected the fire visually, made measurements, and then pronounced judgment. The basis of his conclusion was the black box of his experience inspecting other fires — about which one could only hope that he had drawn the correct conclusions — and a smattering of seminars on fire science he had taken during the 1960s.

As a preliminary, Smyth thought it might be useful to test the flammability characteristics of the carpet in the Knapp children's room. The synthetic carpet in the Pioneer Hotel had been a major driving force in feeding and spreading that conflagration, he had found. If the carpeting in the Knapp bedroom had also burned furiously, that might account for the floor-level burning that the state experts assumed was due to flammable liquid.

That sounded like a fruitful avenue to pursue, Basham thought. But Smyth was expensive. Since fire investigators were well educated and in commercial demand — insurance companies needed them all the time — they charged handsomely. Smyth charged $40 per hour for his time before trial and $300 a day for testimony.

The public defender's office had very limited funds available for experts. Basham could get enough to pay for Smyth's trip to Mesa for the house inspection on February 16, but after that, they would have to reassess the situation.

The day before the house inspection, Judge Hardy heard Hyder's motion to exclude Basham or Diettrich from the case. True to his threats, Hyder had subpoenaed eight to ten defense attorneys to the hearing, whom he wanted to interrogate under oath. Judge Hardy didn't see what they had to do with anything, and he excused them almost immediately.

Like Judge McBride, Judge Hardy was confused by Hyder's vehemence about this entire issue. It wasn't the first time a public defender and a private attorney had worked together defending a criminal case in Phoenix. But if Judge Hardy found the motion perplexing, he did not find it frivolous. He allowed Hyder to question Diettrich at length about the details of his retainer agreement with Mary Knapp, and then he reached a tentative conclusion. Since Knapp was indigent, he could continue to be represented by Basham. But if Diettrich ever formally became a counsel of record — as he would have to if he were to appear before the jury at trial — Basham would have to withdraw at that point. The ruling effectively dashed the defense plan, which called for Diettrich to take the lead in front of the jury, while Basham would play a crucial supporting role.

Strangely, though it seemed as if Hyder had won, Hyder was still not satisfied. Having heard Diettrich testify that he could not possibly handle the case alone, because of the low fee and other trial commitments, Hyder asked Judge Hardy to order Basham off the case immediately and to force Diettrich to take the case alone and against his will. He argued that Diettrich had already effectively entered it, and now Basham had to exit.

At the end of the hearing Hardy decided to consider the question at more length. While he did so, he ordered that Diettrich could attend the house inspection the next morning.

The lawyers began to congregate outside 7435 East Capri at about 9:40 in the morning, along with the defense fire expert, Marshall Smyth. But prosecutor Hyder, who had brought along deputy fire marshal Dale to watch, refused to let the inspection begin until a deputy sheriff arrived with a video camera. Hyder was not only going to watch the defense lawyers preparing their case, he was going to videotape them.

Smyth took photographs and measurements and then sifted through the mound of fire debris that was still piled outside the children's window on the lawn. He photographed some of the objects he found there, including some charred aerosol cans and a roaster pan that had obviously been in a fire. The pan had a paintbrush in it and an unknown substance that had turned into a gooey, crusted mess during the fire.

The charred roaster pan and aerosol cans later became a major embarrassment to the state investigators, who had never mentioned those suspicious objects in their own reports. Aerosol cans can contain butane as a propellant. And insecticides, which often come in aerosol cans, are themselves petroleum products that closely resemble flammable liquids in chemical composition.

Even though all these items had obviously been through a terrible fire and were found in the same pile as all the other fire debris from the children's bedroom, the state later *took the position* that these objects must have been involved in some other fire and been brought to this pile by parties unknown during the three months that had elapsed between the Knapp fire and this inspection. Alternatively, the aerosol cans may have been aerosol "food" cans that did not contain flammable propellants.

Smyth took out from the pile all the pieces of carpet that he could find, pieced them together on the driveway, and then took them into the children's bedroom. It was possible to put most of them back into their locations by comparing them to the burn marks on the floor, baseboards, and walls. Upon doing so, he could see areas of undamaged carpet that had been protected by large pieces of furniture or other objects. From the peninsulas and islands of undamaged carpet, it became possible to figure out where the dresser, bunk bed, and crib support had stood in the room. It was also possible to tell that the entry door had been open as far as it would go — which was not all the way, because it banged up against the corner of the dresser.

Smyth reconstructed the large bed and brought it back into the room, to compare the burn marks on the walls and floor to the bed's apparent location in the room at the time of the fire.

Finally, he cut a sample of undamaged carpeting and pad from the master bedroom to use for further testing. He finished and left at about 6:00 P.M.

A few days later, deputy fire marshal Dale typed his observations of what Smyth had done and forwarded them to Hyder. It is apparent from that report that the day had been a trying one for Dale. He obviously did not like having an opposing expert in the case. (Indigent criminal defendants often had no expert at all.)

Anything Smyth did that Dale had not done could be viewed as an indictment of Dale's work. And it was apparent from Smyth's having taken samples of carpet and pad that he intended to do further work on the case — actual empirical testing. Dale had filed his conclusions way back on November 23, without having performed any such tests.

In Dale's summary he listed nine things that Smyth did during his inspection that Dale claimed were "accomplished with my assistance and/or direction." Smyth had, for instance, allegedly reconstructed the carpeting "at my suggestion," and he had later "properly positioned" it in the bedroom "at my direction." Then Dale listed eleven things Smyth "apparently did not do" during his inspection, which, by contrast of course, Dale had done during his.

Dale also appended to his summary a condescending and scathing critique of portions of Smyth's testimony in the Pioneer Hotel case. When Smyth had used a plain English phrase instead of fire investigator's jargon, Dale scoffed: " 'Reflected heat'? Fire communicates by Radiation, Convection and Conduction. Poor terminology probably indicative of training lack in fire science — even basics may trip him up."

The Monday after the house inspection, Basham learned that Judge Hardy had barred Diettrich from helping him with Knapp's case. If Diettrich ever formally entered the case, Basham would have to leave it.

Basham planned an appeal. In the meantime, Basham handled all dealings with Hyder, who was refusing to speak to Diettrich.

From his jail cell, Knapp wrote letters to his mother and other relatives. As his lawyers warned him they might be, his letters were read and photocopied by the sheriff's office. A few survive, including this one, written on March 18, 1974, to his half-brother William L. Knapp of Radcliffe, Kentucky.

> Dear Bill:
> . . . I now know that I should have ask somebody for help a long time ago. I didn't because I let my foolish pride stand in my way and it has cost me a great deal, the lives of my two children. Since their deaths I have come to know what true sorrow is and why the Lord thy God calls pride one of the seven deadly sins. If I had ask someone for help and had gotten it right away, then I would not have the Coleman fuel in the house. Also, if I hadn't been so stupid, I would have kept the fuel in the storage shed were it belong and not in my house.
>
> I've prayed so much since this has happen, but as far as I know they have gone unanswered. . . . I do have faith in God and pray that he will help me to prove my Innocents. For I am Innocent in the deaths of my children, and I am sure he knows it, and I pray for his help.

I've always wanted the simple things in life, a wife, children, and a happy home. I would have work like a slave just for my wife and children, but now it's all over. My children are dead, may they rest in peace, my wife don't want me. Even if I do get out of this mess, there's a good chance that my wife will divorce me. . . . I am the most hated man in the Phoenix valley. . . . Tell all of the family that I love them very much.

> May God Bless & Keep You Always,
> Your Loving Brother John

Judge Hardy had ordered Knapp's trial to start on April 22. Three weeks before the scheduled trial, the state performed a fire test.

At 1:00 P.M. on April 2, deputy fire marshal Dale, Sergeant Malone, detective Ashford, and prosecutor Hyder all met at the Mesa Fire Department's training facility with several firefighters to perform an experiment for the Knapp case. Corporal Coldren Carnes of the sheriff's office — who had been assigned to assist Hyder with videotaping on the Knapp case — videotaped it.

"On 4-2-74 at 1300 hrs undersigned officer video taped a assimilation [*sic*] of a crime scene . . . at the request of Mr. Hyder of the Co. Atty's office," Carnes wrote in one of two similar sheriff's office reports he filled out that afternoon. Carnes referred to the test as a fire "reenactment/assimilation" in the second document and stated again that the taping had been "requested by the County Attorney's office." He marked the videotape reel "4-2-74 fire assim," put it in a box marked "4-2-74 Knapp Homicide," identified each with the Knapp case number, and checked the tape into the sheriff's office property room "for later court admittance," as he wrote in his report.

The discovery rules required Hyder to show the defense all "results of . . . scientific tests, experiments or comparisons." Nevertheless, the tape was never provided to the defense.* Indeed, no other police or fire department reports concerning an April 2 reenactment/simulation were ever turned over to the defense.

Many years later it was possible to determine that the tape was erased during the pendency of the Knapp case. But when these facts came to light, Hyder and Carnes would each say that he had no recollection or insight into how it got

---

* Hyder later explicitly took the untenable position that he was required to turn over only the results of scientific tests that he planned to use in his case in chief. Accordingly, that may have been the theory under which he withheld this videotape and other documentation about this test.

erased. Notwithstanding the documentary record, Hyder maintained then that he had never asked for such a tape to be made and had never known of its existence. Deputy fire marshal Dale, on the other hand, would state that he had a dim memory of having once actually seen a videotape or film of his fire tests. Because of all these odd circumstances, it is impossible to say what happened at the state's "fire reenactment" or simulation of April 2, 1974.

At the trial, Dale never mentioned an April 2 test. He did, however, claim to have performed a fire test at the Mesa Fire Department's training facility much earlier in the case, on November 27, 1973 — just eleven days after the fire. He also at some point* produced a report purporting to document a test conducted on that date. That report was dated "February 20, 1974" — almost three months after the November 27 test it purported to document, but almost six weeks *before* the April 2, 1974, test. (Though the report listed the people present, it did not list Hyder or Carnes.)

These facts suggest that there were two separate days of testing at the Mesa facility, more than four months apart, and that the second test was wholly concealed. And indeed, many years later, Dale would vaguely recall that there may have been, in fact, two separate days of tests.

But no one else remembers two different days of tests, and those who were present for either one recall seeing very similar events. So it is also possible that there was just one day of testing, on April 2, and that the date of that test was falsified — either accidentally or for strategic reasons — by pushing it forward eighteen weeks. Under that scenario, Dale's report about the test was then backdated by six weeks — either accidentally or intentionally — to indicate that it had been typed up at about the same time that Dale had written his reports about Smyth's February 16 house inspection. The eighteen-week discrepancy about the date of the test, in that event, would have made it appear as if Dale had performed empirical tests of his own before Knapp's arrest and before Smyth's entry into the case, rather than months afterward. The error would have helped make his original prearrest investigation look more thorough than it had been and would have made him appear almost as empirical in his methodology as Smyth.

Hyder later subscribed to a variant of this theory — that the April 2 tests were the only tests conducted — maintaining, however, that the eighteen-week discrepancy about the date was merely an honest mix-up.†

---

* It was most likely turned over either in July 1974, shortly before trial, or in August during the trial itself.

† When Dale first testified about the test, on August 19, 1974, he said that it was performed on No-

In any event, in the report that Dale did draw up, purporting to document tests that occurred at the Mesa facility on the afternoon of November 27, 1973, he claimed that the following occurred.

Dale placed a mattress and a small piece of acrylic carpet inside an enclosed masonry building that was at least three to four times larger than the Knapp children's bedroom. The chamber had no windows and one metal door that, unlike the door in the children's bedroom, opened outward. Dale then poured a full gallon of Coleman fuel on the carpet and mattress.

One of the firefighters, in full turnout gear and holding a mattress as a shield, approached the open door with a match. He tossed it in. Almost immediately a fireball blew out of the doorway and singed the fireman's handlebar moustache. The room became, Dale wrote, "a raging inferno." Fire and smoke rolled out the door for several minutes. The metal door was warped from the heat.

The investigators believed that there was an uncanny correspondence between the fireman's singeing of his moustache upon igniting the fuel, and Knapp's assertion, in his confession, that he singed his hair upon igniting the fuel, when a fireball came out of the bedroom.

Afterward, Dale performed a second experiment, according to the same report. He poured just one-half gallon of Coleman fuel inside the building this time. It triggered a similar blast. Dale then counted out thirty-eight seconds — the length of time it had taken Knapp to get out of bed and walk to the door of the children's bedroom when he reenacted his movements for Malone at the East Capri house.*

---

vember 19, 1973 — just three days after the fire. After a recess he said that he had checked his report and now realized that the test had actually been performed on November 27, 1973 — eleven days after the fire. If the test was really performed on April 2, 1974, it was actually performed 137 days after the fire, and just 20 days before the originally scheduled trial date.

Thus, for there to have been just one test, and an honest mistake about when it occurred, both Hyder and Dale must have failed to notice the discrepancy about the date even when their attention had been focused on it. Indeed, Hyder would have to have failed to notice even though Dale's mistake placed the tests, which Hyder remembers attending, at a time long before Hyder's entry into the case. At least one of the two main investigators on the case, Malone or Ashford, must have also failed to notice the error when Dale testified, since one or the other of those detectives sat at the prosecution's counsel table each day. Both Malone and Ashford had attended the test that was the subject of Dale's report, and Ashford had attended the one that was the subject of Carnes's report.

* If Dale's account is accurate, this fire experiment could not possibly have occurred on the afternoon of November 27, when Dale testified that it happened, and when his report stated that it had. Knapp didn't perform that thirty-eight-second reenactment of his movements at the East Capri house *until later that evening.*

After thirty-eight seconds, Dale instructed a firefighter to try to close the door. The firefighter couldn't do it. The force of the hot air blasting out of the building was too great, Dale wrote in his report. Dale himself also tried to close it, without success. Fire and smoke "literally whistled out of the door," he wrote. "We all agreed that we wouldn't want to be standing in the open doorway at that time."

Clearly, Dale concluded, both Linda and John had been lying when they claimed to have gone to the door of the room and looked in.

But there were other inferences that could be drawn from the "raging inferno" Dale had created in his experiment. Didn't the experiment suggest that if Knapp had really ignited a gallon of Coleman fuel in the tiny children's room that the force of the blast would have blown the window out? Yet four neighbors had seen Knapp knock the window out with a hose nozzle well after the fire was underway.

And since Knapp hadn't been wearing firefighter's gear and shielding himself with a mattress — the way the firefighter had at the Mesa fire test — wouldn't he have suffered more injuries than just singed hair on the top, right-hand side of his head?

Many years later, when defense lawyers found out that a "fire reenactment" or "assimilation" had been videotaped, they wondered whether concerns about this sort of inference could have played a role in Hyder's failure to turn over the tape in the first place and in the tape's subsequent erasure.

As the trial date approached, Marshall Smyth began diagraming the floor of the children's bedroom, differentiating the various degrees of burning in different parts of the room. He hoped to make a diorama of the children's bedroom and place tiny replicas of the various furnishings inside the room, to see what the relationship was between the furnishings and the burn patterns. He also planned a series of burn tests on the Knapps' carpeting and pad and on crib mattresses like the one that had been in the bedroom.

But Smyth had already billed $1,300 on the case. Performing the additional tasks would cost another $2,000. It was a mammoth sum for the public defender's office, and Basham's supervisors refused Basham any more funds.

On April 9, with the trial just two weeks off, Basham asked Judge Hardy to declare Smyth a court-appointed defense expert, so that court funds could be used to pay Smyth. Hyder strenuously opposed the motion. At the time, the U.S. Supreme Court had not yet ruled that an indigent had any constitutional right to have such expenses paid by the state, and the rule of the Supreme Court of Arizona was that an indigent had only a right to counsel, not to "the full paraphernalia of a defense."

In his opposition papers Hyder emphasized that the defense already had in its possession everything it needed to prepare its case. "The state," he wrote, "has conducted tests and investigations to determine the cause and culpability [of the fire] and the defense has been privy to all this material."

The statement was misleading. Hyder had not provided the videotape of the fire test he had performed just nine days earlier or any other information about a test on that date.

Judge Hardy followed the prevailing Arizona law and ruled for Hyder. Smyth would get no court funds.

Today, the courts do recognize that due process sometimes requires that indigents receive funds for experts. Nevertheless, the determination of precisely when funds must be provided is still vague and subjective, with the judge trying to guess the probable value of doing so. It is always a blind call. Until the expert is appointed, no one knows whether what he or she may say will be of *any* help to the defense.

And the determination of how much money, if any, a defendant should get for this purpose does not depend solely on the stakes of the trial — in capital cases, the stakes for the defendant are always infinite — but also on the pool of funds available for indigent defense, which is always very limited.

Basham appealed to the state supreme court both that ruling and Hardy's earlier order barring Diettrich from helping him try the case. The supreme court then stayed the trial until it could decide both matters.

During the delay, an investigator from the county attorney's office, Michael Elardo, continued interviewing Knapp's neighbors. Most of them could tell him only about Linda Knapp; they seldom saw John around the neighborhood. Mainly they related more horror stories about the little girls. One neighbor said she'd once seen the girls walking alone along Broadway — the main east-west road near the development, almost half a mile from their home. Another recalled once seeing Iona, two, all alone in the middle of that highway, apparently trying to cross it. That neighbor had pulled off onto the shoulder, picked Iona up, and driven her back to her home.

By May, six months had passed since the fire — the biggest event ever to hit the little housing development in East Mesa. Neighbors had gossiped, theorized, and traded tales and suspicions. The state's theory of the case had been well publicized in newspapers and television reports.

Much of what the neighbors were saying — especially the hearsay and double hearsay — was flatly wrong. There was a persistent rumor around the development, for example, that John Knapp had prevented someone from entering his house to fight the fire; but neither the police nor investigator Elardo could ever find the allegedly excluded person. Tony Rosales thought it was Dave Contreras, but Contreras said he had entered without any problem. Grace Ellsworth thought it was Leonore Ybarra, but Ybarra said that *debris* had prevented her from getting in the back door, not John Knapp. One police officer thought Molly Cameron told him that Knapp had stopped *her* from entering the house, but she later denied it.

In addition, as time passed, the neighbors' own recollections were metamorphosing. As Elardo's notes reveal, some neighbors were reporting memories that a neutral historian would have discarded as preposterous.

For instance, if there was a consensus about anything that happened on the morning of November 16, 1973, it was that John had appeared unusually cool and unemotional except for occasional outbursts of anger. At least five firefighters had observed that anger, as had Contreras and the bishop's wife, Carolyn Goodman. So had several neighbors who overheard his harsh words to Linda that morning.

One emotion no one had witnessed in Knapp that morning was mirth. But on May 17, 1974, when investigator Elardo interviewed the Knapps' neighbor Susan House, she told him, according to his notes, that John had been "laughing" that morning and that he "actually seemed to be enjoying himself."

House also told Elardo that John was not only clean and neat, but that he was "freshly shaved," his "hair neatly combed," and that he "looked like he had not been asleep at all." Soon Elardo began to hear those exact same phrases — or embellishments on them — uttered by other neighbors. Later that same day, for instance, another neighbor told Elardo that Knapp had been "freshly shaven," his "hair [was] neatly combed," and he looked like he was "ready to keep an appointment rather than just getting up from bed." Three days later, another neighbor told him that Knapp had been "just freshly shaven," his hair was "neatly combed," that he looked "more like he had an appointment with someone rather than just getting up from bed," and that, after the fire, he had been "laughing and having a good time." (Elardo did not tape-record these conversations, so it cannot be determined whether Elardo was suggesting any of these phrases to the witnesses.)

Had all these witnesses really been close enough to Knapp that morning to observe whether he had shaved? Did the state even seriously want to contend that John had gotten up that morning, shaved, combed his hair, detonated a gallon of Coleman fuel in his children's bedroom, and then lain back down in bed next to his wife?

But still more recollections were springing up. On March 1 — four months after Knapp's arrest and long after the media had published and broadcast the state's theory of the crime — one neighbor told detective Ashford that she thought she had smelled "gas or fuel" while the fire was burning. And in May, when Elardo began asking witnesses whether they remembered any suspicious smells, two more said that, come to think of it, they remembered smelling something like gasoline or lighter fuel while the house was burning.

How could this be? None of the neighbors interviewed before Knapp's arrest had ever mentioned smelling fuel. None of the eight firefighters or two deputy sheriffs who had responded to the fire had smelled a flammable liquid on the scene — not, at least, until inspector McDaniel got down on his hands and knees and smelled the oily film on the floor of the children's bedroom. Yet now three neighbors said they had smelled flammable liquids from twenty yards away when they were standing around on nearby lawns.

The state's case was getting stronger with each passing day.

It's impossible to say precisely when it happened. But by June 1974, it had happened to both Basham and Diettrich.

Initially, they would have described the change in their perspectives solely in professional terms: the state's case did not seem as overwhelming as they once thought.

In fact, every aspect of the state's theory was becoming hard to picture. As bad as things might have been in John's life on the morning of November 16, 1973, things were looking up. He had turned the electricity back on the day before and would have been able to turn the gas on that day. His mother would be coming in January to help care for the kids and get the house back in order.

The image of any man waking up and, first thing in the morning, burning his children to death, was intrinsically hard to imagine. In contrast, at 8:10 A.M. — more than an hour after sunrise — the children would very likely have already been up and about. The neighbors said they often saw them roaming outside as early as 6:00 in the morning.

On November 16, it had been cold — 44 degrees outside — and there was no heat in the house. Perhaps the children had tried to do something to keep warm.

Although Knapp had confessed, every detail of the confession was improbable. How had he gotten in and out of bed without waking Linda? How had he buried the Coleman fuel can under a mound of newspapers in the living room closet — just a few feet from Linda's ear — again without waking her? How had he set off a gallon of Coleman fuel without incurring injury or blowing the window out?

In his confession Knapp said the children had been sleeping together in their bed when he set the fire. If so, how had they ended up on opposite sides of the room? Wouldn't a flammable liquid fire have killed them almost instantly?

And then there was Linda, imperturbably sticking to a story that corroborated John's in every respect. She seemed to hate John. Why would she be lying to protect him?

"There's no way he could have done it without Linda Knapp knowing," Diettrich said nineteen years later. "And Linda Knapp would have burned him in an instant if she'd've known, believe me. She would have been there to fry him."

And Linda was scared, as Diettrich recalled it. "The police suspected her from the beginning and — you know what? — to this day still think that Linda Knapp was involved with John in the fire. . . . If she'd have had any knowledge that John was involved in any respect, instead of running she would have said, 'Hey, don't point at me, here's what happened.' Because she was scared to death. She didn't want a bad rap put on her."

And though the state seemed to think Linda was lying, all the details of her story kept checking out. Iona's body was found exactly where Linda said she had seen her; Little Linda was where Linda had heard her. Smyth, the defense fire expert, was telling them the dresser drawers in the room *did* appear to have been pulled out of the chest and sitting in the middle of the room, just as Linda said. There was a crease across the width of the charred crib mattress that suggested that it had been leaning against the crib support in just the odd position that Linda had described. If Linda was telling the truth, then John's confession *couldn't* be accurate.

Other curiosities began to take on importance in the lawyers' minds the more they pondered them. As damning as the neighbors' memories of John were, none of them remembered Knapp wearing glasses that morning. And John always wore glasses — conspicuous, thick, black horn-rimmed glasses. Except, of course, when he just got up from bed.

There was John's strange response when Malone read him his rights inside the cold, dark East Capri house on the evening of November 27. John had said he would answer only questions he had "direct knowledge of." Obviously Knapp was drawing a distinction between what *he* knew and what *his wife* might have known. Why would a guilty person draw such a distinction? In fact, who would say such a thing except someone who suspected that his wife may have been somehow involved and yet wanted to protect her?

Finally — and, of course, this was something they could never argue to a jury — the lawyers were getting to know John. Diettrich and Basham believed they had developed some instincts as defense lawyers.

"I was really a seasoned lawyer for my age," Diettrich said in 1993, the emotion building in his voice, "and I just — after a while you get a feel. Well you add up the evidence, first of all. And then you add up your observations and your senses and things like that, and I just had that feeling about John, there was just no doubt in my mind.

"It's something I knew," Diettrich continued. "I *knew*. And the more time I spent with him, just watching his face, watching his eyes, watching his body language, I guarantee it. I would've known — I would have sensed it. I mean I've spent untold hours working with him.

"You know, there are some times you could be ninety-nine and nine-tenths percent sure about something. But there are some things you just fuckin' know. I *knew*."

And so, by June 1974, it had happened. Neither lawyer would ever recover from the experience.

"It's the worst thing that I think can happen to a criminal defense attorney," Basham said nineteen years later.

Basham and Diettrich had come to believe that their client was innocent.

Six

One of John Knapp's first memories is of giving his baby sister, Iona, a ride in her crib or playpen, by pushing it across the floor. He was about four years old. While doing so, he happened to push the crib up against a heater, catching an end of his sister's blanket on fire. One of John's older brothers put it out. John's father beat John with a hard-soled slipper.

Twenty-four years later, when John Knapp was on trial for his life, prosecutor Hyder unsuccessfully sought to ask questions about this incident in front of the jury.

"He attempted to burn his baby sister to death," Hyder told Judge Hardy. "I think it shows propensity for burning babies." Judge Hardy forbade Hyder from discussing it.*

Knapp's earliest years were spent in Carnegie, Pennsylvania, a small town near Pittsburgh that was dominated by a steel mill and railroad yards. His father, William, was an engineer with the Pennsylvania Railroad. Half German

---

* Hyder's version was apparently based on a misleading hearsay account that Linda told detectives when they interrogated her in Nebraska. According to tapes, Linda Knapp told Malone and Ashford, "[John] remembers setting [his sister Iona's] playpen on fire when he was about five." The words, while literally true, implied that Knapp had set the fire intentionally. The detectives appear to have interpreted it that way, writing in their report: "When his sister Iona was a baby, [John] set fire to her baby blanket." The detectives did not mention John's age in their report.

and half American Indian, William was about five foot ten, big-boned and powerful, with dark hair and a copper complexion. He was bald on the top, with hair around the sides, and was a "good-looking man," according to John's brother Robert.

William's job took him away on business for weeks at a time. John and the other children grew to dread his returns. William was a cold, stern man who lost his temper frequently, particularly with John and Robert, who was five years older.

"When we got punished, we got beat," Robert Knapp later said. "My dad would take a belt to us, or a board. He didn't care where he hit you. . . . The only time I ever saw my dad laugh in sixteen years of living with him was one New Year's eve, when he was inebriated."

John's main memories of his father are of spankings, beatings, and verbal abuse. His father frequently called him a "dumb bastard" or "stupid son-of-a-bitch."

John was very close to his mother, Mary, however.

"Mother was very tolerant and very kind," according to Robert.

Mary was lively, about five foot six, a little heavy, had black hair and very fair skin — a "very beautiful complexion," according to Marilyn. She worked as a cook in restaurants and cafeterias and was an excellent cook at home.

Both Mary and William had children by previous marriages, so Mary raised twelve children in all. John was the youngest of the six boys, and he suspects that his mother may have doted on him. Mary and William had five children together: Robert, Marilyn, John, Janet,* and Iona, born in that order. John was born on August 22, 1946.

In about 1954 the family moved to a rural area between two tiny hamlets called Presto and Federal. They lived in a rustic house that, at first, had no running water, electricity, or furnace. Heat came from a wood-burning, potbellied stove in the kitchen. John's father, who was skilled with tools, fixed up the home largely by himself, installing plumbing and electrical circuitry.

Knapp's brother Robert and sister Marilyn (a pseudonym) have no memory of the incident. They confirm, however, that their sister Iona, who has Down's syndrome, was institutionalized at about the age of two, so that John Knapp, who is three years older than Iona, could not have been more than five at the time the incident occurred.

John's mother, Mary, who had not been present when the incident happened, said she had no knowledge of it when Basham asked her about it in 1974. She has since died, as has John's father.

* "Janet," like "Marilyn," is a pseudonym.

William had his own workshop, but whenever he could not find anything he accused Robert or John of stealing it. On one occasion, when he couldn't find a hammer, he beat John with a two-by-four on the back of the legs, buttocks, small of the back, and shoulders. Although John was screaming, he refused to cry, believing that this would deprive his father of the gratification he sought, he later told a psychologist. His refusal to cry seemed to him to prolong the beating. John's mother ran into the workshop and found the hammer, which William had evidently left on a bookcase he was building. She threw the hammer at her husband. When he ducked, he let go of John, who ran. John remembers his father refusing to apologize and saying that John probably deserved the beating for having done something else William didn't know about.

John's main playmates were Robert, Marilyn, and Janet. (Iona was already institutionalized.) Robert sometimes took John fishing or swimming at a nearby water hole. William was an avid fisherman and hunter, and John was fascinated with his father's tackle box. But William never took John hunting and took him fishing only once — a fact John appears to recall bitterly.

John went to many different schools and did very poorly in almost every subject. He never cared for organized sports, and he developed few close friends.

John's parents had a bad marriage. He once remembers seeing his mother crying, and — assuming that his father had caused it somehow — he started to cry also. He remembers pulling a blanket over his head so no one would see that he was crying.

When John showed affection toward his mother, by hugging her or giving her a kiss, his father would mock them both. — Why don't you give him some nookie, — William would tell his wife. John does not remember his father kissing him or hugging him ever, he told a defense psychologist.

In 1960 John's parents separated. In June they put Marilyn, John, and Janet in an orphanage in Pittsburgh. (By then Robert had left home. He ran away, Robert later said, after he accidentally spilled a wheelbarrow of dirt while doing chores, and his father tried to strike him with a shovel.)

At Christmas, John's parents brought the children home, having patched up their marriage. But as soon as William left on business again, Mary and the children fled to Pottstown, outside Philadelphia, where Mary had some family. Pottstown was a more urban setting than John had ever experienced. At school he encountered switchblades and gang fights. John, who hated arguments of any kind, retreated from his peers. His main solace was sneaking away to a river, where he could fish.

About six months later, John's father showed up at the door, and, much to his son's dismay, talked his wife into returning. They moved to McDonald, another small town outside Pittsburgh. John went to high school there, doing poorly in every subject except science, which he enjoyed. Still largely a loner, he was too shy to have girlfriends. In the evenings he sometimes went to the porch of an old building in town, where he could spend a couple hours by himself, unnoticed.

In February 1965, in the middle of the eleventh grade, he quit high school. He landed a dirty, arduous factory job making bolts for use in coal mines, earning about $1.35 an hour. After a month he took a job as an orderly at a hospital. John bought a used 1955 Oldsmobile for $50, but he recalls his father effectively stealing it from him by simply appropriating it for his own use.

In November 1965 John's half-brother Martin was killed in Vietnam. John didn't cry when it happened. About a month or so later, however, when he was rocking his sister Marilyn's baby to sleep and singing him a song, he thought of Martin and began to cry. To John's surprise, tears streamed down his face, he later told a psychologist.

On January 3, 1966 — two months after Martin's death — John, nineteen, enlisted in the U.S. Army. He was sent to Fort Jackson in South Carolina for basic training, which was awful for him. John liked to sleep long and late, and getting up for reveille at 4:30 was difficult for him.

In the spring he was transferred to Fort Sam Houston in San Antonio, Texas, where he was assigned to work as a hospital supply clerk. He began dating a seventeen-year-old high school girl and became engaged to her briefly, though they broke up the following spring.

It was about then that John learned that he was being sent to Vietnam. After visiting his mother, who had separated from his father and moved to Mesa, Arizona, for her health, he boarded a bus for Oakland, California, where he would catch his flight to Saigon. John began chatting with the young woman next to him, Cheryl, and when she reached her destination in San Diego, they traded addresses and kissed good-bye. John and Cheryl exchanged letters almost weekly throughout John's tour of duty in Vietnam, according to John.

On June 14, 1967, he flew from Oakland to Saigon.

Saigon in June was stiflingly hot, and it rained almost every afternoon. John was assigned to a transportation battalion about fifteen miles to the west, at Phu Loi. The camp, where John served as a supply clerk, guard, and driver, was periodically the target of mortar attacks. After a couple months he got a job he enjoyed, serving as a supply clerk at a medical dispensary in the refugee village of Vinh Son, about four miles from the camp.

Vinh Son was a village of about 1,200 Vietnamese Catholics who had fled North Vietnam. John was taken with the villagers — mainly pig farmers — who seemed astonishingly proud and industrious. John passed out bandages, aspirin, and medicine, treated children whose mosquito bites had become infected, and transported anyone who was seriously ill to a hospital in Phu Loi.

His service in Vietnam, though it had its searing moments, evidently provided John with some of the best times of his life. He made friends and found working with the refugees rewarding. Linda remembers John telling her fondly of the children he treated there and showing her photos of them, which he kept in a shoebox.

In February 1968, the Tet Offensive began, and both Phu Loi and the refugee village came under heavy attack. John was transferred to a base closer to Saigon, but that base, too, eventually came under fire and was periodically shelled during the rest of his stay.

Shortly before his tour ended, Cheryl wrote to him that she had begun seeing someone else.

On June 14, 1968, John flew back to Oakland and then boarded a bus to Fort Bliss in El Paso, Texas.

On his first leave that summer, he went to Mesa to see his mother. His brother Robert was stationed nearby, and Robert's wife, Jane, now lived in Tempe. While John was home, Jane came by with the daughter of a woman she worked with. Her name was Linda.

Linda was sixteen years old, about five foot two inches tall, plump — about 130 pounds at that time — and had strawberry blond hair. John thought she was "pretty in her way," he recalled in 1991. Jane, Linda, John, and John's sister Janet all decided to go swimming at Canyon Lake, a reservoir created by one of the dams that provide power and water to the Salt River Valley. The lake, dramatically set amid red cliffs, was a popular spot for swimming, water skiing, and picnicking.

After an afternoon of swimming, the four headed back across the parking lot to the car. Linda had left her sandals in the car, and the pavement was hot on her bare feet. John picked her up and carried her to the car.

A day or two later John called Linda up, and they took a walk to a park near Linda's home. They lay on the grass and talked. Linda talked about how she couldn't get along with her stepfather, Ken Ramsey, and John talked about how he couldn't get along with his father.

— What would you say if I asked you to marry me? — John said toward the end of the evening.

— Yes, — Linda said.

John and Linda began dating.

Linda's mother, Louise, was born on August 10, 1935, and grew up in Ogden, Utah. Louise was the fifth of ten children. Her father held a variety of jobs — school bus driver, farmer, roofer, gas station owner — and raised the children in the Mormon church.

When Louise was fifteen she married Arthur Holiday (a pseudonym), but separated from him after just three months, when Holiday was arrested for the statutory rape of a different teenage girl (who was about the same age as Louise). Holiday was convicted and sentenced to time in the Utah State Prison.

When Louise separated from Holiday she was already pregnant with Linda, who was born on November 14, 1951. Since Louise had just turned sixteen, her mother, Anna, raised Linda. Anna continued to do so when Louise remarried in 1953. That marriage, too, lasted only a few months and produced a second child, Sybil (a pseudonym).

Louise's third marriage, on July 1, 1954, lasted. Her husband, Kenneth Ramsey, twenty-one, was a nonobservant Mormon. Ken was an electronics technician in the U.S. Navy at the time and later became an electronics instructor in the U.S. Air Force. Ken and Louise raised Sybil and eventually had two children of their own, Kathy and Darlene (pseudonyms).

Meanwhile, however, Linda was still being raised by her grandmother in Ogden, and her aunts and uncles, who brought her up as an observant Mormon. She saw her mother from time to time, but never met her natural father till she was five or six. After his release from prison, Holiday had moved to Nebraska, where he got a job as a truck driver. Sometimes when he was driving through Ogden, he would stop and visit Linda. Linda was not told that he had been in prison. Holiday became an exciting mystery to Linda, according to Louise.

Linda describes her years with her grandparents as happy ones. She was the baby of the family, well cared for, and loved. In her opinion, in fact, her upbringing may have been too sheltered.

"I don't think that people leading Leave-It-to-Beaver lifestyles are living real life," she said in 1993. "I don't think sugar coating helps anything. I grew up in a household that was sugar coated."

When Linda turned nine, her family decided that it was time for her to live with Louise. The transition was dramatic. Unlike Linda's Ogden relatives, Louise and Ken were very nonobservant Mormons; they were chain-smokers and drinkers of alcohol. But more important, Linda went from being the youngest child in one family to being the oldest in another. Louise and Ken thought Linda was spoiled, and Linda thought Ken was a harsh disciplinarian.

"I have six brothers who thought Linda was the greatest thing," Louise later recalled. When she was growing up in Ogden, Louise said, "they took her along on their dates. Anything Linda wanted she got from one or the other of the brothers. But when she come to live with us, she wasn't the only child. She just — I really think I should have never taken her away from my mother."

"She wasn't the baby of the family" was how Ken Ramsey saw it, and no longer had "everybody fussing over her. She thought she was picked on because I insisted she go to school. Linda's a very talented young lady. Her problem has always been getting motivated. . . . She was always very, very hard-headed. If she didn't want to do something, she wouldn't do it. And it didn't matter what kind of punishment you felt like levying on her. One of our bones of contention was her room. It was always a disaster area."

"I wanted out of the house," Linda remembered in 1993. "Me and my stepfather did not get along. Don't get me wrong. Ken Ramsey is a very responsible man. But he could be very violent. I remember him beating me with belts. [But] I have immense respect for the man. We grew up with a sense of values kids don't have now days.

"But I felt left out. I looked like my real father. I'm not his — I'm not real wild about my stepfather. When he's sober, he's a wonderful man. When he drank, I'd rather not be around him."

Since Ken was in the service, the family moved frequently. Linda lived in Utah, Virginia, Connecticut, Arizona, and then Utah again. Though she seemed to be bright, she was an underachiever at school. She liked to draw and, sometimes, to crochet and cook, and she read romance novels. She also liked to write to pen pals, getting her correspondents' names from a pen-pal magazine.

When Linda turned fourteen, Louise decided that it was time to tell her the "truth" about her natural father. "Linda always had this thing about her dad, her dad, her dad," Louise told the author. "Finally one day I set her down and told her just what her dad was like. I told her, 'Hey, your dad isn't what you think he is. If he thought so much of you, he'd at least send you birthday cards.' He never sent her a birthday card, a Christmas card, or a dime of support."

When Linda was sixteen she did some baby-sitting for one of her mother's co-workers, a woman named Jane. One day Jane invited Linda to go swimming with her and her brother- and sister-in-law.

Jane's brother-in-law was John Knapp, a skinny, twenty-one-year-old boy who had just returned from Vietnam. He was almost six foot three inches tall, about 160 pounds, and was wearing a uniform. She liked him, and they began dating.

After John returned to El Paso, he and Linda began exchanging letters. He visited her again on three-day passes and began seeing her regularly after his honorable discharge at the end of February 1969, when he moved to Mesa to live with his mother.

John disgusted Ken Ramsey. Though John had earned his high school equivalency diploma while in the army, he had no plans to go on to college. He landed short-term, low-paying jobs and had only modest prospects for advancement. He was passive, slept a lot, and didn't even seem to have any friends. Sometimes when John visited he would fall asleep on the couch, and Ken and Louise would be unable to wake him.

Ken forbade Linda to marry him until she graduated from high school, which was still two years away. But on May 6, 1969, three months after John moved to Mesa, John and Linda secretly drove to Tucson and got married in a brief civil ceremony. When Ken found out about the marriage he wanted to get it annulled, since Linda was still a minor. But, behind his back, Louise had already granted Linda written permission; the marriage was binding.

Linda moved in with John and his mother, whom Linda soon found very domineering. In July Mary opened her own cafe in Casa Grande, a small desert town south of Phoenix, and John and Linda moved there with her. John briefly found work as a corrections officer at the state prison in Florence but, hating it, quit after about ten days.

By September Linda was pregnant, and she had had all she could take of John's mother. In addition, although the details are unclear, Linda had, by this time, made at least one ostensible attempt at suicide, though it had seemingly little chance of success. While still in Tempe, she took an overdose of an over-the-counter cold remedy tablet; John had taken her to the hospital, where she got her stomach pumped.

"I told her that I felt that she had an emotional problem," John later testified, "and maybe a possible mental problem, and I mentioned a psychiatrist, and she hit the ceiling. She got very nasty about it."

In September Linda and John moved to Ogden, Utah, to put some distance between Linda and John's mother. John found work in a lumber mill, working on a gang-saw, but by January he had been laid off, and he and Linda fell into dire financial straits. Linda pawned her wedding ring, which John had bought for about $350, to help make ends meet.

They returned to Tempe and began living with Ken and Louise. Ken found John work at Frank's Friendly Tavern in Tempe, which a friend of his owned. It paid just $1.50 an hour, but it included free rent in a studio apartment behind the tavern. John and Linda moved into that apartment, and John managed to keep the job for a full year.

During this period, Linda, who had capably performed housework until she got pregnant, suddenly and dramatically stopped doing any. She put on an enormous amount of weight and refused to do almost any tasks around the house. John did not pick up the slack. He regarded housework as Linda's job.

Also during this period John had a sexual relationship with Barbara Vinson (a pseudonym), who was temporarily staying with the Knapps. Barbara was the sister of Bobby Vinson (a pseudonym), whom Linda had previously dated. (Barbara later claimed that Linda had given her permission to have sex with John, but Linda denied it.)

Linda Louise Knapp, a blue-eyed, blond baby girl, was born on May 15, 1970.

Late one night, two or three weeks after the birth, Linda took a cab home to the Ramseys', bringing her infant daughter with her. According to Louise Ramsey, Linda (the adult) had a "black eye, a cut lip, and her face looked like hamburger." Linda said John had beaten her. John later admitted having struck Linda in the face on one occasion. John later told a psychologist that Linda had made a remark about his mother. In 1993 Linda told the author she couldn't remember what precipitated this incident.

Within a few days, Linda returned to John.

With Little Linda's birth, Linda appeared to emerge from her inert phase, and she was a good mother for several months. By the fall, she was pregnant again.

But about six months later, in February 1971, John had a falling-out with his boss at the tavern and quit. That forced him and Linda to move back in with the Ramseys. They were still there on May 12, 1971, when Linda gave birth to Iona Marie, a second blond, blue-eyed girl.

The same week Iona was born, John landed the highest-paying job he had ever had, working for Continental Can Company in Tempe, which had a small plant within walking distance of the Ramseys'. The plant operated at union wage scales — more than $4.00 an hour — but the work was seasonal, with peaks during the summer and lulls during the winter. John's labor was required for just seven weeks that summer, and then he was laid off, with little expectation of being needed again until the following spring. Nevertheless, it was a job worth pursuing since, as John earned seniority, he would eventually qualify for year-round work.

In the fall John's mother found him a job with her brother-in-law, who owned a gas station near Pomona, California. John and Linda moved there and eventually wound up in a house next door to John's mother. But soon he lost his job again. Some trading stamps had turned up missing, and John's boss fired him, suspecting him of having stolen them. John applied for welfare, while his mother helped him make the rent.

Meanwhile, Linda was slipping back into her inert mode. She stopped doing housework and began neglecting the children as well.

Louise and Ken do not regard Linda's inert phases as more than a matter of Linda's personal taste and immaturity, aggravated by a host of John's inadequacies. Neither they nor Linda think it appropriate to characterize these episodes as psychological depressions, although Linda does say that they may have had something to do with unhappiness.

"You've got to know Linda," Louise said in a 1993 interview. "She hated housework with a passion. Just one of those rebellious things."

"Rebellion," Linda said in 1993, explaining her aversion to housework. "When we were kids, mother worked and Ken worked, and us kids were responsible for a lot of housework. Me and my sister Sybil raised Darlene and Kathy. So a lot of it's just rebellion. . . . And I wasn't happy. It's hard. There are a lot of things you get unhappy about that there's not a whole heckuva lot you can do anything about."

It was about this time that the Knapps had their first fire, the one John later mentioned to detective Malone toward the end of his first interrogation session. A flame was left on under some grease in a pan on the stove. Although someone called the fire department, John and a neighbor put out the fire before the trucks arrived.

While John and Linda were in Pomona, they also had a serious argument over two teenage runaways John had befriended while they had been hitchhiking and whom he had brought to the house. This was the occasion on which Linda, according to what she later told Malone during her interrogation in Nebraska, allegedly witnessed John groping with one girl on the floor. John always denied any such incident to his lawyers. Linda eventually notified the police of the runaway's whereabouts, and she was picked up.*

Shortly after the argument over the girl, Linda took more than seventy tablets of an over-the-counter drug in what was then at least her second osten-

---

* In an interview with the author in 1993, Linda said she remembered the runaway, and remembered reporting her, but had no recollection of John's ever having made sexual advances toward her.

sible suicide attempt. Again, John took her to the hospital, where her stomach was pumped.

On Friday, March 3, 1972, John learned from the Ramseys that Continental Can had work for him in Tempe beginning that coming Monday. John drove to Tempe that weekend, promising to come back and pick up Linda and the kids after he drew his first paycheck.

By this time, however, Linda was deep into one of her inert phases. John's mother, who lived next door, worked as a live-in housekeeper elsewhere, and came home only for the weekends. But what she saw on those occasions shocked her.

"Linda left medicine lying around the house," Mary later testified. "She left turpentine in the bathroom [where the children could get at it]. The children were running out on the streets. They were naked, they weren't fed. The house was in squalor. Finally, I had the children removed from her custody."

On Saturday afternoon, March 18, 1972, Mary called the Pomona police, who sent an officer to the Knapp home. The stench of urine and feces hit him as soon as Linda opened the door, he wrote in his police report. He found both girls naked, though it was quite chilly inside the house. Iona was in a playpen, sucking on a dirty bottle that contained a molding liquid. Little Linda had a two-inch-long bruise on her face.

The floors were cluttered with trash and dirty clothes, and it seemed to the officer as if ashtrays had been emptied onto the floor. In the bathroom the tub was half full of cold, dirty water, with cigarette butts floating on the surface. The floor of the bathroom was littered with dirty clothing, and behind the bathroom door was a stack of dirty diapers, still filled with feces.

The kitchen stove was covered with dried, caked food and open cans of molding food. The floor of the kitchen was "covered with trash, dried stale food, and numerous piles of animal droppings," the officer wrote. He found no edible food in the house.

After the officer gave Linda her Miranda warnings, she told him that her husband was in Arizona and that she had just $10 on which to live.

The officer took the children away from Linda and had them temporarily placed in a foster home. He took photos of the house and the girls and took Iona's bottle into evidence.

At about the same time, John was on the highway to Pomona, having picked up his first paycheck the day before, according to plan. When he got to his home, he found Linda crying and the children gone.

He called the Pomona police, but learned that the California authorities were refusing to release the children to him so long as Linda would still be caring for them. John then arranged to have the Ramseys take custody of the children. The Ramseys drove to Pomona and picked the girls up on Tuesday night, March 21. John and Linda and the girls began to live with the Ramseys in Tempe.

Louise and Ken blame the child neglect in Pomona on John, since John was failing to provide for his family. In addition, though the claim is incoherent, Louise blames the incident on John's mother, Mary.

Similarly, both Linda and her mother, Louise, deny that Linda neglected or failed to supervise her children — then or, indeed, ever.

There is no document that can be found today that explains precisely what the arrangement was under which the Ramseys were permitted to take custody of the children. But when John and Linda moved into a trailer park about a month and a half later, the Ramseys allowed them to take the children with them without seeking the approval of the California authorities. Ken and Louise maintain the authorities never forbade them from handing the children back to John and Linda.

After a brief period living at the trailer park, the Knapps moved to the Green Goose Motel in Tempe, where John was supposed to manage the motel in exchange for a free apartment — although he was working full-time at Continental Can, also. This arrangement lasted only a couple of months.

One afternoon while he lived there, John came home from Continental Can to discover that Linda had already put the children to bed. Linda told him that Little Linda had gotten hold of her diet pills and that both girls seemed to have taken some. John went into their bedroom.

"Iona's eyes were glassed over," John later testified, "and I realized that there was something wrong. One of the tenants had a car there and I asked her if she would take us to hospital."

Though Little Linda was okay, Iona was not. "I took Iona to the emergency room," Knapp later testified, "and they put a nasal gastric tube into her, and began to pump her stomach."

After awhile the doctors thought Iona would be okay, so the Knapps started home in a cab. But along the way, Iona suddenly stopped breathing.

Floyd Davis, the cab driver at the time, later testified: "John Knapp was very concerned. He was crying. One little girl was passing in and out of consciousness. John was trying to give her mouth-to-mouth to keep her breathing till she got [back] to the hospital. John was trying to save the child. He was more or less in a panic — frantic."

Davis rushed back to the emergency room, and Iona survived. After this incident, Louise talked Linda into seeing a therapist at a community mental health center, but Linda quit after two sessions.

By fall 1972, the Knapps had moved again, to an apartment in Mesa. The winter lull at Continental Can once again resulted in John being laid off in mid-September. John then got a job with a cab company in Mesa. The pay there was much worse — about $75 per week in salary, plus commissions and tips.

On October 9, one of the Knapps' neighbors called the Mesa police to report child neglect, alleging that Linda would lock her children out of the apartment during the day and fail to supervise them. But when the police arrived Linda denied the accusation and the girls seemed healthy, so the officers suggested to Linda that "a little cleaning of the house would probably keep the neighbors quiet," as one officer wrote in his report.

Toward the end of the year John looked into buying a house in East Mesa. He would be able to afford it if he got back his job at Continental Can in the spring. A small, three-bedroom house in the new development would cost $18,600, and he could qualify for a federally subsidized loan.

In January he signed a contract to buy the house that was then under construction at 7435 East Capri. He could move in by March or April, and the first monthly payment of $126 per month would not come due until the end of June.

In mid-February John was recalled to Continental Can. But by that time, John and Linda were having severe marital difficulties. In late 1972 Linda had rekindled her romantic relationship with Bobby Vinson — an old high school boyfriend — had left Knapp, and had moved in with the Ramseys.

Sometime during this period a relative of Bobby Vinson remembers Knapp coming to her home, furious, threatening to kill Vinson and Linda, and demanding to confront Vinson about his relationship with Linda. To calm him down, she later told a state investigator, she had Knapp show her pictures of the children, which he had with him.

— They are cute little girls, — she said.

— No, they're not. They're beautiful! — Knapp responded.

— When they grow up, you're going to have to fight the boys away from the door. —

— Well, the way it looks now, they ain't going to grow up, — Knapp allegedly said.

On February 21, John filed his own child-neglect complaint against Linda, alleging that she failed to clothe and feed the children and describing Iona's ingestion of Linda's diet pills a few months earlier.

But within a day or so — before the agency sent anybody to see Linda — John called again and withdrew the complaint, stating that he and Linda had reconciled.

Linda and John were separated for several weeks. But the Ramseys were having enough trouble caring for Linda's three half-sisters without taking in Linda and her two children as well. They either talked Linda into returning to John, as Louise and Linda remember it, or they kicked her out of their house, as John later described it to his lawyers.

Linda did return to John, and in April the family moved into the house at 7435 East Capri.

As bleak as John and Linda's marriage was, there were some good, if fleeting, moments. Some of those moments involved the children.

Little Linda was "a little Sherman tank," according to Linda. "She was outgoing. She'd try anything. She was a little tiger.

"Iona was very, very petite. She was real quiet, and extremely intelligent. She walked at eight months. And she talked better than her older sister [did when she was the same age].

"Little Linda idolized her father. She would do anything that man asked her to do. But Iona was his favorite. He made no bones about it, either. He called her his little China doll. She looked frail. She was thin. She'd eat constantly but she never gained an ounce.

"John played with them. He had pillow fights with them. . . . John was big on . . . taking the kids places," Linda told the author in 1993. She remembered him taking them to the circus twice, and to Disneyland, Knott's Berry Farm, and Lion Country Safari, a drive-through zoo in southern California.

Thomas Cunningham, plant manager at Continental Can, also later remembered Knapp as having been a proud father. "John was always speaking highly of his family and Linda, as well as the two children . . . almost to the point of doting over the children and discussing what the girls and the family did," Cunningham later said.

John's colleagues at work believed that he loved his wife very much. In fact, it mystified several of them, because they did not think highly of Linda. "I think she was probably the only woman he could get," co-worker James Beckley told defense investigators.

Beckley and another worker used to make fun of John for being so laughably henpecked by Linda, whom they remember seeing when she came in to pick up his paychecks. "She ruled the roost," Beckley later told a state investigator.

Continental Can was itself an obvious bright spot in John's life. At its small plant in Tempe, which made soft-drink cans, John operated a forklift and a palletizer. The palletizer stacked cans on a pallet, so that a forklift could load them onto a truck.

While his colleagues noticed that John kept his problems and emotions bottled up and that he had problems with money as well as tardiness and absences — and at least one considered him moody and sometimes depressed — most seemed to like him.

"John pretty much kept to himself and went about doing his job," plant manager Cunningham later said. He considered Knapp "dependable" and "hardworking." He allowed only the steadiest people to drive the forklift, he later told a defense lawyer, and John was one of them.

John and Linda's social life was limited. Sometimes they went bowling. Neither drank much. John smoked and constantly drank soft drinks — which he called "pop" — even though his doctors told him to abstain from them because of his diabetic condition. Linda read romances, while John read comic books, science, science fiction, detective magazines, and pornography.

And, despite the appearance of appalling abandonment that the Knapp home periodically took on, John and Linda each made occasional efforts to improve their lot. John made a bookcase and two simple tables, and Linda built a crib support for the baby mattress. John later told his lawyers he believed Linda had been painting furniture or something in the children's room during the month of the fire — either with paint or a Varathane (polyurethane) finish.

Even when Linda was at her most inert, she might still pursue an arts or crafts project that caught her fancy. On her birthday, two days before the fatal fire, she made a small terrarium at a women's meeting at her church.

"It had a glass dome, a wooden base, peat moss, plastic deer, and some dried flowers," Linda accurately remembered almost twenty years later, in a 1993 interview.* She brought it home to adorn her unimaginably fetid home.

In April 1973, when John and Linda moved into the house at East Capri, John began to lose his perpetual battle with oversleeping and tardiness. The new

---

* Her description is corroborated by police photographs of the fire scene.

house was more than fifteen miles from the Continental Can plant, there was no bus service to substitute if his decrepit car broke down, and he had no phone to give his employer notice when a problem arose. The company had a policy of terminating any employee who was absent or tardy three times within a month.

John couldn't meet these requirements, and on April 26 he was terminated. But John was sufficiently well thought of at the plant that plant manager Cunningham and the shop steward agreed to give John another chance. He returned to work on May 10, 1973.

After his return, John worked very long hours for several months. Through the peak summer months he often worked fifty or more hours a week, and he worked sixty-five and a half hours one week in July, according to company records. Accordingly, he was making good money during this period. A forty-hour week would net him close to $140, and with overtime he sometimes took home close to $200.

In late May a door-to-door salesman from a Phoenix outfit called Carpetbaggers sold John wall-to-wall carpeting for the house. John later told his lawyers that he had thought it would be better for the children, who were falling down a lot. He ordered a one-inch tufted-pile nylon carpet with an extra thick butyl rubber pad beneath it. They selected a carpet style the manufacturer called Good Fortune and chose Autumn Gold as the color. With financing it cost $1,915, to be paid off in sixty monthly installments of $32.

In June, however, John began to experience severe headaches at work. Though he had had headaches all his life, they had never been this bad before. He complained of dizziness, nausea, flashes of light, and blindness. Other workers remember him holding his head, wincing, or laying his head down on a table. No one at Continental Can thought John was faking. (John was not paid for any time he missed due to health problems. His health benefits covered his medical care only.) Cunningham arranged to have John get electroencephalograms taken. No organic problem was apparent, so doctors thereafter assumed that Knapp was suffering from tension, vascular, or, possibly, migraine headaches. Prosecutors would later *take the position* that since there was no apparent organic problem, Knapp must have been faking.

In the late afternoon of August 10, John had another severe attack. It was Louise's birthday, and Ken was taking her to Tucson for a few days. As a gift, John and Linda were going to paint some rooms in the Ramseys' house while they were away. In later years, prosecutors and the Ramseys would suggest that maybe John had faked this headache to get out of his painting commitment.

At the time, however, nobody questioned the seriousness of Knapp's headache. Louise's friend Melba Burr was visiting when the headache struck.

"John was pulling his hair out," she later told prosecutor Hyder in a taped interview, "crawling all over the floor, like he was going berserk. . . . He scared Linda to death." Burr drove him and Linda to Tempe Community Hospital, Burr recounted, where "he passed out, and fell, and hit the floor in the waiting room."

"He started pulling hair out by handfuls," Linda recounted in 1993. She, too, remembered Knapp passing out in the waiting room — a claim that is corroborated by the hospital's records. "They had those ceramic tiles on the floor," Linda said, "and he broke one with his head."

Though the headache subsided, John was in the hospital for a week for observation. Late on his second night there, when he tried to phone Linda, he discovered that she was out with Melba Burr at a bar. Consumed with jealousy — or, perhaps, as he later told his lawyers, angered that Linda had left the children in the care of one of her teenage sisters — he checked out of the hospital on a four-hour pass, found Linda, and made a scene in the bar. Prosecutors later *took the position* that Knapp's temporary departure from the hospital showed, again, that he must have been faking the headaches that had led to his hospitalization.

After performing more precautionary tests, including a spinal tap, the neurologist found no organic abnormalities and diagnosed John as suffering from tension headaches. He prescribed the painkiller Percodan and released John from the hospital on August 17. Later, in October, the neurologist switched the prescription to Darvon Compound.

John returned to work on Tuesday, August 21. But three weeks later, while working the night shift on September 10, John had another attack.

"They called me at home," the plant manager, Cunningham, later testified. "John had been working on the palletizer. I went in, and John was very unstable, grasping his head, obviously in pain. It didn't pass."

Cunningham sent John home.

"Linda came in to pick John up," Cunningham remembered. "She was pretty loud and on John's case for having to be picked up and having headaches. In my opinion, it was inappropriate. John didn't say anything in response."

At the end of September the transmission on John's seventeen-year-old Pontiac broke down. John couldn't get to work, and he was terminated. Again, however, Cunningham held out to John the prospect of yet another chance.

"I told John if he could get his house in order," he said later, "so he could be at work on a regular basis and on time, we'd reconsider his employment in six months. He was a very fine worker apart from absenteeism and tardiness."

After three weeks with no work at all, John got a job driving a cab again. But he couldn't keep up with his bills at that point. The truth is — and the reasons for this have never become clear — many of the Knapps' bills were going unpaid even before John was terminated from Continental Can. John and Linda each later blamed the other for an inability to handle money responsibly, and both were likely right.

John told lawyers and prison psychiatrists that when he started driving the cab he gave Linda his tip money — about $40 to $50 per week — for groceries. John later told his lawyers that he and Linda had also even given some money to the Ramseys to help them out, though Ken would "never admit it."

Ken didn't admit it when asked in 1993 and, indeed, scoffed at the notion. The possibility is not preposterous, however. Ken's latest employer, a private electronics company, had gone out of business a few months before the fire, and Louise's salary was not enough to maintain a family of five.

Linda's stories varied. At times she told investigators and juries that John controlled the finances, never gave her money, and ate out at restaurants while she and the girls had no money for food. At other times, however, she said John did give her money and ate out only because he had to — he was always working.

One of the Knapps' neighbors in the East Capri neighborhood, Nancy Hardin, told a state investigator (and the author) that in late 1973 Linda was *giving away* to Hardin many of the groceries that the Mormon church had been donating to her to help her out. Linda gave her a couple dozen eggs, beans, flour, and other staples until Hardin refused to accept any more, insisting that the church meant for Linda's children to have that food.

The gas and electricity were cut off in mid-October. John's first paycheck, for a partial week, arrived in late October, and amounted to just $46, according to John.

The Knapps had started using candles for light, but the children soon knocked one over, causing a small burn on the living room carpet — a burn mark Dale later noticed in his initial review of the fire scene.

"After that incident," John testified, "I told my wife I was going to look around to see if I could find something else to keep light in the house that would not be dangerous to the children. Well, she asked me at that time to buy her one of these big, oversized glass kerosene lamps. You know, we could use that, and it would be decorative. But with the children in the house, I didn't want anything that could be blown in that way, so I had the money from that small paycheck, and I was over in Mesa, and I bought a Coleman lantern and a Coleman stove for the purpose of having light in the house and being able to fix the kids, my wife, something to eat, and have enough money left over to buy groceries."

John also went to Bishop Gail Goodman Sr., the head of Linda's ward, to see if the Mormon church could help them pay the utilities. Goodman invited him to come to his office the following Sunday and encouraged John to attend the church more, Goodman later testified.

John saw the bishop on Sunday, October 27 (and had Iona christened at the same time, according to John). Goodman agreed to issue a parcel of food, and said he would see if the church could do something about the utilities. Three days later Goodman sent checks to the utility companies to pay the Knapps' electric and gas bills. But, in an oversight that must have seemed trivial at the time, *he didn't notify the Knapps.*

"I never followed through to let him know that [the checks] were actually sent in," Goodman later testified.

The checks were cashed by the utilities on November 1 and 2. But the check to the electric company turned out to be short of the required sum, either because John had been confused about the amount owed or because the company had added a disconnection charge to the amount in delinquency. The utility did not notify customers when third parties paid their bills, so the Knapps evidently had no way of knowing that most of the bill had been paid.

The check to the gas service did cover the full amount, but, again, the utility had no policy of notifying customers when third parties had paid their bills. Nor could it turn the Knapps' gas back on without sending an employee to the Knapp residence to make the hookup. So the gas service waited for the Knapps to call to set up an appointment. The Knapps, apparently not realizing that the bill had already been paid, never called.*

On Friday, November 9, Linda wrote to her natural father, Holiday, asking for money to go to Nebraska, and gave the letter to John to mail. He tore it up.

---

* Some prosecutors and police investigators over the years later speculated that perhaps Knapp had purposefully refused to get his utilities turned back on, so that, after burning his daughters to death, he could float the claim that the children had set the fire to keep warm. One prosecutor (not Hyder) even theorized that Knapp hoped the children would accidentally set a fire and burn themselves to death, and that Knapp set the fire himself only after they failed to do so.

"I did get a little upset," John later testified, "because she did not ask me for the money, but instead, she wanted to write her father in Nebraska. I told her if I had to I would contact my mother, get her the money, and if she wanted to go to Nebraska, she could go for six months." In six months, John would be able to get his job back from Continental Can.

That weekend John called his mother in California and asked if she could help them with the utilities and house payments and come take care of the kids. Mary sent a money order to Knapp and two house payments to the federal agency that serviced the mortgage, she later testified. She also agreed to come live with them, but said she couldn't until the first of the year.

On Tuesday, November 13, 1973, Linda wrote her father the chatty letter that began, "Well tomorow I'll be 22 years old."

On Wednesday, John received the money order from his mother.

On Thursday he paid the electric bill, arranged for a future payment of the water bill, and then returned to the East Capri house at about four in the afternoon. He was unable to get a ride to the gas company, he later testified. One neighbor later told state investigators that, at a little after four that afternoon, Linda asked her for a lift to the gas service so she could pay a bill. But the neighbor, who was late for an appointment, had not been able to do the favor.

"So I gave them a call," John testified, "to see if the man could come and turn the gas on, and I would pay him when he come down. I was informed that the man was not bonded, so therefore I would have to go to the office and pay it. And the office closed at five o'clock. So I couldn't make it."

Again, apparently neither John nor the customer service representative realized that John's bill had already been paid.

On the next morning, Friday, at a little after eight o'clock in the morning, one of four things happened: John burned his children to death; or, Linda burned her children to death; or, John and Linda together burned their children to death; or, the children, trying to keep warm or simply playing with matches, started a fire that spread rapidly and claimed their lives.

Seven

On June 24, 1974, the Supreme Court of Arizona reversed Judge Hardy's earlier ruling that had prevented Diettrich from assisting Basham in defending John Knapp at trial. The court found no legal or ethical bar to the arrangement Diettrich and Basham had worked out with Knapp's mother, and it noted that there was something "unseemly" in allowing a prosecutor to play a role in the selection or rejection of an indigent defendant's defense lawyers.

At the same time, however, that court affirmed Judge Hardy's refusal to give any county funds to pay Knapp's expert Marshall Smyth. There was no unfairness in denying Knapp a fire expert, Vice Chief Justice James Cameron wrote, because, "The state is required to make available to the defendant any and all information it might have relating to the cause of the fire."

But while the high court thought Arizona's discovery rules were clear on that point, Hyder thought otherwise. Hyder appears to have, for instance, already been withholding a videotape — and, perhaps, all documentation of any kind — relating to the April 2 fire simulation or reenactment. In the ensuing months Hyder would, indeed, *take the position* — unsupported by the discovery rules — that he was not required to turn over scientific test results that he did not plan to use in his case in chief. (A criminal trial consists of the prosecution's case in chief, followed, if the defense chooses, by a defense case, followed, if the state chooses, by the prosecution's rebuttal case.)

Since the defense expert Smyth was critical to the defense, Basham brought a civil rights suit in federal court to try to force the state to fund Smyth's experiments. In addition, he begged his superiors at the public defender's office to find funds somewhere so that Smyth could perform his experiments.

In the meantime, Judge Hardy held a hearing on July 9 to resolve several remaining discovery disputes — disputes concerning each side's obligation to disclose to the other certain records and documents in its possession.

Discovery disputes are a mainstay of every litigation, civil or criminal. Procedural rules describe in general terms what each side is supposed to give the other. Nevertheless, these rules are always subject to interpretation, and compliance hinges on the judgment and good faith of each side's litigator.

In addition to the discovery rules, which vary from state to state, prosecutors in all states must also comply with a federal constitutional obligation to disclose to the defense any material *tending to exculpate* the defendant — that is, material that supports the defendant's claim of innocence. Because the U.S. Supreme Court began to define this obligation in the 1963 landmark case of *Brady v. Maryland,* such exculpatory information is known as Brady material.*

But, as with any discovery obligation, precisely what constitutes Brady material is a matter of interpretation. If any evidence were so obviously exculpatory that it really proved that a defendant was not guilty, the prosecutor would be obliged to dismiss the case, and all discovery issues would become moot. So Brady material always encompasses a grayer area — material the defense lawyers would think supports their case if they knew about it, but which prosecutors think of as a red herring that crafty defense lawyers will use to confuse the jury.

The exact point at which evidence turns into exculpatory Brady material is obscure and usually left to the prosecutor's judgment. And any litigator, in the heat of battle, has terribly distorted judgment.

Consider, for instance, Linda's *second* letter to her father, the one written on November 13, 1973. Her *first* letter to her father, dated November 9, 1973, had become a critical component of the state's case. The state was *taking the position*

---

* In that case, John L. Brady, who sought to avoid the death penalty, admitted his participation in a robbery, but claimed that his confederate had been the one who actually strangled the victim to death. Prosecutors had withheld from Brady a statement to police in which the confederate had admitted personally committing the murder. The Supreme Court decided that this information should have been turned over. Thus, Brady material encompasses not only evidence that a defendant is actually innocent, but also evidence that the defendant played any lesser role than the prosecution claims.

that when John read that letter and discovered that Linda was leaving him, he flew into a jealous rage that eventually led him to murder his children. That being the state's position, the defense lawyers certainly would have liked to have known about the blithe and prosaic letter Linda wrote four days later, mentioning nothing about divorce and sounding reasonably content with her lot. Yet, from a prosecutor's perspective, the second letter — an innocuous letter from Linda to her father — was a far cry from proof that John was innocent. Was it Brady material?

It is impossible to determine today whether Hyder turned over to the defense Linda's second letter to her father.* We do know that no juror who heard John Knapp's trial in 1974 ever learned of the existence of this letter.

We also know that Hyder refused to give the defense the five to eight hours of tape recordings Malone and Ashford made of their interrogation of Linda in Fremont, Nebraska. Since Hyder had decided not to call Linda as a witness, no *state* discovery rule required him to provide those tapes to the defense, and Hyder was *taking the position* that nothing on those tapes constituted Brady material, required to be disclosed under the *federal* Constitution. Yet Linda had told Malone in that interview that the can in the living room closet — the one used to set the fire according to John's confession — had been *empty* long before the fire and that the only full can in the house was the one on the floor to the right of the door. Didn't Linda's statement tend to exculpate John?

Maybe Hyder had not listened carefully enough to the tape to hear this passage. (The tapes *were* of poor quality.) If he did hear it, maybe he never focused on it.

In any event, an aggressive prosecutor might even *take the position* that such a statement did not rise to the level of Brady material. Linda had obviously just forgotten whether that can was empty, the prosecutor might reason, just as she had mistakenly remembered that the can on the bookcase was empty, when it was, in fact, half full. Though it was unlikely any judge would accept such an argument, no judge was ever going to hear it. At this stage, the prosecutor needed only to convince himself. Enforcement of the Brady obligation depends largely upon the judgment and good faith of the prosecutor.

Although Diettrich did not know what was on the Linda Knapp interrogation tapes when he appeared at the hearing in July 1974, he was incensed by Hyder's

---

* Hyder declined comment on whether he would have considered the letter Brady material and whether he recollected turning it over.

refusal to provide them, a decision that was clearly tactical and antagonistic to the search for truth.

"The only person at the scene of the fire," Diettrich protested, "and they're not going to call her, and they've got eight hours of tape recordings that they don't want us to hear. If that doesn't smack of Brady, I don't know what does. . . . If the state has nothing to hide, why would they not want us to hear [the tapes]?" Turning to Hyder, Diettrich continued, "Your duty is to seek justice, not a conviction."

"Your honor," Hyder responded, "for the record, let it be stated I always seek justice."

Judge Hardy decided to review the state's Linda Knapp tapes himself, listening for Brady material. But having a judge review hours of almost inaudible tapes is a very imperfect way to enforce Brady obligations. Judge Hardy, like any judge at that stage of the proceedings, lacked the intimate understanding of the case he would have needed even to recognize Brady material. He had no inkling of the significance, for instance, of which cans were full and which were empty.

He found no Brady material on the tapes and ordered none of them turned over to the defense.

Although the lawyers for each side had already come to the July 9 hearing with a profound animosity for one another, the proceedings exacerbated the bad blood.

Hyder believed Basham and Diettrich had to be violating their discovery obligations. They had thus far turned over to Hyder notes of interviews with only five or so potential defense witnesses, and some of those notes were illegible, Hyder claimed. He was certain that the defense lawyers must have been withholding notes of other interviews. (There is no requirement, however, that lawyers take notes when they conduct interviews, and many prosecutors and defense lawyers purposefully take none, precisely to circumvent the discovery requirements.)

But Hyder was most infuriated by the defense's failure to provide something that did not exist — a written report summarizing defense expert Smyth's findings. Smyth was still awaiting funds to perform the tests that would form the basis for his findings. In addition, he was under no obligation to create a written report at any time. The defense had to provide only whatever photographs, films, or reports Smyth did create; thus far, he had created none.

Hyder demanded that defense expert Smyth be barred from testifying altogether. In the alternative, he asked to be relieved of all his own discovery obligations because of the defense lawyers' alleged failure to meet theirs. But Judge Hardy refused both requests. Instead, he ordered the defense lawyers to make available Smyth's written test results and findings as they became available.

While Hyder complained bitterly about the defense lawyers' compliance with their discovery obligations, Hyder was *taking positions* concerning his own obligations that were extremely aggressive. He was propounding one implausible interpretation of the rules after another.

Though the rules required him to turn over "all statements" of the defendant that were preserved in writing or on tape, Hyder *took the position* that he had to provide only those statements that he planned to use in his "case in chief."

"[The rule] doesn't say that," Judge Hardy protested. "It says all statements of the defendant are to be disclosed."

Then Hyder *took the position* that he didn't have to turn over the defendant's tape-recorded statements if they had been "reduced to writing."

"Oh, I disagree with that," Judge Hardy protested again.

"Unless the tape recording is still in existence," Hyder responded, apparently proposing a fallback position. But in doing so, he was implying that tape recordings had somehow already been destroyed.

"All right, we're not going to get into a Watergate situation here," Judge Hardy said, meaning that Hyder could not destroy tapes to avoid having to give them to the defense.

"Our gaps are longer," Hyder joked.* But then he continued to suggest that tapes had somehow already been destroyed.

"[The defense] has been given all statements which have been substantially reduced to writing. Now, if the tape recording is no longer in existence, but the writing is superseding that, then that's . . . what they get. I can avow that there is no tape recording."

"You mean," Diettrich asked, "the tape recordings have been destroyed of the interrogation and interviews?"

"There are no tape recordings," Hyder responded, evading the question.

---

* In late November 1973, during the week of the inquest in the Knapp case, the infamous 18-minute gap had been discovered on a tape that White House attorneys had turned over to a federal grand jury investigating the Watergate affair. The erasure had evidently deleted conversations between President Nixon and his chief of staff, H. R. Haldeman, concerning that matter. President Nixon's secretary, Rose Mary Woods, testified that week that she may have caused the gap when she turned to answer the telephone and accidentally pressed the record button.

"There was a tape recording made originally," Diettrich continued, referring to the one Knapp believed officers had made at his first interrogation on November 19.

"That very well may be," conceded Hyder, "but I can assure you there is no tape recording in existence, and any interview which may have been tape-recorded has been reduced to writing."

By "reduced to writing," Hyder did not mean that a comprehensive transcript had been made of the interview, but, rather, that some investigator had drawn up a police report selectively summarizing those parts of the interview that he wanted preserved.

At Diettrich's request, Judge Hardy then ordered the state not to destroy any tape recordings that were still in existence — a remarkable order for any judge to have to give.

Another matter of great concern to Hyder arose for the first time at the July 9 hearing, when Hyder mentioned that he planned to show the jury the horrifying autopsy photographs of the children's charred bodies.

"Just a moment, please," Judge Hardy interrupted. "Photos of the victims? What are they material to prove?"

Judge Hardy thought the grisly photos proved nothing in dispute, since the defense acknowledged that the children were killed by a fire. The photos would obviously just incite the jurors' passions while contributing nothing to their understanding of what had caused the fire.

But Hyder had planned to make the photos literally Exhibits 1 and 2 in his case. That afternoon, when the proceeding resumed after lunch, Hyder asked Judge Hardy to reconsider his decision and submitted a fourteen-page brief. It appears to have been the longest written document Hyder had submitted on any issue thus far. Judge Hardy agreed to reconsider.

On the afternoon of July 22, only two weeks before the case was due to go to trial, Hyder's investigator Elardo interviewed Melba Burr, the histrionic friend of Linda's mother, Louise Ramsey.

For the state, it was a mixture of very good and very bad news. The good news was that Burr could provide very negative spin on everything John did on the afternoon following the fire. Burr said, for instance, that while Linda and her mother, Louise, got shots of a sedative from Burr's doctor, John hadn't. The implication was that John was not sufficiently upset to need a shot. Burr turned out to be verifiably wrong about this recollection — the doctor and his records indicated that Knapp *did* get a shot of the same sedative — but neither Elardo nor Hyder knew that at the time.

Burr also claimed to know that John's other errands that afternoon were not merely callous but were actually committed with calculating, pecuniary motives.

"She said that on the way to the dentist's office," Elardo wrote in his report, "he kept telling her that he owed this particular dentist money for work performed on his two girls' teeth and that he was going over to explain that now that they were dead, he didn't believe that he should pay the bill owed the dentist."

And Burr told Elardo that after she drove John to the insurance office, where he found out that his carpet wasn't covered, "He bitched all the way home. Boy was he mad."

On the other hand there were things Burr told Elardo that unquestionably hurt the state's case. The one comment that towered above all others was what she said when Elardo asked her the stock question he was asking every neighbor or acquaintance: Did you ever see either of the children play with matches?

"Melba said yes," Elardo wrote, "that she had on four or five different occasions. . . . She said that . . . the eldest girl, Linda, would strike the match and then ignite the rest of the book of matches and then discard the matches."

That was odd.

Linda, the girls' own mother, didn't admit ever having seen Little Linda light matches. How could Burr have seen her do so on so many occasions — and have such a vivid recollection of how she had done it? Was Burr simply an unreliable witness?

Or maybe Burr was right, and Linda was lying about the children's ability to set fires for some reason — perhaps to avoid facing her own share of responsibility for the children's deaths. After all, if the fire was set by the children, then it was really John and Linda's joint neglect that killed them.

It is impossible to say with certainty what went through Hyder's mind in late July 1974 when he first read Burr's statements to Elardo. It is possible, however, to infer the sort of dilemma a hypothetical aggressive prosecutor might have grappled with at this point.

Burr's statement to Elardo appeared to be Brady material, which the prosecutor would have to turn over to the defense. If he did, the prosecutor would be providing the defense with precisely what they had been searching for in vain for months: apparent proof that children so young were capable of setting a fire.

On the other hand, what constitutes Brady material is a judgment call. Perhaps an aggressive prosecutor could delude himself into thinking that the information wasn't really exculpatory. If Linda didn't corroborate Burr's claim about the children's ability to set fires — and Linda had to have spent more time with the children — maybe Burr was just mistaken.* It was like Linda's memory that the can in the hall closet had been empty; maybe it wasn't really exculpatory but was just an obvious memory lapse.

Again, it is doubtful that any judge would accept such an argument. But if the aggressive prosecutor wanted to *take the position* that Burr's memory about Little Linda lighting matches was not Brady material, he had to convince only himself. Judge Hardy wouldn't know about Burr's statement unless the prosecutor showed it to him.

But even so, the prosecutor would still face an additional hurdle. If he called Burr as a witness — to testify about all the damaging things she saw John do on the day of the fire — he would have to turn over Burr's statements under the unambiguous command of the state discovery rules.

Or was there some way out? Some *position* he could *take?*

In mid-July Basham lost the federal lawsuit over funds. At that point the public defender's office brass finagled a way to advance Basham money from the coming year's budget so that he could pay defense fire expert Smyth. Basham telephoned Smyth and gave him the green light to do his tests.

Since both Linda and John said it was the crib mattress that was burning most violently when they first looked in the door, Smyth did a series of tests to see how crib mattresses would burn under a variety of conditions.

Unfortunately, there was no way to determine the precise composition of the Knapps' crib mattress. It had been a hand-me-down from neighbors, who had, in turn, been given it by friends of theirs from New Mexico, whom Smyth could never locate.

Seeing no alternative, Smyth purchased four different crib mattresses at different stores in Tucson, each of which conformed to what he did know about the Knapps' mattress: it had an inner spring, a vinyl cover, and sisal and cotton padding. While Linda had told the police that the crib mattress was made of excelsior — wood shavings — Smyth discovered no mattress on the market that contained excelsior. Many, however, contained sisal, another plant fiber,

---

* In testimony many years later, Hyder attempted to minimize the significance of the Melba Burr statement by using exactly this argument. In 1995 Hyder declined to comment as to whether he considered Burr's statement to be Brady material.

which the Knapps may have mistaken for it. The substitution was, in any event, conservative; actual wood shavings would have been *more* flammable.)

On three days in early August, over a period of about a week, Smyth tested the four mattresses — each propped up at the same odd angle as the crib mattress in the Knapp children's room. He documented each test with both still photos and Super-8 movie films. His thirteen-year-old daughter held up cardboard signs at one-minute intervals, displaying for the cameras how much time had elapsed since ignition. He performed the tests in his scrubby, desert backyard at about 4:00 in the morning, when winds would be at their most calm.

He burned the first mattress out in the open with no other combustibles in the vicinity. He just sat one end on a piece of wood and propped up the other end against a metal garbage can. He pulled some cotton and sisal material out of a slit in the top surface of the mattress — since the children had pulled padding out of the mattress on another occasion — and lit the padding with a match. The mattress burned slowly and eventually the fire went out. But Smyth noticed that when he lit the mattress the same way from the lower surface, underneath the mattress, the fire lasted and eventually consumed the entire mattress.

Still, while the mattress was obviously quite flammable, it did not look as if it could cause a conflagration like the one the Knapps experienced.

In the next two tests he burned mattresses inside an open, three-sided Sheetrock chamber, six feet across, four feet deep, with four-foot-high walls. Smyth suspected that the Sheetrock walls — like those present in the Knapp bedroom — would intensify a fire by reflecting heat back onto burning surfaces.

Smyth propped up each crib mattress again, this time against a plywood crib support that he built to duplicate the one in the Knapp children's bedroom. He crumpled two sheets of newspaper and placed them beneath each mattress, and set the paper on fire with a single match. Since the floors throughout the Knapp house were littered with newspapers, magazines rolled like torches, synthetic clothes, and other flammable debris, Smyth theorized that a child could possibly have dropped a match on such debris and that the resultant fire could have eventually found its way under the mattress.

Again, each of these two mattresses burned to completion, but not very dramatically. This scenario still did not create a fire of anywhere near the fury of the one that killed the Knapp children.

On the other hand, Smyth learned at least two interesting facts from these tests.

In each of these relatively lazy fires, the metal springs of the crib mattress had creased at the point where it was propped up against the crib support, and the mattress springs had collapsed — or annealed — unevenly. This was precisely what had happened to the Knapps' crib mattress. Evidently, the uneven collapsing of the springs did not mean, as David Dale had opined, that flammable liquid had to have been poured under the springs that collapsed. A very rudimentary empirical test had proven that theory to be nonsense.

Smyth also noticed something else of interest during the second and third mattress tests. About fifteen or twenty seconds after each fire was started, the vinyl covering of the mattress began to melt and drip to the Sheetrock floor of the chamber. It pooled there and continued to burn. Perhaps, Smyth thought, the dripping vinyl could start a more serious fire if there was something combustible where it was dropping — like carpet and pad.

For the fourth test, performed in the early morning hours of August 7, Smyth covered the floor of the chamber with carpet and pad that he had cut from an unburned room of the Knapp house in February. In addition, he provided a Sheetrock ceiling to the chamber this time, reflecting the fact that the Knapp children's bedroom had a Sheetrock ceiling as well as walls.

He lit the mattress the same way as before, with crumpled newspaper and a match. Within fifteen to twenty seconds the vinyl cover of the crib mattress began to melt. This time the dripping vinyl ignited the nylon carpet below it. The flames then visibly began crawling across the carpet on their own. After just one minute most of the carpet was involved in the fire, and some of the pad beneath it had begun to burn. The crib mattress, as part of this system, burned much more vigorously than it had previously. By one minute and forty seconds, flames from the carpet-and-mattress system were shooting out of the one open side of the chamber in a spectacular way, leaping eight to ten feet up into the desert night. The carpet and mattress in combination burned ferociously. Astonishingly. Voraciously.

After about eight minutes, virtually everything in the chamber had been consumed. All of the carpet and pad had been burned away. The burn "shadows" on the wall behind the crib mattress looked exactly like those on the wall of the Knapp children's bedroom where the crib support had been — showing the same sort of intense floor-level burning that the state's fire investigators thought had to have been caused by a flammable liquid poured on the floor. And on the floor of the chamber, where the carpet and pad had burned away, there were inkblot char marks similar to those that had been found on the floor of the Knapp children's bedroom. In short, there were "flammable liquid runs" — created without the use of flammable liquid!

That morning, Smyth took the film from his still camera to be developed at a local lab, but he sent his movie film to be developed in California, since he knew of no labs in Tucson that processed it.

While Smyth was performing his fire tests, Diettrich and Basham were trying to come to grips with the state's claim that residues of something "similar to" Coleman fuel had been found in the fire residue from the children's bedroom. On July 29, they won a court order allowing them to interview Jack Strong, the forensic chemist who had reached that conclusion, and on August 2, just a week before trial, that interview occurred at the county attorney's office.

Greatly hampering the value of the interview, however, was Hyder's continuing refusal to permit the defense to see the gas chromatograms — the actual charts generated by the chromatograph machine — that were the whole basis for Strong's opinions. Hyder was *taking* another one of his aggressive, implausible *positions*. He was claiming that these scientific tests were confidential "attorney work product," and not the "results of . . . scientific tests, experiments or comparisons," which the discovery rules required Hyder to provide. "Attorney work product," which can, indeed, be kept confidential, is a term of art referring to the impressions, opinions, and strategies of attorneys and, in certain cases, of the people attorneys hire to assist them. But a police chemist's gas chromatograms—providing the crux of the state's proof that the fire was set with flammable liquid—were simply not attorney work product.

"You've been ordered to produce any charts, pictures, photographs, documents," Diettrich protested at the interview.

"Not work product," Hyder responded. "Just reports."

Notwithstanding the state supreme court's ruling just a little over a month earlier in this very case — where that court wrote that "the state is required to make available to the defendant any and all information it might have relating to the cause of the fire" — Hyder was interpreting the rules to create an exception.

Although much of the interview was highly technical, and the defense lawyers were out of their depth, they could understand some of Strong's statements easily enough. While state investigators had always spoken about the gas chromatography results as if they were objective and definitive, Strong spoke about them in a very different way. Backing up Hyder's refusal to turn over his gas chromatograms, Strong stated that another expert wouldn't necessarily understand his charts.

"The problem is," Strong explained, "that unless you actually ran the analysis yourself it's virtually meaningless because it requires explanation of essentially everything that is on there."

At the end of the interview, Diettrich asked Hyder to save time and just let him see the chromatograms right then and there, without a court order.

"Hell no," Hyder responded. "Underline that."

On August 6, Judge Hardy began the pretrial hearings in Knapp's case, at which Knapp's lawyers were trying to suppress Knapp's confession — that is, have it excluded from evidence. They argued that it had been coerced, because Knapp had been suffering from an excruciating headache when it was obtained.

The hearing afforded the defense lawyers their first opportunity to find out how Sergeant Malone would describe Knapp's confession. Would he concede, for instance, that Knapp had suffered from a headache at all? Would he concede that he had asked Knapp leading questions to which Knapp had answered "yes," as Knapp claimed? Or would he say that Knapp had delivered the whole confession in a spontaneous narrative, the way the police report suggested it had happened?

The account Malone gave Hyder during his direct examination turned out to be a mix. While the overwhelming impression left was of a reliable, noncoercive interrogation, there were certain aspects of even *Malone's* telling of it that sounded quite odd — and where his account resembled Knapp's more than it resembled the one in the police report.

"Mr. Knapp started making statements pertaining to spots that were contained on the tile floor in the office at the Mesa substation," Malone testified. "He said he didn't want to look at the spots, that they annoyed him. At that point a chair was put in front of Mr. Knapp that was a solid color, and he was asked to look at the chair."

"Now during the conversation with Mr. Knapp throughout the evening, did he appear to be rational to you?" Hyder asked a few minutes later.

"I would say not at the time that he was talking about the spots on the floor."

That was not an ideal response for the state. The detective was conceding that at the moment Knapp began to confess, he did not appear rational.

In addition, making matters worse, Malone admitted having fed John almost the entire story through a series of leading questions, to which John had answered "yes."

"I believe I asked him if he observed these spots on the day of the fire," Malone testified, "and he said that he had. And I asked him if he observed these spots in his house, and he said that he had. And I asked him did you observe these spots in your children's room, and he said that he had. And I asked him did he observe these spots on his children, and he said it was possible."

So it hadn't been the spontaneous narrative described in the police report. It had been much more like the scenario Knapp had described.

At that point in the examination, Hyder changed the form of his questions. As a result, Malone stopped relating his own questions to Knapp, obscuring the precise manner in which information had been elicited. Accordingly, Malone's answers, like the police report, once again began to convey the impression of a spontaneously narrated confession.

"So after he claimed he was seeing spots everywhere did he tell you what he did?" Hyder asked.

"Yes, sir. He tried to wash the spots away."

"What did he use to wash the spots away?"

"He said that he used water."

"Did he tell you what the water was contained in?"

"Yes. . . . It was contained in a Coleman fuel can."

"Did he ever mention to you where he got the water or the Coleman fuel can?"

"Yes, sir, he did."

"Where was that?"

"Out of the hall closet."

Had Malone first suggested to John that he got the can from the hall closet, or had John volunteered that detail? Due to the change in the formulation of the questions, no one knows.

The transformation of the first confession, involving spots, into the second confession, without spots, was also a police-guided process, it turned out, *even as detective Malone described it.*

"After Mr. Knapp gave the original statement to us about the spots," Malone testified, "I advised Mr. Knapp that I felt that he had been basically honest with us, but that I didn't believe . . . the part about the spots, and I asked him if it wasn't true that he did obtain that can of Coleman fuel from the hall closet, pour it throughout the room and light it. He advised that, yes, he did. I asked him why he had done this. He said that he had read a letter that his wife had written to her father in Nebraska asking for money so that Mrs. Knapp could go there."

Malone provided one more detail during his direct testimony that the defense had never heard before, but which, interestingly enough, tended to support John's story that he confessed to protect Linda.

"After he confessed to killing his children," Hyder asked, "was the fact of his wife's blame or guilt ever brought up?"

"Yes, sir."

"What was said?"

"Something to the effect . . . 'Was she involved?' or 'Did she have knowledge of this fire?' "

"What did he say?"

"He said, 'No, sir, and if you don't leave her out of this, I'm getting up and leaving here.' "

Toward the end of his examination, Hyder asked Malone whether Knapp had suffered from a headache.

"Mr. Knapp advised that he had a headache," Malone testified, "and I advised Mr. Knapp that I had also had one, and we walked out to the other part of the substation where a closet has aspirins in it. I asked Mr. Knapp if he wanted some aspirins, and he said, no, he would wait until he got home. . . . I took two aspirins and Mr. Knapp, he didn't want any."

So Knapp had complained of a headache, but it sounded like a very trivial one.

"Was this prior to admitting that he had killed his babies?" Hyder asked.

"I believe so, yes."

The last answer was not the ideal one, though, from the state's perspective. It would have been better for Hyder to have been able to *take the position* that the headache was not only trivial, but that it hadn't even begun until after the confession — when it couldn't have played any coercive role in securing that confession.

Nevertheless, on balance, the confession as articulated during Malone's direct examination still sounded impregnable.

During Diettrich's cross-examination, however, detective Malone seemed less certain than he had on direct examination about whether John had ever requested his headache medicine, and Malone began to concede that John had behaved as if his headache had been very severe indeed.

"When you offered him aspirin, isn't it a fact he said, 'Aspirin wouldn't help my migraine, I have to have my prescription medicine,' and that's why he wouldn't take the aspirin?"

"I don't recall. I remember offering him the aspirin, and remember him saying he would wait until he got home. That's all I can remember about it."

"Isn't it a fact that the Ramseys volunteered to go get his prescription medicine, but you refused to let them . . . ?"

"I don't recall."

"You're not saying that didn't happen?"

"No, sir. I'm not saying that. I'm saying, I don't recall it."

"Isn't it a fact, Sergeant Malone, that . . . at [one] point Mr. Knapp's headache was so severe he was literally pulling his hair, physically pulling his hair?"

"The time Mr. Knapp pulled his hair . . . *pulled a quantity of hair out of his head*, was at the time he was complaining about the spots and screamed something to the effect of, 'I can't stand them spots,' and he pulled his hair."

"This was before he made his quote unquote confession?"

"Correct."

So the confession, which had looked so open and shut in the police report, was turning out to be rather bizarre, even as detective Malone recounted it. Knapp had been complaining of a headache, screaming about seeing spots, and pulling hair out of his skull a few minutes before he began to confess. That confession had, indeed, begun with a series of leading questions, to which Knapp had simply responded "yes."

As improbable as these aspects of Knapp's story might have once sounded, the interrogator himself had just confirmed them all.

Though Judge Hardy found the confession admissible, Basham and Diettrich could now show the jury that the confession had been obtained under indisputably odd circumstances.

On the morning of August 8, just before jury selection began, the lawyers had another scrimmage over discovery matters.

The focus of Hyder's objections — ironically, since he himself was apparently concealing a videotape and, perhaps, all related materials concerning the state's April 2 fire "reenactment/assimilation" — was that he had still not been given adequate discovery about Smyth's fire tests and findings. He asked, once again, that Smyth be barred from testifying.

Because Smyth's tests had been delayed by the funding problems, it was true that the defense had not yet shown Hyder the movie rolls of the last three mattress tests, since they had not yet come back from the California processing labs. The defense lawyers offered Hyder a postponement in the trial, so that he would have time to study the movies when they arrived, but Hyder rejected the offer. He insisted, instead, that Smyth be barred from testifying. Alternatively, again, he asked that the court suspend all of his own discovery obligations until Smyth finished making all the required disclosures.

Judge Hardy urged the lawyers just to get together in the next few days and exchange everything that was still outstanding.

"Let's arrange that," Judge Hardy said. "Let's get going with the jury here."

But just when business seemed to have been concluded, Hyder interrupted. "I would like to have the court rule on my motion," he said.

"Do what?"

"To not reveal anything to the defense other than Brady material until the state is furnished with a complete disclosure."

"All right, I'll grant that."

The defense lawyers did not even object.

But what had Judge Hardy just done? Perhaps he thought he had merely postponed Hyder's discovery obligations until Hyder's planned meeting with the defense lawyers a few days later. Perhaps, he thought he had postponed Hyder's discovery obligations until the defense provided the movie rolls of the mattress tests.

But, judging from the transcripts of all that followed, something more momentous may have occurred. Hyder had won what he apparently regarded as an open-ended suspension of all his discovery obligations — except Brady obligations — until the defense had provided *in Hyder's opinion* "complete disclosure."

Hyder may have, in his mind, also solved the problem created by Melba Burr's statement to investigator Elardo about having seen Little Linda light matches. As long as Hyder could convince himself that Burr's statement was not really Brady material, he now had the excuse he needed not to turn over her prior statements, *even if he called her as a witness*. Judge Hardy had suspended the Arizona discovery rule that would have required him to do so.

Later that evening President Nixon announced to the nation that, effective at noon the following day, he would resign. He was then facing trial in the Senate on three articles of impeachment, two of which arose from his allegedly having obstructed justice and withheld evidence in connection with the Watergate affair.

The day before Nixon's resignation speech, Phoenix's highest-circulation paper, the *Arizona Republic*, ran a *pro-Nixon* editorial cartoon, ridiculing Congress for hamstringing presidents by forcing them to disclose their private notes and tapes.

Eight

On Friday, August 9, the defense gave Hyder a written description of Smyth's mattress tests and the conclusions they drew from them. On Monday, August 12, they showed him movie reels and photos of those tests and allowed Hyder to interview Smyth for several hours. The only thing the defense lawyers had not yet given Hyder were the movie reels for the fourth mattress test, which had still not arrived from the California lab.

Trial began the next morning, on Tuesday, August 13, 1974. It was a clear summer day in Phoenix, with the temperature rising to 104 degrees at midday.

The State of Arizona's first attempt to put John Knapp to death would take place on the sixth floor of the Maricopa County Courthouse in downtown Phoenix. The courthouse, built in 1965, was a nine-story, box-shaped building sheathed in a composite of brown stone and masonry. Rows of narrow windows looked north and south, but the east and west walls afforded solid protection against the rising and setting Phoenix sun.

Judge Hardy's courtroom was of modest size, with three rows of benches for visitors. Fluorescent lights lit the room, and the walls were lined with metal-bordered panels of medium brown wood.

In the morning a jury of thirteen was empaneled: four men and nine women. If all were healthy at the close of the evidence, one of them, selected by lots, would be named an alternate, and excused.

Because of the large numbers of potential jurors who admitted that they couldn't be fair in the gruesome and highly publicized case, jury selection had lasted three days and required questioning of eighty prospective jurors. In fact, because of the extraordinary publicity surrounding the case, Judge Hardy took the expensive and highly unusual precaution of sequestering the jury from the outset. Accordingly, for the entire trial the jurors were put up at a downtown hotel, so that their access to newspapers and television could be strictly monitored.

Hyder's opening statement was brief and restrained, lasting roughly fifteen minutes.

"The state submits that when all the evidence is in, you will have no reasonable doubt in your mind that John Knapp on the sixteenth day of November, 1973, killed his baby daughters by setting them afire in their bedroom with Coleman fuel. . . .

"The state will put on many witnesses who viewed John Knapp during the fire, that not once did he act like a man who had just lost two baby children in a fire, but instead, he was cool, calm, collected, drinking coffee, smoking cigarettes, and worrying about whether or not he had to pay for his new rug."

Then Hyder prepared the jurors for Dale's critical expert testimony about the flammable liquid runs.

"The evidence will show, like fingerprints, that the spots that appeared on the floor after the scene was cleaned, indicated a fire caused by a flammable liquid fire. . . .

"The evidence will show . . . that while these babies were burning in that flaming hell, they didn't live long . . . which indicates that it was a very rapid, high intensity fire. . . .

"The state submits [Knapp] was confronted with the evidence. He knew he could no longer lie about it, and now he admits it. He tells officer Malone that he walked down the hall to go to the bathroom . . . he looked in upon his children and saw them together, they were cold, he was tired of seeing them cold, tired of seeing them hungry. So he walked down and got the Coleman fuel can, threw it around the room, ignited it, and a ball of fire came out and singed his hair."

The defense lawyers chose to reserve their opening statement until the end of the prosecution case, a rare tactic both then and now. (Basham and Diettrich cannot remember today why they employed it.)

Because Judge Hardy had, by this time, ruled twice that Hyder could not show the jury the horrifying autopsy photographs of the children's charred bodies —

state's exhibits 1 and 2 — Hyder had five of his earliest witnesses describe what the girls' bodies looked like.

"The skull had split open," one fireman said of Iona. "The skin was all burned away. The arms and legs were partially burned off." As for Little Linda, he testified, "The limbs were completely gone. [She was] just bones protruding from the charred flesh."

As he heard this testimony, Knapp "removed his glasses, buried his face in his hands and wept," according to the *Arizona Republic* story the next morning.

But the lead for that day's newspaper story was more dramatic: "As firemen fought a blaze that burned his two daughters beyond recognition, John Henry Knapp stood calmly on the sidewalk sipping coffee and smoking a cigarette, firemen testified Tuesday."

This lead sentence, like the headline on page B1 — "Dad sipped coffee while 2 daughters burned, jury told" — and a similarly worded reference to the story on page A1, were all actually false.

What one firefighter, Monty Brow, had really said — and he was the only one of the seven witnesses called that day who said he had seen Knapp with a coffee cup — was that Knapp sipped coffee sometime *"after we got done removing the [children's] bodies"* from the house. That had happened at about 10:15 A.M., about an hour and forty-five minutes after the blaze was extinguished.

The only person who had implied that Knapp had sipped coffee *while* the fire was burning was prosecutor Hyder, who had done so twice: once in his opening and once during his examination of Brow, when he inaccurately summarized Brow's earlier testimony.

The image of Knapp sipping coffee while the fire blazed was a powerful one. But it made no real sense. Who would have given Knapp that first cup of coffee? Had some neighbor rushed out there during the four-minute period while the firemen were actually putting out the fire and brought it to him?

Still, rhetorically, the image of Knapp sipping coffee while his children burned was valuable and devastating. And, before the trial was over — about a week later — one neighbor did substantiate Hyder's version. That neighbor said she saw Knapp drinking coffee about "fifteen to thirty minutes" after the fire engines arrived, when, by her mistaken recollection, the fire was "still going strong."

Whether it made sense or not, once the neighbor gave her improbable memory, the myth ossified into truth for the purposes of all future legal proceedings. Prosecutors could fairly *take the position* that Knapp had literally sipped coffee while his children burned.

*　*　*

The next morning Hyder had medical examiner Karnitschnig give the jury the sixth description they had heard thus far of the children's charred bodies, having him describe each child's head wounds *twice*.

Iona had suffered "fire decapitation, partial fire amputation of both arms, and fire fractures of both arms," Karnitschnig explained. "The bony part of the top of the head was burned away, and this . . . defect exposed the shrunken dura through which the brain substance had mushroomed out on either side of the skull."

Then — good, tenacious litigator that he was — Hyder made another attempt to persuade Judge Hardy to let the jury see the horrifying autopsy photos. To change Judge Hardy's mind, Hyder had to come up with a plausible argument that the photos actually helped prove something that was in dispute. Pursuing that tack, he had Karnitschnig testify that "the fire decapitation, the explosion of the skull and removing the top of the head, and exposing the brain, *aids me* in making the determination" that the fire was rapid and intense. Hyder then argued that the photos were relevant to proving a disputed issue—how quickly the fire developed. Hyder submitted a second written brief on the issue.

Judge Hardy still couldn't make up his mind. He kept the photos out of evidence for now.

During the rest of the day Hyder called nine neighbors and acquaintances of Knapp, who testified about how cool, calm, and collected he appeared after the fire. One, Susan House, testified that he had "acted like he was at a cocktail party."

During these first two days of trial, a theme became apparent in Hyder's questioning.

"Ever see the children play with matches or gasoline?" he asked neighbor Jim Garrison.

"No."

"Ever see the children play with matches or gasoline?" he asked neighbor Dave Contreras.

"No."

"Did you ever see them play with matches or gasoline?" he asked neighbor Susan Webb.

"No."

"Ever see the children play with matches or gasoline?" he asked neighbor Linda Crumpton (whose deposition testimony was being read to the jury).

"No."

But Hyder did not ask that question of Louise's friend Melba Burr, whom he called on the second day — the woman who had told his investigator that she had seen the children set whole matchbooks on fire on four or five occasions.

If Hyder complied with the discovery rules and with his Brady obligation, he should have turned over to the defense lawyers his investigator's report of Burr's prior statements, which would have revealed that startling statement to the defense. But the transcript of that day's testimony strongly suggests that Hyder never turned over the document.

While Basham and Diettrich had planned to interview Burr themselves a few days before the trial started, it appears that the interview never actually took place, for unknown reasons. However, from the defense lawyers' interviews with John, Linda, and the Ramseys — and, possibly, some conversation with Burr herself — they knew some of the harmful things Burr was likely to say about John. They knew, for instance, that she might testify that John, just hours after his children's deaths, had asked her to drive him to the property insurer to find out whether his carpeting was covered. But the lawyers hoped they could persuade Judge Hardy that any mention of John's trip to the insurance agent should be barred, since property insurance — unlike life insurance — could not provide a motive for the crime. Knapp's trip to the insurance agent, they wanted to argue, was likely to anger and offend the jury in a manner that was out of proportion with what it really proved about the cause of the fire.

When Hyder called Burr to testify, Basham and Diettrich asked for a conference outside the presence of the jury. They wanted to find out exactly what Hyder was going to have Burr say, so that they could challenge those things they thought were inadmissible before the jury heard them.

After an off-the-record bench conference, Judge Hardy excused the jury and continued the discussion on the record.

"Mr. Diettrich," Judge Hardy said, "I understood you to say a moment ago you have received no copy of any statement given by [Melba] Burr."

"No indication from the prosecution of any kind as to what her testimony might be," Diettrich responded. Diettrich then asked for an oral summary from Hyder of what he planned to ask Burr.

Judge Hardy said that the discovery rules did not give Diettrich a right to an oral summary, but they *did* give him a right to any written report recording Burr's prior statements.

Hyder did *not* claim to have turned over Melba Burr's prior statements to the defense. Instead, he said this: "Your Honor, I'd like to call the court's attention to something. . . . The court has granted the State's motion to . . . suspend the

State's obligation under the rules to continue furnishing the defense with discovery material, other than Brady material, some time ago."

That suspension was still in effect, because Smyth's movie rolls for the fourth mattress test had yet to arrive from the California lab.

Though that discovery suspension did not suspend Hyder's Brady obligations, Hyder had apparently convinced himself that the Melba Burr interview did not contain Brady material. And neither Diettrich nor Basham knew what was in the report, so they did not realize that it *did* contain Brady material.

"I'm not bringing up a [discovery] rule for that reason," Diettrich responded, apparently recognizing that the discovery suspension was still in effect. He explained that that was why he was asking only for an oral summary of what Burr planned to say — so that the judge could determine, as an evidentiary matter, whether it was admissible.

Basham then interrupted. "We'd like the record to reflect *we have not received any copies of any statements Melba Burr has given,* and that's not the reason for our objection." Like Diettrich, Basham apparently believed that Judge Hardy had suspended their discovery rights.

Again, Hyder *did not contest* Basham's statement that he had never turned over Burr's statement. Instead, Hyder said that the defense lawyers were sufficiently on notice of what he would be asking Burr, because he had given them two notice documents, each of which still exists, and each of which consists of nothing more than a vague, one-sentence recitation that Burr would be testifying about her observations of Knapp on the day of the fire.

The transcript very strongly suggests that Hyder invoked Judge Hardy's discovery suspension to withhold his investigator's report of Melba Burr's prior statements. Evidently, he had convinced himself that nothing in Elardo's report was Brady material.

Many years later, however, when the Elardo report came to light, Hyder did not argue that the report was not Brady material. Instead, he maintained that, after reviewing the entire record, he believed that he must have, in fact, turned over Melba Burr's prior statements to the defense lawyers and that the portions of the transcript quoted above were misleading.* The defense lawyers had simply failed to use Burr's statements for reasons known only to them, Hyder argued then. But both Basham and Diettrich would swear that they had never

---

* How Melba Burr's prior statements came to light, and more detail about Hyder's claims in response, will be discussed in later chapters.

seen the report before and that it was inconceivable they could have failed to use something so crucial, had they known about it.

The only thing that is certain is that the jury never found out that Melba Burr claimed to have seen Little Linda light matches and, indeed, set whole matchbooks afire four or five times.

When forensic chemist Jack Strong testified on the third day of trial that his gas chromatography showed that fire residue contained vapors "consistent" with Coleman fuel, the defense lawyers still knew precious little about this extremely important aspect of the case against John.

They had found a chemistry professor at Arizona State University in Tempe, Michael Parsons, who had agreed to advise them. The defense had also by this time won the right to see copies of the gas chromatograms — by means of a court order — so that it now had something for Parsons to analyze. (The chromatograms were the actual charts generated by a gas chromatograph machine.) But when the photocopies had arrived, they were illegible.

So while Strong was on the stand, the lawyers finally won the opportunity to make legible photocopies. Since Diettrich still had never had an opportunity to show legible chromatograms to his own expert, his cross-examination of Strong was brief and superficial.

Later that same day, fire inspector McDaniel described all the ways he could tell that the fire was caused by flammable liquid. But during his cross-examination the next morning, Diettrich won an important concession from McDaniel. In reality, McDaniel admitted, most of the "hallmarks" of a flammable liquid fire were really just hallmarks of any rapid, intense fire with floor-level burning.

"In other words," asked Diettrich, "you could have other hot, rapid-burning fires that would leave these same signs you saw in the children's room without having . . . [any] propellant present?"

"If you had a . . . very high amount of combustibles or . . . *if the carpet was highly flammable.*"

"So this is possible?"

"Yes, sir."

When Diettrich asked McDaniel how he knew that the Knapps' carpet could not have significantly contributed to the fire, McDaniel explained that there were areas of carpet that hadn't burned.

"Aren't you assuming," Diettrich asked, "that the portions of the carpet that were not burned were not covered by some object that was [nonflammable]?"

"The carpet that was not burned was located approximately in the center of the room," McDaniel responded.

McDaniel had assumed that the center of the room, where people ordinarily walked, would be free of large debris that could have protected the carpet.

But the Knapp house was no ordinary house. McDaniel had never been told that both Linda and John remembered that the children had pulled the dresser drawers into the center of the room, which photos of the fire damage tended to confirm. The drawers would have protected the piece of carpet McDaniel was talking about.

Finally, Diettrich began to explore with McDaniel the actual mechanics of the state's theory that flammable liquid had produced the char marks on the floor of the room. McDaniel explained that the flammable liquid, before it was ignited, soaked down through the carpet and then through the rubber pad beneath it. When the fire worked its way down to the floor, it set that still unignited fuel on fire and caused the char marks.

Diettrich asked McDaniel if he had ever actually tested this hypothesis.

"It's rather obvious, sir," McDaniel responded. "I know for a fact that I have spilled stuff on my carpet at home, and it's gone through. . . . First time it was some water. Once it was some orange juice. . . ."

That was another theory Marshall Smyth would have to test.

Diettrich also exposed another curious theory McDaniel held about the fire. McDaniel had always assumed that the fire had blown out the window. He explained that flammable liquid fires usually will blow out windows within one to three minutes after they are set, assuming they don't blow them out immediately. In fact, McDaniel recalled, when he was in training as a fire inspector, he had been present once when a gallon of Coleman fuel was detonated in a ten-foot by twelve-foot by ten-foot concrete room, and "we blew all the windows and doors out." (This was a different test from the one or ones Dale conducted at the Mesa Fire Department's training facility.)

McDaniel didn't know that four eyewitnesses had reported seeing Knapp break the window with a hose several minutes into the fire.

From this point forward Hyder began to *take the position* that the eyewitnesses might have been confused about thinking they had seen Knapp break out the window.

*   *   *

Michael Parsons, the A.S.U. chemistry professor, was a very careful and courteous man. He was reluctant to find fault with the work of police chemists, who he recognized worked under very different constraints than academic chemists did.

Still, when he viewed Strong's chromatograms and read Strong's deposition testimony, he was troubled. The sloppiness of Strong's work was jarring. Strong's poor record keeping would have been unacceptable not just at the university, in Parsons's judgment, but at Parsons's previous positions in private industry as well.

A carefully done chromatogram will show a line that has been traced along the baseline of a graph. Periodically the line shoots up in sharp, needle-shaped peaks, and then it returns to the baseline. Each peak represents a compound that has been found in the sample. Done carefully with the equipment available in 1973, a chromatogram for Coleman fuel might have shown more than seventy such needle-shaped peaks.

The line in Jack Strong's chromatograms looked more like the outline of a mountain range with about eight to twelve peaks. Numerous compounds had been compressed together in a short space, and it was impossible to determine with any precision how many compounds were present, what they were, and in what proportions they had been found.

But beyond the sloppiness of the work, Parsons had other important questions about Strong's conclusions. While one of the three samples that Strong had said was "consistent with Coleman fuel" — labeled in Strong's report as "item 5" — contained very small traces of substances that might support combustion, it was really impossible to say what those substances were. While they were "volatile" — that is, they contained compounds that would readily evaporate at room temperature — lots of such volatile residues might remain after a serious fire of innocent origin. These compounds might have been caused *by* the fire rather than having been causes *of* it. In addition, Parsons noticed — although very tentatively — that the pattern of peaks for "item 5" simply did not appear to match the pattern for the vapors from the Coleman fuel can.

Although Parsons didn't know it, "item 5" was, historically, the single most important piece of evidence in the case. Item 5 was the jar that contained the "oily film" that the firefighters thought smelled like Coleman fuel. It was that film that had turned the routine fire overhaul procedure into a criminal arson investigation. Item 5 was the reason John Knapp was on trial. But the pattern of its peaks did *not* appear to be the same as those from the Coleman fuel sample, Parsons thought.

Parsons had a second, very different problem with the two other samples that Strong had found to be "consistent" with Coleman fuel. These samples — items 3 and 4 — were the two "extracts" that had been taken from the floor of the children's bedroom after the debris had been removed and the floor had been cleaned and dried. These were the samples taken by soaking a piece of gauze in the solvent methylene chloride and rubbing it on char marks on the floor.

Ironically, the problem with the extracts was the reverse of the problem with item 5. The graphs of the extracts matched the vapors tested from the Coleman fuel can *too well* — for two reasons. First, the fuel from the Coleman can had not been through a fire. The samples from the floor had been through an inferno that had raged somewhere between fifteen and twenty-five minutes. Many of the lightest compounds of the fuel in the room should have, therefore, either burned off or evaporated away. Yet the graphs from the extracts and from the unburned fuel were almost identical.

And there was a second obvious problem with the extract graphs. Their dominant feature should have been a huge single peak representing the solvent — methylene chloride — with which the gauze had been soaked. That large peak should have been missing from the Coleman fuel graph. Yet, again, the extract graphs and the Coleman fuel graph were almost identical. How could that be?

And, to further complicate matters, the methylene chloride the firefighters had used seemed to have been terribly impure. Its graph should have shown a single sharp peak; instead, it had about eight peaks, by Parsons's count. The impurities were scattered throughout the very same range as the compounds that were showing up in the Coleman fuel graph.

Since the solvent, methylene chloride, was itself a highly volatile substance, Parsons wanted to make certain that the state wasn't confusing the solvent with Coleman fuel.

At about 11:00 A.M. on Friday, while the defense lawyers were in court cross-examining inspector McDaniel, the county attorney's investigator, Elardo, called Parsons on the phone. Elardo secretly tape-recorded their conversation.

Elardo asked Parsons what his findings were at that point. Parsons tried to explain to Elardo, who evidently had no understanding of the science involved, why he was unable to arrive at an opinion at that point.

"I am not convinced that we have distinguished between [the solvent] methylene chloride and the Coleman fuel adequately," Parsons tried to explain.

But Elardo kept pressing for a bottom-line answer.

"This is between you and I," Elardo told him, falsely. "What is your opinion, you know, right now?"

Parsons then explained that the graphs for the extracts and for the Coleman fuel were "extremely similar."

This was what Elardo wanted to hear. But Elardo did not seem to understand that Parsons was saying that they were *too* similar.

Parsons explained that the lighter compounds of the Coleman fuel, if they had been through a fire, "in part should have been burned away and in part they should have been volatilized [evaporated] away."

"Right," Elardo said.

"But yet, they look exactly like Coleman fuel. That bothers me."

He explained to Elardo that the solvent used to make the extract samples was a "highly volatile substance" and he wanted to make sure that the police chemist hadn't confused it with Coleman fuel.

But Elardo kept trying to simplify without understanding what Parsons was saying.

"It does resemble Coleman fuel?" Elardo asked.

"Right. Well, let's put it this way, they're highly volatile organic substances," Parsons responded. Then Parsons tried to explain that he was seeing quantities of very light compounds that he would not expect to see in Coleman fuel that had been through a violent fire.

"This is one of the things that disturbs me," Parsons said. "There must have been an awful lot of quantity of fluid put down for there to be this much residue. . . . I would say that these samples do give a definite positive indication that the residues there were in fact from a volatile fluid that would be capable of supporting combustion. The only question I really have is the question about the methylene chloride background. And that's something that really has to be answered before I would state in court that I agree with the chemist at the Crime Lab."

As they finished up their interview, Parsons turned the tables and asked Elardo one question.

"This isn't the only piece of evidence that the case is really being based on, is it?"

"No, it's not."

"Okay. Good. Because it — there are certain weak points in this evidence. You know, if I wanted to go up and bad-mouth Mr. Strong's techniques and so forth, I could, to a certain degree."

He tried to impress on Elardo that, given the stakes of the case, the police really should have used available analytic techniques that could have given more reliable information.

"Because, you know," Parsons continued, "it would be a bad thing if, in fact, these chromatograms are really [the solvent] methylene chloride, which was used in getting the sample."

"Yes."

"In other words, then there would be a mistake in interpretation of the chromatogram."

"Uh-huh."

"And I don't think that's the case," Parsons continued, "but I would certainly like to have that question answered."

Elardo thanked Parsons for his time and hung up. Shortly thereafter Elardo drew up an investigative report summarizing the conversation.

"Dr. Parsons agreed," Elardo wrote, "that he is of the opinion that a volatile fluid was used in the Knapp fire and that all he was trying to figure out was 'what kind.' He went on to say that he didn't think there had been a mistake in the interpretation of the chromatograms, but that he had a question concerning the methalyne [sic] chloride that was used in gathering the samples."

"I think probably I was leaning toward a flammable liquid fire the instant I walked into the [children's] room," deputy fire marshal Dale testified. "This was, in fact, a classic flammable liquid fire. In all my years of investigation, I have never found as many substantiating factors as I have in this fire."

Dale also provided some expert testimony that would enable Hyder to try, once again, to have the gruesome autopsy photos admitted into evidence. In order to change Judge Hardy's mind, of course, Hyder had to present testimony suggesting that those photos proved something that was in dispute. Dale, it turned out, was able to provide exactly that sort of testimony. It was testimony no other state expert had ventured. In fact, it was testimony that no expert of any description would ever again claim the ability to provide during the long history of the Knapp case.

Dale testified that when he examined the autopsy photograph of Little Linda's charred body, he could detect "flammable liquid runs" on her left cheek.

It was remarkable testimony. Even Dale himself admitted he had never before seen a flammable liquid run on a body before. Dale had never taken any courses in pathology. In fact, though the jury didn't know it, Dale's education was little better than John Knapp's; Dale had dropped out of high school and later earned an equivalency diploma.

Dale had also never actually seen either of the victims' bodies in this case; he was making his determination from the black-and-white autopsy photograph alone.

Dale was making a judgment that the state's pathologist, Karnitschnig, had been unable to make. Karnitschnig said he could not say from examining the body whether a flammable liquid was involved.

Diettrich's objection, on the grounds that Dale was not qualified to render such an opinion, was overruled. Once it was, Hyder asked Judge Hardy — for now the fourth time — to admit the hideous autopsy photos of the children into evidence, so Hyder could show them to the jury. This time, in light of Dale's testimony, the photos were finally relevant to a disputed issue in the case. They proved — at least according to Dale — that Linda had been lying in a puddle of flammable liquid.

Judge Hardy let them in.

Early in the morning, before Dale testified, Smyth had been performing another series of tests in Tucson to see how Coleman fuel behaved.

Having shown in his earlier tests that "flammable liquid runs" could be produced *without* the use of a flammable liquid, he now wanted to see whether "flammable liquid runs" could, in fact, be produced *with* a flammable liquid.

In two separate experiments he poured a pint of Coleman fuel, in different patterns, on small unburned samples of the Knapp carpet and pad. He performed one test out in the open air on a piece of Sheetrock, and the other test inside his little Sheetrock chamber. For his protection while igniting the fuel, Smyth set up a trolley system using wire, pulleys, and clothespins; to ignite the fuel he trundled a flaming rag over the fumes while standing a safe distance away.

In each case, the Coleman fuel burned away in about two minutes, and all of the remaining carpet eventually was consumed as well. Only a portion of the surface of the padding beneath the carpets burned, however. And beneath the carpet and pad, Smyth found, *there were no char marks or heat discolorations of any kind.* The Sheetrock, which had a paper surface, would be quite sensitive to heat discoloration, Smyth believed.

The fuel didn't seem to leak through the carpet and pad before igniting, and it burned away too quickly to eat its way down through the carpet and pad.

Though he had been able to create flammable liquid runs *without* flammable liquid, he hadn't been able to create them *with* flammable liquid.

The next morning, Smyth performed one last test. This one was designed to test McDaniel's opinion, which Dale had later endorsed, that the Coleman fuel had seeped through the Knapps' carpet and pad — just as orange juice had seeped through the carpet and pad in McDaniel's living room — and later ignited, causing flammable liquid runs. Smyth took a sample of the actual pad from the Knapp children's bedroom and formed it into a pouch in his hand. Then he suspended it by strings. He poured Coleman fuel into the pouch and periodically replenished the fuel as it evaporated away, so that there would always be a pool of fuel standing in the pouch. He did this for forty-five minutes. No fuel ever leaked through the Knapps' rubber pad.

Hyder called Sergeant Malone as his final witness, to testify about John Knapp's confession.

Malone's testimony at the suppression hearing two weeks earlier had not gone ideally for the state. Malone had admitted at that time that Knapp had suffered from what certainly sounded like a severe headache, that he had appeared irrational at one point, and that he had been pulling handfuls of hair out of his head and screaming about spots before he ever began confessing.

But, now, testifying for the second time, Malone's testimony went better for the state.

Malone had never intended to suggest that Knapp had been irrational during the interrogation, Malone testified this time. He had meant to say that Knapp was feigning irrationality.

And Knapp had never actually *screamed* about spots, Malone clarified. Knapp had only "raised his voice."

Malone could also no longer remember exactly when Knapp had first complained about a headache; it might have come *after* the confession, not *before*.

There was, however, still one flaw in Malone's testimony, from the state's perspective. Malone's original police report — although it is a little ambiguous — suggests that Knapp said, "Oh my God, I killed them," even *before* he began to complain of seeing spots. That version of the confession was the best one for the state, because it would enable Hyder to argue that Knapp had confessed *before* the onset of the bizarre episode in which he began complaining about spots and pulling hair out of his skull.

The trouble was, Malone never remembered the sequence of events that way. When Malone narrated the story at the August 6 suppression hearing, he had omitted the "Oh my God, I killed them" statement altogether. He had testified, instead, that right after he explained to Knapp that all the other suspects had been eliminated except him, Knapp had begun complaining about spots.

Now, in his direct testimony at trial, Malone *still* did not remember things the way the police report had them. Though he remembered Knapp saying the "Oh-my-God" line this time, Malone testified that Knapp made the statement *after* making his spot-related confession. That was still not the ideal scenario from the state's perspective.

But after the lunch recess, Malone changed his mind. From that point forward he testified that, "after reviewing my report," he remembered that Knapp had actually made the "Oh-my-God" statement *before* he began to complain about the spots.

Finally! The state could now *take the position* that Knapp had confessed *before* the onset of any conduct suggestive of a severe headache.

At about 2:45 P.M. the state rested, and the jurors were excused to return to their hotel. The defense case would start the next day.

Nine

John Knapp, Dave Basham told the jurors in his opening statement, "will tell you . . . the chain of events which led him to believe that his wife was the material suspect for the murder of their two children."

The defense at trial would be that the fire was an accident, probably set by the children. Defense expert Smyth had found that there was nothing about the fire damage that was inconsistent with the apparently accidental fire that both John and Linda described.

But since Knapp maintained that he confessed to protect Linda — while his judgment was distorted due to a severe headache — Basham was emphasizing that John had good reason to believe that Linda needed protecting.

And though Basham never accused Linda of setting the fire, he understood that, for the very reasons the police and John Knapp suspected Linda's involvement, the jurors might well wonder about her as well.

In fact, in terms of personal hunches about who set the fire, Basham and Diettrich differed.

"I suspected [Linda] a lot," Basham later recounted. "She seemed kind of psycho to me. Chuck [Diettrich] felt that the kids played with matches and had started the fire. So we had two sort of roads, and they weren't exactly parallel."

"[John] will tell you," Basham told the jurors, "the facts as he remembers them on the sixteenth, the morning of the fire. . . . He will tell you that his wife was interrogated in front of him and accused of criminal activities in front of him. He will tell you that shortly thereafter, his wife, unbeknownst to him, left the State . . . .

"Linda Knapp . . . will . . . tell you [about] some of the . . . fire accidents that had occurred in the Knapp house out in Mesa and in other houses that they lived in. . . .

"Linda Knapp will tell you the interrogation that went on, on the nineteenth, the accusations that were drawn against her.

"She will tell you why she went to Nebraska and, interestingly enough, she will tell you that when she was in Nebraska many days after John had made his . . . confession, that she was accused by officer Malone and officer Ashford of starting that fire. That they said, 'You might as well 'fess up, Linda. We know you did it.'

"She will tell you that this interview or interrogation lasted about eight hours. . . .

"There's going to be some references to Linda Knapp's involvement in this case. She was around at the time of the fire. . . . I don't want to say that we are pointing a finger at anyone or accusing anyone. . . . That's just not my function at all. . . . Any testimony that we offer regarding Linda Knapp is only going to be used to show the effect on the state of mind of John Knapp at the time he made his confession."

The defense lawyers were in a delicate position. Much of Linda's testimony was vital to John. It corroborated his account of the fire and contradicted the theories of the state's experts. If Linda was telling the truth, John was innocent, and the children had most likely set the fire.

Accordingly, the lawyers couldn't afford to alienate Linda. If they explicitly suggested that Linda could have murdered her children, she might invoke her Fifth Amendment privilege against self-incrimination, in which case she would become completely unavailable to the defense as a witness. If she invoked the privilege before trial — outside the presence of the jury — the jury might be kept completely in the dark about Linda.

Accordingly, the defense needed to play down the Linda-did-it possibility — at least long enough to elicit from her her testimony about the fire. *Then*, after that testimony had been presented, the defense lawyers would be delighted to have Linda take the Fifth — *in front of the jury*. That way both of their goals would be accomplished.

Hyder dreaded that scenario.

In fact, he needed to prevent her from testifying to the extent that he lawfully could. Linda fit nowhere into his case. She contradicted his experts without an apparent motive to lie — unless she was involved. If she was involved, then the state had no idea what the Knapps' joint motive for the crime was, and John's confession was at least partially false. If John's confession was false, the state couldn't prove whether John or Linda or both or neither set the fire.

Once the state admitted that it didn't know if Linda was involved, its case began to unravel — at least to the point of creating a reasonable doubt about John's guilt.

Hyder's chosen posture before the jury was that the state no longer had the slightest doubt that Linda was innocent. And he had already begun bombarding Judge Hardy with the claim that evidentiary rules somehow barred the defense lawyers from calling Linda as a defense witness and then suggesting that she could have committed the crime. Judge Hardy had not ruled on the claim so far.

One of the first defense witnesses was Mary Knapp, John's then sixty-four-year-old mother.

"John was never an emotional child," she told the jury. "He was always calm and collected. . . . He had one brother killed at work. . . . John didn't cry then. He had a half-brother killed in Vietnam, and he did not cry then. . . . I think John kept his emotions all bottled up."

Mary then described Linda's attitude toward the children, based on what she had observed when John and Linda lived next door to her in Pomona.

"The children were baby dolls to Linda," she testified. "She played with them for awhile, then would put them in the bathtub of water — leave them sit for two or three hours at a time without attention. Or she would put them in the yard — leave them there. . . . If she wanted to play with them, okay. If she didn't want to play with them, she just put them aside. . . .

"She didn't care for housekeeping. She would sit and daydream about castles in Ireland."

Mary described Little Linda's behavior with matches when she was still *less than two years old — about a year and a half before the fire.*

"John and I both smoked," Mary said, "and we would leave cigarette butts in the ashtray. Linda would get matches and she would either turn — she couldn't get it lit on one side and she would either turn it over on the other side. She would try to light the cigarette. She was trying to copy her father and I." (Mary apparently demonstrated what Little Linda would do, but what her physical gestures were no one can say today.)

*   *   *

Next, the defense lawyers called those neighbors who supported aspects of the story they needed to tell. But, again, there was a theme to Hyder's cross-examination of these neighbors.

"It is your testimony, is it not, that the children never played with matches in your presence?" he asked neighbor Nancy Hardin.

"Yes."

"Did you ever see the little girls playing with matches?" he asked Tony Rosales, who had seen them playing with fire.

"No, I haven't."

"You never saw the children playing with matches, did you?" he asked neighbor Guenodine Sheets.

"No."

"You have never seen the children yourself playing with matches, have you?" he asked neighbor Ernest Paredes.

"No, sir. I never did."

The point he was making was sustainable, of course, only as a result of his concealment of Melba Burr's statement that she had seen Little Linda light matches on four or five occasions — or, as Hyder would later have it, due to the defense lawyers' unaccountable failure to use that statement after Hyder had duly provided it to them.

When the first day's testimony ended, and arrangements were being made to have defense expert Smyth come up from Tucson to testify the next day, Hyder notified the judge that he might want to have the jury come a half hour late the next morning.

"I have some matters I want to take up with the court in regard to Mr. Smyth," Hyder said.

"I know what you are going to say," Judge Hardy said, alluding to the fact that Hyder was going to try to bar Smyth from testifying again. "You have taken it up about twenty times."

"I have some additional matters," Hyder promised.

And he did. Hyder had still more theories for barring Smyth's testimony.

While the trial may have already been radically distorted by his own sharp discovery maneuvers, Hyder continued bitterly denouncing the defense lawyers for their alleged failure to comply with their own obligations. At a break early on the first day of the defense case, Hyder sought to bar certain defense expert testimony on the grounds that their conclusions had been disclosed to Hyder too late.

Diettrich could not contain his fury. Smyth's tests had been delayed because the courts had, at Hyder's urging, refused to provide the funds required to conduct them. And the main reason defense chemist Parsons hadn't been able to form an opinion earlier was that Hyder had refused to provide copies of the chromatograms.

"Mr. Hyder's reply was . . . 'Hell, no,' " Diettrich recounted to the judge. "Now he's going to have the gall to get up and scream about it. I think it is bordering on unethical conduct. He is not here to seek justice. He is here to seek a conviction. I'm getting tired of it."

"I could care less what Mr. Diettrich's attitude is," Hyder said. "I will state to the Court that they have been given everything they are entitled to be given."

Hyder was winning the discovery battles. The defense lawyers were becoming frustrated and emotional. They couldn't keep up with all of Hyder's *positions*. They never asked Judge Hardy explicitly to lift the open-ended suspension on Hyder's discovery obligations that the judge had ordered on August 8 and then apparently forgotten about. Basham and Diettrich were complaining about being denied discovery, but they were not demanding that it be provided.

"I would like also to say," Basham had said during the midmorning skirmishing, "that there has been so much testimony in this case, in the state's case in chief, that I have not heard before, reports that have not been furnished to us, witnesses that I had no report of. We're going in this blind on at least five or ten of those witnesses."

But Basham's complaint was ineffectual, since he never demanded the reports when they might have done him some good — when Judge Hardy could have ordered them provided.

Judge Hardy still wasn't being asked to do anything, so he didn't.

While the lawyers bickered in court, Hyder's investigator, Elardo, telephoned Dr. Parsons, the defense team's gas chromatography adviser. Elardo had Jack Strong with him on the line, and they offered to clear up any questions Parsons had. Again, Elardo secretly tape-recorded the conversation.

Parsons was, once again, reluctant to suggest criticism of Strong's work. But Parsons did gently ask Strong the questions that were troubling him. Astonishingly, Strong seemed to have never given any thought to any of these issues, nor could he shed any light on them.

Ironically, Parsons was trying to help Strong out — trying to come up with possible explanations for Strong's seemingly impossible results. One possibility Parsons had hypothesized was that perhaps Strong had changed the settings on the machine between tests. If so, Parsons was thinking, Strong's results might make some sense.

No, Strong explained, the settings were kept constant.

"Once you're in the ball park sensitivity-wise," Strong explained, "why, you don't have to change the sensitivity settings . . . at all."

Then Parsons suggested that perhaps the so-called logarithmic display Strong was using might make the methylene chloride look more contaminated than it was.

"Yeah," Strong said, "the logarithmic display really louses up any good quantitation. But qualitative is the thing that I was specifically looking for."

But Parsons realized that even the logarithmic display would not account for the drastic problem he was seeing.

"It would seem to me like there would [still] be an obvious spectrum of methylene chloride [in the extract graphs], and it doesn't appear to be here," he said.

"Yeah, uh-huh," Strong responded.

Strong had no additional insights into how to account for his own findings.

The second day of the defense case was an odd one. Hyder's attempt to block Smyth from testifying ballooned into an all-day affair. Even though the jury was sequestered, and Judge Hardy was holding trial on Saturdays to minimize the length of time that they would be kept from their families, the jury heard no testimony at all on this day.

Instead, outside the jury's presence, Hyder was allowed to interrogate Smyth for most of the day so that he could raise every conceivable objection to Smyth's qualifications and tests. Hyder's main goal was to keep the jury from seeing any of Smyth's crib mattress tests, particularly the fourth one. That test showed that when a crib mattress was propped up against a crib support at an angle, on top of the Knapp carpet and pad — just the way the mattress had been in the children's room — the entire system burst into a ferocious fire just 100 seconds after being lit with a single match and crumpled newspaper.

The state experts who claimed that the carpet would not burn well unless flammable liquid was poured on it were wrong, the test showed. Verifiably wrong. Dead wrong.

But the day's activities showed that it was much easier for prosecution experts to testify than for defense experts to testify.

Based on nothing more than the black box of his "experience," for instance, high school dropout David Dale had been permitted to opine that the autopsy photograph of Little Linda showed "flammable liquid runs" on her cheek. Fire inspector McDaniel had given expert opinions whose only empirical foundation had been his having spilled orange juice in his living room several years earlier.

Today, however, Hyder offered tier after tier of objections to Smyth's methodical and photodocumented tests. Some bordered on the absurd.

Hyder *took the position* that Smyth's tests were inadmissible because they were conducted *at night* instead of during the day! The night sky would prevent the jurors from seeing "the presence of smoke" and "the flames are going to stick out much more greatly than they would . . . in the day," he argued. "Literally, whether it's light or night is a material element." Judge Hardy rejected the argument.

At another point, Hyder argued that Smyth's movie rolls were inadmissible because they contained ten-second gaps when Smyth was reloading the film magazine. (The movie film came in fifty-foot rolls, which provided only about three minutes of continuous footage.) Judge Hardy rejected this theory as well.

But Hyder finally did raise one objection that was not silly. Smyth's chamber was smaller than the Knapp children's bedroom and, in truth, that might well have had some effect. Hyder argued that the small size of Smyth's chamber radically distorted the burning process.

Diettrich and Basham explained that the tests were designed to give the jury an idea of how the ordinary furnishings in the Knapp children's bedroom would burn under a range of circumstances, instead of just relying on Dale's "experience." While the final test was performed in a chamber only one-seventh the size of the Knapp children's bedroom, the amount of combustible furnishings in that chamber was *less* than one-seventh of what had been in the Knapp bedroom.

After permitting Hyder, outside the presence of the jury, to examine Smyth all morning and into the early afternoon, Judge Hardy denied Hyder's motion.

"As I understand him," Judge Hardy said, "[Smyth] intended to establish a range, to show under best of circumstances or worst of circumstances. . . . I think these tests are admissible frankly."

But Hyder kept arguing. Over Diettrich's protest, Hyder argued for another fifteen minutes or so. Then Judge Hardy ruled for the defense again.

But Hyder kept arguing. He persuaded Judge Hardy to look at the films first before he decided. Smyth then showed his films during much of the early afternoon, including the films of the fourth mattress test, which had finally arrived from the California processing lab. After the showing, Hyder resumed arguing. Diettrich protested Hyder's "filibustering" after the court had already ruled, but Judge Hardy agreed to hear Hyder out.

Smyth had created a "barbecue pit," an "oven," and "a little bomb," Hyder insisted. "The law is clear. That's misleading as the Devil. . . . This [is a] controlled, artificial, contrived environment to get a maximum burn. . . . The law is clear on demonstrative evidence. They have to substantially reproduce as close as possible the situation at the time in question. They haven't done that here. They don't even make the attempt."

By 4:00 in the afternoon, Judge Hardy had begun to have second thoughts. Ironically, the ferocity of the burning in the fourth mattress test was *so* exonerating of Knapp that Judge Hardy began to assume that something must, indeed, be amiss. He feared that the low ceiling that Smyth had added in the final test may have been the cause of the extraordinary burning, rather than the addition of the carpet and pad.

"I will say," Judge Hardy noted, "that [in] the fourth test, the walls and the ceiling influenced the nature of the burn, because we didn't see that burn in the other three [tests]."

As court ended that evening, Judge Hardy still hadn't made up his mind.

Sometime after Smyth finished his first day of testimony, the defense lawyers and Smyth took the movie rolls of the fourth mattress test to the sheriff's office so that Hyder could make his own videotape copy of it, as Hyder had requested.

That afternoon, at 4:40 P.M., Hyder had had his videotape technician, Corporal Carnes, pick up some videotapes from the sheriff's office property custodian, including the never disclosed one that had been made of the fire test that Hyder and Dale had performed on April 2, 1974. It depicted either a test the defense knew nothing about at all, or the Coleman fuel tests that Dale inaccurately told the jury he had conducted just a few days after the fire.

It was not unusual for Hyder to check that tape out of the property room. He had sent Ashford or Carnes to check it out, along with several other tapes, on three earlier occasions that month, according to the property log. This time, however, at about 7:50 that evening, Hyder or Carnes videotaped Marshall Smyth's fourth mattress test on top of that videotape, obliterating whatever had lain beneath it.* (From electronic evidence it appears that the state's fire test was

---

* It will be explained in later chapters how the destruction of this tape, and the timing of that destruction, came to light.

erased before Smyth's test was recorded on top of it, in a separate and seemingly pointless act, since any new taping automatically erases whatever has previously been encoded in the tape.)

Hyder and Carnes say they have no recollection of the incident at all, and Hyder says he never knew of the existence of this tape.

So by late August 22, 1974, if not before, the taped record of the *state's* fire test had apparently been obliterated, either accidentally or intentionally.

But the tapes of the *defense* fire tests still remained. Hyder devoted the next morning to trying to keep the jury from ever seeing *them*.

After Smyth testified about his qualifications in front of the jury, the jury was excused yet again, and the lawyers began their second day of argument over whether the jury could see Smyth's tests.

Judge Hardy agreed with Diettrich that the defense was entitled to show that the state's fire experts had been dead wrong in asserting that the flammability of the carpet could have played no role in the fire.

But, unfortunately perhaps, Smyth had not only added the carpet and pad to the fourth test, he had also added the ceiling. Judge Hardy thought the unusually low ceiling — about four feet above the floor of the chamber — was the key factor contributing to the dramatic fire depicted in that test.

Smyth candidly admitted to Judge Hardy that the ceiling would have probably had an effect in the later stages of the test. But he didn't think it would have influenced the earliest phase of the burning.

Accordingly, Judge Hardy allowed the first minute to be shown, so that the jury could see "the plastic dropping off on the carpet, igniting the carpet, and the carpet taking off," as the judge described it.

Hyder argued with that ruling for another fifteen or twenty minutes, but Judge Hardy held firm.

In the afternoon the jurors finally saw the mattress tests, including the first minute of the fourth test.

Even this much of the test, by revealing the flammability of the carpet without the presence of Coleman fuel, was back-breaking to the credibility of the state's fire experts. But in addition, Diettrich was allowed to show — over Hyder's impassioned objections — the final footage from the fourth mattress test showing the fire residue in Smyth's chamber after the fire was out. There, in the photos, was the crib mattress — its springs collapsed in just the manner of the crib mattress in the Knapp children's bedroom. There, in the photos, were the shadows on the drywall behind the crib support — just like the ones in the

Knapp children's bedroom. And there, in the photos, were the supposedly telltale inkblot char marks on the floor of the chamber — the "flammable liquid runs."

After Judge Hardy refused Hyder's request to exclude these photographs, Hyder changed strategy. For reasons known only to him, he decided to let the jury see the entire movie of the fourth mattress test at that point. Perhaps he hoped that doing so would better enable him to argue that the test was bizarre and unrealistic. Maybe he thought the jurors would be less inclined to believe that he was trying to hide something from them.

The following Monday, Linda Knapp took the stand. Judge Hardy had appointed her a lawyer a few days earlier, at Hyder's request. Diettrich had been terrified that the lawyer would advise her to take the Fifth Amendment before she testified, and that he would thus lose the right to call her at all. The jury would then be kept in the dark about Linda. Diettrich suspected that this was Hyder's strategy all along.

But Linda did show up to testify on Monday, and Diettrich's worst fears were past.

But before Diettrich elicited Linda's vital testimony about the fire itself, he asked her about her birthday on November 14, two days before the fire.

"Did you have a conversation with your mother," Diettrich asked, "concerning a dream that you had about the children burning up in the house?"

"I respectfully refuse to answer on the grounds it may tend to incriminate me," she answered — in front of the jury!

Judge Hardy immediately excused the jurors.

While Linda's invocation of the Fifth Amendment was a windfall for the defense lawyers — how could the jury ignore the possibility that she had set the fire now? — she had invoked it too early; the defense lawyers hadn't yet brought out all the testimony they needed from her.

Still, Hyder was furious. Having her take the Fifth in front of the jury was precisely what he had feared most. How could he *take the position* that no one suspected Linda of the crime now? He thought Diettrich had tricked him. He demanded that the judge forbid the defense lawyers to ask any questions that would cast further suspicion upon Linda.

"It would be wholly misleading . . . for them to be able to ask [Linda] questions in such a fashion to make the jury believe that she's under suspicion or that she may be charged with a crime when Your Honor knows and the defense knows . . . that the State at this time has no evidence which would make Mrs. Knapp a suspect."

Of course, in reality, almost every shred of evidence, except the confession, implicated Linda as much as John. To that litany could have been added several factors that implicated Linda alone: a history of mental instability and her hasty departure from the jurisdiction. And the state's chief fire expert, David Dale, had testified at the suppression hearing just three weeks earlier that he still believed Linda was involved.

But Judge Hardy took Hyder seriously, and he did something that neither Hyder nor the defense lawyers had foreseen — something, in fact, the lawyers weren't sure he had the power to do. He granted Linda transactional immunity and ordered her to continue testifying.* As a result, from this point on Linda could never be prosecuted for the murders of her two children, no matter what additional evidence might come to light.

Hyder, having just *taken the position* that the state had no suspicions about Linda, was in no position to protest, and did not.

Now that she had immunity, Linda resumed testifying, giving the jury essentially the same account of the fire as the one she gave at her first interrogation three days after the event. Her testimony supported John's account of the fire and contradicted the arson hypothesis as outlined by deputy fire marshal Dale.

"The way that developed was just perfect," Basham later recalled. "Just storybook. That was a kick in the groin [for the state]."

On the morning of the last day of the defense case, Basham and Diettrich finally called chemist Michael Parsons to address the gas chromatograms.

There had been numerous petrochemical products present in the children's room at the time of the fire, he explained: the nylon carpeting, the butyl pad, the vinyl tiles, and the adhesives used to bind every one of those layers to every other. In addition, there had apparently been large plastic toys, aerosol cans, synthetic clothes, and heaven knows what else, since the fire inspectors had never inventoried the room's contents. Given the poor quality of the chromatograms, Parsons did not believe anyone could say what they were showing.

"There would be substances left, residue from the fire itself," Parsons testified, "and some of these would undoubtedly be in the same volatility range that we're interested in here. And it would be very difficult to, in fact, separate [this] smoke residue . . . from the actual residue of interest."

---

* From time to time during the later history of the case, lawyers on each side questioned if Linda really had transactional immunity, because they doubted Judge Hardy's power to confer it in the manner in which he did. But judges always decided to treat her as if she had such immunity.

Parsons testified that what was showing up in the extract samples might simply be the solvent (methylene chloride) the firefighters had used to lift those samples, together with the impurities that seem to have been present in the solvent.

At about 1:45 P.M., John Knapp took the stand. He described, from his perspective, the days leading up to the fire, what he remembered about the fire itself, and all his subsequent interactions with the police, including his confession. The crux of his testimony has already been related.

During his examination Diettrich also introduced one of the photographs taken by the state's investigators on the morning of the fire. Due to yet another discovery dispute or mix-up, the defense lawyers never saw many of these photographs until a few days before the trial began. But when they finally sifted through them then, this particular photo had jumped out at them. It showed the sofa in the Knapps' living room, after the firefighters had folded it back up into the couch position. And there at the foot of the sofa, folded on the carpeted floor, were Knapp's distinctive, thick, black, horn-rimmed glasses. He always wore those glasses. Knapp must have been roused quickly out of bed that morning without time even to put on his glasses.

Between the impact of Smyth's tests and Linda's unexpected invocation of the Fifth Amendment, the state's case had been seriously damaged.

Hyder presented a brief rebuttal case, recalling deputy fire marshal Dale as his last witness.

Hyder played for the jury the videotape he had made of Smyth performing his house inspection in February 1974. Pointing to Smyth's understandable confusion at certain points on the tape, Dale attempted to portray Smyth as a bumbling amateur who had been rescued from laughable errors by Dale. (Smyth, for instance, had not understood at first why a partially burned headboard had not been more completely consumed, until Dale explained to him that the headboard in question had been recovered from the children's closet; the one from the bunk bed inside the room had been almost totally consumed.)

During his cross-examination, Diettrich responded cleverly.

"Did you bother to videotape or film any of *your* investigation or tests so the jury could see what *you* did?" Diettrich asked.

It must have been a more ticklish question than Diettrich realized. Dale's April 2 fire test apparently *had* been videotaped. But that tape had been withheld from the defense and had then been mysteriously erased.

"We didn't videotape that investigation, no."

"As a matter of fact, you recorded nothing in the way of your investigation, or any work or tests you did, in the way of photographs or videotape or any other form of preservation of the evidence?"

"I didn't realize that service was available. I think it would have been advantageous."

Had both Hyder and Dale forgotten about the videotape that, according to the documentary record, Hyder had ordered made of Dale's April 2 fire test at the Mesa Fire Department's training facility? Hyder or his assistants had apparently videotaped Smyth's test on top of that videotape just one week earlier.

Hyder kept silent.

On Friday, August 30, the attorneys gave their final arguments, the transcripts of which have been lost. Then the judge briefly instructed the jury on the law, and, at about 5:50 P.M., he excused the jury to deliberate.

The jury deliberated all Labor Day weekend, being kept late into the night. When they adjourned at 10:30 P.M. on Saturday, they stood seven to five for acquittal.

At 10:00 P.M. on Sunday, it was six to six.

By 5:20 P.M. on Monday evening, it was seven to five for conviction. But at that point the jurors sent out a note indicating that they were irreconcilably split.

Judge Hardy called a mistrial. Knapp would have to be tried again. Hardy set the new trial for October 15. (See chapter 10 for a discussion of double jeopardy.)

Judge Hardy released Knapp from jail on his own recognizance and gave him permission to go to Houston, Texas, to stay with his brother Robert between trials.

It was an extraordinary decision — turning loose a man facing the gas chamber, and letting him leave the state on nothing more than his word that he would return.

"Hyder was outraged," Judge Hardy later recalled. "I said, 'This guy's too dumb to run away. He wouldn't know where to go.'"

The defense lawyers were jubilant. Each eventually clipped and framed the article from the next day's *Phoenix Gazette* — including a photo of the grinning defense team — and hung it up in their homes. They had pulled off an enormous upset and had, for the time being, saved John Knapp's life. It was the proudest moment either would ever know as defense lawyers.

Yet, at the same time that each lawyer was savoring the moment, each already knew what he wanted to do next: bail out.

After a five-week trial, six days a week in the courtroom, neither could face the prospect of battling Hyder again in another brutal, posturing, low-road litigation, with John Knapp's heartbeat as the trophy.

In fact, Diettrich and Basham competed to get out of the case. Each understood that Judge Hardy probably wouldn't allow them both to drop out at so late a date. It would take another lawyer too long to prepare. One of them was going to have to try the case again — alone.

"I'd rather get my ass kicked than walk away," Basham said in 1993. "That's been a basic rule that I've followed for a long time. But I kind of ended up walkin' away from that one."

Nineteen years later, Basham still could not come to terms with his decision.

"It was staggering for me for some reason to think about doing it again," he said. "Basically, I tried to figure out whose hands John would best be served in. So I guess I made the decision to let it be [Diettrich's] . . . . It seemed like a huge — just something about it — I'm not sure that I was the one to take it on by myself. . . . I'm not sure I did the right thing. . . . It's just kind of — thinking back in your mind, when you're trying to go to bed at night: Did you run away from something? Was it good sense? Was it cowardice? . . . It's something I have to understand."

Immediately after the trial, Basham took a leave of absence from the public defender's office.

"I don't think I went anywhere," he said. "I just went unemployed. Maybe three months. I came back to the office for a very short period of time — [maybe] two months — and then quit. Then I took another leave of absence — from everything."

He went back to school, studying Eastern philosophy. He gave criminal practice another stab in 1976, but in 1978 he left it again.

He became a commercial airline pilot.

"Everyone asks me, 'Why did you get into flying?'" Basham observed in 1993. "'Why did you change your career?' I can't say. I try to figure that out, too. Was I running away? Or was I seeking?"

Diettrich also wanted out.

"I couldn't imagine myself going in and doing it again," Diettrich recalled. "I was wrung out."

And there was a financial problem, as well. Having agreed to take just a

$5,000 fee, Diettrich had astronomically underestimated the hours really required. And even that fee turned out to be hypothetical. Mary Knapp had never come up with much more than half of it.

"It was really killing me," Diettrich remembered. He had neglected all his other cases, and as a young lawyer just getting started in private practice, he could not afford to take charity cases.

While Knapp's lawyers celebrated their anxiety-ridden victory, Knapp walked into freedom. He breathed the fresh, evening air for the first time in nine months.

And then he complained. He hadn't wanted a hung jury, he told a reporter from the *Gazette*.

"I was hoping they'd decide one way or the other."

Ten

On October 7, Judge Hardy refused to allow Diettrich to withdraw from the case.

At that same hearing Hardy also told the lawyers that, for the second trial, he was probably just going to reaffirm all his earlier evidentiary rulings.

But a week later, prosecutor Hyder started up the steady drumbeat of arguments for excluding any testimony from defense experts Smyth and Parsons.

"You can't believe how forceful Hyder is," Diettrich later remarked. "He's relentless. He is relentless."

Hyder's main theory this time was almost incoherent. Smyth's and Parsons's opinions, of course, had been absolutely essential to the defense case. In their opinions, the fire damage and residue were as consistent with an accidental fire as they were with one that had been set with flammable liquid. Their testimony negated almost all the state's evidence, except for the disputed confession.

But Hyder now argued that because Smyth and Parsons did not pretend to know the answer to the ultimate issue — whether the fire was or was not in fact set with flammable liquid — they held no true expert opinions.

Hyder's assertions at this stage were becoming parodies of legal argument. They were torrents of words, ad hominem attacks, legal catchphrases, and mischaracterizations of prior testimony.

"You can't put a man on the stand and ask him a bunch of rubbish to have him come down with a response, stand up and say, well, he is an expert. . . . If

[Smyth] has no opinions on those crucial issues . . . his testimony is not relevant. . . . He stands in the shoes of an ordinary layman . . . and the fact he ran some tests, doesn't have any bearing on that. . . . The law is quite clear. . . . If he has no opinions, he is not an expert."

Diettrich no longer had the patience to respond seriously, as a lawyer must. "I don't know what he is talking about," Diettrich said. "I don't understand if it's Spanish, English, or pig Latin. I can't respond to that."

Hyder came up with still more arguments for excluding Smyth's experiments from the jury. He claimed, for instance, that Smyth's experiment in which he showed that Coleman fuel would not permeate the Knapps' carpet pad might have come out differently if Smyth had performed it indoors instead of outdoors.

"Are you saying that padding is more likely to be permeable in a house with a roof on it than outside a house?" the judge asked.

"Perhaps," Hyder responded, "simply because you don't have the escape and the volatility of the fuel that you had in an enclosed room. . . . I'm not the expert, but neither was [Smyth]. The law, I think, is quite clear."

"I can't believe we're arguing all this again," Diettrich said. "I'm going to withdraw."

But he couldn't.

Judge Hardy's main concern was the same one as at the first trial — whether Smyth's little chamber had properties so different from those of a full-size room that it was misleading to let the jury see his tests.

Diettrich *did* offer a serious response to Judge Hardy's concerns there. If Judge Hardy would approve funding, Diettrich said, he would have Smyth redo his experiments in a full-size chamber — exactly the size of the Knapp bedroom.

But Judge Hardy ultimately ruled that doing so would be too expensive and he denied funds for that purpose.

At the end of the afternoon, Judge Hardy said he would reserve decision on whether Smyth's tests would be admissible.

The bar against double jeopardy, contained in the Fifth Amendment to the federal Constitution, generally prevents prosecutors from trying someone twice for the same offense. But there are several broad exceptions to that general rule, including one that embraces the situation in which a trial ends in a hung jury. Courts have refused to intervene when defendants have been put to trial, under these circumstances, four or even five times for the same offense.

While such retrials do not violate the double jeopardy clause, they may nevertheless frustrate many of the goals that underlie that clause. Memories prove quite malleable when subjected to the heat and stress of adversarial proceedings, especially when those memories have once proven insufficient to secure a conviction. Human memory is not passive and stable, like information stored on a hard disk. Our will shapes our memories. A prosecutor who believes he is bringing a heinous criminal to justice will push his witnesses as far as they will go, and witnesses who believe they are serving that same noble goal may bend under the pressure.

The unseemly changes in testimony and strategy that occur between trials that are repeated underline the gamesmanship and fallibility inherent in the entire process.

Arizona commenced its second attempt to put John Knapp to death on Wednesday, October 23, 1974. With a very few exceptions, the state's witness list at the second trial was identical to that of the first. Nevertheless, every aspect of the state's case was stronger at the second trial.

Predictably, the state's fire experts no longer espoused those opinions that Smyth's experiments had proven false. Neither McDaniel nor Dale, for instance, still believed that Coleman fuel had seeped through the carpet and pad to the floor before being ignited. More surprisingly, however, each now denied *ever having held that view*. Confronted with their prior testimony, each said he had misunderstood the questions that had been asked.

The state's fire experts also modified other opinions they had expressed at the first trial. McDaniel no longer conceded, for instance, that many "hallmarks" of a flammable liquid fire were, in fact, merely the hallmarks of any intense, rapidly growing fire, or that a highly flammable carpet could cause the burn patterns seen in the Knapp bedroom. Instead, he was adamant that some of the damage — for instance, the deep-fissured blistering or "alligatoring" seen in some of the charred wood — could have been caused *only* by a flammable liquid.

At the second trial, Dale now remembered having been much cagier about how much he told Knapp about his theories prior to Knapp's confession. At the first trial, Dale had admitted that he had "pretty well laid out" his theory of the fire to Knapp three days after the fire — long before Knapp's confession. Dale also had admitted telling Knapp that the arsonist must have used about a gallon of fuel. A few moments later in his testimony, however, Dale had retracted his answer, stating that while he "may have" told Knapp how much fuel he thought had been used, he could not really recall. By the time of the second trial, however, Dale had become pretty sure he had *not* told Knapp how much fuel had been used, and, indeed, his memory now was that he "didn't relate any of the specific details" of his theory to Knapp prior to Knapp's confession. Accordingly, Hyder could *take the position* at the second trial that Knapp had volunteered all the details in his confession — which uncannily fit Dale's theory — rather than having simply regurgitated a theory that Dale had already laid out for him.

Hyder's litigation posture — that nobody suspected Linda of the crime — was also stronger now. Though Dale had admitted at both the suppression hearing and at the first trial that he suspected that she was involved in the fire, he now testified that he believed she had played no role in it.

At the retrial Hyder was even able to shore up, to an extent, Dale's most improbable claim — that he could detect a "flammable liquid run" on Little Linda's cheek in the autopsy photograph. Hyder did this by — after one false start — eliciting from Karnitschnig, the medical examiner, a statement that could pass for corroboration of Dale's claim:

"Do you have an opinion what the black peninsular-like mark is on [Little Linda's] face?" Hyder asked him.

"I couldn't really say. *It could be soot or anything*," Karnitschnig said in his counterproductive first response.

"Could it be consistent with skin?" Hyder continued, unfazed.

"Yes, it's consistent with it."

"And would that be consistent with burned skin . . . having been received in a flammable liquid fire with the flammable liquid seeping on the face?" Hyder continued, shamelessly.

"That's consistent with it, yes."

By using the protean lawyer's phrase — "consistent with" — Hyder finally obtained what he needed. In his closing he would read back the last question and answer and then remind the jury: "That's the doctor's testimony. That's not Dave Dale's testimony. That's the doctor's testimony."

Hyder also dramatically bolstered that portion of the state's case that rested on the gas chromatography. This time, when defense chemist Parsons testified about the unaccountable anomalies in the state's gas chromatograms, Hyder confronted Parsons with certain statements he had made on August 16 in the first of his two secretly recorded conversations with Hyder's investigator, Elardo. This was one of the conversations — made with Elardo's assurance that it was "just between you and me" — whose meaning Elardo had so monumentally mangled when he summarized them in his investigative reports.

But Hyder did not use in court the tape itself or the transcript that had been made of it. Indeed, it appears that he never advised the defense that a tape or transcript of the conversation existed.* (Under the discovery rules at that time, no rule explicitly required him to turn such a tape or transcript over; an amendment to those rules, which would have explicitly required such disclosure, became effective about nine months later.)

"Do you remember," Hyder asked Parsons during the cross-examination, "you told [Elardo that] from the amount of residue that you saw on the graphs it must have been one heck of a lot of flammable liquid in that room, is that correct?"

What Parsons had really been trying to tell Elardo, in context, was that the quantity of the highly volatile compounds showing up in the graphs was so great *that he was having trouble believing they had been through a fire.* He was saying that the substance they were seeing in the graphs might well have been either the solvent with which the extracts had been made or, perhaps, some other material that had gotten into the sample *after the fire.* Parsons had said, during that earlier conversation, that he wondered if contamination could have occurred during the floor-cleaning process, for instance, before the extracts were taken.

But without notes or records of the two-month-old conversation, Parsons simply had no idea what Hyder was talking about.

"I don't recall making that statement," Parsons told Hyder. "I do recall being asked to make a conclusion at that point . . . and . . . if we're talking about the same conversation, I did not have the full details of what Mr. Strong had done when we had that conversation."

"Well," Hyder continued, "you're not denying that you made that statement?"

"Well, I don't recall making that statement, but I may have made a tentative conclusion based on incomplete knowledge."

To reinforce the misleading impression just given, Hyder called Elardo as a rebuttal witness to describe his memory of the same telephone conversation.

"[Parsons] said," Elardo testified, "that there was really one area that bothered him. . . . He said, you know, there must have been one awful lot, a large quantity of flammable liquid put down in that room for there to be this much residue."

---

* Hyder declined to comment on what, if anything, he recalled turning over regarding Elardo's taped conversation with Parsons, or what he thought he would have turned over in such a situation.

"Now," Hyder asked, "did he say whether or not the graphs . . . gave any definite or positive indication . . . that there was flammable liquid there?"

"Yes." Again, this was a misstatement. What Parsons had really said was that there was definitely a "volatile" substance present; the problem was that it appeared to Parsons to be a volatile substance that *had not been through a fire*.

"So you're saying that Doctor Parsons's testimony, then, was not truthful or correct?" Diettrich asked Elardo on cross-examination.

"I have to term it 'watered down' from what he told me on the telephone," Elardo responded.

Even if Hyder had turned over Elardo's written summary of the interview in question — which cannot, today, be determined — Diettrich had no way of knowing what Parsons had really said. Only the tape would have revealed that.

The testimony the second jury heard about the confession was also more favorable to the state than what the first jury heard. Detective Malone, now testifying about the confession for the third time, finally remembered it in the ideal way from the state's perspective. Malone testified this time that Knapp had told him, "Oh my god, I killed them," *before* he ever began to complain of seeing spots.

Meanwhile, Knapp's behavior and dress on the morning of the fire had grown even more clownishly suspicious, according to the neighbors. This time when Susan House described Knapp as acting like "a host at a cocktail party" and "laughing" and "really enjoying himself," she was not alone. Molly Cameron also now remembered Knapp "laughing," although she did not appear to have ever told police or investigators that in her earlier interviews.

Perhaps influenced by news media accounts of the neighbor's "cocktail party" simile, some neighbors also remembered Knapp as having worn more formal attire on the morning of the fire. One said Knapp "had on dress clothes," while another testified that he was dressed "about the way he is now [i.e., in court!]. He had on the same [sports] coat and pants and white shoes." This neighbor also remembered Knapp having worn glasses that morning — now that the importance of that detail had become apparent from the previous trial.

Diettrich was able to counteract some of the more extravagant tricks that memory was playing on these witnesses by subpoenaing from a television news station the footage it had taken of Knapp as the children's bodies were being removed from the house after the fire. Knapp is dressed in a pullover polo shirt, is not wearing a sports jacket, nor is he wearing glasses. He is shown solemnly looking down at the ground. He is not laughing and does not appear to be enjoying himself.

Nevertheless, regardless of all the ways in which the state's case improved in its revised edition, Knapp still stood a fair chance until November 7, 1974.

On that Thursday morning Diettrich called defense expert Smyth to the stand. He testified to his inspection of the fire scene on February 16, 1974, but when he began to describe his mattress tests, Hyder objected.

The jury was excused, and Hyder made his arguments yet again.

"This time," Judge Hardy said, "I think Mr. Hyder's argument is well taken, Mr. Diettrich."

Judge Hardy had changed his mind. He was keeping out Smyth's tests.

"[There is] not a substantial similarity of conditions," the judge ruled, "with respect to the intensity of heat. . . . What I'm thinking about particularly is . . . where you got the heat rising up to the ceiling and coming back down again in a small chamber."

Accordingly, the second jury saw no portion of any of the four mattress tests Smyth had performed. The jury never saw the vinyl plastic dripping to the carpet, never saw the nylon carpet igniting within fifteen seconds, and never saw how that carpet, once it got hot enough, burned demonically.

As the case was collapsing in ruins, Diettrich made a record of what was happening, so that an appeals court would understand.

"I'd like the record to reflect that . . . I made request of Mr. Smyth to construct an experiment wherewith he would recreate a room just like the Knapp children's bedroom, so that there would be no objections from the State . . . and that this request was denied on the grounds that there is not sufficient money to permit such tests that would meet . . . Mr. Hyder's legal objections. Therefore, because of the price tag, our right to demonstrate our defense . . . was denied."

"Well, your statement that the request was made and that it was denied because of the expense factor is correct, and the record may reflect that," Judge Hardy conceded.

Thus, the critical evidentiary ruling in the case was determined by Knapp's indigence — his inability to pay for full-scale room burn tests. Judge Hardy excluded Smyth's tests from evidence because Smyth hadn't built a full-size chamber. But he also refused to give Smyth the funds with which to build a full-size chamber. Knapp's lawyers over the years came to refer to this decision as the Catch-22 ruling.

While it is unusual for indigence to play so naked and critical a role in a trial as it did in John Knapp's case, the Catch-22 ruling can hardly be viewed as an aberration — either in the context of the Knapp case or in the context of death-penalty litigation generally. By the time it occurred in the Knapp case, Hyder's attempts to use Knapp's indigence to gain a litigation advantage were a theme of the litigation, not a footnote to it.

Knapp's indigence had served as the basis for Hyder's motions to limit Knapp to a single attorney in the first trial (granted by Hardy, but reversed on appeal), to choose who that attorney would be (denied), to prevent Knapp from having any fire expert at the first trial (granted by Hardy, affirmed on appeal, but circumvented), and, finally, to prevent Knapp from having a fire expert at the second trial (denied initially, but later, in effect, granted). Nor was the Catch-22 ruling the last time the state would use Knapp's indigence to try to win his execution.

Our criminal justice system treats indigence as a handicap that can be corrected by taking remedial steps, such as granting judges the power to appoint attorneys and experts for the indigent. But, in practice, indigence appears to be a prerequisite to receiving the death penalty in this country. When the U.S. Supreme Court struck down most of the country's death-penalty laws in 1972, it did so in part because of its recognition that juries were imposing the death penalty only on a "freakishly" tiny subset of those who had been convicted of first-degree murder, and that that subset consisted almost exclusively of the indigent (and disproportionately of minorities).

It is not, of course, that a defendant with unlimited funds can buy acquittal; he cannot. But there are many steps along the way where a defendant with money to hire topnotch lawyers, psychiatrists, experts, and investigators can at least tip the scales far enough in his favor to avoid imposition of the death sentence or the carrying out of that sentence once it has been handed down.

There are no hard data on the exact percentage of death-row prisoners who were indigent at the time of trial. The most conservative estimates place that number at about 90 percent, and the number climbs as execution approaches, since many prisoners with retained counsel manage to have their death sentences lifted.

During the first decade after the enactment of its modernized death-penalty statute in 1973, Arizona sentenced 80 people to death, of whom 74 were indigent at the time of trial (92.5 percent). None of those 80 had been executed by the end of 1983, but 29 of them had won reduced sentences or new trials by that time. Of the 51 remaining on death row at that time, 50 had been indigent at the time of trial (98 percent). The one exception, Wilmar Holsinger, was *sui generis*, since he had been murdered in prison in early 1982.*

With the accidental fire defense gutted, Diettrich had decided to be more direct about hinting that Linda could have set the fire.

But Hyder kept him from doing that also.

Hyder asked Judge Hardy to bar Diettrich from suggesting in any manner that Linda could have committed the crime. (Since Linda already had immunity, the jury would not see her invoke her Fifth Amendment privilege against self-incrimination again.)

"The law is quite clear," Hyder proclaimed, "he cannot call a witness to the stand with the intention of blaming them or forcing them to . . . deny that they did something."

"The defendant can always attempt to show someone else committed the crime," Judge Hardy countered.

"He can't call that person to the stand and try to elicit that information out of them," Hyder insisted. "The law is clear. . . . If Mr. Diettrich has evidence about somebody else shooting somebody, his remedy is to turn it over to the state for investigation, not to put them on the stand to mislead the jury. . . . The law is quite clear on that."

Judge Hardy rejected Hyder's insupportable claim. Nevertheless, as he considered the matter, Judge Hardy himself finally thought of a more plausible theory under which, in his view, Hyder *could* bar Diettrich from casting suspicion on Linda.

Under Arizona law, the judge remembered, the defendant could not claim that some other specific person committed the crime unless there was some evidence actually linking that person to the crime. In Judge Hardy's view — assisted by the fact that, this time around, both Dale and Malone claimed that they did not consider Linda a suspect — there was not sufficient evidence linking Linda to the crime. Accordingly, he barred Diettrich from arguing or suggesting that Linda could have committed it. Similarly, he prohibited Diettrich from presenting evidence — like the fact that Linda had dreamed that her chil-

---

* These figures were compiled by superior court judge John Foreman when he was a deputy public defender in Phoenix, and were accurate as of December 31, 1983.

dren burned to death two days before they did — that tended to cast suspicion on her.

At the second trial, Diettrich never got to the bottom of any of the discovery problems that had plagued the first trial. Once again, Hyder asked at least seven witnesses whether they had ever seen the children light matches — none had — while neither he nor Diettrich asked the same question of Melba Burr, who would have given a markedly different answer.

In fact, on the next-to-last day of trial, when Diettrich discovered that Hyder had never turned over a Dictaphone tape of a conversation between an insurance agent and John Knapp five days after the fire — which the agent had switched off at one point because Knapp had begun to cry — it became clear that Hyder was still marching to the beat of his own drummer when it came to interpreting his discovery obligations.

"We don't have to reveal rebuttal evidence," Hyder said.

"[Rule] 15.1 doesn't say that," Judge Hardy protested, just as he had on July 9, 1974, four months earlier, when he rejected this very same argument. "It says 'all statements of the defendant.' "

But Hyder, notwithstanding the judge's earlier ruling, had continued *taking the position* that he had to provide only those statements of the defendant that he intended to use in his case in chief.

Hyder then added an even more disturbing argument. He *took the position* that Judge Hardy's temporary discovery suspension, imposed back on August 8, 1974, because the defense had not yet turned over Smyth's last movie reels, was still in force!

"If the Court will recall," Hyder said, "the Court relieved the state of all of its burden to so furnish the defense with further discovery prior to the trial. . . . [The] Court did enter an order relieving the State from having to comply with the rules after the State had repeatedly made requests that the defense . . . furnish us with disclosures."

In Hyder's mind, it seems, that temporary suspension had never been lifted!

Judge Hardy, who did not seem to know what Hyder was talking about, rejected his argument. But Diettrich did not think to demand whatever other documents Hyder might have been withholding under his private theory that the discovery suspension had never been lifted.

Each side rested on Friday, November 15. On Monday, the lawyers gave their closing arguments. As in many jurisdictions, in Arizona the prosecution argues first, the defense responds, and then the prosecutor replies.

"[Neighbor] Susan House saw Mr. Knapp clean, calm, and she smelled the odor of kerosene or gasoline burning," Hyder recounted, "and she testified that Knapp was drinking coffee, smoking cigarettes and laughing, generally enjoying himself. . . . That [it] was like he was a host at a cocktail party. He can't shed any tears for his children, but he can spare a few laughs for the neighbors.

"These people have no motive for testifying in any other way but the truth. Not one. Sue House put John Knapp in the proper perspective, I submit, because only a cold blooded killer who could walk into a bedroom and pour it full of Coleman fuel could sit while his children were burning to death and [have] a good time."

To highlight the impossibility that the children could have set the fire, Hyder stressed that no witness had ever seen the children light matches — an argument made possible only by Hyder's concealment, or the defense lawyers' inexplicable failure to use, Melba Burr's statement that she had seen Little Linda light whole matchbooks.

"What did Mrs. Sheets say? . . . She has never seen the girls play with matches or gasoline. . . . .

"[Mr. Rosales] admitted he had never seen the girls play with gasoline or matches. . . .

"Mr. Knapp admitted the girls never struck matches."

Hyder denounced each of Knapp's experts as little better than a fraud.

"Along comes Doctor Michael Parsons," he said, referring to the defense chemist. "He hedges, you see. 'Well, you know, that methylene chloride was kind of dirty, and you can't really tell what was there.' . . . [But you heard] what he told Mr. Elardo over the phone. . . . 'You know, from the residue, Mr. Elardo, there must have been one heck of a lot of flammable liquid in that room.' "

Hyder urged the jury not even to worry about Linda Knapp.

"They're trying to get her to testify favorably for John Knapp because that will really confuse the people," Hyder argued, "and they will have that reasonable doubt. What a flagrant attempt."

He closed the first half of his summation with a flourish, alluding once again to the improbable testimony of neighbor Susan House:

"I submit . . . that the State has proven the case and shown not only that John Knapp is a liar and without compunction. . . . He is cold blooded. . . . He is guilty, and I think it's about time the party was over for Mr. Knapp. Thank you."

*　　　*　　　*

Though Judge Hardy's rulings on the fire tests had ripped the heart out of the defense case, Diettrich's closing was impassioned.

"Linda Knapp's statement — oh, not very important, I guess. Only that, as the only person in the house at the time of the fire, other than John, [she] testified, one, that John was asleep in bed between her and the wall when she discovered the fire. Two, as he lay in bed within inches of her, she detected no strange odors about him of fuel or smoke. His hair wasn't singed. . . . She didn't feel him or hear him crawl over her and that if he would have she would certainly have been awakened. She didn't hear any unusual noises such as the rattling of a Coleman fuel can under a pile of trash in the closet where it was supposed to have been hidden, according to the state's theory."

By the time he finished, Diettrich was in tears and engaging in emotional argument that was, at times, over the line of propriety.

"There was no arson. . . . It was an ordinary combustible fire. Then why this [trial]? Remember when the jury panel walked in? . . . Every panel that walked in, I guarantee — I sit over there and die a thousand deaths from the looks you get [when the jury is] advised of the charges: . . . arson murder of his daughters. All the looks. There is no presumption of innocence. . . .

"If John Knapp actually set this fire that killed his children, God help him. But for me, as the lawyer charged with his defense, for you, as the judges . . . of the facts, and for judge Hardy, who is going to have to impose a penalty if he is convicted . . . Lord help us if he is innocent."

During his reply argument, Hyder skillfully punished Diettrich for his emotional display.

"I'm chagrined . . . that he would feel that appealing to you in this manner is the proper way to defend Mr. Knapp, because he is an experienced attorney, and if we're going to resort to tears and to broken voice, I suggest his two little girls ought to have some tears shed for them. . . ."

Judge Hardy let the jury deliberate in the main courtroom, since it would be easier on one of the jurors who objected to the others' cigarette smoke. They deliberated the rest of Monday evening until 10:00 P.M., when they were taken to a nearby motel to spend the night.

Then they deliberated all day Tuesday, and into the night.

"I was out drinking and letting down," Diettrich said in 1993. "We really got torpedoed in the second trial by Hyder and Judge Hardy in his rulings. . . . But despite all that, I just believed in the case enough that I believed they were going to acquit him."

At about 11:00 P.M. the judge's clerk notified the lawyers that the jury had reached a verdict, and by 11:15 everyone was back in court.

Across the street, several deputy county attorneys who had been working late ran over to hear the verdict — the end not only of a highly publicized case, but of a brutal, bitter scrimmage between two of the city's best-known criminal trial lawyers. One of the young prosecutors who ran over considered both Hyder and Diettrich her friends. (She requested anonymity when interviewed by the author in 1993.)

She arrived at about 11:25 P.M. and had just missed the verdict. John Knapp had been convicted of two counts of murder in the first degree.

She was happy for Hyder. Having heard about the case mainly from fellow prosecutors, she did not doubt Knapp's guilt. But Diettrich was sitting in his chair, weeping. She became concerned. She had never seen a lawyer behaving this way.

"I saw him melting down in front of me," she remembered nineteen years later.

"I was shocked," Diettrich recounted. "Whether it was realistic or not, I was shocked. And all of a sudden I just fell apart emotionally. It all finally ended. The battle was over and I could let down.

"I don't remember John saying anything. . . . I have a very clear picture of him taking his watch off, taking his ring off, and handing it to me [because he was going back into custody], and just looking . . . perplexed. He didn't say anything. Typical John Knapp reaction. Very little reaction."

Judge Hardy set a date for the sentencing, excused the jury, and left the bench.

Then the young prosecutor who was worried about Diettrich stepped through the wooden gate in the low rail dividing the gallery from the well of the court and approached Diettrich. She told him that he had done a fine job, had done everything anybody could do, but that the jury had spoken and now it was time to accept their verdict. But her words were having no effect.

"He was beyond consolation," she recalled. "I remember what Chuck said. He repeated it twice: 'He's innocent. He's innocent.'"

Knapp was sentenced on January 6, 1975, a mild winter morning. Under Arizona's law, the judge would decide between life and death after weighing certain aggravating and mitigating factors listed in the statute. Judge Hardy found that one aggravating factor applied — the crime had been committed "in an especially heinous, cruel, or depraved manner" — while none of the four mitigating factors were applicable. He then offered Knapp his last opportunity to speak before judgment was pronounced.

"I felt the State was negligent and incompetent in the case," Knapp told the judge, "and I did not burn my two children. And just because Mr. Hyder was able to convince twelve people that I did, doesn't change the fact that I did not do it."

Then Diettrich offered one last desperate plea for Knapp's life. Diettrich argued that there was just too much doubt about Knapp's guilt to impose the death sentence, though the law did not appear to allow Judge Hardy to take such concerns into consideration.

"I didn't change my position," Diettrich explained years later. "I wasn't going to try to shotgun a lot of immaterial [arguments about] sentencing criteria. . . . We're talking about a man who's innocent, and we're talking about an execution."

"You know as well as I do," he told the judge, "there is tremendous question in this case [about guilt]. I think you'd be in a sorry position some . . . years down the road to be sitting on a porch or on a park bench some place and have a question pop in your mind about, 'Gee, I wonder why . . . those children didn't die right away if he was really guilty of setting that fire? I wonder why Mrs. Knapp wasn't aware he was up and setting the fire?' . . . and all the other questions that were unanswered.

"Certainly, you must take these things into consideration in imposing [the] penalty here," Diettrich continued. "There may not be a statutory provision for it, but who cares? . . . I could care less about the statutes at this point. I'm talking about reality. . . . There is no way you can, as an honest, conscientious human being, impose the death penalty in this case with the problems and questions that still loom in it."

Hardy's response was measured.

"Mr. Knapp, before I enter judgment I do want to say this. I think you have been well and adequately defended by both Mr. Diettrich and Mr. Basham, and both these lawyers handled your case in a manner which is a real credit to the profession. They have represented you vigorously all the way, and intelligently, I might add, and well.

"It's my reading of [the statute that] given the existence of aggravated circumstances . . . and no mitigating circumstances, I have no discretion about it.

"I must say, though, if I had discretion, I would enter the same judgment that I'm about to enter. I feel you're guilty. . . .

153

"As punishment, therefore, I'm going to sentence you to die and be executed in the manner provided by law."

Knapp's mother, Mary, who was sitting in the gallery, then lunged at, and struck, a juror, who had also come to see the sentencing, shouting, "I hope you die a terrible, terrible death," according to newspaper accounts in the *Phoenix Gazette* and *Arizona Republic*. Sheriff's deputies had to restrain her.

"I'll never forget standing in court that day," Diettrich remembered in 1993. "I remember I couldn't stop my legs from shaking. It was an experience you can only be aware of if you've gone through it. You can't read about it or be a spectator. I was actually standing there hearing the judge sentencing the guy that I was responsible for to be executed.

"I remember no reaction on [John's] part at all. Not a clearing of the throat even. Almost like he was oblivious to it. Just that strange demeanor."

Later that day Knapp was driven to the Arizona State Prison Complex in Florence, about sixty miles to the southeast, and placed on condemned row.

PART 2.

Tick-Tock, the Game
Is Locked

Eleven

Diettrich was too emotionally involved in Knapp's case to let go now. He decided to handle Knapp's automatic appeal to the state supreme court, though he had handled only one other appeal during his whole career. He had always been a trial lawyer.

And he had serious financial problems.

"I was scrambling," he later recounted, "trying to regain a practice outside of the Knapp case." He had neglected his paying clients for a whole year, and he had a wife and two children to support.

Toward the end of May 1975, Diettrich was preparing for a major criminal trial for a paying client set to begin in Tucson in early June. After he had gotten two extensions of time to file Knapp's appeal brief, and had let both of them pass, Diettrich hired a friend, Catherine Hughes, to do a first draft for him. Hughes, twenty-six, was just two years out of law school and had no experience in criminal matters. But since she had spent a year clerking at the state supreme court, she knew more about appeals than Diettrich.

"I probably unfairly turned over the bulk of the work on the appeal to her," Diettrich said later.

Diettrich gave her a box containing the transcripts of both trials — about 3,700 pages — and a list of five appellate issues he had scribbled down on a sheet from a yellow legal pad. He told her the brief was due in a month.

Since Hughes was working full-time as a civil lawyer with the Legal Aid Society, she had only weekends and nights to devote to the project.

"I never considered that I was 'handling' [the appeal]," she recalled in 1994. She saw herself as a ghostwriter, and her name never went on the brief.

She worked maniacally to meet the deadline. With Diettrich's permission she farmed out one issue to a friend in the public defender's office.

"My memory is that I had asked [Diettrich] to seek another extension and he didn't think he'd be able to get one," she said. "I remember not being satisfied with the product, but it needed to be filed."

Diettrich filed the brief on July 1, 1975, with minimal revisions.

One passage in it, however, bears Diettrich's indelible imprint. Characteristically, it has emotional impact, and no legal weight at all. In it, Diettrich argued that the death penalty should be considered "cruel or unusual punishment," violating the Eighth Amendment of the Constitution.

But he made the argument not because of its cruelty to the *defendant*, but because of its cruelty to everyone else who becomes affected by, and implicated in, the execution.

It is cruel to the family and friends of the one upon whom it is imposed. It is cruel to the judge who must order its imposition. It is cruel to the jurors whose finding of guilt made its imposition possible. . . . It is cruel to the executioner and to the members of this Court who must sit in judgment and to all members of the public who disapprove of its imposition.

The only person Diettrich left out of the litany was the most obvious candidate for inclusion — the tormented defense lawyer who feels personally responsible for the death of his client.

"Case number thirty-one oh six. State versus Knapp," an Arizona supreme court justice* called out at 9:30 A.M. on January 15, 1976, the date of the oral argument of Knapp's appeal.

"The state is ready, Your Honor," answered assistant attorney general Frank Galati in a clear, sonorous baritone.

---

* The voice is probably that of then Chief Justice James Duke Cameron. The supreme court keeps no written transcript of its oral arguments. Its tape recordings do not identify the voices of the justices and, because of the placement of the microphone and the poor quality of the tapes from that period, their voices are difficult to distinguish.

"Is the defense ready?" the justice asked.

Silence.

Diettrich was not there. It was very unusual for a lawyer not to show up for a supreme court argument.

In Diettrich's absence, the court had Galati present the state's argument, even though he ordinarily would have responded to Diettrich's.

Galati, who is today a superior court judge in Phoenix, had had nothing to do with either of the two trials. In Arizona direct appeals from criminal convictions were — and are — usually handled by the appeals bureau of the attorney general's office, rather than by the local prosecutors who obtained the convictions. Consequently, Galati's familiarity with the case came from reading those transcripts necessary to respond to Diettrich's brief.

One justice asked Galati to address the Catch-22 ruling: Judge Hardy's decision to exclude Marshall Smyth's small-scale fire tests while denying funds to perform full-scale tests.

In his hastily drafted brief, however, Diettrich had challenged only *half* of what Judge Hardy had done. Diettrich had protested Hardy's refusal to give Smyth funds to perform full-scale burn tests, but had never challenged Hardy's *exclusion* of the small-scale tests Smyth *had* performed. It was as if Diettrich were conceding that the small-scale tests were in fact too unreliable to have been admitted — which was not, of course, what he meant to do at all.

In defending what Judge Hardy had done, assistant attorney general Galati therefore also divorced the second half of Judge Hardy's ruling from the first half, producing a defense of Judge Hardy's actions that was little short of surreal.

"The only thing withheld from [the defense]," Galati argued, "was another two thousand dollars of county funds to build a complete re-creation of the room. . . . I think [Judge Hardy] said, 'That's not necessary,' because — well, for one thing, Mr. Smyth himself testified at the first trial that 'my tests are valid even though they're not conducted in a house like that. I can do it on a smaller scale and they are valid.' And for him to come back later and say, 'No, I need a whole new room' — Judge Hardy said, 'That's out of line.'"

Of course, the only reason Smyth and Diettrich "came back later" and said they needed "a whole new room" was that Judge Hardy had reversed his earlier ruling and decided not to let the second jury see the smaller-scale tests. One of the justices asked Galati if it wasn't Hardy's ruling excluding the small-scale tests that had, in fact, prompted the defense's interest in performing full-scale tests.

Evidently only now appreciating what had happened, Galati conceded, "That's certainly a plausible explanation for the shift from the first trial to the second trial."

The inquiring justice was concerned that Smyth's full-scale tests, if he had been allowed to perform them, might well have created a reasonable doubt in the minds of the second jury — just as his smaller-scale tests had created it in the minds of five members of the first jury. The smaller-scale tests, even if they hadn't perfectly replicated the conditions of the Knapp house, seemed to disprove some of the pronouncements of the state's fire experts, the justice pointed out.

"If the state's expert is wrong in one area," the justice asked, "perhaps he's wrong in all of them. What about that? Doesn't it raise that point?"

"Probably so," Galati conceded. But then Galati parried with an argument that, from a cold, academic perspective, was supportable by existing law.

"We're talking about *appointed* experts," he emphasized.

Under the constitutional law as it stood, he observed, Knapp — because he was indigent — was not entitled to *public funds* to perform a scientific experiment that merely cast doubt on the credibility of the state's expert. Instead, he was entitled to *public funds* only if the experiment could completely *exonerate* him, which Smyth's tests could not do. While Smyth's tests might raise a reasonable doubt about Knapp's guilt, they could not *prove him innocent*.

Galati's argument was an attempt to distinguish Knapp's case from a 1970 case in which a federal judge had reversed the conviction of an indigent rape defendant because the prosecution had refused to perform a semen test that might have completely cleared him — *proved him innocent*.

"All [Smyth's experiment] does is offer an alternate theory to how the fire started," he observed. "In no way, shape, or form does that *exclude* the defendant as being the cause of the fire. . . . Completely different from [the semen sample case]."

Since Diettrich wasn't present, no one was there to point out to the judges the horror of what was being so placidly argued. What Galati was effectively saying was that an indigent defendant wasn't entitled to funds to perform a scientific experiment *even if that experiment would create a reasonable doubt about guilt and result in his acquittal*. Though, in theory, a defendant was entitled to acquittal if his attorney could raise a mere "reasonable doubt" about his guilt, an *indigent* defendant was not entitled to public funds to establish such doubt.

A distraught Chuck Diettrich arrived at the supreme court about two hours later.

"I'd like to apologize for the late arrival," he began, "but I can avow solemnly to this court that the last notice I received was that [the argument] was set at two o'clock. Nothing's more important to me up to this point in my life than this case. . . . As it is, I'm a little upset and flustered. . . . The bottom of my world sort of fell out when I received a call at nine-thirty this morning that I was supposed to be at the supreme court arguing this case."

The justices allowed Diettrich to present his argument. Diettrich began by making a claim so legally frivolous that his friend Cathy Hughes had urged him to drop it altogether. He argued that retrying Knapp, after the first jury had deadlocked, constituted double jeopardy.

"Do you have any authority to support your interpretation?" a justice asked moments into his presentation. (He was asking for precedents from other published court rulings.)

"Uh — I don't have any authority, no," Diettrich conceded.

But at a gut level, Diettrich thought the double jeopardy claim captured the true injustice of what had happened to Knapp. And his argument — though rambling and legally futile — was exactly right, if emotions counted for anything.

"It wasn't as though [the state] had something new to put on they didn't put on the first time. All they did was present their case again, keep out a major portion of our case, and then the second time around they got him."

As he continued his argument, Diettrich periodically veered outside the rules, bringing up personal asides that the judges were not entitled to consider.

He mentioned that Knapp still denied his guilt each time Diettrich met with him at the state prison. Then he commented that a well-regarded Phoenix homicide detective "was horrified" by Judge Hardy's ruling allowing Knapp's confession into evidence.

"Is that in the record?" a justice asked Diettrich, brusquely.

"No, it isn't."

"All right. Well, stick to the record."

Diettrich finally turned to the Catch-22 argument. But not having heard assistant attorney general Galati's argument two hours earlier, Diettrich never addressed Galati's central contention: that even if full-scale fire tests might have created a reasonable doubt and resulted in Knapp's acquittal, Knapp *still* was not entitled to public money to fund them.

Diettrich closed with one last, desperate, improper argument.

"I first got into this case in late December 1973," he told the court, "and have expended well in excess of a thousand hours on this case, including nine solid weeks in trial, countless hours in investigation, pretrial hearings, and, more importantly — and uniquely to me — private and intimate conversations with the defendant. I'm not naive. I'm not an inexperienced lawyer. I've spent the last eight and a half years steeped in criminal law. As a county attorney, U.S. attorney, assistant attorney general, as a public defender. And ninety percent of my private practice work in the last few years has been criminal work. I solemnly avow to this court that it is my firm and honest conviction that John Knapp is totally innocent of this crime."

A justice told Diettrich that the court obviously could not consider the lawyer's personal opinions.

"I concede that my opinion probably is not material," Diettrich responded. "But, on the other hand, you — as well as being justices of the supreme court — are also human beings. And I wanted to ring the bell, and I don't think it can be unrung."

Diettrich sat down.

Two months after the oral argument in Knapp's case, the U.S. Supreme Court heard oral argument in five capital cases raising a variety of questions concerning the constitutionality of the death penalty. Since the Supreme Court's narrow 1972 ruling in *Furman v. Georgia* — which decided that death-penalty statutes were unconstitutional if they gave the judge or jury total discretion to choose between life and death — 35 states had reenacted death-penalty laws, and about 460 new inmates were now on death row. Most states, including Arizona, had tried to meet the demands of *Furman* by enacting lists of aggravating and mitigating factors that were intended to "channel" the judge's or jury's sentencing discretion. A few states on the other hand had gone to the opposite extreme, eliminating sentencing discretion altogether, and making the death penalty mandatory for certain categories of murder.

On July 2, 1976, in *Gregg v. Georgia* and four companion cases, the Supreme Court upheld the post-*Furman* capital-punishment laws of Georgia, Florida, and Texas, which — like Arizona's — used aggravating and mitigating factors to guide sentencing discretion. At the same time the court struck down the mandatory death-penalty laws of Louisiana and North Carolina, finding that they unconstitutionally interfered with individualized sentencing.

In light of these rulings, the constitutional law governing capital punishment became very tricky. Completely discretionary death-penalty statutes were unconstitutional, but so were completely nondiscretionary death-penalty statutes.

In court, lawyers might say that the two principles were *in tension with* one another. In private, they might say they were contradictory.

The five justices of the Supreme Court of Arizona unanimously affirmed Knapp's conviction on March 9, 1977.

In upholding Judge Hardy's Catch-22 ruling, Justice Jack Hays adopted almost verbatim Galati's argument — the one Diettrich had never heard and, therefore, never addressed.

"The defense theory then was merely an alternative being offered to the jury as to the cause and origin of the fire," wrote Justice Hays. Judge Hardy had not abused his discretion, Hays continued, because he had merely refused to give the defense money to perform "a questionable experiment that would not have legally exonerated the appellant, but only offered a weak alternative theory to the trier of facts."

But while Hays may have considered that alternative theory "weak," five members of the first jury — who had had the benefit of seeing Smyth's tests — considered it strong enough to warrant acquittal.

After losing the appeal, the routine course would have been for Diettrich to move for rehearing, which would have further delayed the issuance of a warrant for Knapp's execution. But Diettrich never filed the motion.

After the Knapp case ended, Diettrich recounted many years later, "I would start . . . going over and over the case, going over and over the evidence, going over and over what maybe could have been done to change the outcome. I would just get deeper and deeper into a depression. And then, of course, the drinking starts. Alcohol — it just makes it worse."

In 1977 a lawyer friend suggested Diettrich see a psychiatrist, and the psychiatrist recommended that he check into a thirty-day inpatient program at a hospital.

"They knew immediately I was an alcoholic. So I've been working on it since then," Diettrich said, sixteen years later.

Diettrich was still in the hospital when he learned that the supreme court had affirmed Knapp's conviction. Either due to Diettrich's physical condition or due to confusion about who was representing Knapp — Mary Knapp was trying to find another lawyer — the motion for rehearing was not filed within the proper time period.

When that period lapsed, the Arizona supreme court issued a warrant for

John Knapp's execution. The two-page document, signed by each of the five Arizona supreme court justices, ordered "that Wednesday, the 29th day of June, 1977, be . . . fixed as the time when the judgment and sentence of death pronounced upon said appellant, JOHN HENRY KNAPP . . . shall be executed by the administering to said JOHN HENRY KNAPP lethal gas."

Most death-penalty advocates believe that capital punishment is necessary to express the unique abhorrence that our society places upon the taking of life. The penalty is, paradoxically, a way of affirming the sanctity of human life.

Figuring out just how to kill criminals, however — the actual mechanics of it — in a way that will also affirm society's reverence for the sanctity of human life has proven to be a challenge.

From the time the United States won its independence until the late nineteenth century, most death-penalty states used hanging as the prescribed means of execution. In 1888 New York switched to the newly available electric chair, which, by the end of the 1920s, had become the method of choice.

In 1921 Nevada's legislature turned to lethal gas, which its sponsors had originally envisioned as being administered to the unsuspecting prisoner as he slept in his cell. The plan proved unworkable, but the state installed a gas chamber instead, and several other states later followed suit.

Like all death-penalty states, Arizona originally used the gallows. But on February 21, 1930, the hanging of an obese, syphilitic woman literally ripped her head off. Determining that such a spectacle was a poor way to express Arizona's reverence for the sanctity of life, the state legislature switched to the gas chamber in 1933.[*]

Diettrich was released from the hospital on April 11, 1977, and was well enough to resume practicing, he thought, a week later. He recruited a University of Arizona law professor, Joel Finer, to seek a stay from the U.S. Supreme Court. The application focused on Judge Hardy's Catch-22 ruling.

At 7:00 A.M. on the morning of June 27 — about forty hours before Knapp's scheduled execution — the Supreme Court granted a stay while it pondered whether to hear Knapp's case. Diettrich drove to Florence to tell Knapp personally.

---

[*] See Crane McClennen, "Capital Punishment in Arizona: Past, Present, and Future," *Arizona Attorney* (October 1992).

"He'd already ordered his last meal," Diettrich recalled. Though Diettrich said he had never seen signs of stress or fear in Knapp concerning his impending execution, he did remember seeing "elation" in his face that day.

"It was one of the few times he apparently was capable of showing much emotion," he said.

In the several months of life granted Knapp, Diettrich had time to pursue a paper-thin lead he hoped might lead to "newly discovered evidence" meriting a new trial.

The lead had arrived the same morning as the stay, when Diettrich's secretary got a phone call from the wife of one of John's former co-workers at Continental Can. The frightened woman, who would not give her name, said her husband remembered Knapp being called home from work one day by his wife because his kids had been playing with matches and had set a fire at their house. This incident had allegedly occurred a few months before the fatal fire.

To pursue this lead Diettrich enlisted the help of Richard Todd, thirty-six, a short, stocky private investigator with light brown hair. Todd had spent sixteen years with the Phoenix police department, most of them as a detective. Diettrich had known Todd for many years.

"Chuck told me we didn't have any money," Todd recalled. "He said, 'You know me, I'm a defense lawyer. I'll give you other cases, but I need your help on this one.' " Though Diettrich got Todd appointed briefly, most of Todd's work was donated.

Todd was a controversial figure. As an investigator, he had a low reputation among some law enforcement officials, who believed he used suggestive and disreputable investigative techniques. Even before he left the police department he had been involved in a celebrated narcotics prosecution in which his testimony about some of his observations of the defendant's home from a nearby alley were later shown to have been physically impossible. An appellate court ultimately upheld the conviction, noting that "while many inconsistencies in [Todd's] testimony are apparent, [they do not] convince this Court that [Todd] was committing . . . perjury."

Whatever his flaws, Todd was diligent. He soon verified that five current or former Continental Can employees remembered an incident several weeks before the fatal fire when Linda had telephoned John and had him come home from work because the children had allegedly lit a fire.

Unfortunately, John Knapp himself could never remember the incident.

Todd began to canvas Knapp's old East Capri neighborhood, trying to find the neighbor whose phone Linda had borrowed to call John home from work that day. On the very first day he did so, Todd located a neighbor three houses down from the Knapps who had — incredibly — never been interviewed before by either the defense or the prosecution. Though the man, John Gregory, knew nothing about the phone call Todd was investigating, his memories of the fire — now four years after the fact — were curious.

Gregory remembered seeing Linda walk past his home on the afternoon before the fire, apparently on the way toward the only convenience store in the community. He had then seen her return about twenty minutes later carrying a gasoline or Coleman fuel can. He also remembered having seen her the next morning, as he left for work sometime before 8:00 A.M., standing in the threshold of the Knapps' front door — perhaps a half hour *before* the fire.

Gradually, as investigator Todd continued his work, he began to subscribe with increasing exclusivity to the Linda-did-it theory of the fire.

Soon thereafter, Diettrich put together a short "post-conviction relief petition" seeking to overturn the verdict based on the little information Todd had come up with so far. If the U.S. Supreme Court denied review of Knapp's appeal, Diettrich would file this petition in state court before Judge Hardy. Though the petition was exceedingly thin—it almost certainly would not warrant reversing Knapp's conviction—Diettrich knew of no other way to buy Knapp time.

Meanwhile, Diettrich's life and practice were falling apart. From late 1977 through early 1978, five clients — including Mary Knapp — filed bar complaints against him for failing to meet court appointments and just "disappearing." Later a bar disciplinary committee concluded that Diettrich's difficulties had resulted from "severe emotional pressure" brought on by his involvement in the Knapp case.

In an interview in 1993, Diettrich refused to "blame" the Knapp case for his dissolution. But he also acknowledged that his inability properly to "deal with" that case did play a role.

"For some reason it threw me," he said. "I wasn't able to deal with it like I did other things. I mean I was always at my best [with pressure] — the bigger the case, the better I am. But for some reason this one threw me. I would dwell on it instead of putting it out of my mind."

He was also losing his passion for law practice.

"It just didn't seem like I had the — I don't know. There wasn't the intensity. I'm not sure if it was due to one, two, three, or ten things. It was a decline."

Diettrich's marriage of fifteen years had broken up. He moved to an isolated valley in the high desert near Payson, Arizona, about sixty miles northeast of Phoenix. He was living in a trailer without a phone, while he was building a cabin nearby. The only way to reach him was to leave messages with an array of friends and neighbors and then hope he eventually called back.

In late February the U.S. Supreme Court declined to review Knapp's appeal, as it does in the vast majority of cases.* Accordingly, it also lifted the stay of execution.

As a result, Knapp's weak post-conviction relief petition, which Diettrich had filed based on the scraps of information investigator Todd had come up with, became Knapp's last hope. A post-conviction relief petition, known as a PCR or a "Rule 32" — after the Arizona rule of criminal procedure authorizing the action — was a proceeding in front of the same judge who had sentenced the defendant. There the defendant could try to win a new trial on the grounds that "newly discovered evidence" tended to show that he was innocent. Knapp's petition was scheduled for argument before Judge Hardy on March 20, 1978.

Diettrich never showed up.

Accordingly, Judge Hardy simply examined the papers Diettrich had filed, found too little to warrant a new trial, and dismissed the petition.

Diettrich, meanwhile, was mired in depression at his home near Payson. He had gotten mixed up about the date of the hearing, he later explained, believing it to have been set for March 27. By then, however, Diettrich had temporarily quit practicing law on his doctor's advice. His psychiatrist had now diagnosed him as a manic-depressive and had prescribed lithium.

"I always knew that I had a propensity to have depressed periods," Diettrich said. "While working I was fine. While I'm involved in something I'm like a rocket. But it's when I back off of something that I start sinking into depressed thought."

---

* For a case to be accepted for review, four of the nine justices must vote to take the case. The Court ordinarily issues no opinion when it denies review, although individual justices occasionally write dissents to such denials.

Predictably, Justices William Brennan, Jr., and Thurgood Marshall dissented from the denial of review in Knapp's case; at that time they were dissenting to the denial of review in *all* death-penalty cases because of their belief that capital punishment was always unconstitutional.

In a more unusual gesture, however, Justice Harry Blackmun *also* wrote an opinion. Signaling his concern over the specific matters raised by Knapp's petition, which had focused upon the Catch-22 issue, Blackmun wrote that he was voting to deny review only because the issue could later be explored in a federal habeas corpus action — a proceeding Knapp could bring in federal district court even after the Supreme Court had declined to review his appeal.

He began trying to pass Knapp's case along to someone he trusted.

"I remember him being absolutely under [the case's] spell to the point where he couldn't function," recalled Michael Benchoff, whom Diettrich had approached, but who ultimately did not take the case. "I remember an emotional — if not mental — condition that precluded him from doing what he most wanted to do: from running with the ball and setting Knapp free."

On March 28, the state supreme court issued the second warrant for Knapp's execution. It called for him to die on May 31, 1978.

A few days after the warrant issued, Diettrich came before Judge Hardy, explained his mental condition, and begged the judge to reinstate Knapp's petition and appoint new counsel. The judge consented, and ordered the public defender's office to represent Knapp. That office would have less than two months to try to get a stay — while coming to grips with a mammoth file whose complex history was fully understood only by an alcoholic manic-depressive with no telephone.

The beliefs of most death-penalty advocates necessarily dictate that Arizona should have killed John Knapp on May 31, 1978. Knapp had been convicted, his conviction had been affirmed, and the U.S. Supreme Court had denied review.

Some death-penalty advocates would also allow Knapp to bring one federal habeas corpus action at this point — the law currently favors that path — but most of those same advocates believe that there are few, if any, issues that Knapp could have properly raised at such a proceeding. Most would have already been either conclusively decided by the state courts or waived by not having been raised there.

In essence, death-penalty advocates *have* to favor killing John Knapp at or about this point.

They may not endorse all the discovery positions Hyder took at the trials; they may feel that Diettrich or Basham could have done a better job defending Knapp; they may not agree with the jury's verdict; they may second-guess some of Judge Hardy's rulings or those of Justice Jack Hays and his colleagues. But *every* case involves questionable lawyer tactics and performance, a debatable verdict, and disputed judicial rulings.

No finite number of post-conviction appeals will guarantee that only guilty people are put to death. An infinite number of appeals *will* guarantee, however, that the death penalty will never be administered. In addition, most death-penalty advocates also concede that if the death penalty is to have any deterrent effect at all, it must be administered reasonably soon after the crime. By May 31, 1978, four and a half years had passed since the fire at East Capri.

Therefore, realistic death-penalty advocates concede that, if we are to have a death penalty, innocent people must periodically be executed. Such rare catastrophes are outweighed, they argue, by the benefits of keeping the penalty: the ability to express society's moral outrage in a manner more commensurate with the heinousness of the crime than a sentence of life imprisonment without parole; the guarantee that the individual executed will never murder again; and the speculation that the prospect of being sentenced to death will deter so many would-be first-degree murderers from committing their crimes — people who, it is claimed, would not be deterred by the "mere" prospect of life imprisonment without parole — that the savings in innocent life will numerically outnumber the losses due to innocents being put to death.

Figures on how frequently innocent people are convicted of capital crimes are necessarily subjective and debatable, because there is no definitive way of determining innocence or guilt. State officials have psychological, political, and legal incentives not to acknowledge errors on this scale.

The most ambitious effort to compile a list of such miscarriages of justice was undertaken in the mid-1980s by two law professors, Hugo Bedau and Michael Radelet, who last published an updated version of their list in 1992. By that time they believed they had documented 416 cases of innocent people who had been wrongfully convicted of potentially capital crimes in the United States during this century, of whom 166 had actually been sentenced to death, and 23 had been put to death.

In October 1993 the Subcommittee on Civil and Constitutional Rights of the Committee on the Judiciary of the U.S. House of Representatives published a report concluding that, since 1973, 48 people had been released from prison after serving time on death row due to the emergence of significant evidence of their innocence, and that in 43 of those cases, the defendant was ultimately acquitted or pardoned, or the charges against them were dropped.

What kept John Knapp alive past May 1978 was confusion — confusion, by and large, that no longer exists. There was still doubt whether Arizona's death-penalty law would survive U.S. Supreme Court scrutiny. More important, there was tremendous confusion about how many times a condemned prisoner could challenge his conviction.

Today most of the key issues concerning the constitutionality of existing death-penalty statutes have been resolved. In addition, the Arizona legislature has amended its laws to ensure that condemned inmates can use the state's post-conviction procedures — the so-called PCR or Rule 32 proceedings — only once, and only within a short period after the inmate's conviction has been affirmed. Similarly, the U.S. Supreme Court has taken forceful steps to limit condemned inmates to a single federal habeas corpus proceeding — the post-conviction relief vehicle in the federal court system — under most circumstances.

But in 1978 the rules were still unformed. Knapp squeezed through loopholes that have since been sealed.

Nineteen days before Knapp's second scheduled execution, federal judge Carl Muecke stayed his execution — and those of all other Arizona death-row inmates — because of an apparent constitutional flaw in Arizona's death-penalty statute.*

Four months later, in July 1978, the U.S. Supreme Court struck down a similar Ohio capital-punishment law in language signaling that, as Judge Muecke had suspected, Arizona's law could not stand either.

Seventeen days later, the Arizona supreme court tried to fix the problem with the Arizona law without having to commute to life the death sentences of all the inmates who had already been sentenced under the unconstitutional law. The court said it would reinterpret the law retroactively, and that all death-row inmates would be resentenced under the newly interpreted law — but they could still be resentenced to death.

Since the constitutionality of the state supreme court's maneuver was itself highly suspect, Judge Muecke kept his stay of all Arizona executions in effect until the federal courts could decide that question. The stay lasted four years, until November 1982, when the federal courts finally decided that the state court could, in fact, do what it had done.

During this period, Knapp's case was handled, in succession, by two more defense lawyers. Charles Hyder, however, remained the prosecutor.

---

* Arizona's law limited the number of factors that the judge could consider "mitigating" to the four explicitly listed in the statute itself: factors including, for instance, the defendant's having committed the crime under "substantial duress," or his having played a relatively minor role in the offense. But because the statute excluded consideration of many other potentially relevant factors in determining whether to impose the ultimate sentence of death — including, for instance, the defendant's age, prior criminal record, and the degree of cooperation he had provided to authorities — Judge Muecke held the law unconstitutional.

Hyder's career, in contrast to Diettrich's, was thriving. In November 1976 he had been elected Maricopa County Attorney — the county's chief prosecutor. Yet, despite his new high position, he continued to handle the Knapp case personally.

Knapp's resentencing was held in May 1979. Before the sentencing, Judge Hardy held a hearing on the post-conviction relief petition Diettrich had initiated two years earlier. This was a new version of the same petition Judge Hardy had dismissed back in March 1978, when Diettrich failed to show up at a hearing. But after learning of Diettrich's disability, Judge Hardy had allowed a public defender to revive the petition, and he had then allowed it to be periodically amended to include additional evidence as investigator Todd found it. The focus of most of the evidence presented at this hearing was the possibility that Linda might have committed the crime. The presentation included two male friends of Linda's who — independent of Todd's investigations — had surfaced in 1978, one of whom had been romantically involved with Linda during the period of the 1974 trials. Each claimed that Linda had admitted to him some responsibility for the fire, though she had told him it had been an accident. Both of the men were highly unreliable — one was borderline retarded and the other was incarcerated for auto theft — and their stories were vague, hard to follow, and seemed to change with each telling. (In 1993 Linda recalled knowing both men, and dating one, but denied having confessed in any fashion to either.)

Judge Hardy found the witnesses either incredible or irrelevant. While the evidence weakly suggested that Linda might have played a role in the fire, it didn't exonerate Knapp, he found.

As for the possibility that the children could have done it, Judge Hardy still didn't believe children that age could set a fire.

"They were just babes," he said.

He sentenced Knapp to death for a second time.

The denial of post-conviction relief and Hardy's second sentence were both affirmed by September 1980.

Upon the completion of that process, Knapp's last court-appointed lawyer withdrew, leaving him with no lawyer at all. Only Judge Muecke's federal stay was keeping him alive. (A third warrant for Knapp's execution was issued in October 1980, but it expired harmlessly because of the stay.)

Death-row inmates are ineligible for school or work at the prison. Accordingly, for the five years since his sentencing, John Knapp had spent twenty-two to twenty-three hours a day in his cell. He could read some books from a library, and he could sometimes watch television or listen to a radio with earphones. For exercise, he would step up and down off his toilet seat.

For about three hours a week he was allowed outdoors into an exercise yard, a cage enclosed by two layers of steel mesh, with a weight machine or a basketball hoop inside. Though Knapp had weighed only 170 pounds when he entered the prison, he gained 18 pounds in the first two years, and he probably weighed more than 200 pounds by early 1981.

When Knapp first entered the prison, condemned inmates were housed in Cell Blocks 1 and 4 of the Florence Complex's Central Unit. Central Unit was surrounded by a 16.5-foot wall — 8 feet thick — topped with barbed wire, razor wire, or razor ribbon. Five guard towers were spaced around the perimeter, and another stood in the center of the yard. Passage in or out of the unit was gained through a double-gated archway in the wall, with one steel-barred gate locking before the other opened. Similarly, entry into each reinforced concrete cell block also required passage through double, mechanically interlocking steel doors, designed so that one could not be opened until the other was closed.

Inside each cell block, the condemned row was housed on the bottom of three tiers of cells. Each cell — 9 feet long by 5.5 to 6.5 feet wide — accommodated one person. All plumbing fixtures were consolidated in a single, metal, T-shaped device, with a seatless toilet curling up from its base and a sink and a water fountain at the top. Each cell had solid walls except for steel bars across the front, with a sliding steel-barred door. There were no windows in the cell, although some daylight filtered in from windows across the corridor in front of the cells.

Although color schemes were in constant transition, when Knapp got to the prison most of the exteriors were what the guards referred to as "baby-shit yellow" with "poo-poo brown" trim, while most interiors, including bars, were pale green.

Inmates wore jeans, denim jackets, blue chambray work shirts or white T-shirts, and boots with a distinctive "V" notched into the sole for easy tracking. In the early 1980s inmates were, for a brief period, allowed to wear civilian clothes if they had them, and to grow long hair and beards without medical or religious justifications. Knapp did grow a long, flowing beard, which made him look deceptively intellectual.

Though routines varied, he was usually fed in his cell, with meal trays being slid through a trapdoor in the cell door. For one hour a day he was allowed into a narrow indoor dayroom a few feet in front of the cells, where he could pace, place collect phone calls, take a shower, and, sometimes, if another inmate had been allowed into the dayroom at the same time, play cards.

In April 1980 he was transferred into the newly opened Cell Block 6, a state-of-the-art maximum-security unit that was designed especially for condemned prisoners and inmates in administrative segregation — prisoners who either presented a special threat or whose lives were especially threatened.

There were few steel bars in Cell Block 6. They had been replaced by solid steel, perforated steel, reinforced cinderblock, and wire-reinforced windows. Living units, or "pods," consisted of two tiers of eight-cell runs. These cells had a narrow, horizontal window near the ceiling at the back of the cell, but otherwise the inmate was almost completely walled off to himself, since the front of the cell was almost entirely faced with solid steel.

Most of the time, Knapp was in total isolation from other inmates — which suited him fine. A month after transferring to Cell Block 6 one inmate managed to attack him, punching him in the face and slamming his head against a steel door, splitting Knapp's lip and bruising his head and throat. About two years later one of the few inmates Knapp did socialize with, Wilmar Holsinger, was murdered by inmate Robert Vickers, who threw a homemade fire bomb — fueled by five bottles of Vitalis hair tonic — into Holsinger's cell. Knapp got along fairly well with the guards, perhaps because he shared their fear of the other inmates.

Knapp regularly attended religious services at Florence and became a progressively more religious Christian, although unaffiliated with any particular denomination. Chapel in Cell Block 6 was often held in the visiting room during nonvisiting hours. The chaplain would sit in one of the plastic molded chairs provided for the general public, separated by wire-reinforced windows and cinderblock walls from the prisoners. Each inmate would listen in on a phone from inside his own, individual, steel-mesh cage, as he sat on a gray metal stool that was anchored to the floor so that it couldn't be thrown through the window or used as a club.

In prison Knapp continued to complain of "severe headaches," "persistent headaches," or "migraines," according to prison records, although the headaches do not appear to have ever been as severe as those he complained of during the last six months of 1973. (His brother Robert recalls that Knapp had had a terrible headache in Houston in 1974, during the period between his trials. "He was totally beside himself with pain," according to Robert, who said he took him to the hospital.)

Every January inmates received an evaluation of their conduct for the previous year. Knapp's was always the same: "o major and o minor disciplinary problems." In 1994, when a prison counselor called up Knapp's record on a computer at the author's request, the counselor appeared astonished at how few notations there were.

The lawyer handling the federal class action that was keeping Knapp and about thirty other Arizona death-row inmates alive was deputy public defender John Foreman, thirty-two. As head of the appeals bureau, Foreman had become the state's de facto death-penalty coordinator. He tried to make sure that every death-row inmate had an attorney.

Since Foreman believed there was a reasonable doubt about Knapp's guilt, he wanted to find someone to represent him in case the federal stay was lifted. (The public defender's office had a conflict of interest preventing it from representing Knapp, because a prosecutor who had supervised Hyder at the time of Knapp's trials had since switched over to the public defender's office.) Foreman began looking around.

One person Foreman could not turn to was Chuck Diettrich.

Although Diettrich had started practicing again in 1979, he was still struggling. The bar disciplinary committee had allowed him to practice on condition that he follow a prescribed rehabilitation regimen, but Diettrich was failing to adhere to it. The bar was considering suspending him.

And Diettrich had another problem.

"It was a social thing," he recounted in 1993. "But I didn't really let it interfere with my practice. I would take off for a couple days, or a day, or three days, or however long, and get it out of my system and then go back to work.

"And I wasn't real secretive about doing cocaine because I thought it was my business as long as I didn't interfere with somebody else. So I became an easy target."

In October 1980 a client who had never paid Diettrich called him to say he finally had the money. Diettrich, who was taking his son to see a boxing match on closed-circuit television that night, stopped to meet the client at a restaurant on his way.

"I didn't even turn the car off," Diettrich recounted. "I ran into the restaurant. There's [my client] sitting there with a guy who looks like a cop who he introduces as his brother. I said, 'Well, do you got the money?' And he says, 'I don't have [all] the money, but I got an eight-ball of cocaine. Would you take that?' I said, 'Jesus Christ. All right, fine.' He says, 'Well it's out in the car.' So we go out into the parking lot, right in front of where my car is pointing. My son sees the whole thing. The guy who looks like a cop — I should have seen the setup coming, here I'm a criminal lawyer — hands me a plastic deal with some cocaine in it. And just then about six camper doors in the parking lot open up, and about fifteen cops come piling out, shove my face down on the hood of the car — guys I'd known — put a gun to my head, the whole deal, 'Don't make a move or we'll blow your fucking head off.' And they take me to jail."

Diettrich made bail, but a few weeks later the police came to his girlfriend's townhouse in Mesa and arrested him again. A different client had gone before the grand jury and testified — accurately, Diettrich concedes — that Diettrich had given him about half a gram of cocaine several weeks earlier while Diettrich was trying to arrange the man's release from the Gila County jail.

Now there were two felony cocaine possession charges against Diettrich, plus one felony count of promoting prison contraband. He pleaded guilty to all three counts and, on April 16, 1981, he was sentenced to 30 days in jail, four years probation, a $3,000 fine, and 250 hours of community service.

With the sentencing came automatic disbarment.

"That was the worst period — after the disbarment in 1981," Diettrich recalled in 1993. "That's when I would disappear for days at a time. I was always extremely active, productive. Anything I was involved in I was involved in to the hilt. All of a sudden I went from being an active, busy trial lawyer to not only [having] nothing to do, but being down on myself. I was really just kind of existing. I really didn't care if I woke up the next morning or not. As far as I was concerned, life was over."

Twelve

In early 1981, deputy public defender John Foreman and his wife went to a backyard barbecue for parents and administrators of a preschool where Foreman's wife worked. It was being hosted by James Scarboro, a commercial litigator at a small, well-regarded civil firm in Phoenix then known as Martori, Meyer, Hendricks & Victor. Foreman started chatting with Scarboro, a short, unprepossessing black-haired man with glasses, who was standing with a tall, thin, craggy-faced partner of his, Larry Hammond.

As they chatted, Foreman started telling them about representing people on death row. It was a conversation Foreman had had before with many civil lawyers.

— Well, — Scarboro said toward the end of the conversation, — if you ever need somebody to help out on one of those cases, give me a call. —

Foreman thought Scarboro was blowing smoke. In Foreman's experience, civil practitioners did not usually like to sully themselves with criminal work, which they viewed as unclean and economically unhealthy.

— Well, we need somebody right now, — Foreman said. — There's a guy who says he's innocent. I think there's a reasonable doubt. And he's gonna die unless somebody helps him right away. His name is John Henry Knapp. —

Scarboro had clerked for Justice Byron White of the U.S. Supreme Court when the Court struck down most existing death-penalty statutes in its 1972 ruling in *Furman v. Georgia*. Like Justice White himself, whose views had essentially prevailed in that ruling, Scarboro did not believe that the death penalty was unconstitutional in all circumstances, but he did think that its application — because it fell so disproportionately on the poor and minorities — frequently was.

Although he did only civil work at Martori, Meyer, Scarboro had a strong interest in criminal law. He had taught it for five years before joining the firm and had co-authored a criminal procedure text. He wanted to take the Knapp case.

His partner Larry Hammond, on the other hand, was ambivalent. — I'm not sure it really makes sense for us to be taking this case, — Hammond told Scarboro, after the barbecue. — We don't have any death-penalty expertise. We really don't know what we're getting into here in terms of lawyer hours. And I can't do anything on it for months. —

Hammond was then immersed in a complicated civil case that was coming to trial soon, in which he was representing a group of homeowners whose community, Hound Dog Acres, had been destroyed by floods.

In fact, it was a bad time to be proposing any new project. The firm's younger lawyers were so overworked that the partnership had recently declared a moratorium on any new work. The firm had even turned away a lucrative litigation opportunity arising from the collapse of the ceiling at a sports arena in town. How could they now ask the firm to make an exception to take on a case of uncertain dimension representing a convicted child-murderer for free?

But Scarboro was insistent.

— This is something personally I just have to do, — he said.

Hammond agreed to accompany Scarboro to meet Knapp. They could decide what to do then.

After being sent to several different gates and windows, a prison van drove them around behind the Central Unit to Cell Block 6, where neither of the lawyers had ever been before. Under a guard tower, they passed through the double-gated entrance into the compound and then through the double steel doors into the cell block.

The lawyers were led to an antiseptic visiting room, which Hammond remembers today as having been very freshly painted in an institutional green.

Knapp, thirty-four, now probably weighed 200 to 210 pounds and was growing bald on the top of his head. Hammond was surprised to discover that Knapp was white. He had always just assumed that he was black.

Hammond remembers a sense of eerie anticlimax.

"I don't know if I expected more drama," he recalled in 1993, "but I kind of felt like he was a bystander. Almost like he was just there for the show."

At some point Knapp told them that he was innocent, but he did so in a matter-of-fact way. There was no pounding of tables or sense of outrage.

Scarboro explained to Knapp the steps that lay ahead.

"I remember John nodding or stating assent to everything Jim said," Hammond recalled. "I remember feeling like it was good that Jim was [explaining things to John] because a lawyer should, but that it didn't matter. John was going to say yes to whatever it was."

In the spring of 1981 Scarboro called a meeting of the eight partners to consider making an exception to the firm's moratorium so that he and Hammond could take Knapp's case.

The meeting was held in a conference room at the firm's brand-new offices. In a mildly venturesome move, the firm had relocated several miles north of downtown, where all the courts were, to a small four-story smoked-glass building recently constructed by a client.

At the meeting Hammond was surprised by Scarboro's candor, given how much Scarboro wanted to take the case.

— I have no idea how long the case will last, — Scarboro told his partners. — I don't know yet what work will have to be done. I was involved in one capital case while teaching, but the truth is, I'm not an expert in this area. And this is a highly specialized and rapidly developing field.

— But I see it as an obligation of citizenship, — he continued. — As a lawyer who lives in a state and a country that administers the death penalty, I feel this is something I need to go through and understand firsthand. —

— Do you really think he's innocent? — one partner asked.

— I don't know, — Scarboro responded. — I'm not God. I met Knapp. He looked me in the eye and said he didn't do it. John Foreman said he thought there was a reasonable doubt. —

— Could we give him a lie detector test? — a partner asked.

— We could, — Scarboro responded. — We could also give your corporate clients lie detector tests. But we don't. —

In April Scarboro told deputy public defender Foreman that he and Hammond would take the case on a pro bono basis — i.e., free, out of civic obligation.

"Within a very short period of time," Foreman remembered in 1993, "I started hearing phrases like 'miscarriage of justice' and 'outrageous' creep into Scarboro's conversation. And so I knew he was hooked."

Working with the time allotted by the federal stay, Knapp's new lawyers began to prepare a federal habeas corpus petition. In such an action, a defendant can challenge in the federal court system the various federal constitutional rulings that the state courts inevitably had to make in the process of convicting him. The Martori, Meyer lawyers would raise a slew of issues, but Hardy's Catch-22 ruling would be the centerpiece.

Mark Wallace, twenty-seven, was beginning his second year as the firm's tax specialist. A slender, blond young man with a receding hairline, Wallace was amiable, something of an intellectual, and a conservative or libertarian politically. He was very much in favor of the death penalty.

A philosophy major at Princeton, Wallace considered himself a utilitarian; he believed that an action was good if it produced the greatest happiness for the greatest number. He was, therefore, intrigued by the role of criminal defense lawyers, whose job might require them to unleash dangerous criminals on society. He believed the justification for the vocation lay in the distinction philosophers drew between "act" utilitarianism and "rule" utilitarianism. While the isolated "act" of defending a dangerous criminal might not produce the greatest happiness for the greatest number, that act could still be moral if it furthered a "rule" that, in the long run, *did* produce the greatest happiness for the greatest number.

Wallace volunteered to work on the Knapp case. Since he did meticulous work and wrote beautifully, Scarboro and Hammond agreed to have him comb through the vast record and write the first draft of Knapp's federal habeas corpus petition.

But as Wallace did so, his philosophy experiment collapsed. Knapp was innocent, Wallace came to believe. "Rule" and "act" utilitarianism were merging. Defending an accused murderer might not only further Justice in the abstract, but it might further justice in this very case.

Ironically, his first suspicions were kindled when he read the Arizona supreme court ruling upholding Knapp's conviction. When Justice Jack Hays recounted the police questioning of John and Linda Knapp three days after the fire, Hays wrote: "Although their statements were not inconsistent with each other, nor with the statements they had made the day of the fire, they were inconsistent with the way the police and [state fire expert] David Dale believed the evidence showed that the fire was ignited."

"That was the first thing that made me start to wonder," Wallace later recalled. "Why is it that the experts' testimony is at variance with the eyewitnesses? Could it be that these, quote, experts are completely out to lunch?"

Eventually Wallace reached Diettrich and invited him to lunch at a darkly lit Italian restaurant in Phoenix.

Diettrich looked haggard, as if he were recovering from a terrible disease. But in arguing Knapp's case, he was still passionate.

— If Linda knew John had done it, — Diettrich told Wallace, — she would have nailed him. —

Wallace came to agree.

"How many mothers," Wallace asked the author years later, "are going to protect somebody who kills their kids? Not many. Then you read the transcripts and you realize, she really hated John. I agree with Diettrich. She would have nailed him."

During 1982, with Knapp still under the protection of the federal stay, Wallace twice visited the county records annex on the far south edge of Phoenix to look at the trial exhibits from Knapp's case. Strangely, when he returned for a third time in December 1982, the clerk told him that the exhibits could not be found.

They were missing.

In early 1982 the federal appellate court in San Francisco upheld what the Arizona supreme court had done to salvage Arizona's death-penalty law, and in November the U.S. Supreme Court denied review.

The Supreme Court then lifted the federal stay that had kept Arizona's death-row inmates alive for four and a half years.

By then Wallace and another associate, Parker Folse III, were putting the finishing touches on Knapp's federal habeas corpus petition. Although the 176-page petition raised numerous challenges to both Judge Hardy's rulings and to the constitutionality of Arizona's death-penalty statute, its most persuasive portion may not have been a legal argument at all, but rather its 44-page statement of facts.

"After all is said and done," Wallace wrote in the brief's conclusion, "how likely is it that a man would awaken one morning and set his children afire for the purpose of keeping his marriage together? . . . Or, on the other hand, how likely is it that children would set their bedroom on fire in an effort to stay warm in a house without heat? These are the competing theories of the case."

Wallace's work won one convert before it was ever filed. Larry Hammond read it in a cabin he and his wife had recently bought near the Tonto National Forest northeast of Payson. He was recuperating there from the fiasco that had become of his Hound Dog Acres case — the case on behalf of the homeowners whose community had been flooded. The jury trial had dragged on for six months — at the time, an Arizona record — and then Hammond had lost.

Despite Hammond's disconsolate mood, Wallace's petition stirred him.

"I became convinced that Knapp was innocent at about the time I read this paper," Hammond later said.

In January 1983, the Arizona supreme court began scheduling executions for all the inmates who had been protected by the federal stay. They were set to proceed at a rate of one per week for the first six months of 1983. Knapp's would be on Wednesday, April 6, 1983.

By the time Knapp's execution warrant was issued, Scarboro realized that serious procedural obstacles lay in the path of Knapp's federal habeas petition. A federal court could not consider an issue unless the state courts had already had a chance to rule on it. But when Diettrich had frantically filed Knapp's appellate brief in 1975, he had not included many of the issues Scarboro and Wallace now wanted to raise. Even the critical Catch-22 issue had been phrased very poorly, imperiling the ability of a federal court to consider the whole problem.

Since there was no legal bar to doing so at the time, Scarboro filed Wallace's petition in state court in February 1983, rather than in federal court. It became Knapp's second state post-conviction relief (Rule 32) petition. If it was denied, he would then file the same petition in federal court. That way, the federal court might be able to hear all the issues they wanted it to hear.

Today, stricter procedural rules enacted in 1992 would probably forbid the filing of this sort of petition.

The Arizona supreme court stayed Knapp's execution to allow time to consider the second petition.

Scarboro, Hammond, and Wallace allowed themselves some optimism. Scarboro and Hammond were eminent civil practitioners, and they were used to having judges take their filings seriously.

"I felt very strongly," Scarboro said later, "that John was ultimately going to get a new trial because of the trial judge's denial of money to do the full-scale experiments. I thought, 'My God, whatever else you can do to the guy, you can't make the case turn on whether the fire was set with an accelerant and then not give him the money to prove [that that's not true]. I don't care how conservative the justices on the Supreme Court may be. I think every one of them will think that that is wrong.'"

Since Judge Hardy had been appointed to the federal bench in 1980, the case was reassigned at random to superior court judge Marilyn Riddel.

By this time, prosecutor Hyder was also no longer involved in the case. His term as the elected Maricopa County Attorney had ended in 1980, and after a short period in private practice, he had become a federal prosecutor in Phoenix.

A far less emotional advocate, assistant attorney general Crane McClennen, was now opposing Knapp's petition.

McClennen, thirty-six, had spent most of his career with the attorney general's office, and most of that period in the appellate arena. He had been involved in one way or another with almost every Arizona death-penalty case. Few people were more justifiably skeptical of any death-row inmate's appeal than McClennen, who had, for years, heard scores of defense lawyers cry wolf on behalf of vicious criminals.

McClennen had longish, graying hair, glasses, and an academic air. He spoke in a halting, deliberate way, and his demeanor was low-key and understated. He strove to maintain an emotional distance from his work.

"[Emotional response] is something that I try to suppress," he related in 1993. "In a death-penalty case . . . somebody has already died and, quite possibly, somebody else will die. An attorney in one of these cases should be driven by the seriousness of the case, because if they're driven by the emotions that they feel — either toward the defendant or to the victims — that may tend to cloud the attorney's judgment."

Scarboro and Hammond's optimism was delusional. Superior court judge Riddel denied the petition without a hearing in a three-page order in June 1983. She found that she was procedurally barred from considering almost every issue in it. If it had been raised before, she was bound by the earlier rulings. If it had not been raised before, it had been waived.

Wallace was embittered.

"It just struck me as [the work of] a judge who wanted to get this case off her docket as quickly as possible," he said. (Riddel, when reached in 1994, had no recollection of ever having been involved in the Knapp case.)

They appealed Judge Riddel's ruling.

Since the Martori, Meyer lawyers had taken over the case, they had had few dealings with Dick Todd, the private investigator Diettrich had brought into the Knapp case, and whose investigations had formed the basis for the first post-conviction relief petition, which had been denied in 1979.

But Todd had continued his independent, completely self-funded investigations on Knapp's behalf. In mid-1982, after learning from Knapp of Todd's continued involvement, Mark Wallace arranged to meet him for lunch.

Though Wallace regarded Todd as "unconventional" and possibly even "a little flakey," he respected the fact that Todd had put in so much uncompensated work on the case.

Todd, who was still firmly ensconced in the Linda-did-it camp, wanted the firm to reimburse his expenses to take an investigative trip to Utah, where Linda now lived.

Although Wallace personally believed that the fire was most likely an accident, set by the children, he thought Todd's was a reasonable request. Wallace wasn't going to turn down an offer of help.

At about the same time, Jill Abramson, then a reporter with the *American Lawyer* magazine in New York, was talking to death-penalty specialists around the country. The magazine's editor, Steven Brill, wanted to take an in-depth look at a capital case in which there was some genuine question about guilt. In September, Abramson recommended that Brill select Knapp's case, and she got a copy of the transcript from Wallace.

Larry Hammond, meanwhile, had been shaken by seeing their masterful petition tossed out by Riddel's perfunctory order in June.

He was seized with panic and guilt.

The firm had not been handling Knapp's case the way it would a paying client's case, he thought. It had waited two years to file its first document, and that document had been drafted by a tax lawyer.

"Mark [Wallace] had read the transcripts with care and with love," Hammond recounted in 1993, "but without background and knowledge. We really didn't know what other kinds of issues we [might be] waiving because we weren't asserting them. We hadn't been systematic about approaching the review of this case."

Hammond still could not devote time to the case — he was about to go to trial in another civil matter — but he wanted Colin Campbell to join the defense team.

Campbell, thirty-one, had returned to Martori, Meyer in January after a two-year stint as an assistant federal public defender in Phoenix. He had far more practical experience with habeas corpus and criminal defense than anyone else at the firm.

Campbell was about six feet tall on the rare occasions when he stood up straight. He had a perpetually rumpled appearance and a dry sense of humor. He was clean-shaven, had short black hair, and wore black-rimmed glasses. As an observant Catholic he opposed the death penalty — just as he opposed abortion and euthanasia — but he was not vocal or passionate on the subject.

Campbell had two four-drawer metal file cabinets dollied into his office and filled them with the Knapp file. Storing these unsightly metal cabinets in his office set Campbell apart from his partners, who usually stored their files in handsome stained-wood credenzas or completely out of view in the firm's communal file room on the third floor.

Predictably, as Campbell systematically plodded through the record, he saw things that had never occurred to Wallace, a corporate tax lawyer.

Because of his recent habeas corpus experience, Campbell was alert to the procedural traps that bedevil any prisoner who tries to make use of the writ. The procedures governing federal habeas actions were tightening during the 1980s, as the U.S. Supreme Court tried to choke off the endless stream of largely frivolous petitions generated by prisoners.

Campbell was not surprised to discover that Diettrich had not adequately preserved many issues for federal habeas corpus review during Knapp's trial and appeal almost a decade earlier. As Campbell recognized, it's the rare lawyer that knows both state law criminal procedure and federal habeas corpus law.

More embarrassing, however, was that Campbell's own colleagues, Scarboro and Wallace, also had not fully "mopped up" these issues when they filed Knapp's second post-conviction petition just six months earlier. Campbell now saw still more issues he wanted to raise that had not ever been properly presented to a state court.

When Judge Hardy made his Catch-22 rulings, for instance, Diettrich had objected using the language of state evidentiary law. But he had not used the federal constitutional terminology that Campbell needed to use.

Diettrich's failure to pose the question in precisely the words Campbell now wanted to use was, at most, an exceedingly technical failing. Yet it could be literally fatal to John Knapp.

Campbell and Scarboro began to contemplate a *third* post-conviction relief petition in state court. Today, under 1992 amendments to the state law, they probably could not file one. But in 1983 there was no explicit ban on it.

Campbell tried to bring to the case the cold, skeptical perspective that he thought befit the seasoned criminal defense lawyer.

"But the problem with the Knapp case," he admitted in 1993, "is that it's the type of case that's hard to remain cynical on."

As Campbell began to believe that Knapp was really innocent, his frustration mounted. The whole goal of the conservative justices on the U.S. Supreme Court, he thought, was to devise mechanisms to sieve out the hundreds of hypertechnical habeas petitions so that courts could devote time to cases of actual possible innocence, like the Knapp case.

Yet Campbell could not push Knapp's case through the sieve!

In early October 1983, investigator Todd came to Martori, Meyer after his trip to Utah. Triumphantly, he handed Mark Wallace a sworn, transcribed statement.

The statement was that of Linda Knapp's second husband, Samuel Jensen (a pseudonym), from whom she was now also divorced. In it Jensen said that Linda had, in fact, confessed to him that she had set the fatal fire in the East Capri house. He said she had poured Coleman fuel around the room the night before, after Knapp fell asleep, and had thrown a match in the next morning.

As Wallace read the statement for the first time, he felt a moment of exhilaration.

But Campbell read the statement moments later with a different eye.

"I think that affidavit was one of the things that started me thinking, 'We don't need to use Dick Todd anymore,' " he later recalled.

Jensen's statement was virtually worthless, Campbell thought. Todd had spoken to Jensen on at least four earlier occasions — going back to 1978 — and this was the first time Jensen had claimed Linda had confessed to him. Jensen acknowledged in the statement that there was a custody battle for his and Linda's seven-year-old child going on, and he obviously hoped his statement would ensure that the child was taken away from Linda. And Jensen was a convicted felon who was currently in jail on a forgery charge.

"This is going to get so chewed up on the [witness] stand," Campbell remembers thinking, "there's going to be nothing left."

Campbell had already had qualms about collaborating with Todd because of his controversial reputation. Now he decided that he really wanted to hire a different investigator.

Nevertheless, he would still submit the affidavit Todd had obtained. Knapp's execution was just sixty days off. While improbable, it was possible Jensen was telling the truth. He was, after all, the third of Linda's friends to claim that she had, in some fashion or another, admitted responsibility for the fire.

In addition, the statement Todd had obtained contained one terribly important piece of information that *did* interest Campbell. In his affidavit Jensen claimed that his decision to finally report Linda's confession had been prompted by a recent incident that made him fear for the safety of his seven-year-old son.

The incident he described, if true, would be easy to verify and document. And it was very odd.

Jensen said that in January 1983 his and Linda's then six-year-old son had suffered burns when a fire broke out in the boy's bedroom at Linda's home after the boy had gone to bed.

In mid-October the state supreme court, with one justice dissenting, refused review of Judge Riddel's ruling denying Knapp's second post-conviction relief petition in the standard opaque language: "ORDERED: Petition for Review = DENIED."

Eight days later the five justices signed the fifth warrant for Knapp's execution, calling for it to occur on Wednesday, December 7, 1983.

Thirteen

During John Knapp's first trial in 1974, Linda Knapp had been "drinking pretty heavy," according to her stepfather, Ken Ramsey.

"She got to where she was partying a lot," Louise Ramsey recounted, "but I've known a lot of people who's gone through similar situations that partied a whole bunch just to see if they could forget. To me, it's a normal reaction."

"I drank quite a bit," Linda acknowledged in 1993, "with my mother, stepdad, Melba [Burr], nameless guys."

At some point during the period of the 1974 trials, Linda's stepfather, Ken Ramsey, also raped her, Linda claimed in later testimony. Ramsey denies the accusation.

In any event, the Ramseys left Arizona during the second trial to go to St. Louis, where Ken had found a job. Linda stayed with Melba Burr during much of the remainder of the second trial, and then moved in with John's mother, Mary Knapp, after the conviction.

Two weeks after John was sentenced to death, Linda wrote a letter to one of her inmate pen pals.

> Hi Sweething
> I got your letter the outher day. . . .
> Well babe I am moving again. . . .

I am still going to come to see you. . . .

John got the gas chamber. I may be cold harted but I can't help but think he got what he diserved.

Well babe I am going to have to make this short. . . . Remember I LOVE YOU.

Love You Always
Peanuts

In February 1975, Linda Knapp took a bus back to Ogden, Utah, where she had grown up. Ogden was then a town of about 67,000 at the foot of the Rockies about 30 miles north of Salt Lake City. Once the site of a major railroad connection, the town was now dominated by military installations and the aerospace industry.

In May she met Samuel Jensen,* a tall, thin, blond twenty-year-old who had recently left the navy and now worked at a warehouse at the Defense Depot, Ogden. Within two months she had divorced Knapp — it is simple to divorce a man who has been sentenced to death — and married Jensen.

Jensen had grown up nearby in a large, clean, well-kept house in North Ogden. Jensen's mother, Patricia, loved children, had raised eight of her own — four boys and four girls — and worked for the Children's Aid Society, an adoption agency in town.

Despite her devotion to children, however, Patricia's own boys were not growing into model citizens. They showed signs of alcoholism, a malady that ran in the Jensen family. Sam had already been arrested for shoplifting and public drunkenness.

Patricia's first impression of Linda was negative.

"She looked like a slob," she remembered in 1993, "and I thought, where did [Samuel] find someone like that. But the day that they was married, it was really interesting, because Linda could clean herself up and could be pretty. She did have some talents also. She made her own wedding dress. It was very plain, but it was a talent I was rather impressed with."

Sam and Linda moved into a small house in North Ogden near Patricia's. Patricia soon noticed that Linda did absolutely no housework. Patricia sometimes did the laundry herself so that her son would have clean clothes to wear to work.

---

* The names of all members of the Jensen family have been changed.

Sam did no housework either. Sam, who was drinking more and more, lost his job at the warehouse and then found and lost several others.

One day Patricia found out how Linda's earlier marriage had ended. Linda showed her an article in *True Detective* that had been published in 1975 about the Knapp case. (A very similar piece was also published as the cover story for the October 1975 issue of *Detective World*, entitled "He Laughed While His Babies Burned.") The article was a strange amalgam of truth and fiction, but it was illustrated with actual photographs used at the trial. An arrow superimposed on one of the photos pointed out the location of Iona's charred, exploded skull in the rubble.

"[Linda] points and says, 'This is Iona,'" Patricia recalled. "She did it with such a coldness. There was never a dint of remorse. Never a tear. There was nothing."

Then Patricia saw the photos of the filth and disarray of the Knapp house.

"It was so frightening," she said, "because I could see the same thing was going on with Samuel — with the house, the conditions, it was almost like I was seeing the exact same [house], except that there was no baby."

Linda gave birth to a baby boy in September 1976. Sam and Linda named him Daniel, after a child of Patricia's who had died at age eleven of an aneurysm. Patricia took a special interest in the boy, baby-sitting for him often.

When Linda brought Daniel over, he would not have been changed in many hours, and he suffered from horrendous diaper rashes. When Patricia went to Linda and Samuel's apartment, Patricia recounted, she saw "spoiled food in cans with spoons in them, dishes stacked all over, filthy clothes, animal feces." Patricia began to take Daniel for longer and longer periods, fearful of leaving him with Linda, and Linda seemed happy to let Patricia take him off her hands.

One evening in August 1977, when baby Daniel was at Patricia's and Linda was waiting tables at a Chinese restaurant, Samuel Jensen was arrested at his and Linda's home in Ogden. He had just sexually molested two little girls from the neighborhood, ages seven and four. He eventually pleaded guilty and was sentenced to one to fifteen years in prison.

Upon arresting Jensen, the police searched the apartment. Detective John Panter was staggered by the filth and stench. Filthy clothes, overflowing ashtrays, cigarette butts, dirty dishes, dried and rotten food, and empty beer cans were strewn about on the floor and furniture of every room. Used sanitary napkins lay on the floor of the kitchen and the bathroom. Stacks of laundry and dirty dishes appeared to have been untended for many days.

Panter filed a child-neglect complaint against Linda and Samuel, and let Patricia care for Daniel until the courts could sort things out. But on the day before a scheduled court hearing, Patricia got a call at work from one of her daughters, who said Linda was taking Daniel from the house. Patricia rushed home and found Linda walking away from the house, pushing Daniel in a stroller.

— You can't take him! — Patricia shouted. — The police said he had to stay here. —

Linda was furious, but Patricia refused to part with Daniel. Later Patricia notified detective Panter of what had happened, and Panter had Daniel placed in shelter care until the hearing.

After the hearing, the judge ordered the Division of Family Services of Utah's Department of Social Services to monitor Daniel's welfare, but allowed Linda to resume custody. He also ordered Linda not to take Daniel out of Weber County, Utah, without the prior permission of Family Services.

About a week later Linda took Daniel and fled to Warner Robins, Georgia, where the Ramseys now lived.

On September 8, the Ogden judge initiated contempt proceedings against Linda for fleeing the jurisdiction. These proceedings were never pursued, however, and since Linda and Daniel were gone, the custody proceedings were also suspended.

In 1993 Linda's memories of these events were greatly at odds with all the arrest reports, court records, and Division of Family Services records.

"[Patricia] instigated taking Daniel away from me in 1977," Linda said. (According to the documents, detective Panter initiated the petition, and Patricia was not present at the hearing.) According to Linda, the judge "gave me back my son. I remember the judge telling [the county officials] they had five days to file another action. I waited five days, got on an airplane, and went to Georgia."

She denies ever having been told not to leave Utah — just as she denies that Sergeant Malone ever told her not to leave Arizona in November 1973.

After six days of searching for Linda, the Utah caseworker found out from a neighbor where she was and contacted Georgia authorities to look after Daniel.

"A girl showed up at the door a couple times [from Georgia's child-welfare agency]," Linda recalled in 1993. "I never hid where I was at. Utah got ahold of the authorities. It was a routine thing. She only came twice."

Linda lived with the Ramseys for about ten months in Georgia without incident.

She returned to Ogden in the summer of 1978. When the Division of Family Services found out, it sent a new caseworker to visit her. Linda made a good impression on her. Linda said she had been having problems before, but was doing better now. She was enrolled in a federal job training program, learning cabinetmaking. Daniel, now twenty-three months old, appeared healthy to the worker. Though she did have some psychological problems, Linda conceded to the worker, she said they stemmed from her difficulty in coping with the tragic deaths of her first two children.

The caseworker recommended discontinuing supervision.

Once back in Ogden, Linda called Patricia.

"She said we could come down and see [Daniel], as long as I minded my own business," Patricia recounted. Patricia began to care for him again, often taking him for weekends or longer.

On one of those occasions, Daniel was crying when Patricia picked him up to take him for the weekend.

"He just reeked," Patricia said. "I got him home and I took the diaper off. He was peeling all through his privates and his bottom [from] urine burn. There were just these big hunks of skin just peeling off him."

After her return, Linda divorced Jensen and, in July 1979, married Richard Hall,* thirty-one, whom she met while waiting on his table at the China Temple Cafe in Ogden. He was a tall, red-haired man who had a good job with the Southern Pacific Railroad.

Patricia liked Hall, since he treated Daniel well. But the condition of the house didn't improve, according to Patricia. "It was always just filthy."

In June 1980 Linda gave birth to a blue-eyed, blond-haired daughter, Lisa.

"She looked just like Iona," Linda said in 1993.

For almost two years thereafter Linda and Dick lived together without attracting the attention of the Ogden police or the Weber County child-welfare authorities.

By 1982, however, the marriage was failing.

"[Dick] liked to cheat," Linda said. In addition, Hall had developed severe

---

* The names of all members of the Hall family have been changed.

problems with alcohol and, later, cocaine. He lost his job with the railroad and, eventually, according to Linda, "he almost died from liver failure and drugs."

In April 1982 an anonymous caller filed a child-neglect complaint against the Halls. Detective Panter once again investigated.

When he arrived, Linda and Richard had just moved out. The landlords told the detective that they planned to sue the Halls, who had left the apartment in astounding filth, with dried food lying about the kitchen and stacks of feces-laden diapers thrown behind the door in the bathroom.

The Halls had separated, Panter learned. Linda, who was pregnant with a third child, had custody of both children and had gone to live with the Ramseys, who were now living nearby in South Weber, Utah.

Jade Hall, Linda's third child since the fire, was born in September. Jade was pretty, blue-eyed, and blond.

The following month, Jade's father, Dick Hall, filed a child-neglect complaint against Linda, who had, by that time, moved into her own apartment in Ogden. Dick had visited Linda's apartment and had found five children there — including one-month-old Jade — all under the care of a twelve-year-old baby-sitter. After a neighbor agreed to watch the children, however, the responding officer saw no need for further action.

Daniel, six, was now old enough to go to school. But the school and child-welfare authorities were discovering that Daniel's behavior was an anthology of severe childhood behavioral problems. He could not control his bowels or bladder, and he played with his feces. His attendance was erratic, and when he did come to school he would steal, destroy other children's toys, and engage in other dramatically antisocial behavior. When the teachers discovered that Patricia — who worked at the Children's Aid Society — was the grandmother, they would call her to let her know what was happening.

"He would come to school just reeking [of urine]," Patricia said. "I was told that they kept a set of clothes there to change him into so that he didn't smell so bad."

On one occasion Patricia remembered that when Linda dropped Daniel off for baby-sitting, his head was shaved. When Patricia asked why, she remembers Linda responding, " '[He] had some lice so I poured kerosene on his head and then I cut his hair.' And I went, 'My God, you did what?' She smokes all the time!"

At about 9:00 P.M. on January 12, 1983, Linda's estranged third husband, Dick Hall, brought Linda's son Daniel to the emergency room of the hospital in Ogden. The six-year-old had first-degree (minor) burns on his chest, left foot, and both hands.

Hall explained to the doctor and nurse on duty that he hadn't been present when the fire started — he no longer lived with his wife Linda or Daniel — but Linda had asked him to bring the boy in.

When Daniel told the nurse that he did not know how the fire started, the nurse called the police.

A uniformed police officer, Roger Van Cleave, arrived at the hospital a few minutes later and spoke to Daniel privately.

— I was asleep, — the boy told him, — and someone came into my room and set my blanket on fire. —

— Who? —

— I don't know who. —

Dick Hall told the officer that Daniel had told him the same story in the car.

Since Daniel's injuries were minor, he was released later that evening, and Officer Van Cleave drove him back to Linda's apartment. The officer was surprised that Linda, when he got there, did not appear more upset.

The officer examined the damage in Daniel's bedroom and found three partially burned matches on the floor.

At the time of the fire, he learned, Linda and Daniel's uncle had been watching television, while drinking beer and smoking marijuana. Each would periodically get up and go to the kitchen. On one of these trips Daniel's uncle discovered the fire and put it out by throwing a dishpan full of water on it.

Linda told Van Cleave that Daniel must have set it.

"I had a box of Ohio Blue Tip matches [on the refrigerator]," Linda said in 1993. "He crawled up on a chair, got the matches from the top of the refrigerator, and then [took them] into his bedroom," she theorized.

The officer made no arrests. His colleague, detective Panter, however, who knew of Linda's previous fires in Pomona and East Mesa, was suspicious.

In February 1983, after a relative twice found Daniel wandering alone in the commercial section of Ogden, Daniel's father, Sam Jensen, who had been released from prison, filed a child-neglect complaint against Linda.

Following up on that complaint, a caseworker visited Linda. When he arrived, Linda's home was clean, the children were bathed, and the kitchen well stocked. Overall, the caseworker was quite satisfied.

There was just one oddity. When he asked about the January fire, Linda said she could not figure out how Daniel could have gotten hold of matches. Yet, even as he was conducting the interview, the worker noticed that there were matches readily accessible to a child on a table in plain view.

Five months later, in July, an employee at a bowling-alley nursery called the police when she noticed suspicious marks on Lisa, three, and Daniel, six, who had been left there. The caseworker who investigated the complaint, Kimberlee Brady, found a long scratch mark across Lisa's back, a welt on Daniel's lower back, and serious bruising on his buttocks. Jade, who was then just ten months old, also had a bruise on her arm. The police officer, caseworker, and bowling alley attendant all also noticed that Lisa seemed to have surprisingly little speech facility for a three-year-old.

But Linda, while acknowledging spanking the children with a spatula, attributed the children's wounds to accidents that had occurred while playing with other children.

In 1993 Linda recounted that her use of corporal punishment had been very moderate.

"[Ken Ramsey] used a belt on our backsides," she said, "[so I] made a vow that nobody would ever use a belt on any of my kids. I used to have a little paddle [instead]. You couldn't hit very hard [with it, because it] would break."

Since caseworker Brady noticed that Linda was neglecting housework again, she reinstituted regular home visits.

Linda moved frequently during this period — about once every three months.

And "her utilities was always being shut off," according to Patricia. "They'd use a different name to get it put back on. Bills would come to Linda Holiday, to Linda Knapp, to Linda Jensen, to Linda Ramsey, to L. K. Ramsey. I said to her one time, 'How come you use all these different names?' 'Well, to get the utilities turned on.' "

In late September 1983, there was another fire at Linda's latest apartment. A mattress lying outside in the yard had caught fire, and the fire department put it out. Firefighters couldn't determine how it started.

In still another fire-related incident that month, Daniel singed his hair while playing with matches by the side of the house.

At the end of September Dick Todd made his trip to Ogden, with the Martori, Meyer law firm picking up his expenses. He interviewed detective Panter, several child-welfare people and, as he usually did on these trips, Sam Jensen. This time he found Jensen in jail, serving a ninety-day sentence for forgery. Because of the January and September fires, Jensen was quite concerned about Daniel's safety. That was why, he told Todd, he was finally willing to tell the truth about Linda's confession to him.

Caseworker Brady was now paying Linda regular visits. When she came on October 24, the apartment was cluttered and deserted. Apparently Linda had moved again — at least her fourth move that year.

Two days later a former roommate of Linda's called Brady to lodge a child-neglect complaint against Linda. She claimed that Linda was now living in a place with no heat, gas, or water, and that the children were filthy. She claimed that Linda would lock the children in their rooms and leave Jade in her crib for many hours on end. She told the caseworker of having once found Daniel in his closet, melting a toy with matches, and having also seen him playing with matches behind a neighbor's house.

On November 1, after a neighbor also called in a second complaint about Linda's new apartment, Brady visited. She found all the children unbathed and some of the rooms cluttered and filthy. But Brady believed Linda was mainly having trouble because she couldn't get the authorities to turn the water on. Brady took steps to help her do so.

On November 2, Steven Brill, the journalist from New York, visited Linda in the course of doing his article about the Knapp case. By this time Brill had reviewed the transcripts from the 1974 trial and had spoken to investigator Todd. Brill reviewed the police reports and child-neglect complaints documenting Linda's history since Knapp's conviction and spoke to some people Todd had suggested.

Detective Panter told Brill that he suspected that Linda might have set the January 1983 fire, though he couldn't prove it. A psychologist who had seen Linda admitted to Brill that he entertained the same thoughts. The psychologist, Clifford Hilton, had evaluated Daniel while on a contract with the Division of Family Services and often spoke to Linda at length when she brought Daniel in for visits. (Since Hilton considered the agency his client, and Daniel his patient, he did not consider his conversations with Linda privileged.) Hilton told Brill that he wondered if Linda might have some sort of split personality and might be setting fires — not to kill her children, but to attract attention, help, or sympathy.

Both Hilton and Panter also told Brill that they considered Linda to be quite bright and exceedingly adept at keeping governmental authorities at bay.

It was now just two weeks before the tenth anniversary of the fatal fire in East Mesa, and Brill found Linda and her children living in squalor almost identical to that he had read about at the East Capri house. Brill, whose first daughter was approaching her first birthday, was then immersed in the world of diapers and its unpleasantries. But the stench of Linda's home and of her babies, who were wrapped in soiled towels that had obviously not been changed in many hours, shocked and sickened him. Linda struck Brill as "spooky," and he was becoming convinced that Linda's pathology had to have had something to do with Iona and Linda Louise's deaths.

It was an opinion shared by almost everyone who had ever witnessed Linda in one of her inert phases — possibly even her own mother.

— Oh my God! What have you done to those children now? — Louise Ramsey had allegedly said, according to two neighbors, on arriving at the scene of the fatal fire on November 16, 1973.

Brill's conversation with Linda in November 1983 only reinforced his suspicions. When he asked her about the January 1983 fire, Brill had the same strange experience the caseworker had had the previous month.

Linda told him she did not know how Daniel had gotten hold of matches, since she did not allow him access to them.

Yet on a low table in plain view Brill saw numerous matchbooks within reach of any child.

And as Brill continued asking follow-up questions about that fire, Linda became upset. She stood up from the couch and went to the front door to call for Daniel — though Daniel had actually been in the room all along, and she simply hadn't seen him because of the garbage and debris.

Then she sat him down in a chair and said, — Tell this man how your bedroom caught on fire. —

Daniel, who had chatted with Brill earlier and had not seemed shy at the time, now said nothing.

— Tell this man how the fire started, — she demanded, her voice rising. — Tell him! —

Daniel remained silent.

— Tell him how you were playing with matches and caught your bed on fire! — Linda screamed.

— No one could have set the fire, — Daniel finally said, — because, whoever did it would have come through the front room. And my mommy was in the front room at the time. So nobody could have come in without my mommy stopping him. —

Brill, who had by then been a journalist for ten years, later wrote in an affidavit: "I have never left an interview more shaken."

Daniel seemed terrified of his mother. Brill was convinced that Linda had set the January 1983 fire — and, probably, the November 1973 fire. He returned to New York to write his article.

While Colin Campbell was rapidly coming to believe that Knapp was innocent, he had not yet decided which theory of innocence was more likely: the accidental-fire-started-by-the-children theory, which Wallace favored, or the Linda-did-it theory, which investigator Todd favored. The new information filtering back from Ogden was swaying Campbell toward the Linda-did-it camp.

But with Knapp's execution just thirty-four days off, Campbell had no time to figure out which competing theory was right. He had to keep the possibly innocent man alive.

On November 8, with twenty-nine days left, he asked the U.S. Supreme Court for a stay, to give itself time to consider Knapp's second post-conviction relief petition — the one Judge Riddel had denied in June.

Meanwhile he and Scarboro continued working on Knapp's *third* state post-conviction relief petition, to which they hoped to append Brill's article.

In addition, he was also preparing a federal habeas corpus petition.

Caseworker Brady visited Linda's home again on November 9. Everything was vastly improved: the water was on, the house was clean, the children were bathed and unbruised. Brady considered ending her supervision of Linda.

But the next day she got a call from Clifford Hilton, the psychologist seeing Daniel. Hilton thought the impending anniversary of the fatal fire — now six days away — was having a strange effect on Linda.

Linda made numerous phone calls to Hilton from November 12 to November 14. She seemed to be getting more and more anxious. Hilton had also begun getting anonymous calls on his private phone line at his office, in which someone would breathe deeply into the receiver. The private line was unlisted, had just recently been installed, and he believed that Linda was the only one who had that number.

At about eight in the evening on November 14 — two days before the anniversary of the fire — Linda called Hilton again. Lisa — then a month younger than Little Linda had been when she died — had poured "lamp oil" or kerosene on her bed, she told Hilton. Linda wanted the children taken away from her for their own protection.

So did Hilton. The next morning, November 15, Linda placed the children with the department's family support center for a couple days, so that they would not be near her on the anniversary of the fatal fire.

Although these events are reflected in Family Aervices records, and in subsequent accounts given by Family Services personnel in interviews and testimony, Linda denies any recollection of them.

When caseworker Brady brought Daniel, Lisa, and Jade to the child support center on the afternoon of November 15, 1983, she noticed some redness under Lisa's left eye, which later matured into the beginnings of a black eye. Later that day an employee at the center also noticed a scratch that ran all the way across Lisa's buttocks. Lisa, whose language facility was limited, told her, "Mom did."

On November 17, Linda told Brady she was not ready to resume caring for the children, and she agreed to have them sent to a foster home for fourteen days.

Meanwhile Brady notified the Ogden police of another instance of possible child abuse. A police officer came to see Lisa that day, took Polaroids of her wounds, and tried to ask Lisa what had happened, but "Mom did" was all Lisa could say.

Linda later told the officer that there was no bruise on Lisa when she gave her to family services and the scratch had been caused by playmates.

Although Steven Brill insisted on adhering to his general policy of not releasing advance copies of his magazine to anyone before it was sent to subscribers — even though the execution was imminent — he advanced the publication schedule and mailed the December issue of *American Lawyer* out on November 14, two weeks early. That same day he faxed page proofs of the article to Martori, Meyer's offices.

The 10,000-word, front-page article, entitled "Innocent Man on Death Row," reviewed the history of the case, discussed the lingering doubts that had always haunted the defense lawyers and then raised the new doubts suggested by Linda's eerie history since the fatal fire. Despite the provocative title, the article did not come out and declare that Knapp was innocent — though Brill obviously believed he was — but argued that there was far too much doubt at this stage to go through with an execution.

Campbell filed Knapp's third post-conviction relief petition on November 17 in state court, attaching Brill's article, and making it the centerpiece of the petition. At the same time he sought a stay from the Arizona supreme court to allow time for that petition to be considered.

Four days later he filed Knapp's federal habeas corpus petition as well and sought a stay from the federal district court.

At that point there were three stay requests outstanding — one to the U.S. Supreme Court, one to the state supreme court, and one to the federal district court.

On November 22 Linda found out about Brill's article, which was eventually reprinted in full as a front-page story in Phoenix's *New Times*, a weekly newspaper. Reporters began trying to reach Linda for comment.

Extremely upset, Linda called caseworker Brady and demanded that her children be returned to her. After checking with the county attorney, who told Brady that the county did not yet have enough evidence to keep Linda's children away from her involuntarily, Brady returned them to her on November 23.

In early December, however, a local television reporter went to Linda's home seeking an interview. On December 12, Linda called Brady to ask that the children be taken away from her again. She said they were too disruptive, she could not cope with them, and the TV reporter was bothering her as well. Brady arranged to have the children placed in a foster home for ten days.

The foster mother reported new concerns to Brady. Daniel had told her that Linda would lock him and Lisa in their bedrooms on weekends. A public health nurse who examined Lisa thought her behavioral development, including her language skills, were stunted, and noticed a vaginal discharge due to uncleanliness.

Brady went back to the county attorney and talked about bringing a hearing to take all three children away from Linda. By now four of Linda's former roommates were willing to testify against her, alleging such neglectful acts as locking the children in their rooms for hours or feeding them soft drinks and crackers as a meal. The county attorney agreed that there was enough evidence to proceed.

On Monday, November 28, the U.S. Supreme Court denied Knapp a stay of execution.

That same morning Campbell, Scarboro, and Parker Folse III — the young associate at the firm — went to federal district court to argue for a stay.

Assistant attorney general Crane McClennen urged the federal judge, Earl Carroll, that he should wait until the state supreme court ruled on the stay application before it, which was scheduled to be heard three days later, on December 1. In fact, McClennen essentially admitted that the state supreme court *ought* to grant a stay and that he planned to oppose it only in a pro forma manner since, otherwise, his office would look bad.

"Naturally, our office is loath to go into court and say, 'Definitely, grant a stay,'" McClennen said. "If the Arizona supreme court grants the stay — which is what ought to happen — then we can get the state litigation finished up."

Judge Carroll agreed to wait.

But at the stay hearing on Thursday, December 1, at least two of the state supreme court justices obviously had no intention of granting a stay no matter how pro forma McClennen's opposition to it was.

"Just stop right there," one justice said, interrupting Scarboro's summary of Knapp's new evidence. "Isn't that exactly the same claim you had, which we reviewed [in an earlier petition] —"

"No, it is not, Your Honor. The claim —"

"The same claim that it was the mother that did it," the justice said, cutting Scarboro off again. "That John didn't do it. He didn't participate or have anything to do with it," he continued, in a mocking voice.

"Your Honor, you did not review any claim involving the evidence that we're now bringing before the superior court below and pursuant to which we ask for a stay —"

"In the original trial, that was the whole thing — we went through it — was that John didn't do it. Who did it? It was the mother. . . . All these things sound familiar. I haven't taken the time to read each of these applications,* but how long do we have to put up with this?"

Later that afternoon the state's highest court announced its ruling. With one justice absent, the court split two to two. A tie counts as a denial.

"It's like being gut-shot," Campbell remembered. "You think you have a very strong case. It's a riveting type of evidence. Then they vote two to two: 'No, we're not even going to hear your evidence.'"

On Friday, December 2, with the execution five days off, federal judge Carroll was obviously irritated. An irascible conservative Democrat who had himself been issuing stern warnings about how he did not plan to tolerate any further delays in the Knapp case, Carroll was now being forced to enter the stay *for* the state courts. It was as if the state court justices were playing chicken with him.

"What do you suggest [I do]?" Judge Carroll asked assistant attorney general McClennen.

---

* On that same day, the court was also hearing another emergency stay application being brought by a second death-row inmate, Jimmie Wayne Jeffers.

"I think this court is probably in a position where it has no choice, other than to grant a stay of execution," McClennen candidly admitted.

"It is obvious to me," Judge Carroll said, "if Mr. Knapp is to be heard on the factual issues presented in his state [post-conviction relief petition] . . . it must be as a result of a stay in *federal* court. I know of no reincarnation for those who are wrongfully [executed], if it is subsequently determined that that is the fact."

Judge Carroll issued the stay.

Campbell called Knapp at Florence with the news.

— Whew, — Campbell remembers Knapp saying.

Fourteen

Since Judge Riddel had finished her criminal rotation, Knapp's third post-conviction relief petition was assigned to superior court judge Cheryl Hendrix. Judge Hendrix, who had been appointed in 1982, was new to the bench, unfailingly courteous to lawyers, and inexperienced in criminal matters both as a lawyer and as a judge.

Hendrix read the voluminous transcripts of both Knapp trials during a vacation immediately after being assigned the case, she said in an interview a decade later. She was troubled by the change in evidentiary rulings between the first and second trial and its apparent impact on the verdict. But she also felt powerless to do anything about that, since the state supreme court had already affirmed.

In February 1984, as the hearing before Judge Hendrix approached in Phoenix, Judge Robert Newey of the First District Juvenile Court in Ogden granted the Division of Family Services protective supervision of Linda's children and ordered that Linda take certain parenting courses. Still, he permitted the children to continue living at home with Linda.

Utah, like many states, has an understandable preference for protecting the family unit against governmental interference. Typically the state must try numerous less drastic measures before seeking permanent adoption.

In preparation for the hearing before Judge Hendrix, Campbell retained a child psychologist to examine Linda's son, Daniel — who was going to be called as a witness at the hearing — and to examine Linda's history and advise him on what he thought might be going on. The reaction of the psychologist, Phillip Esplin, surprised Campbell, who had been leaning toward the Linda-did-it hypothesis.

Esplin told him that persistent fire setting was a common "red flag," or warning signal, of possible child neglect or abuse. Personally, Esplin's intuition after reviewing the record was that Linda probably had not set any of the fires herself. Instead, he thought the cause of all the fires might be Linda's penchant for placing her children in dangerous situations, which Esplin told Campbell might arise from a "destructive motive" at a "possibly unconscious level."

The Ogden fires, the fatal fire, and the Pomona fire were, therefore, all of a piece with Linda's leaving the children in a bathtub unsupervised, letting them walk barefoot near rusty nails, and leaving diet pills, turpentine, Valium, knives, lighters, and matches where the children could reach them.

Linda had repeatedly set up situations, he told Campbell, that put the children at high risk for injury or death. The phenomenon was all the more dramatic, in Esplin's view, because the behavior had continued after Linda lost her first two children. In his experience, people who lost children often became overprotective of the surviving children — often to the point of being phobic. Linda was a vivid exception.

"So I came over time," Campbell later recalled, "to look back at the incidents in Utah differently." They were actually consistent with both of the original theories of Knapp's innocence — the Linda-did-it theory or the accidental-fire-set-by-the-children theory.

In April 1984, Judge Hendrix heard evidence concerning Linda's subsequent fires and history of child endangerment.

Linda Knapp, represented by appointed counsel, invoked her Fifth Amendment privilege against self-incrimination and refused to testify about any of the new fires or the November 1983 incident in which her three-year-old daughter Lisa had allegedly poured "lamp oil" on her bed.

The most important witness was, therefore, Daniel Jensen himself, a terribly frightened seven-year-old boy with blond hair and thick glasses. Judge Hendrix, who had spent a previous rotation handling domestic relations cases, had some toys handy in her chambers. She gave the boy an E.T. doll to play with, to help settle him down while he was waiting.

She heard the testimony in chambers, rather than the courtroom, to put Daniel more at ease.

The judge began by questioning Daniel herself.

"Let's put E.T. over on the desk for a little bit," Judge Hendrix told Daniel. "E.T. wants you to talk real loud."

In response to the judge's questions Daniel said that he set the January 1983 fire, in which he had been injured, by getting a match from the bathroom, lighting it, and throwing it on the bed.

Scarboro then asked him questions. Daniel now testified, inconsistently, both that he had set the fire and that the fire woke him up from his sleep.

Next, assistant attorney general McClennen asked the questions. Apparently attempting to reconcile his two accounts, Daniel said that he threw a match on his bed, fell asleep for about an hour, and then woke up with his bed on fire.

Judge Hendrix then called the boy aside with the court reporter.

"Your mommy will never know what you said inside this room," Hendrix told him. "As long as you tell the truth, you won't get punished. But, if you tell a lie, I would have to make you go to jail, okay?"

Hendrix then secured an alarming admission from the boy followed by a second response whose ambiguity she did not seem to appreciate.

"Have you told us the truth here today," Judge Hendrix asked, "that you were playing with matches, or have you just told us that because your Momma told you to tell us that?"

After a pause, Daniel responded, "My mom told me to tell you what I just said."

"Is that what really happened?"

"Yes."

Judge Hendrix — and, indeed, Scarboro and Campbell at the time — assumed that Daniel was saying, "Yes, I really set the fire." Of course, he may have been saying, "Yes, my mom really told me to tell you what I just said."

On May 21, 1984, Judge Hendrix threw out Knapp's third petition. The evidence "clearly and unequivocally established," she wrote, "Daniel Jensen was playing with matches which caused his blanket to ignite." There was, therefore, no evidence that Linda had engaged in subsequent criminal acts similar to those John had been convicted of. She also rejected all the other defense claims.

In October the state supreme court, with one justice dissenting, refused review in the usual way: "ORDERED: Petition for Review = DENIED."

Less than two months after Judge Hendrix found that Linda's subsequent fires and history of child neglect had no bearing on Knapp's case, Linda had her next fire. It was at least her third fire since the fatal one and her ninth fire-related incident over the years.

In this one, she told her new caseworker, Daniel had set fire to the curtains and the carpet in the front room using a lighter. Daniel must have gotten the lighter from a friend, Linda told caseworker Mary Martinez, since she didn't allow him access to lighters or matches. But Martinez could see through the front window to a low table that was littered with matchbooks and lighters, readily accessible to a child.

Martinez's visit had been prompted after a neighbor called the police after seeing the girls, four and one and a half, wandering barefoot, filthy, and alone along an Ogden street. Since the girls couldn't say who they were or where they lived, the police kept them until Linda called two and a half hours later, looking for them.

Linda's was "the dirtiest home I had ever seen," Martinez wrote in her report. Since the burned carpet had been ripped out, bare nails and carpet tacks were sticking up from the floor. Lisa and Jade were inside barefoot. Dirty clothes and food were strewn about the floor, and the apartment smelled. Linda blamed the mess on the landlord.

Linda said that a nineteen-year-old man who was present, John Seward (a pseudonym), was her baby-sitter. She was letting him baby-sit, she explained, in exchange for her giving him a roof over his head.

Martinez told Linda she would have to clean up her apartment and free it of hazards like bare nails and matchbooks.

"I received a call from Linda that social services was 'snooping around,'" Patricia recalled, "and she was going to bring Daniel out."

When she dropped Daniel off, Patricia discovered that Daniel had a cigarette burn on the inside of his arm. Daniel told Patricia he had walked into Linda's cigarette. Patricia called caseworker Martinez to tell her about the incident.

"I begged for anonymity and confidentiality," Patricia said, because she was afraid Linda might take the children and leave the state again — in which case she might never see Daniel. Patricia also told Martinez that she was becoming concerned about the potential for sexual abuse of Linda's girls, because Linda seemed to use transients as baby-sitters.

In mid-July Linda asked Patricia to take Daniel for the summer, which she did. Patricia also sometimes took the girls on weekends. Once when Linda dropped them off, Patricia noticed lice running on their faces, she later recalled.

"They were just horribly infested," she said.

Patricia also saw that Daniel and the girls had strange eating habits. The girls wolfed down their food, as if famished, and Daniel would "steal food from the fridge or the cupboards, and hide it in his room."

Martinez visited Linda five more times in July, but saw no improvement. Linda blamed the ongoing mess on the baby-sitters and the landlord.

After Martinez expressed concern about the male baby-sitters, Linda said she would fire Seward. A few days later, she told Martinez that she was marrying Seward. After Martinez told her that Seward would have to become part of Linda's "treatment program," Linda told her that Seward was moving out.

Martinez made four more home visits in August, finding minimal or no improvement.

In September 1984, Martinez requested a new court action against Linda, writing, "Linda operates on her own terms. She has excuses for all of her actions, she blames others for her home conditions, and she has manipulated the system very well."

Lisa, now four, still could not make herself understood through speech. Linda insisted to Martinez, however, that Lisa spoke fine when she was at home alone with her family.

Psychiatric caseworker Robyn Hansen, who had been counseling Linda and her family for about nine months, wrote to Martinez: "Individual, family, and group therapy have been . . . quite unsuccessful. . . . My main concern . . . is [Linda's] anger and resentment towards any authority. . . . There was an occasion when Lisa was brought in with head lice and Linda was quite offended when I refused to see her."

In October 1984, after Linda ignored another warning, Judge Newey of the juvenile court placed Lisa and Jade in a foster home pending a trial to determine whether to sever Linda's parental rights permanently.

By April 1985, after living with Patricia Jensen for almost nine months, Daniel was showing tremendous improvement. He had become active in a scouting group and at his church, and his school attendance was almost perfect. His pastor wrote to Martinez to tell her of "a dramatic overall change in the way Daniel relates to people."

But with Lisa's placement into a foster home, the gravity of her problems was just coming to light. Lisa was nearing her fifth birthday but still could not say a full sentence. She was also masturbating with her toys, triggering concerns about possible sex abuse. She was violent toward her sister Jade and once scratched Jade's eye seriously enough to require an eye-patch.

In July Linda's counselor wrote Martinez that Linda was denying that she had ever been a neglectful mother.

Linda moved three times between July and December, and her homes fell into squalor again.

Lisa and Jade were transferred to a second foster family in August 1985. These parents thought Lisa was retarded until testing revealed no innate deficiencies.

In 1986 the new foster mother wrote to juvenile court judge Newey, describing the behavior of Lisa, five, and Jade, three: "Both of them have severe eating disorders. . . . [They] have been frequently caught eating out of the garbage. Jade carries this a step further, by eating paper, [illegible], elastic bands — anything within her reach. . . . Both girls will eat until they vomit. . . .

"Both Lisa and Jade . . . seem unable to play with toys in any aspect except destruction. They will rip arms and legs off dolls and tear toys and books apart, but they seem unable to have any constructive playtime."

The foster mother estimated that the younger child, Jade, was "about one year behind in physical and verbal and motor coordination skills."

But she was more worried about Lisa.

Lisa was "excessively violent with the other children in the family, especially [Jade]. . . . [Lisa] roams through the house at night. . . . Although we have placed [gates] and special doors everywhere in the house to prevent this, she has succeeded in going outside on one occasion. Often in the middle of the night she will sneak in and brutally attack one of the [other] children in their sleep [frequently requiring medical treatment].

"She often defecates in her bedroom, painting the walls and furniture with fecal matter. . . . [She] has deliberately flooded the bathroom and basement several times, ruining an entire bathroom and several carpets. She pounds on windows until they break."

Finally, Lisa was displaying one other symptom of her upbringing. Maybe *hallmark* is a better word.

"She has been caught lighting matches."

In March 1986, juvenile court judge Newey ordered Linda to submit to two psychological examinations.

Linda aced them both. In September 1986 Linda, who had moved again, admitted to psychologist Paul Furlong that she had been a "horrible housekeeper" in the past, but now she was better. Furlong gave Linda a battery of intelligence tests and found that she scored in the "bright-normal" range.

Linda gave Furlong a new explanation of Lisa's language problems. She told him that Lisa had stopped talking abruptly when her father, Richard Hall, moved out when she was two, and that the problem became worse when Lisa was taken away from Linda by the court when she was four. Furlong, who had not examined Lisa, agreed with Linda that Lisa's emotional problems probably stemmed from these two "separation traumas."

In his report Furlong described Linda, who was unemployed, as a "homemaker." She told Furlong that her main problem was that she had "tied into men who have been physically, emotionally, and sexually abusive of her children." In addition, she had gone through "a heavy grieving reaction" due to the loss of her children in 1973. But Linda's new fiancé, Seward, was more loving than Linda's previous husbands, so she — and Furlong — believed that Linda's prospects were bright.

Furlong recommended that Lisa and Jade be returned to Linda.

In March 1987 a second psychologist, Robert Eyestone, was also very favorably impressed with Linda. She was "cooperative, friendly . . . and kept her appointments," he noted in his report. Her responses on a standardized personality test were, Eyestone wrote, "typical of a person who values the traditional American values of being dependable, independent, self-sufficient, and responsible."

But the two psychologists' reports were hard to square with the grim report of a third psychologist, William Bauman, who had examined Linda's children.

Daniel, ten, gave "the impression of someone with deeply suppressed emotional pain, confusion and anger," Bauman wrote. "[He] manifested extreme discomfort when talking about his mother. . . . He has made positive strides . . . [but is] still an extremely confused, deeply hurt, and strongly psychologically damaged young person."

The youngest child, Jade, now four, was doing the best of the three. Bauman believed, however, that she had been "deeply hurt by erratic parental patterns in the past" and was "afraid, due to not knowing whether she will be reintroduced to the previously threatening and overwhelming situation."

Lisa, six, was "perhaps the most damaged of the three children," Bauman wrote. "She has felt totally abandoned, rejected, ignored and unloved. . . . Her testing responses are quite similar to children who have been physically and/or sexually abused at earlier ages. . . . Her references to her mother . . . indicated no actual emotional bond. . . . It is the impression of this examiner that [her] deficits are primarily caused by the extreme emotional deprivation of her earlier childhood."

Bauman believed that Linda was the primary source of the children's problems. "A very similar pattern of deprivation, emotional abandonment, poor physical care and non-consistent parental behavior has been present in the lives of all three of these children. Any attempt on the part of their mother to deny her strong role in providing such negligent and disharmonious parenting . . . should be strongly questioned. . . . Rarely would testing results of three siblings so consistently show such similar deprivation and similar damaging effects without the underlying cause being the same for all three."

Because of the perplexing disparity between Bauman's views and those of the psychologists who had examined Linda, Judge Newey asked Bauman to examine Linda himself. Bauman did so in April and May 1987.

Bauman wrote: "It was apparent that Linda had a strong self-control and an ability to project herself in whatever manner she felt appropriate. . . .

"Linda is a complex personality. She lives on two separate and mostly unrelated planes. . . . She lives one life consciously and another life unconsciously.

"Linda has learned to . . . relate to reality with a fair degree of effectiveness. . . . However, she appears able to maintain appropriate and realistic behavior societally for only limited periods of time.

"Her more deeply buried, unconscious life is one of deep hurt, confusion and emotional pain. . . . She can deal with her external life for periods . . . but invariably that deeper pain expresses itself in ways which are rebellious, strong, numbing and antisocial. . . .

"She cannot explain to herself the fact or reason of her nonfunctional behavior, for to do so would open up the strong inner world of emotional pain/conflict of which she is so afraid. Thus, her style psychologically is to deny the fact . . . of any non-functional behavior on her part. . . .

"This type of personality . . . puts considerable energy [into] 'talking' a positive picture, even actually believing that positive picture. . . .

"Despite her genuine desire [to be a caring parent] . . . she in all probability is not able at the present time to be that . . . parent."

When the parental rights case finally came to trial, in September 1987, Linda switched strategy. She voluntarily surrendered her parental rights but asked that all three children be placed with either the Ramseys or with the family of her sister, Kathy Morrissey (a pseudonym), who lived in the southeastern United States.

The Division of Family Services opposed allowing the children to be placed with the Ramseys, citing, among other problems, Linda's previous use of the

Ramseys as a conduit for recovering Iona Marie and Linda Louise from the California authorities in 1972.

Mary Martinez also warned the court that Louise Ramsey appeared to have a boundless capacity to deny Linda's deficiencies as a parent.

"She has never seen her daughter in the wrong," Martinez wrote.

A family services caseworker in California, who interviewed the Ramseys as possible foster parents, was equally nonplussed upon meeting Louise. Louise told the worker that the only reason Linda's children were taken from her was that caseworker Mary Martinez and Patricia had plotted against Linda.

"This would be a total denial by Mrs. Ramsey," the caseworker wrote in her notes, "as to perhaps what the reality of the situation was."

The judge placed Daniel with Patricia Jensen and her husband, granting them permanent custody in late 1987.

He placed Jade with her then-foster parents, and Lisa with Linda's half-sister Kathy.

In November 1990 the child-welfare authorities of the state where Lisa now lived reported back to the Utah Family Services Division that Lisa, ten, was making good progress, although she still showed "a two-year delay behaviorally, emotionally, academically, and in her speech/language skills." They attributed her ongoing handicaps to earlier "emotional and physical abuse."

When I spoke with her in 1993, Linda denied that she lost custody of her children because of any neglect on her part. She said that Utah won the legal battle to take them away from her "because I voluntarily put them in a foster home where news media could not get a hold of my children."

She also denied that she had really lost them.

"I know where two of them [Daniel and Lisa] are at. There's agencies where, when [Jade]'s eighteen, I can go through to find out where she's at."

She denied that any of her children were injured by her neglect.

"They're alive, healthy, and doing well," she said.

Linda denied ever having neglected or failed to supervise any of her children by any marriage. She also denied ever having seriously neglected housekeeping.

"Look at my apartment right now," she told the author in 1993, speaking in her reasonably clean apartment. "It wasn't much worse than it is right now."

She also denied that she had ever raised any of her children in an unhealthy environment.

"Children are very resilient," she said.

Fifteen

In September 1984, when Jim Scarboro moved to Colorado, Larry Hammond took his place as an active member of Knapp's defense team.

At this stage the battle was expanding, with simultaneous skirmishing in both state and federal courts. Once again a federal stay — Judge Carroll's — was keeping Knapp alive.

While Judge Carroll began working his way through the twenty-four complex claims raised by Knapp's federal habeas petition, Campbell and Hammond filed a *fourth* post-conviction relief petition in the state court in December 1984. Today, such a filing would almost certainly be procedurally barred.

The fourth petition was yet another "mop-up" petition, this time addressing the wording of Judge Hendrix's ruling rejecting their third petition. Since Judge Hendrix had found that Knapp's original lawyer, Chuck Diettrich, had "waived" many of the issues Campbell wanted to raise, by not including them in Knapp's direct appeal back in 1975, Campbell now alleged that Diettrich had provided "ineffective assistance of counsel" at the appellate stage by not including those issues.

In a five-page response, deputy attorney general McClennen argued that, basically, anything Campbell wanted to say at this point had been waived by not having been said earlier.

McClennen was on strong ground. The array of procedural rules that ensure that litigation eventually stops — so-called principles of "finality" — was inexorably funneling Knapp toward the gas chamber.

Hammond was sickened by the spectacle. He likened McClennen's incessant invocation of these procedural bars to the inane logic of children who exclude other children from an activity by chanting, "Tick-tock, the game is locked."

Because the Sixth Amendment to the U.S. Constitution guarantees criminal defendants the right to counsel, courts have inferred that they also have a right to *competent* counsel, or *effective assistance* of counsel. If the right to counsel could be met simply by assigning indigents pathetically inadequate defense lawyers, then the right would be a sham. Accordingly, a defendant whose lawyer provides arguably substandard representation can claim to have been deprived of his Sixth Amendment right and may be entitled to a new trial with competent counsel.

For defense lawyers, occasionally being accused of "ineffective assistance of counsel" simply goes with the territory, especially for those who handle capital cases. A death-row inmate who has exhausted his appeals has almost no alternative except to raise ineffective assistance claims against his original lawyer.

Still, lawyers are human, and being accused of poor professional performance is never pleasant. Accusing Diettrich of having provided "ineffective assistance of counsel" was going to be unbearably cruel. Diettrich was already consumed by guilt from having lost the Knapp case. He had been haunted by it. Ruined by it.

But Campbell and Hammond had no choice. Some of the issues Diettrich had "waived" — including half of the Catch-22 issue — were too critical to Knapp's federal petition.

After disbarment, Diettrich had spent a period living off disability insurance. But by early 1985 he was doing pretty well. He had served out his terms of jail and probation, had not had a drink in eighteen months, had remarried, had a new, fourteen-month-old daughter, and was working as a paralegal in a Phoenix law office. He was applying for readmission to the bar.

Diettrich had always been extremely cooperative with the Martori, Meyer lawyers. He was deeply grateful that serendipity had placed the case in such capable and devoted hands. He remained cooperative as he learned from Hammond of the planned ineffective assistance claim. Diettrich had always struck Hammond as a hard-boiled, "hot-rocks" kind of guy who thrived on pressure, and he seemed to be taking this hurdle in stride.

But one night, as the hearing approached, Diettrich's facade disintegrated. When Hammond met with him in a Martori, Meyer conference room, he seemed nervous.

"At one point in the conversation he was scratching his chin," Hammond later remembered. "He kept doing it and doing it, and first thing you know his chin started to bleed."

Diettrich wiped the blood off with his hand, but it kept bleeding, and it began to drip onto his shirt.

— Look, let's go take care of that, — Hammond suggested.

— No, no, — Diettrich said, brushing Hammond off.

But the wound kept bleeding, and Diettrich kept scratching it and wiping at it. "The blood was all over," Hammond recalled. "The guy was just bleeding like a pig. It was really just a very unnerving experience.

"Almost every encounter I've had with Chuck since then has been a very emotional one," Hammond said. "I've seen him cry at least half a dozen times. I mean bawl like a baby."

Diettrich's testimony at the fourth post-conviction hearing, in March 1985, was candid. "I had lost the perspective that I needed for the purpose of the appeal," he admitted, "and I don't believe I had the expertise that this appeal required."

Hammond once again allowed himself to feel optimism about this petition. Knapp's direct appeal had been, after all, something of a farce. Diettrich's young, inexperienced ghostwriter, Cathy Hughes, had written up what she mistakenly thought would be a first draft, and it had turned out to be Knapp's appeal.

But ineffective assistance claims were common in the late stages of death-penalty proceedings. To block this well-trodden path, courts had heightened the standards for proving attorney incompetence, just as they had heightened procedural barriers to all other avenues of escape.

Judge Hendrix denied the petition in May 1985. She acknowledged that Diettrich's "failure to raise issues was due to counsel's delegation of brief writing to an attorney of limited experience and time, and lack of supervision after delegation."

Nevertheless, rather than decide whether that sort of slapdash approach to a capital appeal constituted ineffective assistance, Judge Hendrix concluded that Diettrich's conduct did not matter because, she speculated, the state supreme court justices would have stumbled across all the important issues on their own as they read through the Knapp transcripts.

"The fact [that] the issues were not specifically delineated in the brief does not mean they were not considered by the supreme court," she wrote.

Judge Hendrix's ruling amounted to a cruel joke. She was saying that for indigents sentenced to death, appellate lawyers were simply unnecessary. The supreme court justices could be relied on to browse through the 3,700-page trial record, spot problems on their own, and reverse a heinous murder conviction without being bidden. Since appellate counsel was superfluous, ineffective assistance of counsel was impossible.

In August the state supreme court, with one justice dissenting, issued its by now familiar shrug: "ORDERED: Petition for Review = DENIED."

Tick-tock. The game was locked.

Hammond began to develop a nearly paranoid vision of the superior court bench in Phoenix. Many of those judges were former members of the county attorney's office or of the attorney general's office. Joseph Howe, who had been one of prosecutor Hyder's supervisors at the time of the Knapp case, was now a superior court judge. Frank Galati, who had persuaded the Arizona supreme court to uphold Judge Hardy's Catch-22 rulings, was now a superior court commissioner — a lower-level judicial officer — who would soon be appointed to the superior court bench himself. Hammond began to imagine the judges making offhand, off-the-record remarks during social banter that might be having a devastating effect on Knapp's ability to find an open-minded arbiter.

And now that he turned his attention to Knapp's federal habeas petition, his apprehensions spread to the federal bench as well. Although Judge Earl Carroll had already saved Knapp's life once, Hammond thought he appeared hostile during court appearances thus far. Judge Carroll's chambers at the federal building were physically next door to those of Judge Charles Hardy, who had moved to the federal bench in 1980. To grant Knapp's habeas, Judge Carroll would have to fault the rulings of his colleague and office neighbor. In addition, three other federal judges in Phoenix had also risen from the state superior court bench, and two of them had ruled on minor matters in the Knapp case when Judge Hardy was unable to do so.

In an abundance of caution, he and Campbell moved to disqualify the entire federal bench in Arizona from hearing Knapp's federal habeas, because Judge Hardy was now one of their brethren.

To their astonishment, Judge Carroll granted the motion, and the case was reassigned to Judge Robert Belloni, a senior federal judge in Portland, Oregon.

Shortly thereafter, deputy attorney general McClennen began picking off, one by one, the more vulnerable claims Knapp had raised in the federal petition. Each time the U.S. Supreme Court or other appellate courts rejected one of the dwindling number of constitutional attacks left to be made on capital punishment, McClennen would move to dismiss that claim, and Judge Belloni would grant the motion.

Campbell and Hammond, in response, moved for summary judgment on their strongest claim — the one challenging Judge Hardy's Catch-22 ruling. At the same time, they submitted a version of Mark Wallace's beautifully written statement of facts — the one originally submitted as part of Knapp's second state petition in early 1983 — hoping to instill in Judge Belloni a genuine doubt about guilt. The Martori, Meyer lawyers had used and reused Wallace's statement of facts in so many contexts by this point that they jokingly referred to it as the sacred Ur-text of the Knapp case.

Judge Belloni scheduled an evidentiary hearing on the Catch-22 issue to be held in Portland on September 30, 1985.

For Campbell and Hammond, this was the main event. Every state petition they had filed — Knapp's second, third, and fourth — had been principally intended to ensure that the lawyers could raise the federal habeas corpus claims they wanted in the language they wanted. And the crux of the federal habeas was the attack on Judge Hardy's Catch-22 ruling.

They hired Marshall Smyth to go with them to Portland and testify once again about what he had done back in 1974. They recorded Smyth's now-antiquated Super-8 films onto videotape, so that they could play them more easily for Judge Belloni.

In addition, the lawyers asked Judge Belloni in 1985 to do what Judge Hardy had refused to do in 1974 — order that public funds be released so that Smyth could perform the full-scale burn tests that he was barred from performing in 1974. The court could then see for itself how they would have supported the defense case.

Although the lawyers had already outlined the case in numerous voluminous written submissions, Judge Belloni agreed with Hammond at the outset of the hearing in Portland that it would be a good idea to refresh his recollection of the facts. Hammond gave him an overview.

Then Campbell showed the films of Smyth's four mattress tests, while Smyth explained what was going on. But, out of context, Smyth's televised

Super-8 movies were not thrillers. Each showed a mattress burning, and in the first three tests, the mattresses burned without much drama. Judge Belloni became impatient.

"How long is this whole thing?" he asked. "You know, for a judge to sit here and watch a tree grow or a fire burn seems like pretty much — "

Hammond never forgot that line. He thought to himself, "If Knapp is executed, that should be his epitaph."

Seeing the judge's impatience, Hammond began to panic. He suggested that Campbell skip over the films and go straight to the argument. But Campbell thought the films were too important. "It's difficult to argue the motion and constitutional issue without having a good grasp of what's happening," he explained to both his partner and the judge.

Campbell suggested that the video technician fast-forward to the next important part of the film. But the fast-forward mechanism on the court's video player was broken! So Campbell had to show Smyth's films at normal speed.

For a long period Belloni asked no questions, and for some of that period he closed his eyes.

Campbell and Hammond believe he fell asleep. (Belloni declined to be interviewed. His court reporter said he doubted Belloni would have fallen asleep. McClennen said he recalled Belloni being bored, but not falling asleep.)

"I remember being deeply offended," Hammond recalled in 1993. "I know it was dry stuff, but to have this guy fall asleep on us was just a nightmare."

Just before the lunch break, Judge Belloni did ask a question.

"Well," he said, "if a test on a larger scale would prove the same thing as the test on the smaller scale, then why do the larger-scale one?"

Judge Belloni had evidently gone through the whole morning without the slightest understanding of what the Catch-22 claim was all about.

Since argument went late into the afternoon, Smyth and the lawyers missed their flight. While they waited for the next, they had drinks in a booth at an airport lounge and shared dreary and bitter thoughts.

The firm had now been working on the case for almost five years. During that period they had brought three state petitions and one federal habeas, and had lost almost every battle they had joined. The one victory — winning the right to have Judge Belloni hear their case instead of Judge Carroll — had obviously backfired.

Some of their partners were growing restless, too. This endless pro bono case was sapping two important partners' time and the firm's limited resources.

Now Campbell and Hammond were coming to grips with the fact that even their cherished federal habeas was a lost cause at the district court level. They would eventually have to win Knapp a new trial at the federal appeals court in San Francisco.

The other possible outcome was not discussed.

PART 3.

Flashover

Sixteen

As the dejected lawyers sipped their drinks in the Portland airport, Smyth said something startling.

— You know, I was thumbing through this collection of technical articles, — Smyth told them, — and I noticed a couple that were kind of in line with what I was finding back in 1974 with my tests in this case. —

— What do you mean? — one of the lawyers asked.

Smyth explained that the articles seemed to disprove a long-accepted belief among arson investigators. Investigators had thought that "spalling" (crumbling) of concrete proved that a flammable liquid had been poured on the concrete in the spot where the spalling had occurred; only flammable liquids, it was thought, could cause the intense burning necessary to cause such severe damage.

But when researchers actually ran empirical tests, Smyth explained, they found just the opposite. They had been *unable* to produce spalling by just igniting flammable liquids on concrete, because the liquid burned away too quickly to cause severe damage. They *had* been able to produce spalling by setting fire to ordinary furnishings (with or without the assistance of flammable liquids).

Although spalling had not been a factor in the Knapp case, Smyth found the studies intriguing, he explained, because he had had an analogous experience in 1974 when he tried to produce flammable liquid runs on a floor underneath a carpet and pad. He could not do it by just pouring flammable liquid on the carpet; but he *could* do it by building an intense fire using ordinary furnishings.

— Does that have any interest to you? — Smyth asked.

Both lawyers stirred from their malaise. What if there were other studies out there that now cast doubt on other supposed "hallmarks" of a flammable liquid fire, including the ones David Dale had relied on? Smyth might be talking about "newly discovered" evidence justifying a new trial.

— Find us out about that, Marshall — Campbell told him. — When you get back to Tucson, why don't you get into the books and research, and hit the phones, and find out everything you can. Don't worry about expenses on this one. Just do it. —

Holy shit, Hammond thought to himself.

Marshall Smyth had just sent him some government studies concerning the flammability of mattresses and other ordinary household furnishings.

He and his firm had been handling the Knapp case for five years, and he had never gotten hold of such reports. What sort of incompetents were they? he thought.

The reports Smyth sent, which had been published in 1977, 1980, 1983, and 1985 — all long after Knapp's conviction — had been performed by researchers at the National Bureau of Standards in Gaithersburg, Maryland (now, the National Institute of Standards and Technology). A research unit there, which became known in 1974 as the Center for Fire Research, had begun conducting experiments in the early 1970s after Congress first began mandating regulation of the fire safety of fabrics used in household furnishings. (In 1991 the center became part of NIST's Building and Fire Research Laboratory.)

The studies had been prompted by several multiple-fatality fires in hospitals, nursing homes, and prisons that had been caused by rapidly combusting mattresses. In these studies, the researchers were discovering that many petroleum-based synthetics — like latex foam and polyurethane foam — had very different burning properties than the natural fibers they had replaced. Some plastics would melt and pool and run, like flammable liquids. Some resisted ignition under certain conditions and yet, under others, burned furiously.

— Marshall, what's this word "flashover" mean? — Campbell asked Smyth in a phone call.

Campbell kept coming across the word in the Center for Fire Research publications he was reading.

Smyth himself still had only a very vague idea, having only recently encountered the word himself.

— Well, it's when materials, you know, burn like crazy, — Smyth said. — What difference does it make? —

But Campbell focused on the concept. He began to speak directly to some of the fire experts Smyth had found.

He learned that the precise origin of the modern concept of flashover was hard to fix in time. The term had been around for a long time and had been used in different ways by different people. But the modern understanding had begun to gel at the Center for Fire Research in the early 1970s. Investigators there and at a few other laboratories set fire to furnished test rooms fitted with devices to record the temperatures and gas levels at various locations throughout the duration of the burn. The tests were exceedingly expensive; a single test could take a year to set up and analyze, and could cost $25,000 to $50,000.

The investigators had gradually discovered that a fire in a room, whatever its origin, would create a layer of hot gases at the ceiling. That layer gave off powerful radiant energy in every direction, including back down to the floor. When the temperature of that gaseous cloud reached about 1100 to 1200 degrees Fahrenheit, the flammable materials in the cloud ignited, glowed red, and emitted radiant energy so strong that it would swiftly ignite everything else in the room — all the way down to floor level.

The investigators were realizing that ordinary household furnishings, ignited by a match or cigarette or burning paper, could progress to flashover conditions shockingly fast — without the presence of any flammable liquid. That was especially so, the center discovered in a study published in 1985, in a room composed of Sheetrock walls and ceiling — like those in the Knapp children's bedroom — which provided excellent reflective surfaces.

And it was especially true, every study was showing, in a small room — like the Knapp children's tiny bedroom — where the gaseous cloud could quickly fill the ceiling volume and radiate energy back toward the floor. In one test done in 1975, a furnished room much larger than the Knapp children's bedroom had progressed from ignition to flashover in only six and a half minutes, without the use of flammable liquids. In a 1977 test, a single mattress, ignited by flaming paper in a wastebasket, had flashed over a room larger than the Knapp children's room in less than four minutes.

Campbell and Hammond obtained videotapes of two of those early tests.

"I remember being in a conference room and looking at those films," Hammond later recalled. "Your heart just goes boom, boom, boom."

The speed and power of flashover were breathtaking. So was the damage it left in its wake.

Many of the ordinary clues arson investigators might look for, in trying to determine the point of origin of a fire, could be obscured or annihilated by the intensity of the post-flashover stage of a fire.

As a result, in a flashover fire of innocent origin, investigators might not be able to locate the original point of origin. Instead, they might find only fairly equal deterioration of all four walls and baseboards, formerly thought to be a "hallmark" of a flammable liquid fire.

A flashover fire could easily warp steel, once thought to be a sign of a flammable liquid fire.

Radiant energy reflecting down from the ceiling during flashover could cause intense floor-level burning, another "hallmark" of a flammable liquid fire.

Radiant energy could shine into the so-called dead-air spaces in the corners of a room and cause heavy burning there, another "hallmark" of a flammable liquid fire.

Uneven reflection of radiant energy from the ceiling could cause irregular char marks on the floor indistinguishable from flammable liquid runs.

"We could see this whole thing just coming apart," Hammond later recounted. "Everything David Dale said could have been caused only by a flammable liquid could in fact be the result of flashover."

"With flashover," recounted Campbell, "you could explain everything."

As the lawyers read more and talked to fire researchers, they realized that other aspects of the state's case against Knapp had also disintegrated over the years since his conviction.

"Every time you'd see an article you'd see something in it," Hammond said in 1993. "I remember over those months finding just one thing after another after another."

It was no longer tenable, for instance, to claim that the low levels of carbon monoxide found in the girls' blood were too low to have been brought about by an ordinary household fire. Studies begun in 1981 — eight years after Knapp's conviction — showed that people who were trapped in a room with a fast-burning accidental fire might die showing very low levels of carbon monoxide in their blood. Until shortly before flashover the carbon monoxide levels in a room remained quite low, especially low to the ground where small children would be breathing. As flashover approached, carbon monoxide levels skyrocketed. A person caught in such a room would often die from other causes before his or her carboxyhemoglobin level rose above 30 percent. The Knapp girls' levels, of 8 percent and 23 percent, were within this range.

There was also now more documentation that very young children could set serious fires using both matches and lighters. Using improved methods of fire reporting and record keeping that had developed since the time of the Knapp conviction, investigators in the mid-1980s had recognized that a substantial number of fatal house fires were set by unsupervised small children playing with matches, lighters, candles, or the like. One study had determined that, of all children under five who died in fatal fires between 1978 and 1982, one-third of them had set those fires while playing — usually with matches or lighters. Even among children two or younger, 14 percent had set the fires themselves.

Often house fires were set in the morning by children who awoke before their parents, the researchers were finding. Most often, the children managed to set fire to bedding, mattresses, pillows, or other furnishings in their bedrooms. The children often failed to escape even when there was time to have done so, perhaps because they feared being punished, researchers speculated. Instead, they tended to hide in closets or under beds. Fire battalion chief Geary Roberts and a deputy sheriff on the scene both thought Little Linda had tried to hide under the bed, judging from the position in which they found her body.

So the notion that children the age of Little Linda, three and a half, were incapable of lighting matches had also buckled over the years since the conviction. (At this stage, of course, neither Hammond nor Campbell knew that Louise Ramsey's friend Melba Burr claimed to have *seen* Little Linda light matches. The document that would have revealed that fact was not present in the defense files that Martori, Meyer inherited in 1981.)

In early February 1986 the law firm — which had recently changed its name from Martori, Meyer to Meyer, Hendricks, Victor, Osborn & Maledon — filed Knapp's *fifth* petition for post-conviction relief, alleging that newly discovered scientific evidence concerning flashover and related concepts warranted giving John Knapp a new trial.

Today, because of state legislative reforms designed to speed up executions, this filing might well have been procedurally barred.

Assistant attorney general McClennen approached this latest filing as he had all the others. He argued that an array of procedural obstacles prohibited even considering the petition, whether or not it had merit.

Initially, McClennen argued that in order for evidence to be "newly discovered," it had to have *existed* at the time of trial, but only have been *discovered* later. Since Knapp's lawyers claimed that the new scientific evidence had not *existed* in 1974, it was not truly "newly discovered," and therefore could not warrant a new trial.

Alternatively, if the evidence *had* existed at the time of the 1974 trial, McClennen argued, then Knapp's original lawyers should have found out about it back then, and their failure to do so constituted waiver.

Finally, even if the evidence had not existed in 1974, it had clearly begun to emerge in the 1980s, after the Meyer, Hendricks lawyers took over, so their failure to raise this issue in Knapp's second, third, or fourth petitions for relief constituted waiver.

Tick-tock, the game was locked.

Since Judge Cheryl Hendrix had, by now, completed her rotation through the criminal docket, the case was assigned to superior court judge Stephen Gerst. Gerst was beginning his third year as a judge. Unlike Judges Hendrix or Riddel, Gerst had extensive experience in criminal law. He had been a prosecutor for three years until 1969, and had then gone into private practice, where he had handled many court-appointed criminal defense assignments until he gradually built up a practice more dominated by civil work.

Although Campbell had heard some defense lawyers complain that Gerst had become pro-prosecution since taking the bench, Campbell thought he sounded like a good draw.

Knapp's fifth petition drew very little press attention.

"There wasn't anything newsworthy about some guy on death row going through his umpteenth attempt to get released," Gerst later remembered.

Nevertheless, Judge Gerst, unlike Judge Belloni of Portland, happened to find the issues intriguing.

"When they outlined what [their claim] would be, and told me they had gone to people who were the top fire experts in the country, they would be showing videotapes of actual bedroom fires being lit and burned to demonstrate the scientific theory they wanted to sell, and they were going to be bringing these people into the courtroom, it was fascinating."

In April 1986, over McClennen's fierce objection, Judge Gerst agreed to hold a hearing to listen to Knapp's new scientific experts.

Knapp had a judge's ear.

John Knapp was transported from Florence to Phoenix to attend the hearings. He was housed at the county's new Madison Street Jail, which had just opened the previous year. Madison was a hulking, ten-story beige poured-concrete structure just across the street from the old Main Jail. There were several rows of squinting horizontal recesses in the facade which, though unrecognizable as such from the street, were windows near the ceilings of inmates' cells. More prominent were large square patches of metal louvers, which formed the outer walls of the inmate exercise yards.

On each morning of a court date Knapp would be awakened at about 5:00 and led, in leg irons and handcuffs, to the basement of the jail. Then he would be guided through a 500-foot tunnel about 20 feet beneath Madison Street to the basement of the old Main Jail, and from there up to the seventh floor of the same courthouse where he had been convicted in 1974. Knapp was then taken through internal corridors to the sixth floor, where he was disgorged into a holding cell near Judge Gerst's courtroom, and his handcuffs and leg irons were removed.

Knapp was now decidedly overweight — about 245 pounds — bald, clean-shaven, and forty years old. He had a pronounced habit of twiddling his thumbs. He wore dentures, which gave his speech a soft, palatalized quality. Since he spoke quickly, he was sometimes difficult to understand.

As they prepared their presentation, Campbell and Hammond began to think of the state's scientific case against Knapp as a tripod supported by three legs: (1) David Dale's interpretation of the fire damage and burn patterns; (2) medical examiner Karnitschnig's testimony about the low carbon monoxide levels in the children's blood; and (3) Jack Strong's testimony that gas chromatography had found substances in the debris from the children's bedroom that were "consistent with" Coleman fuel. Though they were now prepared to challenge the first two legs of the tripod, they had not reexamined the last, concerning the gas chromatography.

The original samples taken from the floor of the children's bedroom could not be retested, using today's improved scientific techniques, because the county clerk's office had lost the glass jars that contained those samples, along with all the other trial exhibits. The best the defense lawyers could do was have new experts reexamine Jack Strong's original chromatograms from 1973.

Unfortunately, Strong's original chromatograms had *also* been lost by the county clerk's office, since they, too, had been trial exhibits. The photocopies of the chromatograms in the defense file were horrendous. Due to sloppy photo-copying, pertinent portions of the chromatograms had been cut off.

Campbell tried to get better copies from Strong's employer, the Department of Public Safety, but it, too, had somehow lost or destroyed its only copies of the Knapp chromatograms. All of Strong's notes concerning his tests had also been lost or destroyed, the defense lawyers were told.

So the poor-quality photocopies in the defense files were all that the lawyers could show to anyone.

Campbell discovered that one of the experts they had been working with al-ready, Dennis Canfield, was qualified to read gas chromatograms. Canfield, a burly forensic scientist at the University of Southern Mississippi, had been a po-lice chemist in New Jersey from 1971 to 1976 — the same era as the Knapp case.

On the Monday evening before the hearing began in September 1986, Campbell and Hammond showed Canfield the photocopies of the chro-matograms that were in the defense files.

Like the original defense chemist, Michael Parsons, Canfield was immedi-ately struck by their poor quality. But unlike the original defense chemist — the polite, cautious, academic Parsons — Canfield was spontaneous, unrestrained, and profane. A big, animated man, who gesticulated with his whole body, Can-field mixed crude and scientific terms in a way Hammond found comic.

— Can you believe this shit? — Canfield shouted. — The peaks on this chromatogram are not appropriately differentiated! With charts like these, you couldn't distinguish Coleman fuel from bug spray! —

Campbell showed Canfield the chromatograms of the "extract" samples lifted from the cleaned floor of the children's bedroom with pieces of gauze soaked in the solvent methylene chloride.

Canfield agreed with Parsons. While these graphs matched the one taken of vapors from a seized Coleman fuel can, such a match did not make sense. The residues showed no evidence of having been through a fire, and they showed no additional peaks representing the solvent used to make the extract, which should have been their most prominent feature.

Then the lawyers showed Canfield the chromatogram for "item 5" — the jar that contained a sample of the "oily film" that firefighters had found floating on top of the water on the floor — the film that the firefighters said smelled like Coleman fuel. Was item 5 truly "consistent with" Coleman fuel?

— This is a negative, — Canfield said. — As negative as it can be. It's not Coleman fuel. I don't know how another scientist could say otherwise. —

Back in 1974, in his own much more tentative way, the academic chemist Parsons had also testified that item 5 did not appear to match the Coleman fuel sample. "They are not of the same pattern as the liquid," he had testified about the peaks of item 5, without elaboration.

Canfield, on the other hand, was blunt. In his opinion, Strong had perjured himself.

The emerging picture smelled very bad to the defense lawyers. How had the Department of Public Safety lost its copies of Strong's chromatograms and notes for this case? They even began to wonder about how the clerk's office had lost all the trial exhibits — including the original sample jars and chromatograms — from an active death-penalty case in the first place.

A day and a half after Canfield looked at the chromatograms, Campbell filed papers alleging that Strong had committed perjury at trial.

A week later McClennen called Strong as a witness to rebut the charge. But Strong's testimony ranged from murky to unintelligible. At first Strong said that too much of the chart for item 5 had been cut off in the photocopy for him to draw any conclusions. "I would not make a determination strictly on [what's left]," he said.

When Campbell directed Strong's attention to the portions of the chart that did exist, however, Strong conceded that that portion did *not* match the Coleman fuel chart. Strong maintained, however, that the heat and degradation resulting from the fire may have accounted for the absence of a match between the fire debris sample and the unburned Coleman fuel in that area.

The trouble with Strong's explanation, however, was that what remained of the chromatogram was the portion that should have been *least* affected by the heat of the fire, since it depicted the *heavier* molecules present.

"Wouldn't you expect your lighter molecules [to] have boiled off before your heavier molecules have been boiled off?" Campbell asked.

"To a degree yes," Strong answered.

So if he didn't have a match at the heavier end of the spectrum, Campbell asked, then he certainly would not expect a match at the lighter end, would he?

"It's rather unpredictable just what does occur," Strong responded, "so I don't believe an absolute conclusion can be made."

*   *   *

Judge Gerst was unwilling to conclude that Strong had intentionally lied in 1974, especially given the fact that the defense's own expert, Parsons, had been so tentative about challenging Strong's conclusions at the time. He disallowed Campbell's motion to add an allegation of perjury.*

Nevertheless, Canfield had pointed out that the emperor had no clothes. The gas chromatogram of item 5 — the oily film that smelled to the firefighters like Coleman fuel — was *not* "similar to" or "consistent with" Coleman fuel. And once Canfield said so, no state expert would ever again claim that it was. Instead, prosecutors and state experts from this point forward would *take the position* that too little of that chromatogram remained to draw any conclusion one way or another. But, when asked directly, state experts would concede that what *did* remain of that chromatogram *was not a match*.

While Judge Gerst was uncertain what to make of the gas chromatography leg of the state's case, he was impressed with the testimony of the defense experts concerning the other two legs.

---

* Assistant attorney general McClennen also *took the position* — one that later prosecutors from time to time recycled — that the defense chemist, Michael Parsons, had *himself* testified at a hearing in May 1979 that Strong's chromatograms showed the presence of a flammable liquid. This was not true.

At that hearing — Knapp's first state post-conviction relief petition hearing — Knapp's lawyers, relying on the evidence unearthed by investigator Dick Todd, were focusing on the Linda-did-it possibility. Because of the nature of the other evidence Todd had found, the defense theorized that if Linda had set the fire, she had probably used *gasoline* rather than Coleman fuel. The defense lawyers therefore wanted to retest the original fire debris samples.

Prosecutor Hyder opposed any retesting by the defense, just as he had repeatedly and strenuously since 1974. Ultimately, however, after Judge Hardy decided to allow retesting, Hyder won a modification of that order narrowly constricting the scope of that testing and ensuring that it would be performed by the FBI, rather than by Parsons. Accordingly, in late 1978 the FBI examined the samples for the *limited purpose* of measuring their lead content. The defense theorized that the lead levels would be elevated if gasoline were present, since all commercial gasolines contained lead at the time. Coleman fuel, by contrast, contains no lead.

The FBI found that lead levels were, in fact, elevated. But the FBI expert also said he could reach no conclusions based on that fact, since too little was known about other sources of lead that might have been in the room — for instance, hand-me-down furniture possibly painted with old-fashioned lead-based paints.

Defense expert Parsons then testified, as he had in 1974, that he could draw no conclusions from Strong's original chromatograms as to whether a flammable liquid was present in the samples or not. If, however, one were to hypothesize that a flammable liquid *were* present, it was more likely gasoline than Coleman fuel, because of the high levels of lead that had been found.

"They did everything they said they were going to," Gerst later recalled. "It was compelling."

Gerst speculated that Crane McClennen "was caught a little bit flat-footed, in that he didn't have any experts to counteract what I was hearing."

McClennen denies having been caught flat-footed. He had simply become convinced — and is still convinced — that the defense team's evidence was not "newly discovered" at all. Deputy fire marshal Dale and Chief Roberts were assuring him that they had known all about flashover back in 1974 and that nothing important had really been learned since then.

But McClennen, whose strength was appellate work, was not a polished trial lawyer. At this hearing his instincts proved flawed. The state's experts, who were now faced with the unbearable possibility that they had testified mistakenly in a capital case, responded with unconvincing intransigence — and anger.

Chief Roberts, who was now a fire chief in Tennessee, testified that he had learned about flashover during his training in 1965. But Roberts, who had testified in 1974 that a normal fire would take thirty to forty-five minutes to progress to full-room involvement, still said he doubted flashover could occur in less than ten to fifteen minutes.

In an attempt to change his mind, the defense lawyers showed him government studies documenting that ordinary combustibles could cause flashover in as little as four minutes. Indeed, they showed him — and Judge Gerst — a videotape of an early Harvard experiment in which a bedroom had flashed over in less than seven minutes.

"When you read those studies, did you learn some new things about fire behavior in a room?" Campbell asked him.

"I learned other people's opinions of them," Roberts responded.

But through his resistance Roberts only proved the defense argument: fire science *had* evolved since Roberts had received his training.

Deputy fire marshal Dale, who was still the chief fire investigator for the state, now claimed to have understood in 1974 that "flammable liquid runs" could be created by burning plastics and other innocent causes. But he could not account for his testimony at Knapp's second trial that such patterns could *only* have been caused by flammable liquids.

Dale's voluble memory tried to supply him with a new set of facts to work with. Dale now thought he remembered, for instance, that the ventilation register near the ceiling of the children's room had been open. That would have allowed hot gases to escape, preventing flashover from occurring. But Campbell showed Dale that he had testified in 1974 that the register had been closed.

Medical examiner Heinz Karnitschnig was adamant that the children would have shown higher carbon monoxide levels in their blood had they been in a room with a serious fire for longer than two or three minutes.

Hammond showed him studies reaching the opposite conclusion. Then he described one study in which researchers actually lay inside a fire-involved room breathing the fresh air at floor level for several minutes until shortly before flashover, when they retreated.

"It's very nice to have these scientific and experimental tests here," Karnitschnig sneered. "Apparently there are some people stupid enough to go in there and inhale carboxyhemoglobin. Maybe they've done it before. Maybe that's why they do it again; they had brain damage."

Though Hammond wanted to explore the original fire inspector James McDaniel's understanding of flashover — McDaniel had never mentioned the concept in his testimony in 1974 — McDaniel ended up never testifying in front of Judge Gerst. Though McDaniel, was a full-time employee for the city of Scottsdale, he told Hammond and McClennen when the court hearings approached that he preferred not to testify because of a severe back problem. When Hammond insisted, McDaniel did come to court, as required. But a few minutes before he was due to testify, his back seized up. Fire department paramedics were summoned, and they took him to the hospital.

About a month later Hammond tried taking a videotaped deposition of McDaniel at a law office near McDaniel's home, so McDaniel would not have to come back to court. But eleven minutes into it, McDaniel protested that, due to back pain, he needed a break. After fifteen minutes more he said he was unable to proceed at all.

Hammond gave up at that point.

In his post-hearing brief, deputy attorney general McClennen argued that the evidence was not "newly discovered." He pointed out that two of the earliest videotaped bedroom burn tests had actually been conducted in June and July of 1974 — just *before* Knapp's first trial — although no written reports analyzing those tests were produced until after Knapp's conviction. He also stressed that one bedroom test fire had been conducted in July 1973 and was the subject of an unpublished manuscript dated July 1974 — the month before Knapp went to trial — and may have, therefore, been available from the researchers at Harvard University and the Factory Mutual Research Corporation who had conducted it.

McClennen was *taking the position* that Diettrich and Basham, as they frantically prepared for trial in July 1974, should have found out about these obscure unpublished technical experiments and should have understood their significance long before the researchers themselves had.

McClennen, who is a decent and intelligent man, still adheres to this implausible and, in context, brutal argument today.

"What I thought was interesting about [Knapp's fifth petition]," he said in 1993, "was that two of those tests were done prior to Mr. Knapp's first trial. One of the films was dated prior to the date of Mr. Knapp's first trial. So this wasn't what would normally be thought of as 'newly discovered' evidence."

Tick-tock.

In Arizona, to grant a defendant's motion for a new trial based on newly discovered evidence, a judge must find that the new evidence would *probably* have changed the verdict. To make this judgment, Gerst had to read the entire transcript of Knapp's 1974 trials.

"That was obviously the most troublesome part of this whole thing," Judge Gerst said. "I had no problem concluding that there was development in the area of fire science. . . . But Mr. Knapp had confessed. My inclination, like most people, is that people don't confess unless they've done something."

Although Judge Gerst signed his ruling on Wednesday morning, February 11, 1987, he waited until Friday to release it. He had been bracing uncomfortably for the press response to his opinion, and some of the other judges told him that if he released it midday on Friday, it would get covered only in the Saturday papers, which were the least read.

So on Friday the thirteenth, 1987, Judge Gerst's secretary notified the attorneys for each side that his written ruling was now available at his chambers. In accordance with Judge Gerst's custom when reporters had expressed interest in a case, she also called down to the courthouse press office to let them know the same thing.

There was little conversation as Campbell and Hammond drove to the courthouse in Hammond's pickup truck. Campbell was steeling himself for another loss. It was too painful to get his hopes up and then have them shattered. As a defense lawyer he had generally come to see judges as an arm of the prosecution. Almost without exception his successes in the criminal arena had been before juries. The history of the Knapp case was right in line with his experience.

Hammond, on the other hand, was trying to "cabin his optimism," he recalls. He was beginning to think that they just might have something this time.

They went up to Gerst's seventh-floor chambers. An *Arizona Republic* reporter, Venita Hawthorne James, happened to have just arrived as well, to pick up her copy.

Gerst's secretary gave Campbell the opinion. Hammond thought Gerst's secretary gave him a little smile, which he hoped was more than just a gesture of politeness.

They stepped back out into the hall. Campbell flipped to the last page, as Hammond strained to read over his shoulder:

"IT IS ORDERED granting the Petition for Post-Conviction Relief, vacating the conviction and sentence of the Defendant, and granting the Defendant a new trial."

Campbell and Hammond embraced. Tears formed in Hammond's eyes and an embarrassing sound escaped his lips.

"Knapp's attorneys," the reporter James's front-page article declared the next day, "let out a whoop of joy as they read the seven-page ruling."

"I remember a childish shriek," Hammond recalled in 1993. "I was embarrassed about it as soon as I did it."

Gerst had concluded that "the foundation of the state's case rested upon the opinion of expert witnesses that the fire damage and the carboxyhemoglobin levels in the children's blood could only have been caused by an accelerant such as a flammable liquid having been poured throughout the room. . . . The new scientific information relating to the flashover phenomenon and carboxyhemoglobin studies directly impact on the State's basic premise and offer a strong alternative explanation to the State's theory of an arson-caused fire."

The original prosecutor, Hyder, now a federal prosecutor, was also quoted in reporter James's story the next morning.

"It just seems to me that [Judge Gerst] is rejecting the jury's finding and substituting his own opinion," Hyder had told the reporter. "As far as I'm concerned, it's just a rehash of what they had before."

Based on the tenor of McClennen's arguments in the ensuing weeks, as he asked Gerst to reconsider his order and then challenged the order on appeal, Hammond's perception was that McClennen was stunned by Gerst's ruling — just incredulous.

But, characteristically, McClennen denies having had any emotional reaction at all.

"I don't get surprised one way or the other," he recalled in 1993. "I make a motion. You respond. The judge rules. . . . That's where you are at that point, and you move on to the next step."

McClennen also indirectly suggested that Gerst's opinion may have been motivated by Gerst's craving for publicity.

"The one thing that did surprise me," McClennen said, "is that apparently the press was alerted [that] the decision would be coming out at one o'clock this particular day. I'm not sure that immediate notification of the press is an essential component of the judicial process."

Was McClennen really suggesting that Judge Gerst's decision—freeing a convicted child murderer—was a way of playing to the press?

"I think I'll just leave it, I'm not sure why they were alerted when they were."

Even before they left the court, Campbell called Jon Sands, a young associate at the firm, to have him start drafting a motion to have Knapp released pending the new trial.

The lawyers then returned to the firm so they could call Knapp. By the time they got back, Sands had spread the word of the stunning victory through the firm. As colleagues crowded about them with congratulations, Hammond felt pangs of guilt about celebrating while Knapp still did not know.

He and Campbell made their way to Mark Wallace's office on the fourth floor. From there they called Florence and asked the guards to have Knapp call back — the necessary routine.

With the speakerphone set up, they waited. For once, a guard found Knapp quickly.

— John, — Campbell told him, — you won. You won a new trial. —

Today Campbell remembers Knapp's reaction as nonverbal, an exhalation of relief.

"He didn't believe it," Campbell told the *Republic*'s James that day. "He was speechless. He said he's going to call his brothers and sisters back East and tell them the news."

Press and television cameras crowded around the west exit from the Madison Street Jail on March 11, anticipating John Knapp's walk to freedom after thirteen years and twenty-five days of incarceration. Mark Wallace and Colin Campbell waited outside while Sands and Hammond managed, after administrative hassles, to get back to see John. Knapp was dressed in his inmate's blue jeans and work shirt, with the denim jacket slung over his shoulder. He carried a red accordion file under his arm.

— It's time, John, — a jailer called at about 12:30.

The guards unlocked the first of the two interlocking steel doors in an

S-shaped passage leading to the exit, letting Hammond and Knapp into a poorly lit interim chamber. The first door slammed shut behind them. After an eternity in this cramped no-man's-land — had they somehow been forgotten? — the second door electronically clicked open.

That left one last door, the one to the street, but Knapp could shove it open himself, with a push-bar.

Squinting in the blinding Arizona sunlight, Hammond and Knapp trotted down a few steps and waded out into the reporters.

"I'm glad to get out," Knapp told Channels 5 and 12. He looked down at the ground, showed a slight dolphin-like grin — was it a smile or just the shape of his mouth? — pushed his glasses up his nose, and scratched behind his left ear with his index finger. "All told, I've been locked up for thirteen years and thirteen days* and I'm just glad to be out now."

"I'm going to get something good to eat and go to Texas," he told the *Republic* and the *Gazette*.

Amid dozens of unanswered questions, Hammond guided Knapp to his truck, which was parked just a few yards away, and took him to the law office.

Knapp had a beer at an impromptu party in the reception area near the elevators. He met the lawyers, paralegals, and secretaries who had been working to save his life for years, or funding the effort. Others came just to see what a man looked like when he had come back from the dead.

— This floor's so soft — Knapp remarked to the associate, Sands, referring to the novel experience of standing on carpeting.

Conversing with Knapp was awkward.

"To us, John was the fact-pattern," Sands recounted later. "And now he was here in flesh and blood. And what could he talk about? His life stopped in 1973."

Outside Knapp's presence there was nervous humor among the lawyers, who were arranging for Knapp to fly to Houston that evening, where his brother Robert would pick him up. They tried to imagine his conversation with the passenger seated next to him. So, what have you been up to?

After about an hour, the elevator doors parted and Chuck Diettrich and his wife walked in. Diettrich had driven in from his home near Payson.

"He was blubbering like a baby," Hammond recounted. "He cried and cried and cried. I didn't know what to say. It was one of the most awkward things."

---

* His numbers were either slightly off or based upon a correct computation of his time as of February 27, 1987 — the day Judge Gerst ordered his release. Knapp had remained in jail twelve more days, however, while the supreme court considered whether to review that order.

While the party continued a wire service reporter came by and gave Hammond a black-and-white photograph depicting Hammond and Knapp as they had walked out of the jail just a couple hours earlier. Someone suggested Knapp inscribe it for Hammond.

Knapp agreed. He wrote: "To Larry, from John."

Colleagues later kidded Hammond about his client's understated gratitude. But, to Hammond, the inscription seemed just right.

Knapp's older brother Bob and his wife picked John up at the airport in Houston.

"He looked very beat," Bob recounted in 1994. "He looked about ten years older than I did."

There was no celebratory mood.

"He didn't know my wife," Bob explained in 1994. "I'd been divorced and re-married. That was kind of a scary thing for him. He was very reserved, quiet, withdrawn. He really didn't want to talk about it — his experience in jail. He just wanted this to be gotten over with and him left alone."

Bob took John to his own home in Bay City, on the Gulf Coast. (Knapp's mother had died in 1983; his father, in 1976.) At Bob's, Knapp stayed up all night, reading *People* magazines.

The Meyer, Hendricks attorneys donated more than $450,000 worth of attorney hours bringing the fifth post-conviction petition alone — beyond the hundreds of hours they had already spent on the second, third, and fourth petitions, and on the federal habeas corpus action.* They also expended more than $50,000 of the firm's money for experts and other expenses. The firm put in for the $20,492.99 it spent on the fees and expenses of the two experts Judge Gerst had agreed to appoint — out of a total of four used — and Judge Gerst ultimately authorized $14,804.70 in reimbursement, which Hammond and Campbell considered generous. If Knapp had been appointed a lawyer who had been unwilling to donate hundreds of hours of time and more than $35,000 in out-of-pocket funds, Knapp would not have been able to bring this petition.

---

* The firm did receive compensation for its attorneys' time on the federal case at the then-standard, federal court–appointed hourly rate of $40 for out-of-court time and $60 for in-court time.

PART 4.

Trial By Fire

Seventeen

Though McClennen tried to appeal Judge Gerst's ruling granting Knapp a new trial, the supreme court declined to hear the matter in September 1987. Knapp's case then returned to the Maricopa County Attorney's office for re-prosecution. But since that office now had a technical conflict of interest — a former public defender who had played a minor role in Knapp's defense had since moved to the county attorney's office — the case was bounced back to the attorney general's office in November.

— How would you like to reprosecute the John Knapp case? — chief assistant attorney general Steven Twist asked.

— Sure, — David Powell responded.

It was, of course, an honor to be entrusted with such a high-profile case.

Powell, thirty-four, was a clean-cut, athletic, amiable man, with short, curly, salt-and-pepper hair and a moustache. He was smart, good-natured, low-key, and, in the view of defense lawyers, a "straight-shooter."

From everything Powell had heard about the Knapp case, it was as awful a crime as any imaginable. So he set out to retry it.

The issue of *whether* to retry Knapp — whether reconstructing the case fourteen years after the event was really worthwhile — never came up.

Hammond and Campbell were always dumbfounded that the state decided to reprosecute. In granting the new trial, Judge Gerst had read all the evidence against Knapp and had ruled that the new scientific evidence would "probably" change a jury's verdict. Wouldn't the prosecutors themselves have a reasonable doubt now? the defense lawyers thought.

And even if the prosecutors still believed Knapp was guilty, Knapp had already served more than thirteen years in prison. He presented little ongoing threat to society. The case would be terribly expensive to resurrect, and there was no public clamor for retrial.

When they later tried to imagine how and why the state had decided to retry Knapp, Hammond and Campbell pictured in their minds some sort of formal review proceeding at the attorney general's office. They imagined the line prosecutors and upper-level supervisors gathering around a conference table, painstakingly reanalyzing the evidence and balancing the societal, political, and institutional costs and benefits of trying Knapp a third time.

No such thing ever happened.

"There was never a period," chief assistant attorney general Twist said in 1993, "when the attorney general's office said, 'Is this worth doing again?' It was a serious crime that needed to be brought to trial again."

Crane McClennen was the only one in the office who really knew the facts of the case, and nothing in the hearing before Judge Gerst had made him question Knapp's guilt. From the perspective of the prosecutors, well-heeled, clever lawyers and their hired-gun experts had snowed Judge Gerst.

In addition, of course, it is possible that when prosecutors have been trying to kill a man for thirteen years, there is psychological resistance to considering seriously the possibility that that man might be innocent. Such resistance might be especially strong when people in the prosecuting agency are emotionally and ideologically committed to the proposition that, in the real world, innocent people are never sentenced to death.

In November 1987, a couple of months after Judge Gerst's new trial order became final, Hammond and Campbell got a letter from Ray Girdler Jr. The letter had a familiar return address: the state prison in Florence.

"Like Mr. Knapp," Girdler wrote, "I also protest my innocence of the crime and further contend that there was, in fact, no crime in the first place. It has been my contention that the fire that caused the deaths of my wife and daughters was one of accidental origin."

Hammond smiled and took the letter down the hall to show Campbell.

— I wonder how many of these we're going to get, — Hammond mused.

Girdler's name was familiar to both lawyers. There had been a grim pas de deux between the Girdler and Knapp cases for some years now. Girdler, who had lived near Prescott, Arizona, was convicted in 1982 of burning his wife and three-year-old daughter to death, by setting fire to his mobile home with gasoline in November 1981. He was sentenced to consecutive life terms plus twenty-one years by superior court judge James Sult.

At Girdler's sentencing hearing in 1982, in an attempt to persuade Judge Sult to sentence Girdler to death, the prosecutor had recalled to the witness stand deputy fire marshal David Dale, who had testified at the trial that the Girdler fire was an arson. Comparing Girdler's crime to Knapp's, Dale suggested that Girdler's may have been even worse. While Girdler's victims had been conscious, Dale testified, there was evidence that the Knapp children may have been *beaten unconscious* before the fire started. Accordingly, the Knapp children may have felt no pain.*

Dale's testimony was wrong and irresponsible. But it spurred a flurry of interest from the Knapp lawyers because, ironically, if true, it could have helped Knapp. If the children were unconscious when they died, then the crime might not qualify as "especially heinous, cruel, or depraved" — the "aggravating circumstance" Judge Hardy had relied on in sentencing Knapp to death.

After the Knapp lawyers started making inquiries, Dale submitted an affidavit in the Knapp case stating that he "did not have . . . knowledge of any injuries to [Little] Linda and Iona Knapp other than the injuries caused by the fire." The tempest in a teapot then blew over. (Dale was never reprimanded in any way for having negligently given misleading testimony under circumstances that seem tailor-made to have led to Girdler's execution.)

Girdler was now asking the Meyer, Hendricks lawyers to represent him.

It was out of the question. The firm was still reeling from the expense of its six-year pro bono representation of Knapp.

But the firm decided that it could at least send Girdler photocopies of the transcripts of the hearings before Judge Gerst. If he could make some use of those, fine.

*   *   *

---

* Dale's new theory rested in part on the fact that on the day of the fire the Knapps' cat had had a red spot on its paw that looked like blood. But Dale did not tell the sentencing judge in the Girdler case that scientific analysis on November 23, 1973, had established that the red spot on the cat's paw was *not* blood. Dale had gone on to speculate that the low quantities of carbon monoxide in the Knapp children's blood suggested that they had had a depressed breathing rate, perhaps because they had been beaten unconscious before the fire started. Such a theory had never been broached by any witness in the Knapp case.

Assistant attorney general Powell's first task was to figure out what had happened to the trial exhibits. Now that prosecutors, rather than private defense attorneys, were asking the questions, some answers emerged.

The exhibits were not exactly lost, as Mark Wallace had been told back in December 1982. Rather, a court clerk had ordered them thrown out in September 1982, after allegedly having mistaken them for inactive files. Although there were elaborate procedures to follow before exhibits of any kind could be thrown away — lawyers on each side had to be notified and given an opportunity to claim the exhibits — everyone forgot to go through them in this instance.

Accidents happen.

"I don't buy it," Hammond said in 1993. "I do not believe it is possible that anyone could have just absent-mindedly picked up the Knapp exhibits and thrown them in a dumpster with that guy on death row. It's not clerk's office behavior. It's so antithetical to the way these people act."

And the timing of the exhibits' disappearance also seemed suspicious to Hammond — just around the time that Mark Wallace had first begun nosing around down there. The disappearance of those exhibits had, among other things, prevented the Meyer, Hendricks lawyers from retesting the contents of the jars of fire debris by improved scientific techniques.

Whatever had happened to the exhibits in 1982, their absence at this stage *benefited* Knapp. Without any trial exhibits, Powell would have to ask several state agencies to comb their files for copies of documents and photographs to replace the lost originals that had been trial exhibits.

In addition, Powell would have to bring himself up to speed on fourteen boxes of transcripts, witness statements, and other files. Since these tasks would take time, Powell had the case dismissed in December 1987, with the understanding that he could bring a new prosecution at a later point.

Since Powell had many more pressing matters on his plate, the Knapp case began to sit.

— Larry, you've really got to climb in your truck and get on up here, — Jack Williams told Hammond over the phone.

Williams was a solo practitioner in Prescott. He was now representing Ray Girdler.

Using the transcripts sent to him by Meyer, Hendricks, Girdler had written Judge Sult himself, trying to explain their relevance to his own case. Judge Sult had appointed Williams to represent Girdler.

After reviewing the record, Williams thought that Girdler's conviction was even more suspect than Knapp's.

The fire in the Girdler trailer had struck at about 2:45 A.M. on November 20, 1981, about forty-five minutes after Girdler went to sleep. His story was that his wife and he woke up, smelling smoke. He had run for a fire extinguisher, which was outside in his car, while his wife had run to get the baby. He had fallen in the dark, and by the time he got back to the trailer the fire was out of control.

The defense had assumed that the fire must have been started by a smoldering cigarette — Girdler smoked and drank — or perhaps by a homemade generator.

Unlike Knapp, Girdler had never confessed to police,* and no flammable liquid residues had been found in his mobile home.

The evidence against Girdler had rested largely on the expert testimony of David Dale and of one of his subordinates. They had found "classic" liquid accelerant runs on the floor of the trailer, and numerous other indicators, that pointed unequivocally — in their minds — to arson.

In Girdler's case, as in Knapp's, some neighbors believed that Girdler was insufficiently hysterical after the fire. He was "calm as a cucumber," the prosecutor had told the jury. He had been seen drinking coffee and smoking cigarettes. Though there was no insurance on his wife or child, there was property insurance on his mobile home. Since he was behind in his bills, the state theorized that gaining the insurance money and getting rid of his costly dependents was the motive for the crime.

Although there were differences between Knapp's case and Girdler's, even those were instructive. While experts had testified in the Knapp case, for instance, that the low carbon monoxide levels in the Knapp children's blood were consistent with a flammable liquid fire, Dale had testified in Girdler's case that *the high levels* of carbon monoxide in the fire victims — 74 percent and 88 percent — were consistent with a flammable liquid fire.

Hammond agreed to join Williams in handling Girdler's post-conviction relief petition — again on a pro bono basis.

About a year and a half passed in which Powell took almost no action on the Knapp case. Meanwhile, however, his investigator, Debora Schwartz, located

---

* A cell mate with incentives to lie claimed Girdler had confessed to him; he later recanted his claim to a journalist, J. W. Casserly, and then, later still, recanted the recantation. See J. W. Casserly, "An Innocent Man?" *New Times* (a Phoenix weekly newspaper), August 22–28, 1990, p. 22.

negatives of the photographic exhibits and had 185 new blowups of the crime scene made — the most important physical evidence against Knapp.

By this time Powell realized that he could not rely on David Dale as his fire expert at a new trial. Though Powell personally still considered Dale honest — "It's not an exact science," Powell noted in 1993 — he also realized, as a strategic matter, that he needed someone the defense could not denigrate as old-school or unscientific.

At the hearing before Judge Gerst in 1986, Knapp's lawyers had often relied on *Kirk's Fire Investigation Handbook*, whose second edition had been revised by John DeHaan. Powell asked DeHaan, who was now a criminalist with the California Department of Justice, to evaluate the evidence. After all, DeHaan *wrote the book* on fire investigation, it could be said.

After the California attorney general gave his blessing, DeHaan agreed. Powell visited DeHaan in Sacramento in May 1989, bringing photographs and select transcripts.

DeHaan, then forty, was tall, paunchy, and clean-shaven. He had grown up in Chicago and had taken criminology courses at the University of Illinois at Chicago Circle.

"I'm probably in this business because of Sherlock Holmes," DeHaan told the author in 1993. "Read him in high school. Read him again in college."

Today, DeHaan keeps a bust of Holmes in his cramped and cluttered office near Sacramento, and he frequently quotes Holmes's aphorisms. He belongs to a society of forensic scientists who periodically convene to "solve" famous old mysteries, like the cause of the Great Chicago Fire of 1871.

After graduating from college in 1969, DeHaan worked with county, state, and federal crime labs in California, and, since late 1987, he had taught at the California Criminalistics Institute.

In 1980 DeHaan had been invited to revise the *Kirk's* handbook, since he wrote well and had experience with both fire scene investigation and laboratory analysis. Once the revision came out in 1982, DeHaan became, by definition, an authority on the subject.

Yet, precisely how extensive DeHaan's relevant experience was at the time of the Knapp case is not easy to quantify. Most of his time over the years had been spent doing lab work, and much of his time had been spent in areas unrelated to arson: trace evidence, fingerprints, shoe prints, and tire prints. By his own estimate, about 80 percent of his case load at the federal Bureau of Alcohol, Tobacco and Firearms had involved explosives. DeHaan said in 1993 that he had testified in "something like three hundred trials," but he estimated that only "maybe twenty" of those appearances related to fire in any way and that a "smaller number" involved actual cause-and-origin investigations, which is what he was being asked to do in the Knapp case. In fact, he could identify only one such case by name — a case in which his brief appearance for the defendant consumed only thirty pages of trial transcript.

At the time he became involved in the Knapp case, DeHaan claimed to have performed or participated in 200 to 250 full-scale "structure fire tests" — one of his chief sources of expertise. These tests were performed not with an eye toward solving any particular crime, but only with the general goal of observing the behavior of fires and the damage they produce. DeHaan believes that these tests are in many ways more valuable than the tests that fire protection engineers perform in laboratories.

"There's only so much you can do in the laboratory," he said. "If you predict fire behavior based on what happens in a laboratory situation, and you get to a real fire, what's the chances you're really going to be able to predict what the fire's going to do and in what time frame?"

Unlike the highly instrumented and scrupulously documented tests performed by, for instance, the Center for Fire Research, DeHaan's tests were often very casually documented, if they were documented at all. A few had been videotaped; a great many slides existed of the burn damage created by some of them; and he had written some articles based on some of them. But the only comprehensive storehouse of knowledge concerning the precise conditions under which these tests had been conducted existed within the memory of John DeHaan.

DeHaan is superficially precise, fastidious, slightly eccentric, and supremely confident — the way a reader might imagine Sherlock Holmes to be. His vocabulary is well chosen when he describes fires and explosions. He does not speak of lighting flammable liquids but rather, more correctly, of igniting flammable liquid *vapors*; it is, technically, the vapor rising from the liquid that actually ignites. He does not talk of "explosions" but rather of "overpressure situations" that "fail the walls" and "lift the ceiling" while issuing an "audible report."

Yet DeHaan is neither precise nor fastidious when it comes to answering probing questions. Instead, he often appears evasive and even willfully imprecise.

"After decades as an expert witness," he told the author in 1993, "if you get really tired of a particular line of cross-examination, you can sometimes offer a response that is truthful and responsive but it's just slightly off target. And then hope that the cross-examiner follows you down that particular line so you can saw it off behind him."

Every forensic expert, whether for the prosecution or the defense, ultimately relies upon his "knowledge" and "experience," which is largely a black box that is difficult for an opposing lawyer to probe. DeHaan protects his black box zealously.

For instance, some of DeHaan's "structure fire tests," for which he does have videotape documentation, are crude experiments that shed very little light on the Knapp case. They involve, for instance, detonating explosive devices inside abandoned and unfurnished shacks, sheds, barns, or other structures bearing no similarity whatsoever to the Knapp children's bedroom.

It would, therefore, be valuable to know which of those 200 to 250 structure fire experiments DeHaan was really relying on in drawing his conclusions, and to be able to find out the precise conditions under which each of those tests had been run.

But quantifying and verifying even the crudest information about DeHaan's 200 to 250 structure fires tests is very difficult.

Precisely how many involved flammable liquids? How many involved explosives? How many involved innocent scenarios?

"Well, there's no way to tell," DeHaan said. "There's no way to even guess."

When was the last time he had performed one of these structure fire tests before he became involved in the Knapp case in May 1989?

"There's no way to tell," he said again. He guessed it had been three or four years earlier. Maybe he had done one more recently somewhere in the San Francisco Bay area.

DeHaan examined the Knapp materials over a period of about two weeks.

The case did not look very complicated to him. The damage to the children's bedroom had been severe, while the damage to the rest of the house had been minor. That suggested to him — just as it had to deputy fire marshal Dale — a rapid, intense fire. An innocent, unaccelerated fire would have taken far too long to produce that sort of damage, DeHaan thought, probably from a half-hour to an hour. A flammable liquid, on the other hand, could have produced that damage in about fifteen minutes, which was closer to a timeline that fit all the other facts.

In addition, after examining the photos of the burn damage, DeHaan concluded that the room may have never reached flashover conditions at all. And if it had, those conditions could not have been sustained for any length of time —

certainly not long enough to account for the burn damage that would otherwise indicate a flammable liquid fire. There were sections of carpet near the center of the room, for instance, that had suffered only very minor burn damage. Had there been flashover, he reasoned, the carpet there would have shown intense damage. Since it did not, flashover had probably not occurred.

Without performing any tests — or even asking to see those that Marshall Smyth had performed in 1974 — DeHaan also felt confident that neither the nylon carpet nor the butyl rubber pad could have contributed significantly to the fire.

Finally, DeHaan, just like Dale, believed that a number of types of burn damage he saw in the room — burning in corners, under the bed, inside the perimeter of the dresser — could have been produced only by flammable liquids.

In October DeHaan got back to Powell with a telephone call. After spending thirty-eight hours on the case, he had reached his preliminary conclusion. He would have felt comfortable testifying in court even then, he later told the author.

— I think it's an arson fire, — he told Powell.

— Then I guess we're going to go ahead with it, — Powell responded.

Even before hearing DeHaan's opinion, Powell had been developing a certainty about Knapp's guilt that was comparable to the defense lawyers' certainty of his innocence. He did not see how anyone could confess to such a crime if he had not done it. But once Powell talked to DeHaan, there was just no doubt left.

"I mean, that made it so much stronger," Powell said. "I think [DeHaan's] the leading expert in the country — that's why we went and got him."

Accordingly, the state of Arizona would try to put John Knapp to death a third time.

In the ensuing months, DeHaan would learn that many of the premises for his fateful conclusion — that the fire was arson — were verifiably wrong. Like a good scientist, he would, therefore, abandon or revise those premises.

But never his conclusion.

In December 1989, when Powell was asked to head the office's narcotics unit, he had to give up the Knapp case. Since Powell had made slow progress on it while trying to handle a normal caseload, his supervisors decided to assign an attorney who could handle it alone, with no distractions.

Assistant attorney general Susan Sherwin had expressed an interest in switching from the civil liability defense division of the office to the criminal division. She had had experience as a prosecutor in Chicago from 1975 to 1981. They assigned her the case.

Sherwin had wavy light brown hair, glasses, and a far more aggressive style than Powell. She threw herself into her new assignment — her first criminal prosecution in eight years — with great vigor. Without other cases to manage, she made rapid progress.

Sherwin met DeHaan for the first time in January 1990. She was terribly impressed with his expertise and professionalism. In addition, she and DeHaan shared Chicago roots, a love of dogs, and lifetimes devoted to law enforcement. They developed a close professional relationship. He recommended arson-related seminars she could enroll in, and she recommended him as a speaker at law enforcement training seminars and forums.*

In preparing for the Knapp reprosecution, DeHaan and Sherwin began to anticipate the defense contentions that they would have to deflect. Accordingly, DeHaan studied more attentively the transcripts from the 1986 hearing before Judge Gerst.

DeHaan was contemptuous of much of what the defense experts had said.

"A lot of stuff introduced in the [post-conviction relief] hearings was bullshit," he said in 1993. "There's no other word for it. It was there to generate confusion, which it successfully did."

DeHaan considered disreputable the manner in which the defense lawyers had offered testimony about the high flammability of polyurethane furnishings. While DeHaan agreed with the defense experts that a polyurethane mattress pad could have caused a very rapid, intense fire, he was adamant that there could have been no polyurethane in the room.

"They talked and talked about polyurethane," DeHaan said, "what a terrible hazard it is, and how fast it spreads fire, and [so on] — and nobody said, 'And what does that have to do with this case?' Because there was no polyurethane. . . . In my professional ethics, if someone is trying to misuse the

---

* Sherwin declined to be interviewed for this book. She was familiar with a July 1991 magazine article the author had written about the case as it then stood. "I do not believe you intend to be either [fair or accurate]," she wrote in 1994, in response to a letter seeking cooperation. "There are other perspectives on this case other than the blatantly single dimensional one you are pursuing."

Although the main purpose of her letter was to threaten legal action if false information were printed about her, she did note in the letter the intensity of her belief in Knapp's guilt and the source of that belief. "I do emphasize that I am as convinced now of John Henry Knapp's guilt for the murder of his daughters as I have ever been. John DeHaan's 1980s and 1990s research into fire behavior corroborates Mr. Knapp's 1973 confession."

information I'm giving in court, it's my responsibility to make sure that doesn't happen if it's within my power."

Though DeHaan was not himself an expert in fabrics, he eventually spoke with a colleague at the California Bureau of Home Furnishings, who was. DeHaan's understanding of what the expert, Gordon Damant, told him was that polyurethane foam "saw virtually no use" in upholstered materials until about 1973, as DeHaan later testified. Accordingly, DeHaan concluded that the hand-me-down crib mattress in the Knapp children's bedroom in 1973 could not possibly have contained polyurethane.

But when Damant was finally interviewed by the defense lawyers in 1991, he did not corroborate DeHaan's claim. "Polyurethane foam started to be used commercially in bedding products to any extent," Damant told the defense lawyers, "from *approximately the mid-1960s.*"

DeHaan also became convinced that there had been no polyurethane in the room because none of the firefighters and investigators had mentioned seeing any in their reports and because DeHaan himself could not see polyurethane residues in the black-and-white photos of the fire scene or on those scraps of surviving carpet that were still stored in the sheriff's office basement.

But none of the original firefighters or investigators had ever reported *not* seeing polyurethane either. Indeed, there was no evidence that they had ever given the matter any thought in 1973.

"There may well have been polyurethane in [the larger] mattress," Dale had readily conceded at Knapp's first trial in 1974, in response to Diettrich's only question about that — at the time — very peripheral issue.

Nevertheless, DeHaan became confident that there had been no polyurethane in the children's room — and that the defense experts had, therefore, perpetrated a major deceit upon Judge Gerst in 1986. Since DeHaan believed that polyurethane furnishings were the only thing that could have possibly brought the room to flashover within the necessary time frame, other than flammable liquids, he felt that the fraud went to the core of Judge Gerst's ruling.

DeHaan's belief resonated with the prosecutors. Just as they had suspected, Judge Gerst had been snowed by the unprincipled defense lawyers and their hired-gun experts.

The sides were becoming ever more polarized.

In January 1990, thinking that the Knapp case was over, Colin Campbell left Meyer, Hendricks to be sworn in as a superior court judge in Phoenix. Hammond became Knapp's lead lawyer.

Hammond spent the early months of 1990 working on the post-conviction relief hearing for Ray Girdler, the man serving consecutive life terms largely because of the expert testimony of deputy fire marshal David Dale. Hammond and his partner Ed Hendricks assisted Girdler's court-appointed lawyer, Jack Williams, donating all their hours. Together, the trio presented evidence of the new advancements in fire science that cast doubt on Dale's earlier testimony.

Hammond and Hendricks together donated about 2,000 hours to the Girdler case — they normally billed their time then at about $235 an hour — and the firm spent about $77,000 in fees and expenses for expert witnesses. The presiding judge, James Sult, later ordered the county to reimburse the firm for $47,800 worth of those expenses, an extraordinary sum.

In September, Judge Sult — who had himself sentenced Girdler to consecutive life terms back in 1982 — granted Girdler a new trial, and in December he released him. Girdler had been in custody for nine years.

To help the state decide whether or not to reprosecute Girdler, Judge Sult appointed an independent fire expert to examine the exhibits from Girdler's case. In a scathing report, the expert, private consultant, John Lentini of Atlanta, concluded, "There is no credible evidence to suggest that there were any flammable liquids used to accelerate this fire."

At the end of his report, Lentini noted grimly that it was not unusual for him to reach this sort of conclusion when he reviewed fire investigations.

"Fire investigators are engaged in a field of scientific inquiry," he wrote, "yet the vast majority of practitioners have no scientific training. . . . Myths are created and replicated and passed on from one generation to the next. . . . When asked to review another fire investigator's report, I find that I must disagree with the conclusions on approximately 50 percent of the cases."

Girdler was never reprosecuted and is now a free man. Had he not stumbled across lawyers nine years after his conviction who were willing to work for free and, indeed, advance him $77,000 from their own pockets, knowing that a large portion of that sum would never be repaid, he would still be in prison. Had he been sentenced to death in 1982, as prosecutors had urged Judge Sult to do, and had that sentence been expeditiously imposed — as every death-penalty advocate favors — he would be dead.

Still, David Dale remained the chief fire investigator for the state of Arizona. In the law enforcement community, Girdler's release, like Knapp's, was dismissed as just another instance in which crafty lawyers had pulled the wool over a judge's eyes.

David Dale said in 1991, referring to Knapp's new trial and Girdler's release: "It's all balderol" (*sic*).

In April 1990 investigator Debora Schwartz, having done a remarkable job locating witnesses from the 1974 trials, began reinterviewing them. (That their memories were now poor was not critical, since their prior testimony could be introduced at a new trial.)

In that same month DeHaan performed seven full-scale structure fire tests designed to shed light on the Knapp case. Earlier, DeHaan had put out word in the law enforcement community that he was looking for structures in which to perform such tests, and, by April, some had become available. The first three tests were performed in a condemned triplex in Phoenix, and the last four were done in abandoned townhouses in Jefferson Parish, Louisiana, near New Orleans. He furnished each room with items found in thrift shops, attempting in a very general way to approximate the fuel load of the Knapp children's bedroom. At each test site, local fire and law enforcement authorities donated their time, treating the tests as training exercises for their own people.

Basically, DeHaan wanted to compare Coleman fuel (arson) fire scenarios and nonaccelerated (innocently set) scenarios. He set three Coleman fuel fires, and four fires involving no flammable liquids.

In his four innocent-scenario tests — two in Phoenix and two in Jefferson Parish — DeHaan dropped matches on the upper surfaces of various furnishings inside his mock-up bedrooms. In each case, the fires built up very slowly — too slowly to fit the Knapp-fire timeline. Thus, these four tests generally supported DeHaan's theory that the Knapp fire had to have been arson.

Yet, in none of these four tests did DeHaan try lighting the bottom side of a crib mattress that was propped up at an angle — the scenario that mechanical engineer Marshall Smyth had discovered in 1974 could lead to an exceedingly rapid conflagration. Smyth had considered that possibility worth testing because, in the actual Knapp children's bedroom, the burn damage showed that the crib mattress had, indisputably, been leaning up against the crib support in that very odd, dangerous way when the fire started. In addition, Linda had always said that the fire was coming from that crib mattress when she first opened the door to the room. Every room in the Knapp house had been littered with clothing, paper, toys, and other flammable debris, and it seemed logical to assume that the children's room had been no exception. Such debris could have quickly carried a flame under the mattress even if the match had fallen elsewhere.

But DeHaan thought Smyth's scenario too improbable to test.

"I didn't consider it to be a realistic scenario to have a malnourished,* mal-treated three-year-old able to build a bonfire," DeHaan said in 1993. "It's possible to make the fire happen in the way [Larry] Hammond would like to convince the jury it happened. But it requires too many twists. And Sherlock Holmes said, 'You twist the theories to suit the facts, not the facts to suit the theories.'"

When it came to the Coleman fuel fire tests, DeHaan encountered some difficulties with his theory of the fire.

One of the first things DeHaan had to determine was how explosive Coleman fuel was when it was ignited. DeHaan knew that lighting flammable liquid vapors in a closed room created an overpressure situation — a situation that could cause an explosion. In 1974 the state fire experts had all agreed that if Knapp set off a gallon of Coleman fuel in the bedroom, it would have blown out the windows within one to three minutes, if not instantly. They claimed to have performed or seen tests of Coleman fuel supporting their views. Prosecutor Hyder had, therefore, *taken the position* in 1974 that those neighbors who said they had seen John break the window out with the hose, several minutes into the fire, were mistaken.

But DeHaan's review of the photographs of the fire debris had convinced him that the neighbors' and the Knapps' accounts of the fire were *correct*. Based on the relatively contained damage to the eaves outside the window, DeHaan believed that the window could not have failed until "some many minutes" into the fire, as he later testified.

That fact created a major challenge for the state. If the fire was really arson, Knapp had to have set off a large quantity of Coleman fuel in the room without breaking the window out for "some many minutes."

Though DeHaan had set many flammable liquid fires, he had never before set one using Coleman fuel — as opposed to, for instance, gasoline. (Since gasoline is cheaper, few arsonists use Coleman fuel.) As a consequence, DeHaan did not know how explosive it would be. Accordingly, as he began to prepare his first Coleman fuel test fire in one of the bedrooms at the Phoenix triplex — the first fire he set in Phoenix — he wanted to make sure that he did not cause a major explosion.

---

* Although neglected, the Knapp children were, in fact, "well nourished," according to medical examiner Karnitschnig.

"I knew I had to get two more tests out of this building and I didn't want it compromised," he told the author in 1993. "That was a nonreinforced concrete block structure."

To make sure that the room would not blow apart, DeHaan explained, "we blocked the door open by an inch, so it wouldn't close all the way." DeHaan knew from prior experience, he told the author in 1993, that if he left the door open a few inches and ignited a large quantity of Coleman fuel in the room, the overpressure situation would slam the door shut and then overpressure the room — blowing out windows or knocking down walls. So he placed a chock of wood in the doorway. That way the expanding gases could not slam the door shut all the way; the gases would be able to vent out the space left in the doorway, rather than blowing out the window or knocking down walls.

When DeHaan set off about three quarts of fuel in the room with the door artificially propped open in this manner, the walls and ceiling held firm. Though the window bulged outward, it did not immediately break. (It broke after forty-one seconds, when touched by flame, and it fell out seventy-one seconds after ignition.)

That test was quite encouraging to DeHaan. He began to develop the theory that igniting Coleman fuel *on carpeting*, the way he presumed the Knapp fire was set, might lessen the severity of the overpressure situation. Maybe Knapp *could* have set off the fuel without breaking the window out.

He tested that theory further in his second and third Coleman fuel tests, which took place in Jefferson Parish. To protect the safety of the person igniting the fire, he ignited each of these fires remotely, using an electric match, with the door to the room shut from the outset.

In the second Coleman-fuel test — the first of the Jefferson Parish tests — he used only two quarts of Coleman fuel, which was less than half what Knapp said he had used in his confession.

But the test exposed a major problem with DeHaan's theory. Because he did not artificially block the door open this time, the overpressure situation blew the window out immediately upon ignition. Glass shards from the window, which was on the second floor, were blown about thirty feet across a courtyard below.

Despite the carpeting, the overpressure situation was still strong enough to blow the window out. That result contradicted DeHaan's theory of the case, since DeHaan conceded that the window in the Knapp children's bedroom had stayed intact "some many minutes" into the fire.

At that point, DeHaan told the author, he thought to himself, "Well, maybe we had too much fuel. So we did it again with less fuel."

So, for the third Coleman fuel test, DeHaan now dropped down to using a single quart of Coleman fuel — just one-fourth of what Knapp said he had used in his confession — in an attempt to set an accelerated fire without blowing the window out.

"And we blew it out again," DeHaan continued. Indeed, once again, according to his notes, glass ended up as far as thirty feet away.

At that point, having been unable to set off any quantity of Coleman fuel inside a closed room without blowing the window out, DeHaan gave the matter further thought. He decided that *artificially propping the door open with a block of wood* — the way he had managed to get the window to stay intact in Phoenix — *had actually been the best way to perform the test all along.*

"Had I all of the tests to do over again, I would've blocked the doors in Jefferson Parish, too," he maintained.

Why? The Knapp bedroom door had not been artificially propped open with a block of wood.

No, DeHaan explained, but the door in the Knapp house could not slam shut "because someone was standing there dropping the match in the open door. . . . Where's the door going to go? You're in it!"

But this was a very odd new theory. Knapp's confession — as related in both detective Malone's report and testimony — had always left the impression that he had set the fire from outside the room, by tossing a match inside.

"[Knapp] advised," Malone had testified in August 1974, "that . . . he poured the Coleman fuel throughout the [room] . . . returned the Coleman fuel to the hall closet . . . returned back down the hall to the children's bedroom, at which point he struck a match and threw it inside. . . . A large ball of fire came out, and that was how he singed his hair."

And even if Knapp momentarily stood inside the door, wouldn't he — unlike a block of wood — quickly step out of it upon igniting the fire? By DeHaan's estimate, a significant overpressure situation would last anywhere from about one to five seconds after ignition.* Why would Knapp stay inside a room full of flaming Coleman fuel for one to five seconds after ignition? Wouldn't he want

---

* And his estimate may be very conservative. According to the report deputy fire marshal Dale drew up in 1974 concerning his tests at the Mesa Fire Department's training facility, gases were still venting out the door so strongly thirty-eight seconds after ignition that firefighters lacked the strength to close the metal door (which, in that test chamber, opened outward). "The fire and smoke literally whistled out of the door when we attempted to close it," Dale wrote.

to get away as fast as he could, to avoid getting hurt? And once he did, wouldn't the door then slam shut and the window blow out?

"The door was open all the way," DeHaan protested to the author in 1993, defending his theory. "The burn patterns indicated that the person who started the fire was likely inside the room."

But, in all the court proceedings that occurred throughout 1990 and 1991, DeHaan never claimed to be able to tell from burn patterns where the arsonist stood — an improbable feat. And what the burn patterns showed, DeHaan had testified in 1990 and 1991, was that the door had been *closed* or *nearly closed* during the early stages of the fire, and had only been opened later, once the fire was well underway — just as Linda Knapp had always said.

So DeHaan's theory for why the Knapps' window did not break out — because the door was either so wide open that it could not slam, or it was being propped open by the arsonist's body — was *not* based on burn patterns, but on speculation. Further, it was a theory DeHaan had never tested, although it would have been simple to do so. Indeed, it was a theory he had never even postulated until after he had experimented with more logical scenarios and found that he could not keep the window intact that way.

But DeHaan became quite confident about his untested, remedial theory of the fire. After all, the only other possibility was that the fire was not a flammable liquid fire at all.

Eighteen

In Texas, John Knapp lived with his brother Bob and Bob's wife in a three-bedroom house on a residential street in Bay City.

At first, Knapp simply familiarized himself with the everyday, civilian world. After wearing canvas slippers for so long at the Maricopa County jail, it took time to get used to hard shoes again, he told the author in 1991. He liked to take long walks and drives, going nowhere in particular. He learned about new appliances that had not existed when he was jailed, like microwave ovens and videocassette recorders. He was confused by new cultural developments, including two-screened movie theaters, which he, at first, mistook for double features. The most difficult thing, he said, was dealing with actual freedom — not being told what to do every hour of the day.

"He did no dating in Bay City," Bob recalled in 1994. "He didn't have much to do with any women. I think he was probably a little afraid of 'em."

Bob bought John a used Ford Fairmont for about $200 so he could get around, and Knapp began to find sporadic work as a short-term laborer or painter — jobs that required very minimal references.

By late August 1988 John had enough references to land a job doing industrial janitorial work for a contractor on the South Texas Nuclear Project, where Bob worked as an electrical inspector. For $7.40 an hour John helped clean the turbine generator building and other facilities inside the power block.

A secretary there remembered Knapp as clean, well-groomed, "well-mannered," and "a little shy." His supervisor remembered him as a good, reliable worker who never gave him any problems. The supervisor said he knew Knapp had spent time in prison, but thought Knapp had been "cleared" or "pardoned" and that the problem was over for good.

In November, however, after a routine background check, Knapp was denied the security clearance required to work in the more sensitive areas of the plant. Until then, Knapp had been allowed to work in those areas with an escort. But once he was actually denied a badge, Knapp had to be transferred to the "environmental yard."

Because of the sudden transfer, Knapp's co-workers guessed that he had a criminal record of some kind, though only a few clerical workers knew any details. In the environmental yard Knapp did other forms of janitorial work, including filling metal drums with various kinds of hazardous wastes — oily rags, grease, paints, cleaners — tightening the drums, and loading them onto eighteen-wheelers to be taken to disposal sites.

Without a security badge, Knapp's future with the plant was bleak. As construction was being completed, there were fewer and fewer tasks he was authorized to perform.

Knapp was the oldest member of his four-person crew. A co-worker, who was just eighteen at the time, remembers initially thinking of Knapp as a quiet, mild-mannered guy who kept to himself. At lunches when the other workers talked about "girls" or other "guy talk," Knapp did not join in. And when they asked him questions, he rebuffed them.

— None of your business, — Knapp would say, according to this worker, who requested anonymity.

One day while Knapp and he were tightening a drum, the young man asked Knapp a second or third time about some topic Knapp had declined to discuss, possibly women.

Knapp slammed a wrench down on the drum, showing sudden and intense anger.

— I told you, that's none of your business. —

Knapp's outburst frightened the young man, who already knew that Knapp had a record of some kind. He asked to be transferred away from Knapp. Later, he asked a secretary what Knapp's record was, and she gave him some version of it.

"I don't know the full details," the young man recounted in 1994. "It was something about a fire. He burned his house down, and got off on a technicality."

Knapp stopped showing up at the plant in mid-December and never came back. He later told his lawyers that his employer did not give him enough over-time, and one of his co-workers was trying to find out about his past.

In 1991, the author asked Knapp if he had ever discussed the fact that he had been on death row with any of his co-workers.

"No. It's none of their damn business," he had responded, sounding suddenly very angry.

By mid-December, John's brother Bob had gotten a different job, which re-quired him to work in Ft. Worth.

"I wasn't home all week long," Bob recalled. "My wife would come up to see me on weekends. John was kind of left in a situation he wasn't comfortable in."

Sometime around Christmas John loaded up his car with what little belong-ings he had and told Bob's wife he was going to Pennsylvania.

"It was abrupt," Bob said. "I didn't find out about it till after he left."

Knapp drove to a small town outside Pittsburgh, near where he had grown up. At first he lived with his sister Marilyn. Marilyn, who was nineteen months older than John, was divorced and living on welfare.

As always, John was very quiet, Marilyn remembered, and he liked to take long walks. But he did not have a job, did not contribute to rent, and after awhile she "got a little upset with him," she said. "He was in a rut."

After she pushed him to find his own place, he took up residence in a room-ing house, where he had a single room equipped with a bed, dresser, table, hot plate, refrigerator, and a coffee pot. He used a common bathroom in the hall.

In May 1990 he found a job at a plant that made glass for use in lamps and lightbulbs. For the first time since his release, he was living independently and supporting himself.

With the passage of time, Knapp's lawyers sounded ever more optimistic whenever they called. They did not think that he would ever be reprosecuted.

Knapp, however, never believed them. He always knew they'd try him again, he told the author in 1991. He just knew they'd never give up.

On July 25, 1990 — three years and four months after his release — he was walking home when he saw two police cars parked in front of his rooming house.

He walked up to one of them and bent down to the window.

— I'm the one you're looking for, — he told the officers.

Knapp was rearrested and charged with having burned his daughters to death almost seventeen years earlier.

It was "splurge day" toward the end of Larry Hammond's vacation with his family. His children were agog at the splendor and views from the castle where they would be spending the night—a pull-out-all-the-stops, storybook hotel at the top of a mountain in Lucerne, Switzerland.

But there was a message waiting for Hammond at the hotel desk when he registered. He was supposed to call his secretary about an emergency concerning John Knapp.

Was he sick? Had he died?

— John's been arrested, — his secretary told him in the phone call.

— What did he do? —

Hammond thought maybe he had been in a barroom fight or some such thing. The possibility of rearrest for the 1973 fire had not even occurred to him. In February, assistant attorney general Sherwin had written him, "As you have previously requested, I will advise you of any decision on this case when it is made." He also thought Sherwin had promised to let Knapp surrender voluntarily in Phoenix if she planned to go forward.

Sherwin declined to respond to a letter inquiry into whether she ever made such a commitment.

The decision about whether to arrest a defendant or to allow him to surrender voluntarily is a difficult one for prosecutors, and a common source of friction with defense lawyers. But Hammond was furious.

"She had made a commitment to us, and she breached it," Hammond said later. "And she breached it in a way that did irreparable damage to this man's life. I couldn't forgive her, and I never will forgive her."

Relations between Hammond and Sherwin deteriorated.

At his original trials in 1974, John Knapp had had far better representation than most defendants in capital cases. Charles Diettrich had been a virtuoso courtroom lawyer, and David Basham was a diligent and clever young deputy public defender.

Nevertheless, neither Diettrich nor Basham had been standout performers in the area of discovery. Prosecutor Hyder had won those scrimmages hands down.

This time, however, Knapp's representation was being led by an entirely different kind of lawyer.

Because of the uncompromising thoroughness, vigor, and scope of the defense he mounted, Larry Hammond would try the patience not only of opposing counsel, but of partners at his own firm, who were underwriting most of this project, and of the judges of Maricopa County, who came to fear that their indigent defense budget would be bankrupted by Hammond's zeal.

From Hammond's perspective, all he was doing was holding himself to the same standards he observed every day in garden-variety civil litigation for corporate clients.

But that was precisely what the system was unprepared to accommodate. Hammond's attempt to provide competent representation — as he had come to understand the term in the commercial context — to an indigent criminal defendant on trial for his life was viewed as aberrant, bizarre, and subversive.

Larry Hammond was born in Wichita, Kansas, in 1945 to religious Episcopalian parents. His father, a wholesale druggist, and his mother, a music teacher, moved the family to El Paso, Texas, when Hammond was five.

Hammond had a crippling stutter as a child. Nothing the psychologists or speech therapists did seemed to work, and much of it made matters worse. Just being taken out of class to go to the speech therapist was a humiliation.

"It was like carrying a badge around with you that said you were defective," Hammond later recalled.

While his stutter handicapped his school performance, asthma held him back as an athlete. And though he loved baseball, his athletic skills were modest. In contrast to his younger brothers, who were sports standouts on their way to becoming high school football stars, Hammond struggled.

But if Hammond was never destined for stardom as a player, he found that he could still serve baseball in a different capacity — as a fan, historian, statistician, and record keeper.

When he was about nine Hammond was given a spinner-and-dice baseball board game. Hammond prepared shadow lineups for each of the then sixteen major league clubs, mirroring each team's actual player roster as closely as possible. Then, each spring, he set out to play a complete shadow season of the major league baseball schedule — 1,232 games in all. As he played each game, he also *scored* it, using the standardized code by which a fan records for posterity a game's action, inning by inning, batter by batter. (He never achieved his goal of completing an entire season.)

When Hammond went to college at the University of New Mexico, his stutter was still debilitating.

"I just could not convince myself that it was anything other than a sign of intellectual inadequacy," he recounted.

Noticing that the stutter seemed to go away when he spoke in foreign languages, Hammond chose to major in Russian and began contemplating a career in foreign service. But when he transferred to the University of Texas in Austin, which had a more competitive Russian program, the stutter returned.

Hammond became disgusted with himself for having run from his problem. The following year he entered law school at the University of Texas, in part to force himself to confront the handicap head-on. He would sit in the front row, he decided, and he would accept that, when called on, he would have to stand up and stutter in front of a large lecture class. He vowed, however, that no one would mistake his stutter for lack of diligence or aptitude.

"I had note cards for every case," he remembered later, "and I made sure that the note cards were evident — on my desk — so that when I was called on the professor would know that [the stutter] wasn't because I wasn't ready."

Law school, it turned out, captivated him.

"I'd never done really well at anything like that before," he said, "and it sort of fed on itself."

He became editor in chief of the law review, where his research and writing skills were unhampered by his speech problem. Upon graduating he won a clerkship with an eminent federal appellate judge in Washington, D.C., and then applied to become a law clerk at the U.S. Supreme Court — the most prestigious job in the profession for a recent graduate. He applied only to Justice Hugo Black, whose opinions he admired, and who, as the Court's only Southerner, had a reputation for venturing outside Harvard and Yale when selecting clerks.

As it happened, Black also had a penchant for choosing people who labored under a disadvantage of some kind. Hammond's stutter, oddly enough, finally worked in his favor. (His closest rival for the post was a stammering editor in chief of the *Yale Law Journal*.)

Though Justice Black died just four months after Hammond began working for him, his successor, Justice Lewis Powell Jr., kept Hammond on. Then, on January 17, 1972, just ten days after Powell was officially sworn in, he and the other justices heard oral argument in the landmark capital-punishment case of *Furman v. Georgia*.

For Hammond's future partner Jim Scarboro, who was then clerking for Justice Byron White, working at the Court during that period was exhilarating. For Hammond, however, it was excruciating.

Powell, whom Hammond admired greatly, felt strongly that capital punishment was constitutional. Powell was also optimistic that, by writing a convincing draft opinion, he might be able to persuade the two still undecided justices — White and Potter Stewart — to join his camp, which would have created a majority vote broadly upholding all capital-punishment laws. He entrusted to Hammond the task of writing the first draft of that opinion.

But during the course of his research Hammond came to side with those who believed that the penalty was unconstitutional, at least when imposed in the arbitrary way that the discretionary statutes of the time permitted.

"I never told him that I disagreed with him," Hammond admitted in 1993, "and I may have misled him into thinking I was as enthusiastic about this opinion as he was."

More than 600 executions had been held up awaiting the Court's decision, Hammond knew. The opinion he drafted, if joined by Stewart and White, might unleash the greatest legal bloodbath in American history. "The other law clerks around the Court thought the opinion was trash," Hammond later recalled. "There were even a couple who were saying it was disreputable of me to try to help Powell write an opinion on something that might wind up killing people."

On the last Friday of the term, Justice Powell learned that the two wavering justices had rejected his views, creating a five to four majority to strike down virtually all existing capital-punishment laws.

"I think it was one of his lowest moments," Hammond recounted. "He came to share it with me in my office. [But] I could not hide my glee. I don't know what was on my face, but it became clear to him. It hurt him. I think he probably in a second or two replayed three or four months of intensely personal conversations about this. I could have killed myself."

On the following Monday, Powell handed Hammond a sealed letter as he took the bench.

"I thought it would be some sort of termination letter," Hammond recalled. "But it was this very touching thing about . . . what a remarkable thing it was that somebody could work with him when they disagreed as much as I must have. . . . And that nothing would please him more than if I would stay [and be his clerk for another term]. I cried like a baby."

After serving Powell for another full term, Hammond joined the Watergate Special Prosecution Force under Archibald Cox. While John Knapp was being prosecuted in 1974, Hammond was a member of the task force prosecuting former U.S. Attorney General Richard Kleindienst, who was accused of having lied to Congress to cover up wrongdoing by President Nixon.

In late 1974, when special prosecutor Leon Jaworski approved a lenient plea agreement for Kleindienst, Hammond and two colleagues quit. After a friend's wife read about his resignation in the newspaper, the friend invited Hammond to join the tiny, exclusive firm of Martori, Meyer — later Meyer, Hendricks — in Phoenix. Hammond became the firm's tenth lawyer (and fifth former U.S. Supreme Court clerk).

Soon thereafter, while representing the plaintiffs in a school desegregation case, Hammond was called on to speak in a cavernous old courthouse in Tucson. The podium was fitted with a microphone, so the lawyers could be heard throughout. When Hammond heard his voice resounding through the room over the microphone, his stutter magically subsided.

The phenomenon was later repeated when Hammond returned to Washington, D.C., in 1977, for a stint with the U.S. Justice Department's Office of Legal Counsel — the principal source of legal advice for the White House. (There Hammond eventually won the Justice Department's "distinguished service award," the highest honor conferred — one per year is awarded — by the attorney general.) In that job Hammond testified before Congress often, and each time he leaned toward the microphone he found again that his chronic disability vanished. His stutter began to recede in other contexts as well, and when Hammond returned to Meyer, Hendricks in November 1980, he was free to excel as a courtroom lawyer.

Infuriated by Knapp's pretrial incarceration, Hammond wanted to get Knapp freed pending trial as soon as possible. He thought his pretrial detention was abominable, given that Judges Hardy and Gerst had both freed him on his own recognizance, and he had never fled. From Switzerland he arranged for Knapp to waive extradition. The sooner Knapp got to Arizona, the sooner they could get him a bail hearing and try to get him freed.

Still, with administrative hassles, Knapp spent two weeks in custody in Pittsburgh before even being flown to Phoenix. And when Knapp was finally brought to a small courtroom inside the Maricopa County jail for his initial appearance on August 11, the low-level judicial officer who presided did not think he was empowered to set bail for Knapp. According to the Arizona constitution, a defendant is completely ineligible for bail when the "proof is evident and the presumption great" that he has committed a capital offense. Although Hammond thought it was obvious that the proof of Knapp's guilt could not be "evident," since otherwise Judge Gerst would never have overturned his conviction and released him in 1987, the judicial officer ruled that Knapp would have to wait till his case was assigned to a superior court judge before he could make that sort of claim.

So Knapp was back in custody.

In August 1990 Larry Hammond, having returned from Switzerland, began to plan the modern-day defense of John Knapp. To start with, he consulted death-penalty experts and the guidelines published by the American Bar Association advising how to handle capital cases.

"The ABA guidelines on this stuff are very good," Hammond noted in 1993. "And almost nobody has the money to follow them."

Hammond, as Knapp's lead attorney, was appointed by the court. Though Meyer, Hendricks ordinarily billed Hammond's time at $235 per hour, the county would pay him the standard fee for court-appointed attorneys: $45 per hour, later increased to $50 per hour. (That fee was far more generous than that of many jurisdictions, because it was uncapped. In Alabama, for instance, a lawyer in a death-penalty case was limited to $2,000 for all time spent preparing outside court, plus $40 per hour for his actual time in court.)

Because ABA guidelines recommended that at least two attorneys be engaged to defend any capital-punishment case, Hammond applied to have a second appointed. The request was denied.

Reimbursed or not, Hammond would have other attorneys involved on the case. He hoped that one of them would be Tom Henze, one of Phoenix's most accomplished criminal defense lawyers. In late 1989, when Colin Campbell decided to become a judge, Campbell had asked Henze if he would assist Hammond in the event that the Knapp case were ever reprosecuted.

Henze had agreed to do what he could, but the commitment had been vague, and it had been made more than a year earlier. Hammond would have to find out whether Henze was still willing and able — especially since his time might go completely uncompensated.

Hammond also wanted to lure Jon Sands back to the firm from the federal public defender's office, where he had moved in 1987. Sands, the associate who had worked on the successful petition before Judge Gerst, was a friendly, stocky former high school football player, who was hampered as a courtroom lawyer by a pronounced stutter — more noticeable than Hammond's. But he had an easy manner and a self-deprecating sense of humor that were strongly countervailing; jurors liked him, as did his colleagues, court personnel, and even opposing counsel.

Sands agreed to return to the firm in January 1991, in time to work on the case as it approached trial. Though he would then be working full-time on the

Knapp case, the firm would receive no reimbursement for any of his work unless Hammond could eventually win his court appointment.

Sigmund Popko, a young corporate law associate at Meyer, Hendricks, also became a member of the team. An excellent researcher and writer, Popko was slight and boyish in appearance, cautious in speech, and conservatively dressed and groomed. With the Arizona economy mired in a slump, Popko saw that the firm's corporate lawyers were now being conscripted into bankruptcy work, which he preferred to avoid. He had enjoyed interning with a criminal defense lawyer in Tucson one summer, so he volunteered for the Knapp case. All of Popko's time on the case would be uncompensated.

To assist on the written work Hammond called in his markers with his former partner Jim Scarboro. Scarboro now headed the litigation department of the Denver office of Arnold & Porter, a Washington, D.C.–based firm. Scarboro's firm agreed to let three associates in the Washington office work on the case during the pretrial stage. All of their work would be uncompensated.

Hammond's former secretary, Deborah Heller, who was now a paralegal with the firm, would organize and cross-reference documents. Heller, whose services were ordinarily billed out at about $70 per hour, would be paid $20 per hour by the county for her work on the Knapp case. Heller virtually commanded a staff of her own, since she drew on the services of firm librarians, more junior paralegals, photocopiers, and messengers. In addition, Hammond valued Heller's perspectives on strategic matters as well. A slender woman with long, blond hair, Heller was smart and blunt and often saw things with a distance that Hammond knew he could lose when immersed in a case.

Hammond wanted at least three investigators appointed: two to locate and interview witnesses and a third to prepare the so-called mitigation case, which they would have to present if Knapp were ultimately convicted. Mitigation evidence included any evidence — good deeds, military service, a cruel upbringing — that might conceivably persuade a judge* to spare a defendant's life even after he had been found guilty. Hiring a separate investigator to prepare the mitigation case was recommended by the ABA guidelines.

Again, the court refused funds for the purpose, however. In August the court appointed one investigator for all tasks, compensated at $25 per hour.

---

* In Arizona the judge makes the sentencing decision in a capital case. In most death-penalty states, the jury makes the decision.

From the start it was obvious that the biggest expense for Hammond's firm would be the fire experts. This time Hammond would perform full-scale fire tests. As Hammond saw it, Knapp had been sentenced to death in 1974 because he had been unable to afford full-scale tests. No matter what they cost, Hammond was doing them this time. He was optimistic, however, that he could persuade the court to reimburse a hefty portion of these costs.

In August Knapp's case was assigned to superior court judge William Moroney, who scheduled a preliminary hearing for August 24. The preliminary hearing and the bail hearing were going to have very similar purposes; in each case the state had to show that it possessed enough evidence to meet certain minimum threshold standards. For the preliminary hearing (which is required in all Arizona felony prosecutions that have not been initiated by grand jury indictment) the state had to show that it had "probable cause" to believe that Knapp was guilty. At the bail hearing, in which the state was trying to prove that Knapp was ineligible for bail, it had to meet a higher standard, establishing that the "presumption" was "great" that Knapp was guilty. Judge Moroney put off the bail hearing until after the preliminary hearing.

On August 17, in an effort to support her position that the "presumption" was "great" that Knapp was guilty, prosecutor Sherwin filed papers in which she argued that Judge Gerst's 1987 ruling was an "aberration" and that the case against Knapp was overwhelming.

Hammond, who was flying to Dallas that day for another case, took Sherwin's papers to read on the plane.

"I remember being utterly mesmerized by this document," Hammond later recounted, "and landing in Dallas and believing that I had just taken off."

The document provided Hammond with his first glimpse of what the state's new, improved case against John Henry Knapp would look like.

Appended to Sherwin's papers was a thirty-four-page "summary of interviews" prepared by investigator Schwartz. It contained short, adversarial encapsulations of what sixty-six witnesses would allegedly say if called to testify, or of what they had said in prior testimony.

The document contained dozens of curious new odds and ends, but two dwarfed all the others. One was highlighted in Sherwin's memorandum, while the other went unmentioned, and was buried in the appended summary by Schwartz.

What was highlighted was new evidence from Louise Ramsey's friend

Melba Burr. Burr had been interviewed at least three times by Hyder's investigator Elardo and once by Hyder himself in 1974. Hyder had then called her as a witness at each of the 1974 trials, where she gave very damaging testimony about Knapp's suspicious behavior on the afternoon of the fire. To both Hyder and Elardo she had described driving Knapp to the dentist's, to the insurance office, and then home again. Knapp had been so angry when he left the insurance office, she told Elardo in July 1974, that he had "bitched" all the way home.

But now, seventeen years after the event, she remembered it differently, according to Sherwin and Schwartz's document. After leaving the insurance office, *Knapp had confessed*.

According to the document:

> Knapp shouted at her, "They won't pay me one dime for the girls, not one dime for the house, not one dime for the carpeting. Can you believe it? I killed them for nothing!" When [Burr] demanded to know what he meant, Knapp told her he had killed the children so that Linda would not leave him and take the children to Nebraska to stay with her father. Melba Burr said she kicked Knapp out of the car at Frank's Friendly Tavern and proceeded directly to the Tempe Police Department on 5th Street. She said she was hysterical and told the desk officer to go arrest Knapp at Frank's Friendly Tavern because he had just killed his two children. She said the police did not take her seriously.

How could Burr have failed to tell Hyder or his investigator about this confession? If she had told them, how could Hyder have failed to use it? How could the Tempe police department have ignored a woman who was telling them about a confession to a double murder connected to a highly publicized tragic fire that had occurred just that morning a few miles away? How could Burr have failed to tell the Ramseys or anyone else about this confession at the time? How could she have blithely continued dropping by the Ramseys' house, where John Knapp lived after the fire during the next eleven days before his arrest, if Knapp had confessed to her?

Hammond was chagrined that a professional prosecutor would offer this confession — which could only be fantasy or perjury — in a capital case. How could any rational adult credit such a thing?

Yet Sherwin was using this new evidence as one of the bulwarks of her claim that the prosecution's case was overwhelming, that Judge Gerst's release of Knapp in 1987 had been an "aberration," and that Knapp was, therefore, ineligible for bail.

The other oddity in the document Hammond discounted the first time he came across it; the passage seemed to be some sort of mistake. The document said that the fingerprints on two of the Coleman fuel cans were identifiable.

That was wrong, Hammond thought. The fingerprints were *smudged*. The experts could tell that they were adult prints — that's one of the reasons the children could be eliminated — but they could not tell which adult they belonged to. That had been one of the few undisputed parts of the case over the first seventeen years of its history. Hammond scribbled, "How can this be?" in the margin of his copy.

But Hammond later read the document again more carefully. The document definitely meant to say what it said. And there was more.

The fingerprints were actually smudged on only one of the cans — the can that had stood next to the door. That was the least significant can, because it was full; it, therefore, could not have been the can used to set the fire.

The prints on the other two other cans, however — the half-full can from the bookshelf and the empty can from the closet — were identifiable!

The can from the closet was the can Knapp said he had used to set the fire in his confession. That can was, in fact, *covered* with identifiable prints. *Eleven identifiable lifts* — each consisting of one or more prints — had been taken from various surfaces of that can back in 1973.

In June 1990 a fingerprint expert from the Department of Public Safety had run comparisons on the identifiable prints from the alleged murder weapon and from the half-filled can from the bookshelf.

A few prints did not belong to either John or Linda; they presumably belonged to a firefighter or deputy sheriff or storekeeper who had handled the can.

The rest of the prints were Linda's.

None were John's.

"I was wondering, what is this all about?" Hammond recalled in 1993.

There was a tantalizing mystery here. How had it come about that the jury that convicted John Knapp believed that the prints on the alleged murder weapon were smudged, when, in fact, they were identifiable — and Linda's?

To begin to track down the answers, Hammond, associate Zig Popko, and paralegal Deb Heller would have to scour the record from the very beginning. When had the false story arisen? How had it been preserved?

Nineteen

Judge Moroney started the preliminary hearing on August 24, but after three days of hearings he adjourned for two weeks to take a long-scheduled vacation.

By this time Knapp had already been incarcerated thirty-seven days without a bail hearing. Hammond asked the presiding judge, Ronald Reinstein, to find another judge to hold a bail hearing immediately.

Judge Reinstein refused.

"While it is not the defendant's fault that the judge is on vacation," Judge Reinstein said, "that is just kind of the way it is."

Hammond threw his pen down on the counsel table in anger and frustration.

— Calm down, Larry, — Knapp quietly told Hammond at counsel table, with a nervous laugh. — It's no big deal. It's just another ruling. —

Later that evening when Hammond got back to his office, his secretary, Mary Unkefer, told him that she had gotten a rare call from the jail from John Knapp. Unkefer had been puzzled by Knapp's message.

— He just wanted me to tell you not to worry, and not to take things so hard, — she told Hammond.

Hammond appealed Judge Reinstein's ruling and, eventually, won. On September 18 — by which time Knapp had served fifty-six days in custody — the supreme court ordered that a bail hearing begin within forty-eight hours. But by then Judge Moroney had already completed his vacation. He converted the hearing into a joint bail and preliminary hearing, and Knapp remained in custody.

When Hammond showed up for the third day of the preliminary hearing on August 29, he noticed a tall, paunchy, youthful-looking man sitting in the first row of the gallery. It was Sherwin's next witness, John DeHaan.

During the 1986 hearing before Judge Gerst, when Hammond had often cited John DeHaan's revised edition of *Kirk's Fire Investigation* as an authoritative source, he had never actually met DeHaan. At that time he had imagined him to be everything he felt deputy fire marshal Dale was not. Even his name — European and exotic — contrasted sharply with Dale's simple, banal American one. While Hammond saw Dale as something approaching a snake-oil salesman, he imagined DeHaan to be the quintessential scientist: neutral, meticulous, cautious. Hammond's assumptions extended to a sillier realm as well. Since Dale was tall and vigorous, he imagined DeHaan as correspondingly short, frail, and professorial. Perhaps DeHaan would have a foreign accent.

Above all, DeHaan would be the genuine article. In short, Hammond had rested exactly the sort of consummate faith in DeHaan that prosecutor Hyder had rested in Dale.

While meeting the man instantly punctured Hammond's silly assumptions about DeHaan's physical appearance, his other assumptions endured longer.

Sherwin's direct examination of DeHaan filled three half-days of testimony — Moroney was spending the other half of the day on other matters — ending on Friday, September 14.

In certain respects it was apparent to Hammond that, as he had suspected, some of DeHaan's opinions were based on simple misunderstandings of the facts that would be easy for Hammond to set right. DeHaan's opinion, for instance, that flashover had probably not occurred in the Knapp bedroom, was based in part on a large triangular area of undamaged carpet in the center of the bedroom. Hammond could see that the prosecutors simply had not explained to DeHaan that the drawers from the dresser had been pulled out into the center of the room, where they had protected the spot in question.

Yet, in other respects, DeHaan's testimony was surprisingly close to Dale's.

"Nylon doesn't burn all that well," DeHaan testified confidently, "and the jute backing with latex coating . . . is also fairly fire resistant. The pad underneath is an additional barrier against the flame spread because the butyl latex rubber . . . does not support combustion."

Because DeHaan insisted that the carpet and pad were resistant to fire, he also believed that the deep burning in the Knapp bedroom, through both that carpet and pad and down into the floor, showed that flammable liquid fuel must have been poured on the carpet in those locations.

"The only kind of localized fuel," he testified, "that will produce a burn through the carpet and through that kind of pad that I've been able to duplicate is with a flammable liquid."

DeHaan's phrase was terribly powerful, since it sounded as if his conclusion was based on empirical testing. But DeHaan never stated precisely when or where he had successfully "duplicated" such burn damage using flammable liquids. Nor did he explain the precise conditions under which he had attempted to duplicate such damage without flammable liquid, but had been unable to do so.

Whatever DeHaan's database, he continued to draw on it with impressive authority. DeHaan saw many burn patterns in the room that could *only* have been caused by flammable liquids. The burning in the corners was a "feature that I have only been able to produce by [using] flammable liquid." Similarly, the burning inside the perimeter of the dresser was "almost certainly" produced by accelerant, DeHaan testified. "The only way I've been able to produce that kind of damage is by adding an accelerant."

Although DeHaan described briefly the seven full-scale tests he had performed, Sherwin did not want to display or turn over to the defense the videotapes of those tests at this early stage of the case. But, at Hammond's insistence, and with Judge Moroney sympathetic to Hammond's demand, she ultimately agreed to bring the ten hours of videotapes on Monday morning, September 17, when Hammond began his cross-examination.

For the first morning of Hammond's cross-examination, still never having seen those tapes, Hammond tried to tie DeHaan down about his theories of the fire.

"I've always been a believer in the importance of fixed targets," Hammond later explained. If he knew what the state's theory was, he had something he could test and disprove.

He asked, for instance, just how much flammable liquid DeHaan thought Knapp had used.

But DeHaan was vague.

"A considerable quantity," he said.

Hammond asked him what that meant.

"Well, anywhere from, say, three ounces to as much as a gallon."

Though DeHaan was certain that flammable liquid had been used, he could not say whether it was three ounces or 128 ounces!

Still, Hammond continued to regard DeHaan as the august authority he had always thought him to be through the first two mornings of his cross-examination. But then, when the proceeding was interrupted for a week, to accommodate DeHaan's schedule, Hammond finally had an opportunity to pore over the ten hours of videotapes of DeHaan's seven fire tests.

"He is somebody different than I thought he was," Hammond later recounted.

Hammond was viewing DeHaan's work against the backdrop of all the fire tests he had seen performed in the Knapp and Girdler cases. His own expert, mechanical engineer Marshall Smyth, had driven Hammond to distraction in the Girdler case by insisting on identifying the precise composition of each and every combustible object that had been present at that fire scene. Similarly, the videotaped burn tests run by the Center for Fire Research and other research organizations had all been painstakingly planned, instrumented, and documented so as to generate scientifically useful results.

DeHaan's seven tests, by contrast, were appalling.

"I kept thinking," Hammond recounted later, "maybe somebody else did these and [DeHaan] just came in at the last second."

There had been no serious attempt to match the composition of any of the furnishings of the test rooms to what had been present in the Knapp children's bedroom. The precise furnishings differed from test to test, and in most of them the beds, dressers, mattresses, stools, carpet pads — and in some cases a wall or floor — were made of materials that were obviously different from those that had been in the Knapp children's bedroom. None of the crib mattresses — if they existed at all — were innerspring mattresses; none were constructed of sisal or anything similar. Most or all of the furnishings picked up from thrift shops had presumably been treated with fire retardants — required by the government since 1974 — which would not have been present in the Knapp furnishings.

The dimensions of the rooms were wrong, as were the arrangements of the furnishings within the rooms. In the four Jefferson Parish tests, the rooms were about 70 percent larger than the Knapp children's bedroom.

"How hard would it have been to put up a piece of Sheetrock [to get the dimensions right]?" Hammond later recalled wondering. "My brother and I could have done it in an hour and a half."

Knapp's defense, ever since Smyth performed his fourth mattress test in August 1974, had always hinged on the flammability of the carpet in the children's room. Yet the carpet had received only slightly more attention in DeHaan's tests than had any of the other furnishings. Though DeHaan had found carpets that were nylon with jute backing, like the Knapp carpet, DeHaan had done no empirical tests to ensure that those carpets had burning properties that were comparable to those of the actual Knapp carpet. Nylon carpets had been manufactured in myriad ways over the seventeen years since the Knapp fire, using different weaves, piles, weights, styles, adhesives, and dyes.

Hammond later asked DeHaan, when cross-examination resumed, how he had determined that the test carpets had burning properties that were comparable to those of the Knapp carpet.

"I conducted a visual comparison," DeHaan responded, "and estimated that it was suitably similar — that the fire's behavior would be expected to be parallel."

He had just looked at it!

"This is a joke," Hammond thought, as his new image of DeHaan gradually came into focus. "For these people to be calling themselves scientists? In a death case?"

From Hammond's perspective the cruel kicker was that none of DeHaan's seven tests could have possibly satisfied the standard that Judge Hardy had applied in October 1974, when he excluded Marshall Smyth's four mattress tests from evidence at Knapp's second trial.

Knapp spent twelve years on death row because Judge Hardy thought Smyth's low-ceilinged tests had not sufficiently replicated the conditions of the Knapp bedroom. Yet Smyth had tested the *actual* Knapp carpet, the *actual* carpet pad, and four different versions of vinyl-covered, sisal-stuffed, innerspring-constructed crib mattresses that were the closest anyone could come to recreating the actual mattress then or now. Three of these mattresses had been propped up at precisely the right angle against wood crib supports that had been specially built to duplicate the one in the children's room. Smyth had then burned these materials in chambers composed of Sheetrock — the same material as the walls of the Knapp children's bedroom.

Now, sixteen years later, the state was trying to put Knapp back on death row using seven new tests — performed in chambers of the wrong size filled with furnishings of the wrong materials.

The only thing that was truly clear to Hammond about DeHaan's seven tests was that they did not form anything like an empirical basis for DeHaan's authoritative interpretations of the burn damage in the Knapp children's bedroom. And if DeHaan's testimony had *not* been based on these seven tests, then what was it based on — the 200 to 250 tests he said he had performed earlier in his career? But if these seven conscious attempts to recreate the Knapp children's room had rendered such scientifically useless results, how much pertinent information could those earlier tests have really yielded?

Hammond would have to try to pin DeHaan down during cross-examination about the precise nature of those 200 to 250 prior tests.

On the morning of September 28, however, when the hearing resumed, Judge Moroney announced that he was limiting Hammond's cross-examination to the rest of the day. Moroney felt the hearing was getting out of hand.

Using the time he had left, Hammond spent the morning trying to learn the basic details about DeHaan's seven tests. But the task proved disconcertingly difficult. DeHaan had, for instance, never measured or recorded precisely how much Coleman fuel he used in his accelerated tests. In one case, where an assistant's notes indicated that DeHaan had used a half gallon, DeHaan testified that that was merely the assistant's "working assumption" and that DeHaan recalled the amount as having been closer to three quarts. DeHaan himself had made no record of the amount used.

Hammond also wanted to see the burn patterns left on the floor after DeHaan's Coleman fuel test fires. During his direct testimony, DeHaan had testified, "The only kind of localized fuel that will produce a burn through the carpet and through that kind of pad that I've been able to duplicate is with a flammable liquid." But if DeHaan had, in fact, "duplicated" any such burns, Hammond could not find any photographs of them among those that Sherwin had turned over to him.

And what seemed especially suspicious to Hammond was that, in the two Coleman fuel tests in Jefferson Parish, the fuel had been poured in conspicuous Y and X patterns, as if DeHaan had planned to go back afterward and look for burn damage conforming to those shapes. If DeHaan had tried to create flammable liquid runs on the floor *and failed*, that was important evidence favorable to Knapp.

For seventeen years now, Hammond thought, experts had been opining that flammable liquid, when poured on carpet and pad, would burn through both and leave flammable liquid burn patterns on the floor below. But Smyth had not been able to do it in 1974, and it was beginning to look to Hammond as if DeHaan, in 1990, had not been able to do it either.

"When am I [actually] going to see a burn pattern?" Hammond wondered.

DeHaan did not know whether there had been any burn patterns left on the floor after his first Coleman fuel test — the one in Phoenix — since he had never removed the carpet and pad from that room.

What about the second Coleman fuel test — the first of the two done in Jefferson Parish?

DeHaan testified that he "noted a good correlation between the damage to the carpet and where I saw [a colleague] pour the fuel."

"What about damage to the floor underneath?" Hammond asked. "Did you do a comparison of the damage to the floor where the Coleman fuel had been poured?"

"I noted where the carpet had failed and where the padding beneath it had been involved. And I noted a correlation between that and the distribution of the fuel, yes."

Was this one of DeHaan's "off-target" responses? DeHaan had not answered the question. Hammond was not asking about the carpet or pad; he wanted to know about the *floor* — beneath the carpet and pad. Deputy fire marshal Dale had stressed the "tell-tale" burn patterns on the *floor*.

Hammond started over from the top.

"You took out the carpet and the pad after the fire was over, is that correct?"

"Yes."

"Did you then go back in and look for burn patterns on the floor?"

"I did not. I asked that the burn patterns, if any, be photographed."

"And were they?"

"I believe they were, yes."

"And did you compare those burn patterns on the floor with the areas where the Coleman fuel had been spread?"

"Yes, I did."

"And what did you find?"

"I found that there was generally good correlation."

"What do you mean by generally good correlation?"

"From what I could tell . . . it was good agreement between where the . . . most significant damage *ended up on the carpet and pad* to the distribution of that fuel."

Somewhere along the line, wittingly or unwittingly, DeHaan had started giving off-target answers again. He was talking about the *carpet*, not the *floor*.

"I was asking you about the *floor* inside," Hammond persisted.

"Oh, I'm sorry. *I don't remember. It's been awhile since I've seen the photographs of the floor or documentation of it.*"

Well, what about the last of DeHaan's three Coleman fuel burns? That fire had lasted sixteen minutes — just about exactly what DeHaan estimated to have been the length of the Knapp fire. The fuel had been poured in a very pronounced X pattern.

"Was the floor examined after the carpet was removed?" Hammond asked. "It was, but not by me," DeHaan responded. "*I don't know the results.*"

Hammond emerged from his cross-examination of DeHaan personally chastened. He had cited DeHaan's book as authority at numerous court appearances in the past without ever having had the slightest understanding of who DeHaan really was.

DeHaan, for his part, left the preliminary hearing assessing Hammond as "very well-prepared" and "very smart," he told the author, and "methodical almost to the point where it may be a liability."

And, like a chess master praising a worthy opponent, DeHaan spoke admiringly of Hammond's failure to fall for one of DeHaan's intentionally "off-target" answers. (DeHaan could not recall which answer it was.) "I started this with Hammond in the preliminary hearing," DeHaan recalled, referring to his technique of giving off-target answers. "[Hammond] walked over [to a spot where] the judge couldn't see him, and just went" — making a face — "meaning he knew exactly what I was going to try to do and it wasn't going to work with him," DeHaan recalled, laughing broadly. "So I went back to straight answers."

Hammond said he had no recollection of the incident.

Twenty

Although DeHaan's testimony dominated the lengthy hearing, Judge Moroney ended up according little weight to it. Expressing despair about how any judge could determine whether "proof" was "evident" without conducting a full trial, Judge Moroney decided in early October that Knapp's confession provided both proof evident and probable cause to believe Knapp was guilty.

Accordingly, Knapp would have to undergo a third trial, and he would have to wait for it in jail.

Knapp was formally arraigned on murder charges on October 15. That event triggered assistant attorney general Sherwin's obligation to turn over discovery materials to the defense. She made two major productions of documents within the next two weeks.

On the afternoon after a messenger picked up the second batch of materials from the attorney general's office, Hammond thumbed through the bulging red accordion-style folder before heading home for the day. He picked up a cassette tape labeled "Knapp T-Tape, 11/28/73" and took it with him. As he turned left out of the parking garage and headed home, he fed the cassette into the dashboard tape player and punched "play."

A man was placing a long-distance collect call to a number in the 402 area code. Then that man handed the phone over to a second man.

"Deanna, is Linda there?"

It was the voice of John Knapp — only seventeen years younger.

Hammond pulled to the side of the road.

Deanna went to get Linda.

"What?" said Linda, when she took the phone.

"Hello, honey."

"Don't call me that."

"Hey, dear."

"What?"

"I didn't do it."

"Yeah, I'll bet you didn't. Then why in the hell did you say so?"

"I thought they was going to get you, baby. That's the only reason. That and I had a splitting-ass headache last night and they would give me no medicine whatsoever to take care of it. And I started pounding the walls."

It was the phone call to Linda that Knapp always claimed he had placed from jail on the evening after his arrest. He had really done so — and it had been taped!

"You even told them how you did it," Linda protested.

"They supplied that for me. . . . I swear by the grace of God, I did not do it. . . . My [headache] medicine was at Mom's* house and I could not get it."

The conversation ended with John begging Linda for a kiss, which she would not give.

"Okay. Be that way then," John says. "Good-bye, honey."

Linda had remembered this conversation only sketchily each time she testified in 1974. And Linda's credibility had been poor, since the state was taking the position that she was probably lying to protect John — though it never specified which issues she was allegedly lying about. When she described this conversation at the suppression hearing in front of Judge Hardy in 1974, prosecutor Hyder cross-examined her about it, seemingly implying that she might be mistaken in her recollection about when this conversation had occurred.

But Hyder knew exactly when it had occurred; he had a tape of it.

Hyder had argued in 1974 that Knapp's justifications for his confession — that he was protecting Linda at a time when he was under the stress of a severe headache — were fabrications he made up after the fact. He stressed that Knapp never told Linda's stepfather, Ken Ramsey, either of those reasons for

---

* Knapp called his mother-in-law, Louise Ramsey, "Mom."

having confessed when he spoke to him minutes after the confession on the morning of November 28, 1973. If he had really confessed for those reasons, wouldn't he have said so to the first "friendly face" he saw? Hyder had argued. The Arizona supreme court had expressly cited that argument as persuasive in its ruling affirming Knapp's conviction.

But Knapp *had* promptly explained his reasons for confessing — later that same day. He had just done so to someone he loved rather than to someone he hated. And he had done so *on tape*.

Why had Diettrich never introduced this tape at the suppression hearing back in 1974? Why had he never played it for Linda so she could refresh her recollection about the details of the conversation when she testified at trial? Why had he never used it to rebut Hyder's argument? And why wasn't the tape in the defense files Hammond had inherited in 1981?

Under the discovery rules, Hyder had to turn over such a tape to the defense. Had he?

Hammond was still just scratching the surface. As he and Zig Popko and Debbie Heller methodically examined the discovery documents, they found notes of about two dozen interviews of witnesses that had been performed by the state in 1974 that they had never seen before. Most of these had not been discoverable in 1974, for various technical reasons, but several should have been turned over. Had Hyder done so? Basham had repeatedly complained at trial about not having been provided certain witness statements — but he had never clearly demanded them either. Had Hyder withheld them on the basis of one of the many aggressive *positions* he had *taken* concerning his discovery obligations? Had Basham failed adequately to take all steps he could have to demand these documents?

One report — which unquestionably should have been turned over — stood out above all others: the witness statement from Louise Ramsey's friend Melba Burr, the garrulous prosecution witness who had described Knapp's callous actions on the afternoon after the fire with such damaging verve and spin.

After handling the case for nine years, the Meyer, Hendricks lawyers now read, for the first time, Elardo's report of his interview with Melba Burr.

Melba was asked if she ever saw the Knapp children playing with or striking matches. Melba said yes, that she had on four or five different occasions. . . . The eldest girl, Linda, would strike the match and then ignite the rest of the book of matches and then discard the matches.

This was Brady material pure and simple — evidence suggesting that the defendant might be innocent. Why hadn't it been in the defense file they inherited in 1981? Why had neither 1974 jury ever heard about it?

That fall, while Hammond kept stumbling across puzzle pieces he never realized were missing, there was one large piece he had been hunting for all along but still could not find. He wanted to hear the tapes of the five- to eight-hour interrogation of Linda Knapp that had taken place in Fremont, Nebraska, on December 1, 1973. But the state had provided only three hours of tapes for that interrogation, and those were almost totally inaudible. Two to five more hours of tapes appeared to be missing.

At the same time, Hammond was trying to figure out the significance of a baffling videotape that Sherwin had provided. It was labeled "4/2/74 Knapp Case Fire Assim." Had the state performed a fire simulation or test in April 1974? If so, such a test had never been disclosed before.

And when Hammond played the videotape, there was nothing on it that corresponded to the label. Instead, there was just a copy of defense expert Smyth's fourth mattress test — with a strange, barely audible audio track. It was a jazz radio program.

What the hell was this?

Hammond assumed that Sherwin must have sent over the wrong item. But when he asked her about it, she assured him that the original, from which she had made Hammond's copy, showed the same thing.

— It seems like they might have taped over it at some point, — Sherwin said.

In the ensuing months, with the assistance of investigator Mary Durand and an electronics expert — hired at a cost to Hammond's firm of $10,000 — Hammond dogged Hyder's trail as relentlessly as Hyder had once pursued Knapp's. He brought to bear on the Knapp case a lesson he had learned from a mentor at his first job in law practice, as a Watergate special prosecutor.

"When you find fraud or wrongdoing in an organization," Hammond said, "there's no such thing as diminishing returns. Keep looking. You will always be rewarded."

From electronic analysis of the surviving Linda Knapp interrogation tapes Hammond learned that those tapes were most likely copies, not originals, and that the pattern of electronic "start" and "stop" marks encoded in these tapes indicated that deletions had been made.* Where were the originals? What had been deleted?

Hammond also unraveled much of the history of the long-suppressed April 2, 1974, "Fire Assim." videotape. Sheriff's office records and logs indicated that Hyder had had the tape made in April 1974; that it had been checked into the property room the same day; that it had been checked out of the evidence room and returned by Hyder's assistants three times in August 1974 during the first trial; and that it had been checked out for the last time at 4:40 P.M., on August 22, 1974. Then, at 7:50 P.M. the same night, Hyder or his technician made a copy of Marshall Smyth's fourth mattress test on that same videotape, obliterating whatever lay beneath.† (The tape appears to have been erased first, according to Hammond's electronics expert, and the new material recorded on top of the erasure.) After obliterating a marked and vouchered piece of evidence — either accidentally or otherwise — Hyder did not have the tape promptly returned to the property custodian, as he had on the three earlier occasions he had checked it out. Nor does he appear to have notified the property custodian of any accidental erasure or obliteration. Rather, Hyder kept the altered tape for months, according to the custodian's logs. Only after the second trial ended did Hyder's technician return it. When he did so, he made no notation on the tape's label, nor on its box, nor in the evidence room log, to reflect that the contents of this piece of evidence had been obliterated or erased, accidentally or otherwise.

The mysteries were mounting up, and, as Hammond saw it, there was a consistent drift to all of them.

Both juries in 1974 had been given false information about the fingerprints, and the key fingerprint analysis reports that would have revealed the truth were not to be found in Meyer, Hendricks's files — until 1990.

Neither jury in 1974 was told that Melba Burr claimed to have seen Little

---

* There were a series of "start" marks with no "stop" marks between them; the tape had, therefore, been stopped, wound backwards, and then started again prior to the previous stop, recording over and obliterating previously recorded material, including the earlier stop mark.

† When Smyth's test was recorded onto the tape, the video recorder inadvertently picked up the signal then being transmitted from a powerful radio antenna from the top of a hotel just six blocks north of the sheriff's annex. That station was broadcasting a jazz radio program, and the disk jockey happened to inform listeners of the date and time. Thus, it was possible to determine the exact moment when the taping had occurred.

Linda light matches four or five times, and the document that would have revealed that fact was not in the law firm's files — until 1990.

Neither jury (nor Judge Hardy at the suppression hearing) heard about Knapp's taped phone call to Linda from jail, and the tape wasn't in the firm's files — until 1990.

Neither jury heard about a videotaped fire test that Hyder and Dale had conducted on April 2, 1974, and no documents concerning such a test were in the firm's files — until 1990.*

The case was beginning to emit an odor.

"At some point in time," Tom Henze recalled in 1994, "this [case] began to focus on Chuck Hyder. It caused me what I would phrase as a personal/professional dilemma."

Henze was the veteran criminal lawyer who had told Colin Campbell that he would help Hammond if the Knapp case were ever resurrected. He had been honoring his commitment ever since Knapp's rearrest.

But Henze was a long-time close personal friend of Hyder's. Henze had worked alongside Hyder at the county attorney's office in the mid-1970s and had later served as a pallbearer at the funeral of Hyder's wife, who had committed suicide while suffering from a terminal disease.

"In my friendship with Chuck," Henze continued, "I believe that he was a warm-hearted, caring man. In my personal relationships with Chuck I found him to be all those things you would want a friend to be.

"I don't think Chuck would tolerate — my opinion was that he wouldn't tolerate impropriety," Henze said, beginning to speak more haltingly. "The problem here is, is that — it begins to — I'm talking about it on a theoretical plane. It begins to break down when different people have different opinions about what's allowed and not allowed. Where do you cross the line between hard-hitting and aggressive prosecution and improper prosecution tactics?"

Henze was never convinced that Hyder committed deliberate wrongdoing during the 1974 Knapp trials, he told the author in 1994.

---

* As discussed in chapter 5, the defense may have been provided a *written* report concerning this test, if Dale's report of "February 20, 1974" — purporting to document a test that occurred on "November 27, 1973" — was in reality a misdated or backdated report about this April 2, 1974 test. (There is independent corroboration from fire department logs that a test really occurred at the Mesa Fire Department's training facility on April 2, 1974. There is no independent corroboration for such a test on November 27, 1973.)

"I think the evidence showed that things were withheld," Henze said, "and that tape recordings or videotapes were erased, and recorded over, and that it was awfully coincidental that those things seemed [like they] could've been helpful to John. On the other hand, can I sit here today and say that I know that that was a deliberate act on anybody's part? No, I can't do that."

Henze did know, however, that he lacked objectivity. And he could see what the evidence looked like to others, including Hammond.

"I remember feeling, 'This does not look good for Chuck [Hyder],'" he said. "We suffered no disagreements about what your duties are when you see that. You bring it to the court's attention."

Hammond began contemplating a motion to dismiss the case based on Hyder's alleged misconduct at the original trials.

"Throughout this question of misconduct," Hammond remembered, "I had a conscience constantly on my shoulder: Henze. I don't know if it's just because Henze's an excellent trial lawyer or because of his prior association with Hyder, or because of his need to continue to have a relationship with these people, but Henze was always a very gentlemanly Doubting Thomas. . . . I remember Henze telling me, 'Well, before you assume that Diettrich and Basham didn't have this stuff you better sit down and ask them.'"

Finding Diettrich was never easy. His home was still his rustic cabin in the high desert near Payson, and his phone was often disconnected. His problems had never cleared up. In February 1988 he had been reinstated to the bar on the condition that he stay off drugs and alcohol. But less than three months later Diettrich had refused to submit to a drug test. A few days later he submitted to one, but failed it. He was suspended again and eventually disbarred for a second time in September 1989.

By early January 1991 Hammond had managed to set up an afternoon conference with him at the Meyer, Hendricks office. With Henze's warnings on his mind, Hammond tried to maintain a neutral tone as he asked Diettrich to listen to a tape they had received.

He then played Diettrich the tape of John Knapp calling Linda Knapp from jail.

Hearing John's voice undid Diettrich, as Hammond later recalled it. Diettrich broke down and wept again.

— I've never heard that before, — Diettrich said. — I never knew it was taped. —

Hammond let Diettrich go for the evening, so he could compose himself.

The next morning Hammond put him in the small conference room down the hall from his office and gave him the stack of witness interview reports Hyder's investigator Elardo had made in 1974.

— I'd like you to read these and then tell me which ones you can remember seeing before, — Hammond said.

Later that day Diettrich came to Hammond's door gripping the report from Elardo's interview of Melba Burr. He was agitated, emotional, spewing out his words. Next to the portion concerning Little Linda lighting matches, he had scrawled a star in the margin.

— There's no way, — he said. — If I had ever seen this, I would've used it. Talk to Basham! He'll tell you the same thing. —

Diettrich then told Hammond essentially what he later related to the author: "Dave [Basham] and I personally canvassed the neighborhood. We went door-to-door. That, to me, was the key to the case. If I could have found a neighbor that could've really enlivened our theory that the children started the fire. The prosecution's theory was: These children were too young to start a fire. They were at a borderline age. It really hurt not having that evidence. I would've given anything for this evidence. That was our theory. And all the time it was sitting there in a typed report in Hyder's office!"

Eventually, as he prepared to file his motion to dismiss due to alleged prosecutorial misconduct by Hyder, Hammond obtained affidavits from Diettrich, Basham, former deputy public defender John Foreman (who was now a judge), two other defense lawyers who had represented Knapp before the Meyer, Hendricks firm took over in 1981, and the three Meyer, Hendricks lawyers who had worked on the case during its early years. They swore that they had never before seen the Melba Burr statement; had never known that the fingerprints on the Coleman fuel can were identifiable, not smudged; had never heard of an April 1974 fire test — videotaped or otherwise; had never known that John Knapp's telephone conversation with Linda Knapp from jail had been taped; and had never known of a variety of other sundry information that suddenly came to light when the state complied with its discovery obligations in October 1990.

Twenty-one

By January 1991 the trial, scheduled for mid-April 1991, was just three months away. Hammond began grappling with the key strategic issues he would face at trial.

Since mock trials, focus groups, and professional jury consultants were too expensive for a pro bono case, Hammond set up a day-long conference, where he would stage a compressed, adversarially presented version of the case. He invited the extended family of Knapp lawyers, including investigators, paralegals, and former Knapp attorneys like James Scarboro, who flew in from Denver, as well as several outside lawyers and investigators. Due to an oversight that Hammond later recognized was foolish, paralegal Debbie Heller was the only woman present.

Ironically, one of the most valuable insights to emerge from the meeting, held on January 8, 1991, occurred a few minutes before it formally began. Hammond, who had already been in his office for more than two hours preparing for the 8 A.M. conference, was chatting in his doorway with Jon Sands, Zig Popko, and Debbie Heller when it happened.

Hammond said something in passing which none of them now remember, but which presented John Knapp in an endearing light. It struck a nerve with Heller.

— He is *not* St. John, — Debbie shouted.

It is not every day that a paralegal screams at a senior partner. Everyone swiftly dispersed from the uncomfortable scene.

Heller had recently reread a great many of the police reports in the process of preparing a chronology of the early events in the case. As of January 1991 she had a very different perspective on the case than anyone else on the team.

"I thought he was guilty as hell," she recalled in 1993. Though Heller later developed a reasonable doubt about Knapp's guilt, at this point Knapp's confession was decisive to her.

"I could never understand how a man could confess to murdering his daughters unless he did it," she said. "And that's purely subjective. That's from the viewpoint of a parent, of a mother."

And Heller never forgave Knapp for the way he had brought up his children.

"The most offensive part was that he could allow those children to live in the conditions that they were living in. And, while Linda was as guilty as he was, the idea that anybody would think that she was the only one responsible because she was the one at home . . . was bullshit."

"Larry's such a nice guy," she continued, "he always sees the best in people. Larry had put John Knapp up on a pedestal like a savior. Like a saint. And he was by far no saint."

"Debbie's words — 'He is not St. John' — really grabbed me," Hammond recalled. "Debbie is a very controlled person, not given to saying things out of anger. . . . That conversation, and everybody's sort of stunned silence — you could see she was just raging inside — caused me to want to be very careful about not making John Knapp out to be a great human being. He's just a guy, and I needed to be careful about that."

The strategy session was held in 20 East, a twentieth-floor conference room at the firm's new offices. In November the growing firm — now sixty lawyers — had moved a few blocks further north to one of two matching high-rise towers in a new office-hotel-and-shopping complex. It was a handsome trapezoidally shaped skyscraper, with rows of smoked glass embedded in a pinkish, polished granite facade.

Jon Sands, who had just returned to the firm from the federal public defender's office, played the prosecutor at the mock adversarial presentation. Hammond was Knapp's lawyer. They each gave openings, presented evidence in summary form, and delivered summations.

In presenting the defense case, Hammond explained that John Knapp, because he was asleep when the fire began, simply did not know how the fire had started. It could have been set by the children or by Linda. Hammond then presented the evidence that supported each theory, candidly admitting that the defense did not know what the truth was.

Afterward, however, there was great resistance inside the room to that approach.

— I don't think you can ride both horses like that, — someone said. — You can't ride the Linda-did-it horse at the same time you're riding the children-did-it horse. It's too confusing for the jurors. It sounds two-faced. —

Initially, Henze, who had a roll of Bandit smokeless tobacco pressed between his gum and lower lip, defended the two-horse approach.

— This is a death case, — Henze said. — The presumption has to be that we go with everything we've got. If we're going to hold back something, we had better have a very good reason. Otherwise, we're committing malpractice. —

Everyone understood that they would be arguing that the children set the fire. The question was: What would they do with all the evidence that had piled up over the years implicating Linda? Like it or not, by this time there were three people — a former friend, a former boyfriend, and a former husband — who claimed she had admitted to them responsibility for the fire. There were neighbors who thought she had behaved suspiciously before and after the fire. Linda had dreamed that her children would die in a fire two days before they did. There were the fires in Linda's homes before and after the fatal fire. Could the lawyers just conceal all that from the jury?

On the other hand, how could they use it without undermining the defense team's real belief, which was that the fire was probably set by the children?

— Our experts think the fire damage is consistent with an accidental fire, and *not* consistent with a flammable liquid fire, — Sands pointed out. — If we say Linda could have set the fire with Coleman fuel, we undermine our own scientific experts. It sounds like we don't really trust them. —

— Jon, I agree that it would be better to have one theory, — Henze said. — Juries understand one theory better, and you gain credibility by being consistent. But you just can't ignore some of this evidence about Linda Knapp. Particularly the parts about the subsequent fires and what happened to her other kids. I find this to be a real dilemma. —

Debbie Heller vehemently opposed riding the Linda-did-it horse. As always, she spoke bluntly.

— If I were a juror, — she said, — and you sat here and told me the case the way I just heard Larry tell it, it would turn me off. It's like, 'Well, the fire science shows it was the children. But, if you don't buy that one, let me tell you about his crazy wife and her fires in Utah.' I would think, 'This is a trick. What are you trying to pull?' —

Once again, Heller's forcefulness stemmed in part from a unique perspective. Heller had worked on the case a long time, and she had always done so as the only woman on an otherwise all-male team. Many of the male lawyers had unwittingly offended Heller over the years.

"Just how they'd talk about her," she recalled. "It was as if she [Linda] was just nothing but a fat pig."

— I've read the Utah reports, — Heller told the room, referring to the welfare agency records concerning Linda's history of child neglect. — I think I have an idea of what Linda Knapp is. She isn't a murderer. She is a very neglectful, very sick mother. But you ought to be very careful about accusing a mother of setting fire to her kids without having more evidence than you've got. You've been dragging her into this thing for years, — Heller continued, accusing all the male Knapp lawyers present. — Maybe John Knapp didn't set the fire. But John Knapp started the whole thing in motion by confessing. For whatever reason, he confessed. He brought it down on him. She got dragged into all of this because of what he did. —

Heller's passion was chastening to both Henze and Hammond. Accusing Linda of the crime could backfire in ways they had not considered.

Toward the end of the discussion, Henze suggested a way of steering a middle course.

— Maybe there's a way where we could focus on the accidental fire theory, — Henze said, — and yet at the same time we could make available to the jury the information about Linda's subsequent fires. We don't have to say that Linda Knapp set the fire, or even that she *may* have set the fire. We can tell the jurors about the subsequent fires in Utah and let the jury make of them what they will. There's nothing unethical about doing it that way. That stuff really happened. We didn't make it up. It's too important for us to keep from them.

— Juries like to discover, to explore, to have their own theories, — Henze continued. — They like to play Sherlock Holmes. And they're far more inclined to go with a theory that they reach on their own, than to just go with something because some lawyer told them that's what they should decide. —

Hammond thought Henze's advice sounded wise. It was obvious to Hammond that he could not do what he had done that morning.

"You can't go before a jury in a case of this complexity without having a defined theme," he later remembered thinking. "We cannot stand up in opening statement and say, 'We don't know. It could've been either [the kids or Linda].' You've got to tell 'em how the fire happened."

The day before the strategy conference in 20 East, a new Arizona attorney general had been sworn in downtown. Grant Woods, a reform-minded Republican, was replacing conservative Republican Robert Corbin, who had stepped down after twelve years. Woods had defeated Corbin's man, Steven Twist, in the primary.

Woods began reorganizing the office immediately and took bold steps to ensure that the Knapp prosecution received top priority under his administration.

Each move was a colossal blunder.

Woods's first miscue came during an interview with an *Arizona Republic* reporter in his new office, just hours after his inauguration. As he unpacked boxes and selected a spot for his life-size cardboard cutout of John Wayne, Woods outlined his dramatic plans for the future.

"I'm going to try cases myself," he told the *Republic*. "Today, I've assumed supervision of . . . the John Henry Knapp case."

But Woods had been a deputy public defender in the early 1980s, when that office's most high-profile client had been John Henry Knapp. Formally, then, Woods was now leading the attempt to execute a former client on the very matter in which he had once defended him. Though Woods had never personally defended Knapp, he still had a technical conflict of interest.

Hammond knew of Woods's earlier service at the public defender's office and had been watching to see what Woods did when he assumed office. If Woods cordoned himself off from the case, Hammond thought, pledging no personal involvement in it, his office would probably be permitted to continue handling the prosecution.

But Woods had done just the opposite. Within hours of being sworn in, Woods had personally barged into the center of the Knapp case, possibly handing over to Hammond the power to disqualify Woods's entire office.

During his second day on the job Woods further doomed his office's ability to prosecute Knapp. As part of a dramatic housecleaning, he fired eleven attorneys and an investigator and put out word through his official spokesperson that another forty attorneys might eventually be removed or replaced. (Though others were laid off, the cuts never went as deep as threatened.)

Hammond happened to speak to Sherwin on the phone either that day or the next.

— I'm glad it's not another person calling with their condolences, — Hammond remembers Sherwin saying.

Sherwin then explained, according to Hammond, that some people at the office had apparently seen a list of those slated for termination and that her name was on it. People had been calling her to tell her that it was not fair and that they were sorry for her.

In the ensuing days, however, Hammond learned from Sherwin that she had not, in fact, been terminated. Indeed, had Woods fired Sherwin he would have thrown the Knapp prosecution into crisis. Sherwin had already answered "ready" in the Knapp case, which was set to begin on April 23. Nobody except Sherwin could possibly be prepared by then.

But Sherwin was quitting, she told Hammond.

"It was too late as far as she was concerned," Hammond said, recalling the conversation. "They had begged her to stay and she had said, 'You can't treat me this way,' and she said she was going to the county Attorney's office."

And she did. By mid-January she gave notice, and by mid-February she was a prosecutor at the Maricopa County Attorney's office.

Sherwin neither confirmed nor denied having received condolence calls from people who mistakenly thought she was being fired. She did deny, however, having left the office due to any offensive actions by Attorney General Woods.

"I was approached regarding going to work for the Maricopa County Attorney's office weeks before Grant Woods took office," she wrote in a letter to the author, and at the time of the post-inaugural firings "I was already involved in the county hiring process." She declined comment on why she abruptly left after answering "ready" in a complex, high-profile case she had been handling for more than a year.

A spokesman for Woods said he had no idea why Sherwin resigned and denied that there was ever any document listing the names of people Woods planned to fire.

Although communications with the prosecutors at this stage were imperative — to schedule scores of witness interviews and to exchange myriad documents — for the next several weeks the defense lawyers did not know who was representing the state. At first the defense lawyers were told that Woods's newly appointed chief trial deputy, Steven Mitchell, would be trying the case, along with Sherwin. But on February 12, the next court appearance, assistant attorney general David Powell showed up representing the state.

In truth, the prosecutors themselves did not know who was representing the state. Powell's understanding at the time, he recalled in 1993, was that Sherwin, despite moving to the county attorney's office, would still be trying the case with him. (The county attorney's office no longer had the technical conflict of interest that had led to its disqualification in late 1987.)

"I talked to Susan and it was like, yeah, 'Let's do it together,'" Powell recalled. "But I said, 'Listen, Susan, you're first chair. . . . Let me just do the lay witnesses, you do the scientific witnesses.' And that was the understanding."

Sherwin denies there was ever such an understanding.

"I . . . completely turned over the Knapp file to Steve Mitchell and Dave Powell in early January," she wrote in a letter in 1994. "Dave Powell had been assigned to the Knapp case for two years prior to my involvement in it, and it was never anticipated that it would be necessary or desirable for me to try the case for him."

The only thing certain about Woods's inauguration and Sherwin's departure is that they left the Knapp prosecution in utter turmoil.

Meanwhile, the state's fire expert, John DeHaan, refined his theories about the fire.

DeHaan's perspective on the case began to hinge increasingly on an assumption that had nothing to do with fire, arson, or explosions. It rested on child psychology, a field in which DeHaan had no known expertise.

"I've been involved in fire investigation long enough to realize that the time factor was the critical issue of the whole thing," DeHaan said in 1993. "How did the fire develop so quickly that two youngsters would've been trapped in that room and not been able to get out? Even as young as they were, there should've been some time for escape."

Though there were studies showing that it was not uncommon for small children to fail to escape fires they had set, even when there was time to do so — perhaps, the researchers speculated, because the children feared punishment or were paralyzed by fright — DeHaan was increasingly predicating his theory of the fire on the children's failure to escape. That fact proved to him that the fire must have killed them or knocked them unconscious instantly, the way a flammable liquid fire would have.*

But, having concluded that the children must have been killed or knocked unconscious instantly, DeHaan now had to explain Linda Knapp's testimony,

---

* See Source Notes for further discussion.

which contradicted his theory. She said that her children were still alive when she opened the door to the burning room; she had seen and spoken to them.

Although DeHaan could have dismissed Linda's testimony as lies, he was not prepared to do so. Too much of her description of the fire was now corroborated by the fire damage. So DeHaan believed her testimony — *except when it contradicted his own theories.*

"The part about her talking to the kid was a fabrication," DeHaan recalled. "Not necessarily conscious. I think it was more wishful thinking. I think she realized what had gone on and she thought, 'Oh my god. The kids are dead. I've got to make up something to make me feel better.' But everything else that she talked about . . . that all fits."

Thus, DeHaan dismissed as fiction Linda's most vivid, searing, consistent memory of the fire — her last glimpse of her children.

"[Iona] had on a yellow nylon top with white diamonds, and her blue shorts," Linda had told detective Malone in her tape-recorded interrogation two weeks after the fire, in Nebraska. "She had a ponytail in her hair."

But for DeHaan, discarding the portions of eyewitness testimony that contradicted his theories was a routine and necessary part of the criminalist's job.

"What it comes right down to," he said in 1993, "is that in twenty-four years of investigation I've learned that eyewitness information is reliable less than fifty percent of the time."

So Sherlock Holmes's advice — that the investigator should twist the theory to the meet the facts — turns out to be very difficult advice to follow. Since eyewitness testimony is "reliable less than fifty percent of the time," the criminalist must often twist the facts to meet the theory.

On Thursday afternoon, January 31, 1991, a fire broke out in a mobile home in Kingman, Arizona, about 180 miles northwest of Phoenix.

Three young boys died in the trailer. Their father, Dennis Lea Miller, later said he had been asleep when the fire broke out and that he awoke to his boys' screams and cries. He told authorities that he suspected that one of his boys — the oldest was five — must have been playing with fire. Miller, twenty-seven, was separated from his wife and had no criminal record.

Chief deputy fire marshal David Dale examined the scene and found flammable liquid runs and other classic hallmarks of a flammable liquid fire.

Although there were no flammable liquid containers found on the property and chemical testing turned up no sign of flammable liquid residue, prosecutors presented the case to a grand jury on the strength of Dale's testimony and that of a colleague. Investigators theorized that Miller lit the fire hoping to rescue the children and become a hero — and thereby win back the love of his estranged wife.

On February 14, 1991, Dennis Lea Miller was arrested and charged with first-degree murder, a crime punishable by death.

In February, relations between Powell and Sherwin grew strained.

Powell liked to keep his desk and files very neat and tidy. Sherwin had had a different style.

"You'd go in her office," Powell recalled, "and it was just boxes up the walls to the ceiling. . . . It was an organization that only Susan could understand."

Powell asked investigator Debbie Schwartz to reorganize the files in a separate room devoted just to the Knapp files. As Schwartz did so, she discovered a cardboard box full of thirty-two or thirty-three tape recordings inside one of Sherwin's file cabinets, according to Powell.

These tapes included recordings of witness interviews made by Hyder's investigator Elardo back in 1974, as well as some made by other investigators for Knapp's post-conviction relief petitions between 1977 and 1985. Although Sherwin should have turned over these tapes in October, she had apparently forgotten about them or never even noticed them. (No one on either side suspects her of intentionally withholding them.)

"For some reason she thought they weren't in her file cabinet," Powell recounted, "and that Debbie Schwartz had had them, and [that Schwartz] was pointing the finger at Susan. Which wasn't the case, because I saw them in there."

Sherwin declined to comment on these tapes. Powell and Schwartz notified the defense of their existence the day after finding them and provided copies soon thereafter.

Wherever the tapes had been, their emergence would require the addition of several more paragraphs to the motion to dismiss Hammond was preparing based on Hyder's alleged misconduct back in 1974. Among them were tape recordings of Elardo's telephone conversations with the defense chemist Parsons in August 1974 — the conversations Elardo had so monumentally misunderstood and mischaracterized when he testified about them in 1974. There was also a tape Hyder himself had made of his own telephone conversation with Melba Burr a week before she first testified. None of these tapes were in the defense files when Meyer, Hendricks inherited them in 1981, and no previous Knapp lawyer knew of their existence.

*   *   *

In late January and early February, Hammond was deciding whether to try to disqualify Attorney General Woods's office. On the one hand, the disarray in the prosecutor's office obviously benefitted Knapp. But the same disarray was preventing Hammond from obtaining dozens of pretrial interviews with prosecution witnesses, which are allowed under Arizona discovery rules. Hammond just did not feel ready for an April trial in a death case. In addition, he thought it was irresponsible in such a case not to raise every plausible legal issue he could. If he lost the motion and Knapp were later convicted, it would give Knapp a strong, possibly life-saving issue on appeal.

As Hammond grappled with the disqualification issue, he also had to answer to an unremittingly cruel superego.

"I knew," he said later, "we were not doing this at the same level that you would do a fully paying civil case. We were scrambling all the time. We were begging assistance from every source. There's this constant pressure to extract the same level of performance out of people who aren't getting paid as you do out of people who are. And finding day after day that there are things that aren't getting done — that you ought to put another lawyer on it, put another investigator on it. And it didn't happen. We had some real strained nerves around here. Everybody is in a state of near anger. We have a thousand things going on. And dealing with the firm telling me I'm doing too much, and my colleagues telling me I'm doing too little. I'd never felt that kind of pressure before."

Meanwhile, Hammond had another plan brewing.

"I was trying," Hammond recalled, "to take this case off of what I thought was just a crazy collision course with a jury trial."

Hammond could not believe that Attorney General Woods appreciated the sorts of public resources he was about to pour down the drain in a futile attempt to try John Knapp for a third time. With a new, reform-minded attorney general coming in, Hammond saw an opportunity to derail the case from its insane path.

Hammond set up a meeting with Woods. He planned to emphasize how expensive the case would be and how hard it would be for the state to prevail. But, in addition, he would propose what he called "Grand Rounds." Hammond used the medical term, somewhat loosely, to evoke the image of a doctor presenting a lecture to a group of medical students about a patient with perplexing symptoms and then leading a nonadversarial discussion about it afterward.

Hammond suggested that the prosecution and defense put all their experts in a room and let them try to diagnose, in a nonadversarial format, the Knapp fire.

Hammond would simply ask Attorney General Woods to listen to what the experts had to say when they were done. There would be no other strings attached.

Of course, Hammond had no doubt that the scientists would reach a consensus that there was a reasonable doubt about Knapp's guilt.

Woods would then have the politically honorable excuse he needed, Hammond theorized, to free himself of this terrible albatross and explain to the electorate that the case had not been evaluated sensibly under the previous regime.

Henze and Sands were skeptical, but Hammond won them over.

"I was just captivated by the creative way in which this guy Hammond approached problem solving," Henze later recalled.

On Tuesday, February 19, the defense team drove to the attorney general's office, a long, low, rambling white concrete box with black smoked-glass windows. The attorneys signed in with the guard, donned visitors' badges, passed through the metal detector, and waited for an escort to lead them to a large conference room decorated with scenes of Arizona and a poster of Michael Jordan.

There, the defense team met with Grant Woods, Steve Mitchell, and David Powell.

— You have one hour, — Woods said, starting the meeting.

Hammond delivered his pitch. As Hammond remembers it, the only taboo topic on his own agenda was the issue of actual innocence. Mentioning his opinion that Knapp was innocent would be incendiary, he thought. No lawyer was ever in a position to presume that sort of knowledge. And Hammond judged that for him to express such an opinion would be especially offensive, since he was a civil lawyer with little experience in the criminal trenches.

However, at the end of Hammond's presentation, Henze did delicately approach that taboo topic.

— I've been in and out of this office many times on behalf of many clients, — Henze said, — and I want you to know that not once in all the times I have come here have I ever said that my client was innocent. But there is much here that would lead anybody to believe that this man, John Knapp, didn't do it. That he did not set the fire. —

As Henze remembers it, he was always just talking about evidence and what could be proven, not offering his personal opinion, which would be offensive and unprofessional.

"I was trying to reach that chord in Grant [Woods]," Henze recalled, "that would make him feel like this was a dilemma for him in carrying out his very lofty role as the guardian of the Arizona justice department."

At the same time, Henze was in a ticklish situation. He was coming back in front of Woods a few weeks later to make a presentation for another client in a different case. If he urged Woods that Knapp might really be innocent, but did not make a similar pitch for his other client, how would it look?

Hammond was moved that Henze had come so close to discussing actual innocence. He thought it was powerful coming from a veteran like Henze.

In reality, however, the meeting had gone poorly.

To Powell, Grand Rounds sounded like a logistical nightmare, and he feared that the other side would just use it as a discovery tool. (Henze had feared the same thing.)

And he knew what Hammond was thinking.

"They wanted to have their experts try to convince our experts they were wrong," Powell recalled. "Which I didn't think was going to happen. Because John DeHaan is as good as there is, and he was positive."

In addition, Powell's memory is that Hammond or one of his colleagues *did* bring up Knapp's innocence at some point. And it *did* offend Powell.

"I remember," Powell said, "they would say, 'Look at us. [Judge] Colin Campbell, [Judge John Foreman,] this person, that person. How could a guilty man dupe us all? Therefore, he must be innocent.' Which is kind of a backhanded slap in our face. Like, 'You guys are just idiots.' "

Though Hammond has no recollection of making the argument at this meeting, he said he may have, at some point, observed that all the experienced lawyers on the defense team felt there was a genuine doubt about Knapp's guilt.

Powell and Woods interpreted Hammond's comments about the expense of the case and the difficulty of winning a conviction as an attempt to intimidate Woods by threatening him with a politically humiliating defeat in court — which was not completely off base.

"They were just telling me how they were going to kick my ass," Powell remembered.

Three days later, Powell came to Meyer, Hendricks's offices for a meeting around a square, wood table in the small conference room known as 20 South. It was a Friday afternoon, and everyone was tired and irritable.

It was clear from Powell's comments that he was not taking Grand Rounds seriously. He had also made little progress on a host of information-exchange issues Hammond had hoped to clear up.

Hammond became frustrated.

At the end of the meeting Sands saw Powell out to the elevator bank.

— This is silly, — Hammond told Henze. — We have a perfectly good basis for having them disqualified. It's a good, straight-faced argument that responsible lawyers ought to make. —

When Sands returned, he opened the door and looked at Hammond and Henze, slouched in their chairs.

— Let's disqualify the bastards, — Sands said.

On March 1, the defense moved to disqualify Woods's office. A hearing was set for April 1, just three weeks before the trial was scheduled to begin.

Twenty-two

Hammond now turned his attention to what he knew would become either the linchpin of the defense case or its downfall: the full-scale room-burn tests.

He had known from the start who he wanted to do them, if he could get him. In the mid-1980s, fire engineer Richard Custer had helped produce two films depicting how flashover develops in a room. Hammond had shown these films at Ray Girdler's hearing in 1990.

Custer, fifty, a beefy man with salt-and-pepper hair and a white beard, was a former firefighter who became a geological engineer and then a fire engineer. He had spent eight years with the National Bureau of Standards's Center for Fire Research (and its predecessor fire research unit) during the 1970s, and now taught fire engineering at the Worcester Polytechnic Institute in Massachusetts.

Custer flew to Phoenix for a two-day meeting with Hammond and Marshall Smyth in late December 1990. Hammond discussed the sort of tests they needed to do and suggested they might be able to find a room in some abandoned house slated for destruction that they could fix up to replicate the bedroom.

Custer rejected the idea. There were too many variables that he could not control doing the test outdoors in an already existing structure.

— I wouldn't have confidence in the results, whatever they were, — he told Hammond.

The way to do it, Custer said, would be to construct a room exactly the size of the Knapp bedroom inside a large indoor facility equipped to monitor burns. He would outfit the room to the degree possible with exactly the furnishings they knew had been in the Knapp room and instrument the room to record temperatures, gas concentrations, and radiant energy as the fire progressed.

Even so, Custer cautioned, no fire could be duplicated. Each fire had its unique artifacts. And there would be important differences between the test chamber and the Knapp bedroom, no matter what. A freestanding test bedroom inside a warehouse would behave differently than a bedroom that was part of a larger house standing outdoors, for instance.

But all told, burning a full-scale test room inside an indoor laboratory was the best way to do it, short of reconstructing the entire three-bedroom Knapp house.

Custer struck Hammond as bringing to the task just the degree of compulsiveness he wanted. Hammond had Marshall Smyth and Custer begin pricing the handful of test facilities available. They envisioned setting six fires, testing various scenarios, with and without Coleman fuel.

Wherever they were performed, the tests would be expensive. Six tests, Smyth estimated, would cost about $146,000, including $109,000 for the materials and the facility, and $37,000 for Custer's time.

As far as what he could spend from the law firm's coffers, Hammond's marching orders were vague.

"It was becoming clearer and clearer to people here," Hammond recounted later, "that this was going to become an enormously expensive undertaking. The message I was getting was, 'People have confidence in your judgment, but don't get carried away.' People would trust me. But it was a little bit like me telling my son, 'I'm going to trust you to drive carefully.' It was like they were saying they knew it wouldn't happen."

If he could get the judge to order county funds to pay a sizable chunk of the bill for these tests, maybe he and his partners could make up the rest.

He would petition the judge.

After the preliminary hearing had ended in October, the case had been assigned to Judge Frederick Martone to handle the trial. Martone, forty-seven, had been on the bench for more than five years, and had spent twelve years before that in private practice at one of Phoenix's best civil firms. A moderate Republican who had been appointed by a Democratic governor, he had presided over both civil and criminal cases in the past, had served as the associate chief presiding judge for the entire superior court, and was currently a "special assignment" judge — one who handled trials that were so unwieldy or complex that they would disrupt the calendars of judges hearing more run-of-the-mill dockets.

Martone was soft-spoken, cautious, scholarly, intelligent, and supremely logical. He had a boyish face that sat atop a slightly paunchy medium build, and was polite with lawyers, jurors, and court personnel.

Martone had majored in abstract mathematics at the College of the Holy Cross in Massachusetts. When he later turned to the law, getting his degree at the University of Notre Dame and an advanced degree at Harvard Law School, he found that his earlier mathematics training was not completely irrelevant. It assisted him to think clearly, to criticize rigorously, and "to avoid, at least, logical error," he said in 1993.

Though he was thoughtful and considerate, he could be remote and cold in his logic and decision making — almost bloodless. As Martone became acquainted with the Knapp case, he became puzzled by the emotions it generated among the adversaries on both sides.

"When I saw how passionate the [original] lawyers on both sides of the case had been sixteen to eighteen years [earlier]," he later observed, "and then I noticed that same level of passion and intensity in connection with the proceedings before me, it certainly made me wonder whether we were able to put the case in perspective in the universe of both our legal system and the troubles of the world. There are tens of thousands of felony cases in the United States, and we have thousands of them here in Arizona, including hundreds of first-degree murder cases, including hundreds of death cases. . . . I never came up with a useful guess as to what separated this case from the others."

By the end of 1990, Judge Martone was beginning to see a need to get a grip on costs in this case. Marshall Smyth, who had been appointed as a defense consultant for the preliminary hearing, had already cost the county $10,327.50 for his work relating to that hearing, and he had just put in a new bill for $9,891.64. (He had been analyzing DeHaan's seven full-scale tests and working on plans for the defense tests.)

Martone ordered Hammond to write out a budget for the entire case, so that he could get an idea of the dimensions of this enterprise and put some pragmatic limits on it.

Hammond tallied up what it would cost to do the case right. In addition to the $146,000 needed for fire tests, he would also need, at the very least, mechanical engineer Smyth and the three other fire-related experts who had testified at the 1986 hearing — a fire safety engineer, a gas chromatographer, and a toxicologist. For the trial he would also need a forensic pathologist.

Plus, Hammond wanted to call psychologists and psychiatrists to address a multitude of issues: child fire-setting habits; the varying ways in which people express and display grief; the severity and symptoms of migraine headaches; how and why people falsely confess to crimes without the use of physical coercion.

And Hammond needed an electronics expert and a fingerprint consultant to help him pursue prosecutor Hyder's trail — to find out if evidence had been concealed and destroyed back in 1974.

His anticipated budget for experts alone came to $285,000.

When he threw in estimated attorneys' fees, investigators' fees, paralegal fees, transcript costs, witness travel costs, graphics costs, and other sundries, the budget came to $513,000.

Hammond's budget request was "unreasonable *per se*," Judge Martone wrote in an order in December 1990. If granted, the Knapp case would consume almost 25 percent of the county's entire fiscal-year budget for indigent defense.*

"When there are thousands of defendants that come before the court," Martone later observed, "you have to ask yourself: . . . How do you make sure you don't rob Peter to pay Paul, and shortchange thousands of faceless defendants for whom the resources won't be there?"

Hammond was — and still is — dumbfounded by Martone's ruling. Hammond had proposed what, to him, as a civil lawyer, was a shoestring budget. At the time, Hammond was involved in a civil matter in which each side was spending about $1.5 million on experts — just at the pretrial stage. That case involved a dispute between PGA TOUR, Inc., and a Phoenix-based manufacturer of a golf club known as a Ping; PGA TOUR wanted to adopt a rule that would have effectively banned the use of certain Pings at their tournaments, because of the shape of the grooves in their heads.

With each side dropping $1.5 million on experts in a dispute over golf clubs, how could it be "unreasonable *per se*" for him to seek less than $300,000 for experts to show that the defendant in a death-penalty case might be innocent?

---

* That is, the budget for those indigent defendants who cannot, because of conflicts of interest and other reasons, be represented by the public defender's office, which has its own budget.

Still, Hammond was placated by the fact that Judge Martone had explained in the same order that he planned to let Judge Stephen Gerst decide how much money to give Hammond. Since Judge Gerst had handled Knapp's 1986 post-conviction relief hearing, Judge Martone felt Gerst would have a better grasp of how much money Knapp really needed. Hammond assured his partners that Gerst would surely reimburse a healthy portion of the costs of full-scale fire tests.

But Hammond still did not see. A reasonable budget for an indigent defendant was not determined by what was at stake. What was at stake — a man's life — was infinite. A reasonable budget was determined by the size of the county's budget for indigent defense — which, for fiscal 1990–91, was a little over $2 million.

Judge Gerst allotted $50,000 to compensate all of Knapp's fire experts.

He allotted nothing toward doing the full-scale tests themselves. Zero.

He allotted nothing for psychologists, psychiatrists, electronics experts, and fingerprint experts.

He agreed to appoint an additional investigator, but not a second attorney.

"There is a backdrop," Judge Gerst said later. "The backdrop is: other cases. Some standard [is required]. This case has gotten more money than any case I know of in recent history."

But Hammond was shell-shocked.

"At the very least I had to have four fire experts," he recalled. "Well, it comes out to $12,500 for each one." Smyth had billed almost $20,000 already. "I just thought that was a hopelessly unrealistic number."

And then there was the real irony. Knapp had spent twelve years on death row because Judge Hardy refused to give him funds for full-scale tests in 1974. Gerst had even alluded to that injustice in his 1987 ruling granting Knapp a new trial. But now, in 1991, Knapp *still* wasn't going to get funds to do full-scale tests.

"Christ God, I'll never understand it," Hammond said.

Hammond pressed forward with plans to do the tests anyway. They would scale back. Instead of six tests, they would do two: one using Coleman fuel, one without. He told his partners he would ask Judge Gerst and Judge Martone to reconsider.

But the tests would be done.

Custer began gathering the furnishings for the tests. He examined photographs of the remains of the original crib mattress under a binocular microscope in order to determine its precise innerspring structure. Then he took the photos to a mattress manufacturer in Massachusetts who had agreed to custom manufacture four cotton-sisal crib mattresses out of materials that had been used in the late 1960s and early 1970s. The factory agreed not to use the federally mandated fire retardants — required since 1974 — so long as Hammond executed a document protecting the company from liability and pledging that the mattresses would never be used for sleeping or placed in the stream of commerce.

At the same time Smyth was looking for an appropriate carpet. Although there were still some undamaged samples of the actual Knapp carpet that had been stored in the Maricopa County sheriff's office, too little remained to use. Smyth eventually located a source of 1970s-vintage nylon carpets. He selected for Custer two samples that had weaves, piles, backings, and weights that were comparable to the Knapp carpet. Custer then tested the burn properties of two of the carpets in a calorimeter and compared those results to those of the actual Knapp carpet, which he also tested. He then chose a sample that was, in fact, a little *less* flammable than the Knapp carpet.

"We were trying to be conservative," Custer explained. "You start your analysis by making your conditions most favorable to the other side. Then if your results favor your position, you're in pretty good shape."

Hammond was developing tremendous enthusiasm for the full-scale tests.

Jon Sands, on the other hand, was quite worried about what Hammond was up to.

Hammond was pretty much on his own in this project, since Henze was handling a criminal trial in California at the time. And Hammond was not thinking like a criminal defense lawyer, Sands feared. A defense lawyer did not *create* evidence; he *suppressed* it.

Any evidence they created they would be stuck with. Suppose these tests — for whatever reason — did not turn out the way Hammond hoped.

Custer readily conceded that no two fires would burn alike; each always left unexpected and unexplainable artifacts.

And what if Knapp was guilty? It was irresponsible for a defense lawyer to act blithely under the assumption that his client was innocent and that, therefore, any accurate test would exonerate him.

In theory, if things went badly, they could lawfully choose not to call Custer as a witness, and then they could lawfully avoid disclosing his tests to the state. (Unlike the state, which has to disclose any scientific tests it performs, the defense could shield its tests to this extent.)

But any of the defense experts who knew about the test would certainly have to be dropped as witnesses also, since they could not pretend that those tests had no bearing on their opinions. And all the defense experts would know about them.

The bottom line was, if the tests came out poorly, the defense case was eviscerated.

Ultimately, Hammond chose just to risk it. He believed Knapp was innocent. Custer was confident that flashover would occur quickly in a room the size of the Knapp children's bedroom and that it would cause damage generally similar to that of the Knapp children's bedroom.

"We became convinced," Hammond recalled, "that if the tests were done competently, we could let the chips fall where they may."

They performed the tests at a facility in Longview, Washington — just over the border from Portland, Oregon — which was run by Weyerhaeuser. There the forest products company tested the fire resistance and burn toxicity of its own products as well as, under contract, those of other manufacturers. A crew of eight would follow Custer's instructions in constructing the room, furnishing it, instrumenting it, and documenting every phase of both the setup and overhaul with videotape and still photography.

On Tuesday morning, March 26, Hammond and the experts began flying into Portland, Oregon, and then taking rental cars to a motel near the Weyerhaeuser facility.

The first day was devoted to some preliminary mattress testing. Among other goals, Hammond wanted to correct a flaw in Smyth's methodology back in 1974. Smyth thought he had shown that a crib mattress, ignited with a match and crumpled newspaper, could ignite the carpet and pad beneath it and set off a ferocious fire.

That is what had happened in Smyth's fourth mattress test. But prosecutor Hyder had convinced Judge Hardy that it was the addition of the low ceiling in that test — creating a "little bomb," "oven," or "barbecue pit," as Hyder put it — that had caused the inferno, not the addition of the carpet and pad. Indeed, John DeHaan had dismissed the value of Smyth's tests on the same grounds in 1989 and 1990.

So Hammond and Custer redid Smyth's tests, using no ceiling at all this time. They burned one cotton-sisal crib mattress alone, and one with the carpet and pad beneath it. (Neither mattress contained any polyurethane.)

The tests were performed in a vast, empty, rickety wooden warehouse that had been painted yellow a very long time ago. The warehouse was about sixty feet long and forty feet wide, had a twenty-four-foot ceiling and a cement floor, and could be accessed by trucks through outsize garage-style doors. From the center of the ceiling hung a sixteen-foot by sixteen-foot metal hood. The hood ushered gases to an exhaust duct that ran along the roof, where instruments gathered data and computed the heat-release rates, in kilowatts, of the objects being burned beneath the hood. The heat-release data were then relayed to a computer monitor inside a glass-windowed booth at one end of the warehouse.

In one test, a cotton crib mattress was set up at the proper angle to the crib support, just like the one in the Knapp bedroom, and placed in front of a single piece of Sheetrock, which played the role of the south wall in the Knapp children's bedroom. The whole assembly stood in the center of the room, under the hood. Then the mattress was ignited from below with crumpled newspaper and a match.

It burned modestly and unimpressively, as had the mattresses in Smyth's first three tests in 1974.

But when Custer performed the identical test with the carpet and pad below it, the scenario was very different. At first, the mattress burned modestly. In fact, after about a minute and a half, it looked like the fire was going out. But three minutes after ignition the flames suddenly became visible again, rising to a height of about two feet. The carpet beneath the mattress then ignited, and the pace of the burning picked up geometrically. By the four-and-a-half-minute mark flames were leaping all the way up the eight-foot Sheetrock wall and deep into the metal hood above, ten or twelve feet above the floor. The mattress was shooting flame like a Roman candle.

With carpet and pad beneath it, the crib mattress released about seven times the heat of an identical mattress burned in isolation.

The carpet seemed to contribute enormously to the fire, even outside Smyth's little chamber.

"It was stunning," Hammond remembered, "to see it go from a flame that was going to die out to just completely filling the room with fire."

At the end of the experiment, a staff member doused the flames with a hose. Hammond and Custer then inspected the remains, while a staff member video-taped.

— Look at that! — Hammond shouted. — Look at that! — There was a rainbow-colored oily film floating on the water in the debris.

Hammond believed it was just such an oily film, discovered by a firefighter in the Knapp bedroom, that had turned John Knapp from an awkward, hapless cab driver into a filocidal murder suspect.

There was also a pungent odor coming from the melted latex of the carpet underlay. Hammond speculated that the firefighters, having seen Coleman fuel cans around the house, might have mistaken the odor for that of Coleman fuel.

It was an auspicious first day.

On the next morning Hammond arrived at the yellow warehouse at about 8:00 A.M. The eight-member crew was already busily assembling the room under the great metal hood. Originally, the test was scheduled for the early afternoon, but Custer kept postponing it. Holes had to be drilled for cameras, floodlights, and for the cables leading from the forty various measuring devices to their respective computer ports. The crew had to lay down the pad and the carpet, install baseboards, an entry door, a closet door, the window. The furniture — the dresser with the drawers pulled out of it, the bunk bed, the homemade footstool, the crib mattress and crib support — all had to be placed to correspond with the photographs of the burn debris, which Smyth and Custer were continually examining through a microscope. Toys and clothing were also sprinkled around the room.

To moot DeHaan's objections — whatever their merit — there was no polyurethane in either mattress.

On one occasion, when Hammond's and Smyth's memories conflicted about a certain detail, Custer lost his temper.

— Look, we can't do it this way, — he said, getting agitated. — Just get the transcript. — Hammond called Debbie Heller in Phoenix and had her fax trial transcripts so they could get the detail right.

In the course of creating this reenactment, Hammond began to appreciate, really for the first time in his nine years of involvement in the case, how tiny the children's bedroom was. The two beds alone nearly filled it. When all the known furnishings were stuffed in there, it was just packed.

A crew of firefighters in yellow turnout gear took up their positions about 7:45 P.M., with hoses poised. But they had to stand around for yet another hour as last-minute fine-tuning continued. Custer checked each thermocouple and made sure it was calibrated properly. He did a walk-through to make sure everyone knew their roles.

The director of Weyerhaeuser's team, James White, was standing in a glass-windowed instrument booth, where he could announce the readouts of the heat being released, in kilowatts. The readouts would actually show up on his monitor after a thirty-second delay, since the gauges in the exhaust duct on the roof were analyzing gases that had been released by the fire about thirty seconds earlier. By Custer's computations, it would take about 700 to 900 kilowatts of energy to cause flashover in a room of this size.

There was more tension in the room than Hammond expected. Despite their experience with fires, the Weyerhaeuser crew, the firefighters, and Custer all seemed on edge. The notion of a "controlled" burn, especially one that might reach flashover intensity, was a fiction.

The door was left open about two inches, the way Linda had described finding it. A crew member was to open the door the rest of the way once the flames reached the ceiling, since that is what Linda said she saw when she opened it.

At a little before 9:00 P.M., an electric match ignited two crumpled pieces of newspaper that had been stuffed under the cotton-sisal crib mattress.

For the first forty-five seconds, nothing could be seen from outside the room except a gradually building stream of light gray smoke slipping out the gap in the doorway. Just a minute and a half (1:30) after ignition, however, orange flames were already visible through that gap, and they were spreading across the ceiling above the door. At 1:53, the door was swung open to simulate Linda Knapp entering the room. At that point a measuring device in the doorway indicated that the temperature was very hot, but bearable — about 130 degrees Fahrenheit.

By the two-minute mark (2:00) dark smoke filled the room almost halfway down to the floor, and shortly thereafter flames began leaping out the doorway. At 2:19 the fire seemed to be enveloping almost everything in the room. At 2:22 the window glass began cracking, and by 2:32 it was falling out. Just three minutes after ignition, everything in the room was in flame.

From the point that the door was opened, the fire's intensity had been taking off. Just one minute after the door was opened, the temperature in the doorway had risen to about 1,650 degrees Fahrenheit. By that time temperatures elsewhere in the room had reached 2,260 degrees Fahrenheit.

All the while, Jim White, Weyerhaeuser's crew leader, was calling out the kilowattage of heat being released.

"Seven hundred kilowatts," Jim White had called out in his soft Texas accent, shortly before the window began to crack. That was just about what was required to produce flashover, according to Custer's calculations.

"Two point five *mega*watts," he called out, several seconds after the window first began cracking. It had suddenly shot up to 2,500 kilowatts — about three times what was required for flashover.

"*Four* megawatts," he shouted. It was far more heat than anyone had expected.

"*Five point five* megawatts," White called out.

"*Six* megawatts. It's peaking."

White was wrong. He was reading the measurements on a thirty-second delay. The temporary dip he was seeing now was one that had occurred inside the room just *before* the window cracked. But once the window shards fell out, fresh oxygen flooded into the room, and the heat release rate skyrocketed.

"*Eight* megawatts!"

There was fear in White's voice. Though his assistants were speeding up the exhaust fans in the hood, the fans couldn't keep up with the thick black smoke that was gushing from the room. It was pouring out of the hood and into the room. Black clouds of smoke plunged a portion of the room into darkness — and did it so swiftly that workers thought the lights had failed.

There was a whooshing sound from gases being sucked into the room and then being exhausted out of it. The whole room was breathing.

"Hit it!" White yelled, and staff members unleashed a sprinkler system that had been set up inside the room. When that system proved inadequate to douse the raging fire, firefighters put it out with hoses and carbon dioxide.

The delayed readouts of heat-release rates kept climbing after the fire was extinguished. They peaked at a stunning *12.25 megawatts* of heat — about fifteen times what was necessary to flash over the room.

Later analysis showed that the room had reached flashover after about 140 seconds. And it had done so without — as Hammond would later tell the jury — so much as a thimble of flammable liquid.

An unaccelerated fire would *not* necessarily need thirty to sixty minutes to build to flashover, as DeHaan had testified at the preliminary hearing. Even in the total absence of polyurethane, this unaccelerated fire had reached flashover in less than two and a half minutes.

Immediately after the tests Custer took a video camera inside the room and filmed the damage, which would be photodocumented in far more detail in the coming hours and the next morning. Hammond brought with him David Dale's list of the indicia of a flammable liquid fire that he had seen in the Knapp bedroom.

To Hammond the test results were devastating. One by one he checked off Dale's hallmarks of a flammable liquid fire.

There was floor-level burning, burning on the underside of the bed and the footstool, "alligatoring" of wood, charring of the baseboards on portions of each of the four walls. There was fairly equal deterioration of the four walls and the ceiling. The bedsprings had collapsed, the bed rail had been deformed, the aluminum window frame had melted away. Clothing and other debris had protected peninsulas and archipelagoes of carpet, creating patterns of burned and unburned carpet that could have been mistaken for places where flammable liquid had been poured.

DeHaan's predictions had also been savaged. There was, in fact, burning in corners. There was, in fact, burning under the bed. The carpet inside the perimeter of the dresser was completely burned away. DeHaan had testified at the preliminary hearing that he had never been able to reproduce such burning inside a dresser without the aid of a flammable liquid. But how many tests had he actually ever performed that could have realistically shed any light on that claim? Hammond had done it in his first and only try.

And, even though the firemen had begun putting out this fire just three and a half minutes after ignition, the radiant energy from the ceiling had in several places already burned holes through the nylon carpet and butyl rubber pad all the way to the floor.

"The only kind of localized fuel that will produce a burn through the carpet and through that kind of pad that I've been able to duplicate," DeHaan had testified, "is with a flammable liquid."

Again, how many times had DeHaan conducted experiments that could have realistically shed any light on the question?

The next morning Hammond awoke at about 5:00 A.M. to take his morning jog, before heading back to Weyerhaeuser to set up the second full-scale test. He ran along a canal that flowed past his motel. The morning was foggy and cool, and the path was lined with pine trees and cultivated fields. Hammond was trying to enjoy the humid air and the exotic smells that were so different from the arid norms of Phoenix.

But the brief euphoria of the previous day's test had already lifted, and there was a lawyer's anxiety gnawing in his gut.

Today, he and Custer were supposed to do the full-scale burn using Coleman fuel. But Hammond kept seeing in his mind the image from the day before of the test room just before ignition. When they had finished putting all the furniture, clothing, and toys in the tiny room, Hammond had been astonished at how packed it was. Though there was no question about the size of the children's room or the major pieces of furniture that had been in it, the image bothered him.

It looked contrived. A skilled prosecutor could mock the test for that reason.

"Of course the test room went up like a tinderbox," the prosecutor would say. "Look at the preposterous way they've packed it."

The jurors would miss the point. In reality, according to what Custer was telling him, the crib mattress and the carpet and pad *alone* were probably sufficient to flash over the room. Nevertheless, a sarcastic prosecutor could easily steal away the thunder of the excruciatingly painstaking experiment. Maybe, Hammond thought, he should junk the planned accelerated fire test — the one using Coleman fuel — and just do a second *un*accelerated test using far fewer furnishings. It was vital to prove that an innocent fire could account for the damage in the Knapp bedroom, even if the prosecution argued that the room must have contained fewer furnishings.

On the other hand, Hammond dreaded asking Custer to make such a drastic last-minute adjustment after all his scrupulous, methodical preparations. And what if Custer's predictions were wrong, and the minimal furnishings test fizzled?

But he feared that the change had to be made. He interrupted his jog, turned around, and ran back to the motel.

There was an urgent phone message from Custer awaiting him at the desk. Custer, it turned out, was also wondering if a second *un*accelerated test might be a wiser use of resources. Adding accelerant, he thought, would probably just push the fire to flashover even more quickly. It was more important to show how easily an *un*accelerated fire could go to flashover, and that the first test had not been contrived, or a freak. Over breakfast in the motel coffee shop they decided to make the last-minute switch.

For the second test, Custer and Hammond eliminated the larger bed and almost all the clothing, toys, and other debris. They would run the test with just the cotton-sisal crib mattress and support, the homemade footstool, the dresser (without any drawers), and the carpet and pad.

Custer predicted that this fuel alone was sufficient to bring the tiny room to flashover.

Hammond called Sands to tell him of the change of plans.

— When did you guys come up with this idea? — Sands asked.

"Holy cow," White shouted about three minutes into the second test. The readouts were surging even higher than in the first one. "Put it out!"

The second fire reached flashover after about 150 seconds, and after 250 seconds it was releasing an astounding *13.35 megawatts* of heat, even more heat than in the first test.

In retrospect, Custer and Smyth thought that the unexpected power of this second fire probably resulted from the fact that the carpet, having fewer items of furniture and clothing shielding it, was free to contribute even more than before. (DeHaan, who always discounted the significance of the carpet, later opined that the test conditions must have accidentally hit on an optimal balance between the combustibles and oxygen present in the room.)

For his time spent preparing, attending, and analyzing this test, Smyth billed about $35,500 in time and expenses to the case after the preliminary hearing.

William Lowry, the toxicologist — who was, among other things, monitoring carbon monoxide levels in the room — billed about $14,000 for his work prior to trial.

Custer, the fire reconstructionist, billed about $42,000 worth of time on the case before turning off his meter and donating another $20,000 worth of time.

Weyerhaeuser's costs for its facility, materials, and eight-man crew came to $41,000.

Fire engineer Richard Bright, who had testified at the 1986 hearing before Judge Gerst, returned to assist at the trial, billing the firm about $30,000 for his time before he, too, stopped keeping track and donated the remainder of his time.

Gas chromatographer Dennis Canfield never sent Meyer, Hendricks any bills; his donated time would have otherwise come to about $12,000. A second gas chromatographer, who assisted Canfield, billed about $2,500.

The costs to the Meyer, Hendricks firm for the fire-related portion of the case — *above* the $50,000 allotted by Judge Gerst — therefore came to about $115,000. (The firm would still have to spend tens of thousands more for psychologists, psychiatrists, the electronics expert, and a fingerprint expert.)

Back in February, while Hammond had been preparing for the burn tests, he had agreed to take a day out of his schedule to meet with Lee Novak, a young deputy public defender from Mohave County, northwest of Phoenix, who wanted to talk to him.

Novak represented Dennis Miller, the man in Kingman who had been charged with capital murder on the basis of deputy fire marshal David Dale's readings of the burn damage from his mobile home fire in January. Hammond gave Novak a crash course in fire science, and Novak then made a presentation to prosecutor James Zack.

To his great credit, Zack was concerned. On April 4 he consented to release Miller on his own recognizance, and then he joined Novak in urging the judge to appoint an outside fire expert to render a second opinion. The outside expert found no evidence of a flammable liquid fire.

The charges against Miller were dropped.

Twenty-three

By late February and early March, assistant attorney general Powell was coming to realize that the state's case was in crisis.

Sherwin did not share his understanding that she would be handling the scientific aspects of the trial.

"Eventually, we had to have a meeting with [Sherwin's boss, Maricopa County Attorney Richard] Romley, whereby she was ordered to assist," Powell recounted.

"The meeting . . . that I believe you are referring to," Sherwin wrote to the author, "was to establish some guidelines so as to enable me to assist them without neglecting my own responsibilities at the County."

Shortly thereafter Powell had a Saturday meeting with both DeHaan and Sherwin, where the personal tension between Sherwin and Powell was palpable, according to both Powell and DeHaan. Powell then gave up on the idea of teaming with Sherwin, he recalled.

"As to the meeting with John DeHaan," Sherwin wrote, "the account and chronology you relate is false." She declined to provide her own.

Powell finally told Judge Martone that he simply could not be ready by the scheduled April 23 trial date.

In this atmosphere, Judge Martone held the April 1 hearing to determine whether the attorney general's office should be disqualified because of Attorney

General Woods's technical conflict — his previous stint in the public defender's office when that office had represented Knapp.

Woods testified at the hearing that he had never known that the public defender's office had ever represented Knapp until the defense filed its motion to disqualify a month earlier.

But Judge Martone disqualified Woods and his office the next day. In his written ruling Martone expressed skepticism about Woods's testimony and obvious irritation with whatever it was Woods had done that had caused Sherwin to leave, scuttling the scheduled trial.

"We conclude," Martone wrote, "that a lawyer in the office which defended the defendant should not become that person's personal prosecutor. This is especially true where this case was ready for trial in the hands of an Assistant Attorney General before Woods chose to personally become involved in the prosecution."

The defense team's celebration was brief. Disqualifying the attorney general's office turned out to have been a grave error.

"I was relieved when I found out who got the case," Powell told the author. "Dave White is as good as there is in the state of Arizona."

David White, forty-one, was a career prosecutor who had recently moved from the Tucson branch of the attorney general's office back to the Pima County Attorney's office in Tucson, where he had previously worked. White had handled the retrial of John Serna, a prison inmate who was accused of murdering another inmate. Though many in the defense community thought Serna was truly innocent, and Serna's first trial had ended in a hung jury — with the jury deadlocked ten to two *for acquittal* — White had won a conviction and death sentence the second time around after persuading the judge to change certain rulings. (Serna won the right to a new trial in June 1994, after new evidence of innocence came to light. He was released in December 1994 after pleading "no contest" to a lesser charge — an ambiguous result whereby Serna could win his freedom while the state could win a "conviction.")

White is a tall, robust man with a quick, keen mind and a good, sarcastic sense of humor — one of his potent weapons as a trial lawyer. He is a man's man, wielding a personal charisma attractive to both men and women. His stagey body language projects supreme confidence in himself and a withering disdain for the contentions of his adversaries. He speaks sharp, plain English with a Western, cowboy twang and sometimes refers to himself as "just a country lawyer."

White never entertained a sliver of doubt about Knapp's guilt.

"I have two children," White later said. "I would never, ever — I just think it's hard not to personalize — there's no way I would ever confess to killing my children if I didn't do it. No way in hell."

White's team was smaller than the defense team — a reversal of norms that made White feel that he was David battling Goliath.

"Oftentimes it's the awesome power of the state against some poor defendant," White said. "[Here] it was the awesome power of a large Phoenix law firm . . . who'd been working on the case for years versus two lawyers, a law clerk, and an investigator who really had no clue about the facts of the case till right before trial."

White's main assistant, deputy county attorney Catherine Shovlin, would be getting her first trial experience, after having worked in the appeals bureau of the office. She would help mainly with the written work and preparing witnesses.

Reagen Kulseth was an intelligent, idealistic young law student who was clerking for the Pima County Attorney's office. (She later joined upon graduation.) She performed paralegal-type functions, comparable to Debbie Heller's role for the defense.

Charles "Bud" Miltenberger, fifty-three, was a retired homicide detective and a highly experienced investigator with the county attorney's office.

Though Miltenberger was low-key by nature, the rest of the prosecution team soon developed a fever-pitched commitment to the case. They accepted without skepticism every damaging allegation that had ever been leveled against Knapp by three people whom the defense team considered pathologically unreliable: Linda Knapp, Linda's mother, Louise Ramsey, and Louise's friend Melba Burr. Accordingly, they saw John Knapp as a full-fledged monster. All responsibility for the deplorable conditions of the Knapp house rested solely on John, in their view.

"John Knapp was clearly the boss of that family," White said. White was relying on the accounts of Linda and her mother and disregarding those of all the people who worked with Knapp, who remembered him as comically henpecked, submissive, and doting toward his wife.

In White's eyes Knapp was a wife beater, though Linda and her parents had alleged only one specific instance in which he struck her. He was also a child beater, because Linda and Louise alleged that Knapp once slapped Little Linda, leaving a red mark on her cheek. (Louise claimed that on that occasion Knapp's "hand print stayed with that child for two weeks.")

Though Linda may have had mental problems, Knapp was, in White's eyes, the cause of those problems.

"Much was made," White recounted, "about Linda Knapp being suicidal [and] unstable. . . . [But] her suicide attempts, for the most part, . . . were linked to things that John Knapp did to her. . . . For instance, one of the times she expressed suicidal ideation was when she came home and found John Knapp basically having sex with a fourteen-year-old girl."

White was alluding to Linda's uncorroborated claim, made when she was interrogated in Nebraska, that she had once discovered Knapp on the floor with a teenage runaway.*

"[Linda] made a statement," Kulseth said, referring to a remark Linda once made to Elardo, "that [John] preferred girls twelve to sixteen years of age."

Knapp was a sexual pervert, they believed.

The defense team — though Debbie Heller was less forgiving of John than the others — tended to dismiss Linda's stories (which Knapp denied) as the ravings of an untrustworthy, possibly deranged woman who was then suspected of murder herself and had strong incentives to divert all suspicion onto John.

The accusations were, in any event, irrelevant to the charges, the defense lawyers felt. Knapp was not the only one in the case who had ever been accused of sexual improprieties. Linda's natural father, Art Holiday, had served time for statutory rape. Linda had accused her stepfather, Ken Ramsey, of having raped her in 1974. One of the state investigators who testified against Knapp in 1974 had been accused of rape by *his* stepdaughter — who, by coincidence, happened to be yet another prosecution witness against Knapp. Were all these men capable of burning their children to death?

But the prosecutors saw Linda's accusations about John as virtually the answer key to the case. They provided a rare glimpse into Knapp's true character, and they explained away Linda as well.

Kulseth believed Linda was "probably in the battered-wife-syndrome type thing," she said. "The physical abuse, the mental abuse, the no food, the no heat, the I-don't-care-about-you, you're-a-second-class-citizen [attitude]. I mean, everything he did made her feel like she did not matter, she did not count."

Both White and Kulseth were frustrated that the rules of evidence would

---

* Linda herself said she had no recollection of this alleged incident when interviewed by the author in June 1994.

likely prevent them from trying to depict Knapp as a wife beater, child beater, and sexual pervert.

"What we were allowed to present," Kulseth said in 1993, "was a man who wasn't a great father." The defense could therefore argue, she continued, " 'Gee, he didn't feed his kids or clothe them, but basically he was an okay, swell kind of guy. How could he possibly burn his children to death?' Our case was, 'No, take a look at the real character of this man.' Then, burning his children is just one more logical step in his twisted logic. . . . That's the next thing he would do to accomplish what he thinks is important in his life."

At a scheduling conference on April 29, Judge Martone put off the trial until September, to give White time to prepare. But that was not really much time, since Martone ordered the pretrial hearings to begin in mid-June, just a month and a half away. White would immediately have to prepare to defend the admissibility of Knapp's confession and other evidence and fend off the motion to dismiss based on prosecutor Hyder's alleged misconduct at the 1974 trials.

Ever since November 1990, when he began seeing evidence of misconduct by Hyder, Hammond wanted to file a civil rights suit against Hyder and the other state investigators on Knapp's behalf.

But Henze strenuously opposed all "sideshows," as he called them.

— If you're trying a death case, Larry — he told Hammond, — you've got enough things to worry about without worrying about civil lawyers trying to depose your client and all that other nonsense. I can't believe we're wasting time even thinking about it. —

Hyder would be hard to sue in any event, since prosecutors have *absolute immunity* from civil suit for anything they do *as prosecutors* — including, courts have held, such criminal and quasi-criminal acts as suborning perjury, lying to the court, and withholding evidence.

Henze also opposed filing a bar complaint against Hyder. Though lawyers are required under the ethical rules to report evidence of wrongdoing by other lawyers when they become aware of it, Henze thought such a filing under the circumstances would look like a tactical maneuver.

In any event, Hammond thought, tactical concerns actually counseled *against* filing a bar complaint. If one were brought, Hyder would get a lawyer to defend him at those proceedings. Then White would have an ally to assist him at the prosecutorial misconduct hearings before Judge Martone.

Following Henze's advice, Hammond filed neither a civil suit nor a bar complaint against Hyder.

However, when he filed the motion to dismiss based on prosecutorial misconduct, he sent a copy to Knapp's former lead lawyer, Colin Campbell, who, though now a judge, still had an intense ongoing interest in the case. As soon as Judge Campbell read it, he saw it as his ethical obligation to file a bar complaint against Hyder, and did.

Just as Hammond had feared, the county appropriated funds to allow Hyder to hire a lawyer to defend himself in the bar proceedings, because the alleged misconduct had occurred while Hyder was with the county attorney's office. Hyder hired a prominent civil lawyer, Donald Daughton, whom the county agreed to reimburse for up to $20,000 worth of billings — later increased to $30,000. While the county was paying Hammond $45 per hour to defend Knapp's life, it was paying Daughton $200 an hour to defend Hyder's reputation.

Twenty-four

Typically, legal motions are repetitive, drab, and stuffy, rarely using adjectives more colorful than "substantial," "significant," or "meritless."

For the misconduct motion, Hammond junked that template.

"This is a sordid story," the motion began. "If Knapp had kept any one of his appointments with death, the facts we are about to describe would never have been known."

The motion unfolded in a suspenseful narrative and concluded: "The horror at the dark heart of this case is that the prosecutor himself, aided by those who assisted him in the prosecution, chose to lie and hide from view the evidence of Mr. Knapp's innocence."

The prosecutors were infuriated. Assistant attorney general Powell, who was still handling the case when the motion was first filed, noticed the unusual writing style of the Meyer, Hendricks lawyers on this and other Knapp motions.

"You could tell their pleadings were written for the press," Powell said later. "I don't like it when defenses are tried in the newspaper."

Hammond did not specifically deny Powell's accusation, responding instead: "I did and do believe that [the misconduct] is the horror at the dark heart of this case."

Though Hammond's motion was at first overlooked by local newspapers, by May they had discovered it. The "This-is-a-sordid-story" line and the "horror-at-the-dark-heart" line were both quoted prominently and repeatedly in May,

June, and July 1991 — at least once each on the front pages of the *Arizona Republic* and the *Phoenix Gazette*. Thereafter, almost every day of the hearing resulted in a new story, usually on the first page of the second sections of the papers.

"We thought it was not only appropriate but necessary," Hammond recalled later, "that we do what we could within the bounds of propriety to create as favorable an environment for Knapp as reasonably possible."

The first Knapp trials in 1974 had been tried in a community that had learned from media coverage that Knapp was suspected of one of the worst crimes conceivable. Upon Knapp's arrest newspaper stories immediately explained the state's theory that "camp lantern fuel had been doused on the rug in the bedroom occupied by the children." Detective Malone had told newspapers that laboratory tests had confirmed "the presence of fuel" on the carpeting and said that Knapp had been arrested after being interrogated and given a polygraph test.

"In talking to [Dave] Basham," Hammond recalled, "one of the things that made the pressure of that [1974] trial intolerable to him was this conflict that he's representing somebody who he thinks is innocent, but everybody out there is saying [is] a heinous murderer. . . . That made his job much, much harder. It's better to be cooperative with the press, to let them know our story, so that when this trial starts, we will not be dealing with a jury pool that has been prejudiced against us."

Prosecutor White's terse response to Hammond's misconduct motion was unusually personal in its tone, countering Hammond's ethical charges against Hyder by trying to raise ethical charges against Hammond.

"This is, indeed, a sordid tale," White shot back. "These inflammatory accusations [against Hyder] are leveled without credible evidence and, in several particulars, are made in complete disregard to the factual record available to defense counsel. . . . This conduct does violate the responsibility of all [lawyers] to be candid in their dealings with the tribunal."

White's response did not detail precisely what he thought was misleading about Hammond's charges, but he promised to demonstrate Hyder's complete innocence at the upcoming hearing.

In early June those hearings began before Judge Martone. Though the first week was devoted to motions to suppress the confession and other evidence, the next five weeks were devoted solely to Hyder's alleged misconduct.

The misconduct hearing was, thus, longer than either of Knapp's 1974 trials. And every bit as bitter.

White was as convinced of Hyder's absolute innocence as he was of Knapp's absolute guilt.

"That bogus misconduct hearing," he dismissively called it in 1993. He also alluded to Hammond's "personal vendetta" against Chuck Hyder — the theory, casually advanced by Hyder's lawyers and allies at the time, that Hammond, who had never met Hyder until he interviewed him in March 1991, was being driven by an irrational impulse to sully Hyder's reputation.

In 1991, Charles Hyder portrayed himself in a manner that was sharply at odds with the one that was revealed in the 3,700 pages of transcript during the 1974 proceedings and trials. The man who had refused to turn over gas chromatograms of the fire debris without a court order, telling Diettrich, "Hell no," and claiming they were not "results of scientific tests" within the meaning of the discovery rules, now presented himself as a paragon of propriety in discovery matters.

"To the best of my recollection," Hyder told Hammond in a taped interview in March 1991, "the defense got everything. Because that's the way I practice."

White's strategy for defending Hyder, as it unfolded at the hearing, amounted to a "reasonable doubt" defense. White did not offer a coherent, innocent scenario that would account for each odd event that had unquestionably occurred at the 1974 trials; instead, he raised a variety of reasons to doubt the sufficiency of Hammond's proof of deliberate wrongdoing.

The defense files, White accurately pointed out, had changed hands many times before they reached the Meyer, Hendricks firm, and files may have been lost during that process. The mere absence of documents from the Meyer, Hendricks files did not prove that Hyder hadn't turned them over to Diettrich and Basham, Knapp's original lawyers.

Indeed, it was likely that some things *had* been lost from the file. But even so, why was there the suspicious correspondence between the key missing documents — the fire reenactment videotape, the taped telephone call John Knapp placed from jail, the fingerprint reports, the Melba Burr statement, several written and taped witness statements — and the key pieces of seemingly useful evidence that Basham and Diettrich had inexplicably never used in any manner at the hearings or trials in 1974?

White speculated that the defense lawyers may have been following strategies that we could not divine today; they may have failed to recognize the usefulness of the documents; they may have failed to use them out of simple oversight; and Diettrich may have been drunk. And while Diettrich had been a highly regarded lawyer in 1974, his subsequent dissolution into alcoholism, drugs, and crime in the late 1970s now helped White make his case.

"Chuck Diettrich," White argued to Martone at the hearings, "is a convicted felon and [has] been disbarred twice. . . . I don't like talking about these things . . . but they are important because his memory is key here. He's saying, 'I never got this stuff.' . . . He is an alcoholic. . . . And it is clear and obvious . . . that with that kind of condition, it's going to impair his memory. . . . He was drinking even back then. Heavy drinking. . . . If he's drinking during the day, he's going to have a problem remembering what he's doing, what he's getting, what he's seeing, what he's reading."

As for the tape of John Knapp's telephone call to Linda from jail, Hyder said at first, in a March 1991 taped interview with Hammond, that he vividly recalled turning over a copy to Diettrich seventeen years earlier and even remembered some of the conversation he had with Diettrich about the tape at the time.

By the time of the July 1991 hearings, however, Hyder realized that he could not have turned a copy over to Diettrich, since, during the early stages of the prosecution, Hyder had been refusing to deal with Diettrich in any manner — temporarily even winning a court order forcing Diettrich off the case. At that point Hyder testified that he recalled having handed the tape over to *Basham*.* (The chief investigator in the case, detective Malone, testified in 1991 that he never knew about the tape.)

As for the April 2, 1974, "fire assim." videotape — which, according to documents drawn up at the time, had been made "at the request of Mr. Hyder" — Hyder testified that he had never known about such a tape. If such a tape existed and had been erased, it must have been erased accidentally.† The April 2, 1974, fire test and the November 27, 1973, fire tests must have been one and the same test, according to Hyder. The four-month discrepancy about the date of that test — which went unnoticed at trial by Dale, Hyder, Malone, and Ashford, all of whom remembered having been present at at least one test — must

---

* Most likely Hyder withheld the tape on the untenable theory that he was not required to turn over defendant's statements that he did not intend to use in his case in chief. He repeatedly *took* this *position* at the 1974 trials, although Judge Hardy rejected it each time. Hyder declined to comment to the author on why he would have taken this position with respect to certain of the defendant's statements, but not with respect to this tape.

† Most likely Hyder withheld the videotape on the untenable theory that he was not required to turn over the results of scientific tests that he did not intend to use in his case in chief. He *took* this *position* at the first 1974 trial.

have been an innocent mix-up, as was Dale's two-month backdating of his report about the test.

As for Melba Burr's statement that she had seen Little Linda lighting a whole matchbook on fire on four or five occasions, Hyder testified that he must have turned that statement over to the defense as required. The defense lawyers must have just failed to use it out of some unknown strategy or inadvertence. Hyder said he could infer that the defense lawyers must have received Elardo's report of Melba Burr's prior statements from certain oblique hints and suggestions in the transcript, including the fact that the defense lawyers seemed to know in advance certain things that Burr was going to say. (But they could have learned those things from numerous other people, including John Knapp, Linda Knapp, Mary Knapp, Ken Ramsey, Louise Ramsey, or even from brief encounters with Burr herself.)*

And, finally, there were the fingerprints.

The state's story in 1974 was that the fingerprints on the Coleman fuel cans were smudged, adult prints. That was one of the reasons it was possible to eliminate the children as suspects; they could not, for instance, have spilled the fuel around their room while playing with the cans, since their prints were not on them. But it was not possible to identify which adult had touched the can.

That story, of course, was now known to be false. The prints on two of the cans, including the alleged murder weapon, were actually identifiable, and, as investigator Schwartz of the attorney general's office had discovered in June

---

* Most likely Hyder withheld this statement on the theory that Judge Hardy had suspended the discovery rule that required him to turn it over — and having somehow convinced himself that it was not Brady material. Hyder appears to have said as much on the record. See Chapter 7. Hyder declined to comment to the author about how long, in his opinion, Judge Hardy's discovery suspension was supposed to last; whether, in his opinion, it was ever lifted; and whether, in his opinion, the Elardo report was Brady material.

At one point in the misconduct hearing, Hyder claimed to *remember*, from across the seventeen-year abyss, sending the defense the Melba Burr statement.

"My recollection is the statement was mailed with [the notice of disclosure,]" he said, referring to a one-sentence notice apprising the defense of the general subject of Burr's testimony.

In reality, however, it is doubtful that Elardo's typewritten report of Burr's statement even existed on that date. On Thursday, August 1, 1974, the day before Hyder mailed the notice, Hyder conducted a telephone interview of Melba Burr, which Hyder recorded. During that interview Hyder mentioned that Elardo was on vacation and had not yet typed up his handwritten notes of his interview with her.

Unless Elardo returned from vacation the very next morning, a Friday, with his notes already typed, the typewritten report did not exist when Hyder testified that he sent it.

1990, most of those identifiable prints were Linda's. The investigators couldn't find any that were John's. (Later still, in late August 1991 — after the misconduct hearings were completed — the state's fingerprint examiner went back and reexamined the cans one last time and finally found one of John Knapp's prints on the alleged murder weapon. But that print was *underneath** one of Linda's, meaning that Knapp could not have left it there while committing the crime. If he had used the can to set the fire, of course, he would have been the last to touch the can, and his print would have been on top of Linda's prints, not beneath them.)

By the time of the hearing, Hammond's exhaustive search through the record had turned up an extraordinary train of facts.

In the days immediately after the fire, investigators seized three Coleman fuel cans from the Knapp house and tested them for identifiable fingerprints and to see if there were any children's prints on them. On *one* can — which was full or nearly full and, therefore, could not have been the murder weapon — there really were smudged, adult prints. A police report referring to the fingerprint analysis for *this* can *was* turned over the defense in 1973 or 1974, and it was found in the defense files when Meyer, Hendricks inherited them in 1981.

But the fingerprint reports for the other two cans, including the alleged murder weapon, stated that numerous identifiable lifts were taken from each can. (There were no signs that either can had been handled by cloth or gloves.) These reports were *not* found in defense files that Meyer, Hendricks inherited in 1981.

John Knapp was arrested early in the morning on November 28, 1973, and was fingerprinted during the routine booking process. In addition, investigators took his *palm* prints — which was not routine. Since there were latent palm prints on the can from the closet, it might seem as if someone wanted to run comparisons.

Comparing identifiable prints on the alleged murder weapon to the suspect's prints might seem to be as basic a homicide procedure as can be imagined. Investigator Schwartz of the attorney general's office obviously thought so when

---

* That Knapp's print was underneath one of Linda's came to light only because Hammond took the precaution, exceedingly rare in the case of an indigent defendant, of hiring his own fingerprint analyst. That analyst, Steven Anderson of the Scottsdale police department, discovered and demonstrated that John's print was under one of Linda's. The state's expert later conceded that Anderson was right. Anderson's cost to the Meyer, Hendricks firm was about $11,000, none of which was reimbursed by the court.

she ran such comparisons in 1990. Nevertheless, in 1973 and 1974 comparisons were either never performed — or they *were* performed, but the results, because they tended to cast doubt on the confession, were kept secret.

How was it that the defense lawyers never realized that the fingerprints were identifiable in the first place?

Hyder asserted that he, certainly, had kept nothing from the defense lawyers. He said that the original prosecutor at the local justice court, where the case was filed before being transferred to superior court, had presumably turned over those fingerprint reports to the defense at a December 1973 hearing, before Hyder even got involved in the case.

The original justice court prosecutor, Hugo Zettler, ultimately supported Hyder's theory, claiming to be able to deduce from certain surviving documents and the "office policy" in effect at the time that he must have turned over the fingerprint reports to Basham at a court hearing on December 4, 1973. There were serious flaws in Zettler's logic, however, and it was at least as likely that the reports were never turned over due to simple administrative oversight.*

If Zettler really did turn over the reports, as Hyder and his allies theorized, defense lawyers Basham and Diettrich must have then failed to look at them, since there is no question from their subsequent actions that they never understood that the fingerprints were identifiable. The defense lawyers or their successors must have also later lost those reports, so that they were never passed along to Knapp's later lawyers.

But whether the reports were turned over or inadvertently withheld, it is difficult to construct an innocent explanation for the series of events that followed.†

In early August 1974, when Diettrich was trying to suppress Knapp's confession at a pretrial hearing, he submitted a brief mentioning that the defendant "had been advised by the sheriff's detectives and the fire marshal . . . that the children were eliminated . . . in that no child's prints were found on the can [*sic*] of Coleman fuel but only adult smudge prints."

---

* See Source Notes for a more extended discussion.

† Of course, a meticulous defense lawyer could have easily demanded the fingerprint reports, if they had not been provided. But for a busy defense lawyer, focused on other crises, who thinks he already knows what those reports say — that the prints are smudged — doing so might be a low priority. From the perspective of a defense lawyer, smudged prints would have sounded like good news, since the state, which has the burden of proof, would not be able to prove that Knapp's prints were on the cans. Accordingly, the defense lawyers may never have even noticed that they did not actually have two of the three fingerprint reports.

A few days later Diettrich again mentioned in court his mistaken understanding: "There are no fingerprints on the cans other than adult prints — smudges — they can't say whether it was Mr. or Mrs. Knapp's."

Hyder did not correct Diettrich, merely commenting a few moments later, "Mr. Diettrich's theory of the case . . . and his appreciation of the evidence is much different than mine." At the 1991 misconduct hearings Hyder conceded that he had known that Diettrich was telling the judge incorrect information, but he claimed that his own response had set Judge Hardy straight.

At the first trial in 1974, Hyder called as a witness the fingerprint analyst who had examined the alleged murder weapon. In Hyder's private trial folder — which assistant attorney general Powell turned over to Hammond in March 1991 — there was a piece of paper on which Hyder, in his famously methodical way, had typed out the questions he planned to ask and the answers he expected the expert, William Watling, to give. The planned examination would have elicited that there were numerous identifiable prints on the can.

Yet at trial Hyder did *not* follow that script. Instead, Hyder tiptoed through the examination in a way that did not reveal that the prints were identifiable.

During Diettrich's cross-examination of Watling, Diettrich's ignorance of the true situation again became apparent.

"And you found no fingerprints on the can you could identify?" Diettrich asked.

"I found some latent prints on the can," Watling responded, "but none that could be considered to have been made by a child of the ages listed."

"Were you able to identify the prints you found on the can?" Diettrich persisted.

"No, sir, I was not."

Watling's answer was exceedingly misleading. He was *able* to identify those prints, he had just never been *asked* to identify them, as both Watling and Hyder knew. Hyder conceded at the 1991 misconduct hearings that he had known the fingerprints were identifiable at the time Watling gave this misleading answer, but he claimed to see nothing wrong with Watling's answer. Watling asserted at the misconduct hearings in 1991 that his answer would have been correctly understood by a fingerprint specialist, although he conceded that he could not say whether jurors would have understood it.

At the second 1974 trial, Hyder did not traverse the same perilous ground. Instead of having Watling testify in person again, Hyder and Diettrich entered into a *stipulation* to have Judge Hardy simply tell the jurors what Watling supposedly would have said if called. Hyder falsely told the jury that Watling would say that he had found only adult, smudged prints on the can. Diettrich, still in the dark, consented to the stipulation. Then Judge Hardy relayed Hyder's false message to the jurors, who would convict Knapp: "You can take it as a fact," he told them, "there were no children's fingerprints on any of these cans, and the fingerprints that were there were so smudged they could not be identified."

Shortly before entering the false stipulation, Hyder had also stood by silently as the jury and Diettrich were misled yet again about the truth about the fingerprints, this time by the chief investigator on the case, detective Robert Malone. Malone inaccurately testified on cross-examination that fingerprint analysis showed only "smudged fingerprints of adults and no fingerprints of children." Finally, in his summation, Hyder falsely argued to the jury that "a lot of smeared, unidentifiable adult prints were found on the cans. No children's prints."

Malone's testimony and the stipulation that was read to the second jury — the jury that convicted John Knapp of a capital crime — were both false. If Hyder knew that this testimony and stipulation were false, it is difficult to overstate the enormity of the fraud he was perpetrating. In 1974 in Arizona, to commit or suborn perjury at a murder trial was a felony punishable by up to fourteen years imprisonment; if the perjury procured the execution of an innocent man, the perjuror was himself subject to a mandatory sentence of death.

Hyder's responses to this gradually snowballing mass of evidence evolved over time. Originally, when Hammond interviewed him in March 1991, Hyder said that he had never realized that the prints were identifiable. The fingerprint experts must have mistakenly told him that they were unidentifiable.

But Hyder later changed his mind in light of the documents from Hyder's trial file* showing that in 1974 Hyder himself had written out the answers that he expected Watling to give — including the fact that the prints were identifiable.

Hyder then acknowledged that, in fact, he must have known during both the suppression hearing and the first trial that the prints were identifiable. He tes-

---

* The document from Hyder's trial file was confidential attorney "work product." Prosecutor Powell could, therefore, have chosen to withhold it from the defense. But Powell was sufficiently disturbed by what the documents revealed — particularly the disparity between the planned Q&A and the actual Q&A — that he felt Hammond ought to have it, Powell told the author.

"I have a tremendous amount of respect for Chuck Hyder," Powell said. "But it was his battle to fight at that point. He had to come forward with the explanation, because I couldn't formulate one."

tified, however, that *he must have forgotten that fact during the month-and-a-half hiatus between the first trial and the second trial.*

"I'm not sure exactly what happened," Hyder told Hammond at the hearings. "It's my opinion that there was an honest mistake by myself, Mr. Diettrich, and Judge Hardy."

There was still one wrinkle to be ironed out. Since Hyder was now conceding that he *had* known that the prints were identifiable during the first trial, the question arose: Why had he never asked that they be compared to Knapp's?

White maintained at the hearing that they were never compared because such comparisons would not have shown anything important. He maintained that since everyone knew the cans belonged to John and Linda, one would expect their fingerprints to be on the cans. All the investigators cared about was whether there were children's prints on the cans. As long as the children's prints were not there, the children could be eliminated as suspects.

And White forcefully argued that, because it is physically possible for someone to touch a can and not leave fingerprints, the absence of Knapp's fingerprints was meaningless.

Yet evidence can carry weight without being completely dispositive of an issue. If Knapp's confession was true, he had emptied a gallon of fuel all around the children's room and had then buried the can in the closet. If that can was covered with identifiable prints — and showed no signs of having been handled by gloves or cloth — one might have expected his prints to be among the ones observed.

If the fingerprints were literally meaningless, why had Hyder presented evidence about them at all? Indeed, if the absence of John's prints was literally meaningless, then the absence of the children's prints would also have been meaningless, and Hyder would have been conning the jurors in suggesting that they could eliminate the children as suspects because of the absence of *their* prints on the cans. To the extent there was any force to White's argument, it did not exonerate Hyder; it only changed the focus of the fraud Hyder was perpetrating on the jury.

If the absence of the children's prints on the cans *eliminated* the children as suspects, why didn't the absence of John Knapp's prints on the cans eliminate *him* as a suspect?

It was a question that intrigued the logician, Judge Martone. Martone sought an answer from the state's witnesses at the misconduct hearings in 1991, but in vain. He tried most persistently with the witness Joseph Howe, who had been an administrative deputy in the county attorney's office during Hyder's first prosecution of Knapp in 1974. Howe, a former evidence professor, had become a superior court judge in Phoenix by the time of the misconduct hearings.

"Do you have an opinion as to why," Judge Martone asked, "as a matter of logic, the absence of the children's prints would tend to exclude the children, but the absence of the defendant's prints would not tend to exclude the defendant?"

"Well," Judge Howe responded, "I think probably because the presence or absence of adult prints belonging to the parents would not tend, from an impact standpoint to the jury, to mean much. But I think that the absence of any children's prints at all, to the jury, would tend to be important."

Judge Howe, the former evidence professor, was speaking gibberish.

The notion that there could have been a plausible reason why homicide investigators would choose not to compare latent prints on the alleged murder weapon to the known prints of the murder suspect suffered another severe jolt on June 27, 1991, about midway through the hearings. That's when it came out that, in fact, *comparisons apparently had been done.*

That truth was finally volunteered by John Jolly and his supervisor. Jolly was the fingerprint examiner who, in June 1990, compared the latent prints from the Coleman fuel cans to known prints from John and Linda Knapp. He testified briefly at the misconduct hearings on June 17, 1991, but was not asked questions that would have elicited what Jolly knew was important information. About a week later, with his conscience bothering him, both he and his supervisor had come forward to volunteer what they knew. (Prosecutor White, who had not known of this information previously, notified Hammond as soon as he learned of it. Though prosecutor Susan Sherwin had known about this information since June 1990, she had attached no significance to it, she later testified.)

When Jolly had gone into the old latent print files in June 1990 and fished out the cards from the Knapp case, he had discovered that a number of the cards were *folded*. Folding was something that was done during the process of *comparing* two sets of prints. The cards were folded so that the analyst could put two prints next to each other under a magnifying glass. Ironically, Jolly's supervisor had been aggravated about Jolly's discovery from a purely bureaucratic perspective. He was annoyed that Jolly was wasting his time on redundant comparisons.

But then he and Jolly discovered that there was no earlier comparison report. And that was very strange. It was contrary to procedure to perform a comparison and not draw up a report.

Neither Hyder nor White conceded that comparisons had, in fact, been done between the latents and John Knapp's prints in 1973 or 1974. Instead, White speculated that perhaps the analysts in 1974 had compared the latent prints *not* to John Knapp's prints, but to other *latent* prints. Though such a possibility had never occurred to either Jolly or his supervisor, White managed to secure from the original fingerprint analyst, Watling, the concession that, indeed, analysts sometimes *did* compare latents to latents. They might do so, Watling explained, if they found latents on several different objects and wanted to find matches in order to make their job easier *when the time came to compare those latents to known prints*.

But doing such a latent-to-latent comparison would still only make sense, then, if the analysts anticipated eventually comparing latents to known prints — which Hyder claimed had never been contemplated. A latent-to-latent comparison in the context of the Knapp case did not make any sense. Still, it was a scenario White could cling to, rather than concede the horrendous, obvious alternative.

In its final serpentine form, White and Hyder's innocent scenario explaining what happened with respect to the fingerprints in this case — one of the most high-profile Arizona homicide cases of its time — goes something like this:

Justice court prosecutor Zettler turned over the fingerprint reports to Knapp's defense lawyers, who did not look at them, or forgot what they showed, and then lost them. Hyder and the state investigators knew that there were identifiable prints on the alleged murder weapon, but chose not to compare them to John Knapp's prints, seeing no point to it. Comparisons were performed, nevertheless, between those latent prints and other unknown latents for unknown reasons, and the results of that comparison were never recorded anywhere. Then, sometime during the month-and-a-half break between the first and second 1974 trials, Hyder *forgot* that the prints were identifiable and told the judge and jury that they were smudged. Meanwhile, the chief investigator on the case, detective Malone, either never knew that the prints were identifiable, or he did know, but *also forgot* that fact. As a result he, too, falsely testified at the second trial that the prints were smudged.

Twenty-five

In late June, in the midst of the misconduct hearings, the East Valley daily newspaper, the *Mesa Tribune*, received an anonymous fax addressed to Lynn DeBruin, the reporter covering those hearings.

The short message (from which names have been deleted because of the lack of corroboration for the fax's allegations) read approximately* as follows:

> An old fireman knows that when the gas samples from the carpet in the Knapp children's bedroom were first submitted for examination, the results were negative. [Name A] then 'doctored' the samples and resubmitted them. They were then found to have Coleman fuel in them. The following people know about this:
> [Name B]
> [Name C]
> [Name D]

The typeface of the fax was small, so the clerk who first picked it up from the machine had enlarged it on a photocopier, which also had the advantage of

---

* Although the *Tribune*'s lawyers allowed Hammond to see the fax, they placed certain strictures on its use. This account of the fax is taken from a sealed letter Hammond wrote to the court, which quoted the fax "approximately" but did not append it.

transferring the message off the curling, fading thermal paper onto conventional paper. Then she gave the enlarged copy to DeBruin and threw out the original. In the process of enlarging the fax, however, the clerk had inadvertently cut off the transmission information inscribed along the upper edge of the original, which might have identified the telephone number of the sender's machine. Before anyone thought to look for the original, it had been forwarded along its untraceable path to the dumpster.

DeBruin asked Hammond about the fax the next day, and Hammond went to the *Tribune*'s offices to see it later that week.

Several things struck him from the start. The gas chromatography aspect of the case had received almost no press coverage either at the 1974 trials or since Knapp's 1990 rearrest; the subject was too complex. Nor was it a topic at the prosecutorial misconduct hearings. In addition, the names of the individuals designated here as A and C had never appeared in the newspapers since 1974 — and had been minor presences even then.

But the most remarkable thing about the fax was that its allegations dovetailed with what defense chemists Parsons and Canfield had been saying all along: the chromatograms simply could not be what they purported to be. Specifically, both of them — and, by this time, they had been joined by a third chromatography specialist from Dallas, whom Canfield had brought into the case — maintained that the graphs for the "extract" samples lifted using a solvent-soaked gauze pad were *too* similar to the one allegedly produced by the Coleman fuel can from the Knapp home. The volatile substance showing up in the extract samples did not show signs of having been through a fire, and it did not show any extra peaks reflecting the presence of the solvent that the pads had been soaked in.

"I believe it's true," Hammond said in 1993, of the accusation contained in the fax. "Like many other things in this case, I would be surprised to find that it is precisely accurate — so much time has passed. . . . But I think it is substantively true."

But what could Hammond do with the accusations contained in an anonymous fax? There wasn't even a trail to pursue.

Jon Sands put an oblique ad in the *Tribune*, seeking to contact an "old fireman" concerning a matter of "life and death." He got no responses.

Hammond could not ethically bring such accusations up in front of the jury without more to go on. The fax remained an anonymous, unsubstantiated allegation that never surfaced at trial.

*   *   *

Judge Martone's reactions to what he was hearing at the misconduct hearing had gone through phases. At the outset of the misconduct hearing, he had been obviously shocked by how misleading the testimony of Hyder's original fingerprint analyst, William Watling, had been at the first trial in 1974. When Martone found out that Watling had testified that he was "unable" to identify the prints on the murder weapon, when in fact he was *able* to identify them, but had simply never been asked to try, Martone had interrupted the proceedings.

"What level of detail must a lawyer go through," he had asked in disbelief, "to get the whole truth and nothing but the truth when asked?" (Watling claimed that his answer would have been correctly understood by fingerprint experts and that he had been trained not to volunteer information in court.)

After that exchange, Hammond was euphoric.

"I think we're approaching the end game," he told the author at that time, pronouncing the words slowly and evenly, as if he feared jinxing what might be in the works.

Even Knapp had shown flickers of optimism.

— Do you like to fish? — Knapp had asked Hammond, shortly after Martone had grilled Watling.

Hammond told him he had done it only once or twice.

— Maybe one day, when this is all over, I'll take you fishing, — Knapp said.

But White also scored points during the hearing. The files inherited by the Meyer, Hendricks lawyers in 1981 had passed through many hands before reaching them, and there was evidence that things had been lost. It was impossible to prove that something missing in 1981 had never been turned over in 1974.

And by mid-July, as the twenty-two-day hearing drew to a close, Hammond could tell that something had gone wrong. Judge Martone obviously wanted to wrap up the hearing; he curtailed Hammond's cross-examination of Hyder and then limited final arguments to a brisk one hour per side.

What had gone wrong was that Judge Martone was simply unwilling to read the precedents in the expansive way Hammond and his colleagues had hoped.

As Martone understood the law — and, strange as it may sound, he was on strong ground — he could dismiss the case only if the purpose of Hyder's alleged misconduct had been to avoid an acquittal by goading the defense lawyer into asking for a mistrial. If, on the other hand, the purpose of Hyder's misconduct had been merely to win Knapp's conviction — and death — Knapp was entitled only to a new trial, which he was already getting.

The change in Martone's attitude came as a body blow to Hammond.

"The motion will be denied," Hammond solemnly told the author the day after the hearing ended, but weeks before Martone issued his ruling.

Paralegal Debbie Heller recalled Hammond's brutal disappointment: "He was so sure we were going to win the misconduct hearing. He was just positively sure. I think that's part of why this trial took its wear and tear on him. He put all his energy into this hearing. . . . For nothing."

Shortly after returning to Meyer, Hendricks in January, Jon Sands had assumed the responsibility of visiting John Knapp at the jail every Sunday.

Sands would sign in, show his bar card, walk through a metal detector, clip a plastic visitor's badge to his shirt, and then sit and wait. When his time came, a deputy sheriff dressed in brown slacks and khaki shirt, with a metal badge shaped like the state of Arizona, escorted him through the double, sliding, blue steel doors. The deputy would take Sands in a large, bare metal elevator up to Level Four, which housed the visiting rooms.

Though the general public could visit inmates only by talking to them through a telephone while viewing them through a wire-mesh-reinforced sheet of tempered glass, attorneys could meet with clients in person. Sands would be let into one of a row of small, unadorned rooms of white cinderblock, furnished with a particleboard table and two or three molded plastic chairs.

While Sands waited, the process of getting Knapp began. A message would be sent to the central, air-conditioned guard tower on Level Six, where maximum security inmates were housed. A guard there would eventually throw a switch that would electronically open the solid metal sliding door to Knapp's cell, allowing Knapp to emerge into the yellow, mercury-vapor lighting and hot, stale air of the "dayroom" in front of the fifteen cells of his pod. The pods and dayrooms were cooled by an evaporative system that, by July, was no match for Phoenix's 110-degree heat and rising humidity. Most of the sweaty inmates went shirtless this time of year, displaying tattoos concerning sexual, Nazi, or gang-related themes.

A second guard unlocked the steel door to the pod with a foot-long key and allowed Knapp into the corridor, where a strip of black-and-yellow-striped tape along the concrete floor marked where inmates could step and where they could not. He was led to a side room, strip searched, and then, sometimes, shackled with leg irons and handcuffs. The cuffs were threaded through a loop on a leather body cinch around his waist, to prevent him from raising his arms. He was then led to Level Four.

Sands's visits were combinations of business and social calls. He always brought a list of questions to ask about obscure details of the case.

— The night of the fire, would there have been any sheets on the bed the children were sleeping in? —

— I don't think so. I think there was just a blanket. —

— Are you sure? Sheets might have helped the bed catch fire faster. —

— No. I just remember a blanket. —

Sands would bring Knapp up to date on developments in the case, showing him motions they had written, or photographs of the Weyerhaeuser tests, or recounting witness interviews they had conducted. But Sands was reluctant to leave documents with Knapp, and when he did, he was careful to collect them at his next visit. His overriding fear, which Knapp shared, was of inmate informants or "snitches" — prisoners who would fabricate claims that other inmates had confessed to them and then try to barter favor from prosecutors by offering to testify to the "confession" in exchange for leniency for their own crimes. (Ray Girdler, Knapp's doppelganger, may have been victimized by such an inmate.) In order to fabricate a credible confession, a snitch had to learn as much about the other inmate's case as he could. Sands therefore insisted that Knapp keep close tabs on every document.

Knapp needed little prodding in this regard. He already clipped articles about his case out of jail newspapers to keep other inmates from reading them, and he asked Sands for advance warning of television stories so that he could try to have the dayroom television tuned to a different channel when they aired.

Whenever the defense team planned a major strategy decision, Sands would have to get Knapp's permission. But Knapp's response was invariable.

— Do whatever you think is best. —

Knapp's only recalcitrance as a client appeared to stem from the emotional pain he experienced when he looked at certain documents. Since Knapp would eventually be testifying, Sands had to familiarize him with hundreds of pages of his earlier testimony and related documents. But Knapp protested that it was painful to read Hyder's cross-examinations of him, and he also resisted Sands's attempts to get him to read detective Malone's police report recounting his confession.

— I've never read it, and I'm not about to now, — he told Sands at one point. Sands kept pressing him.

Sands also talked to Knapp about his demeanor in court. During both the misconduct hearings and the preliminary hearings in 1990, several journalists had written about Knapp's disinterested demeanor, and how he had twiddled his thumbs or smiled or joked with his lawyers.

Knapp, on the other hand, complained to Sands about how humiliating it had been for him to sit at those hearings dressed in the ill-fitting blue surgeon's scrubs that jail inmates now wore. Knapp, whose weight was up to about 255 pounds, was hard to fit. When the pants were too small, they rode low on his waist and barely concealed his buttocks, which were turned toward the packed gallery when he sat at counsel's table. Out of shame and modesty he would slouch down in his chair, which observers interpreted as lack of alertness or interest.

During the social parts of Sands's visits, Knapp often asked after Sands's daughter Madeline, who had just been born in February. Knapp commented about how odd it was to watch the children of his lawyers grow up over the years, seeing only the disjointed maturation that photographs record.

They would discuss news, sports, or movies. (During that period, the jail showed videocassette movies on the dayroom televisions on Friday and Saturday nights.) At Knapp's request, the Meyer, Hendricks lawyers had gotten him subscriptions to *Scientific American,* both when he was on death row in Florence and now, again, at the Madison Street Jail. Knapp told Sands about articles he had read about the oars used by the ancient Iraqi navy or about the different kinds of longbows used by English archers and Mongolian horsemen.

Knapp also talked about religion sometimes. While Knapp had already become a religious Christian during his long years on death row, during the past year Knapp had begun to identify himself specifically as a "born-again" Christian. Most of what differentiated the various denominations of Christianity, he explained in 1991, was superfluous ritual that had been added to the Bible by men. "Fundamentalism strips all that away," he said.

If Knapp needed money — to buy toiletries, candy, soft drinks, or batteries for approved earphone-equipped radios — Sands or other defense lawyers would deposit ten or twenty dollars of their own money into Knapp's jail account.

Knapp and Sands would also chat about other inmates and their fates. When one inmate was allowed to plead guilty in exchange for time served — meaning that he was released from jail and could go home — Knapp mused about whether he could ever accept such a plea.

— I've spent so long in jail already that pleading might not be such a bad thing, — he said. — On the other hand, I didn't do anything wrong. —

Then Knapp paused.

— I might be willing to plead to something like criminal negligence, — he said. — I am responsible for letting Linda keep the house in such a shambles. —

Sands paid Knapp one of his regular Sunday visits on the morning of July 21, 1991, three days after the end of the misconduct hearing. Though Judge Martone had not yet issued his ruling, Knapp had picked up the same ominous signals that Hammond had.

— I don't think Martone's going to grant any of our motions, — he said.

— I think you're probably right, — Sands admitted.

Knapp's mood was low, and there were long silences at this visit.

— Martone knows what the state did, — Knapp said. — He knows the state hid the fingerprint stuff. But they're not going to get punished. It's wrong. —

He commented that other inmates got out on "technicalities." Why couldn't he get out no matter what happened?

Knapp began to cry.

"While there was substantial evidence in this case in connection with withheld evidence, the destruction of evidence, and inaccurate representations," Martone wrote on July 31, 1991, there was no evidence that such conduct was committed for the one narrow purpose that, as Martone read the precedents, would warrant outright dismissal. "If there was prosecutorial misconduct, it is clear that its purpose was to maximize the possibility of conviction, not to goad the defendant into moving for a mistrial."

As Martone saw it, Knapp's only remedy was a new trial, which he was already getting. "The remedy for professional misconduct lies with another body," Martone wrote — an obvious allusion to the state bar of Arizona.

Judge Martone also denied all of Knapp's other motions.

Martone's ruling never discussed the specifics of the allegations against Hyder. In fact, following a common practice in judicial opinions concerning allegations of prosecutorial misconduct, Judge Martone never even mentioned Charles Hyder's name.

Since the bottom line was that the motion to dismiss was denied, it became possible for Hyder's allies to *take the position* that Judge Martone had exonerated Hyder. Which was a lie.

Though they remained outwardly professional, Larry Hammond and David White emerged from the misconduct hearings with a profound animosity toward each other.

"I really developed a dislike for White," Hammond acknowledged. "He was willing to do anything. They took one thing after another out of context. And White would just stand up there and do it. And do it well."

Ironically, White's description of Hammond was almost identical.

"[Hammond] would take what a witness said out of context . . . which gave it a whole new meaning," he said. "I don't do that. I don't think it's appropriate to do that. Mr. Hammond does that as a technique."

From this point forward, Henze or Sands handled most of the person-to-person dealings with White on scheduling and other administrative matters.

Since the case was now going to trial, Henze now finally had to decide whether to serve as Hammond's actual co-counsel at trial.

While the Meyer, Hendricks firm was making huge sacrifices to handle the Knapp case, its thirty-five partners were sharing that burden, and its lawyers were still drawing regular salaries. Tom Henze, on the other hand, was a solo practitioner with a wife and four children. His office overhead expenses came to about $15,000 per month. He was going to absorb the hit all by himself.

He had made no money in March or June, due to intense work on the Knapp case, and doing the trial would mean making little or no money for the next three or four months as well.

But the case had sucked Henze in. Everyone in Henze's family agreed to adjust their standard of living, and Henze agreed to be Hammond's co-counsel.

"I think I put my head in the sand," Henze later said.

After the pretrial motions were completed, the pro bono committee at Arnold & Porter, Jim Scarboro's firm, decided that it could no longer contribute attorneys to an Arizona case that was already in good hands. By that time that firm had donated $126,202.50 in attorneys' fees and $18,729.08 in out-of-pocket expenses to the Knapp case.

In mid-July the defense team made a mistake. Immediately after the misconduct hearings ended, Hammond kept a long-standing promise to his family and used nonrefundable airline tickets to take a ten-day vacation to Europe. But before leaving there had been miscommunications between him and Zig Popko about the filing of a list of additional witnesses the defense team wanted to call. When Hammond got back the list still hadn't been filed. They filed it then, but it was late. At prosecutor White's request, Judge Martone barred several of the witnesses listed in it from testifying.

Hammond was furious that evening in 20 South — his anger probably fueled, he later suggested, by his sense of guilt over having been "off fooling around in Bavaria" in the first place.

Though ultimate responsibility for the error rested on Hammond, Popko felt his share of the horrible burden. What if he had contributed to the stupid little clerical error that would now cost the life of an innocent man?

"It was my job," Popko said later. "I was and am responsible."

But no one on the defense team directed anger at Popko, especially since every one of them had been living for more than a year with a phantom hovering over their every act in the case: the phantom of Roger Coleman. In 1986 their erstwhile co-counsel Arnold & Porter, one of the nation's preeminent law firms, had generously agreed to donate its time to handle the appeal from a state post-conviction proceeding for Coleman, an indigent defendant sentenced to death for a rape-murder in Virginia. Ignorant of an obscure Virginia appellate rule, the lawyers miscalculated the date by which their notice of appeal was due; thinking they were filing it two days early, they in fact filed it one day late. As a result, Coleman lost his right to appeal and then, in a catastrophic domino effect, lost the right to raise in federal court every issue that could have been raised in that now "waived" appeal. (Coleman was executed in May 1992.)

Against that backdrop, the late filing of Knapp's supplemental witness list was trivial. And with everyone on the team petrified that the next error would be costlier — and theirs — people were very supportive of Popko.

In early September the lawyers picked sixteen jurors, of whom twelve would deliberate. The alternates would be determined by lots at the end of trial, and excused.

The defense lawyers hoped to get well-educated jurors, who might be receptive to the complicated scientific aspects of the defense case. Following conventional wisdom, they also favored strong personalities — the type of people who would hold out for acquittal even if they were in the minority. Strong personalities might also clash with each other, resulting in a hung jury. A deadlocked jury is generally considered a victory for a defendant, since, without a conviction, the state can impose no penalty and may choose not to retry the case.

Sands thought that Cheryl, a fifty-year-old single woman, might have a strong personality. Although she had two brothers who had been police officers — a fact that weighed against her in the defense calculus — she was a quality manager at an aerospace company and had a couple years of college-level courses, which weighed in her favor.

A young mother named Dolores, a twenty-seven-year-old accounts receivable clerk with a high school education, also seemed strong-willed to Sands. She had been willing to raise her hand in front of a room full of prospective jurors to ask to go to the restroom.

Sunny, fifty-one, and Gladys, fifty, also seemed to have forceful personalities. They were each grandmothers who were raising one of their own grandchildren. Gladys, Hammond knew from a questionnaire the jurors had to fill out, had had child protective services take her grandchild away from her own daughter, because she felt her daughter was subjecting the child to a bad environment. Hammond thought Gladys might identify with Knapp's mother, Mary — who had called the Pomona police when she saw how Linda cared for her children — and distrust Linda's mother, Louise, who had returned the Knapp children to Linda's neglectful custody.

Of the sixteen selected — nine women and seven men — five had college degrees, and all but one had high school diplomas or the equivalent.

Accordingly, Hammond was pleased with the panel, the most well-educated jury he had ever been before.

In most respects the jury was much like any other — almost a complete mystery despite each side's crude efforts to mold it.

In one respect, however, the jury in a death-penalty case is necessarily unlike one that sits in any other case, civil or criminal. No juror in such a case is permitted to have serious moral qualms about the death penalty, if those qualms might impair the juror's ability to impose that sentence.

The rule makes perfect sense. Such a juror is unable to apply the law. But the rule also excludes a significant cross-section of the American population that would ordinarily qualify to sit on juries — many observant Catholics, for instance.

Lawyers have wondered if this process of "death-qualifying" juries systematically combs out a segment of the population that would generally be considered more "liberal" on criminal justice issues, less trusting of law enforcement authorities, and more cautious about casting a vote to convict. If so, then — ironically — the jury in a death case might actually be prone to convict more readily than a jury in any other case.

In 1968 the U.S. Supreme Court expressed concern about this problem, but said that no empirical studies yet existed demonstrating the hypothesized distortion. In 1986, after such studies had been performed — and appeared to establish the feared correlation — the Court addressed the question a second time. But by then its membership had changed, and the new majority found that, even if death-qualification did statistically correlate with a bias toward conviction, such bias was not unconstitutional.

As a result, John Knapp's jury in 1991 was composed of sixteen people who had no serious qualms about capital punishment.

"I believe in the death penalty," Jim, a forty-four-year-old marketing consultant on the jury, said in 1993, adding that he also believed it should be carried out promptly. None of this "ten years later, they execute you."

Gladys, a court clerk, likewise had no problem with it — especially in a case involving the murder of a child. "I'd drop the pellets," Gladys told the author, referring to the cyanide pellets that, when submerged in acid, produce the lethal gas used in gas chambers. "It wouldn't bother me one bit."

Twenty-six

Arizona's third attempt to put John Knapp to death began on Thursday, September 12, 1991, on the thirteenth floor of the Central Courthouse. This courthouse, built in 1977, closely resembled the one next door, now known as the East Courthouse, where Knapp had originally been tried and convicted.

Judge Martone's courtroom was a little smaller than Judge Hardy's had been, but otherwise it, too, was reminiscent. In both, witnesses walked down a short center aisle, past three rows of wood benches, and then passed through a low wooden gate into the well of the courtroom.

Judge Martone's bench stood in the far right-hand corner of the room as viewed from the gallery, while the jury box was in the far left-hand corner, and each was slanted symmetrically toward the center of the room. The witness box stood between them, adjoining the judge's bench.

The state's case would be fought out under many different premises than it had been in 1974.

This time around, for instance, the state would be *conceding* that children the age of the Knapp children were capable of lighting matches. This would accommodate the better information about child fire-setting that was now available,* as well as the fact that the 1991 jury was going to find out that Melba Burr said she had actually seen Little Linda lighting matches.

And while Hyder had been able to *take the position* in 1974 that Linda was not a "suspect," that was no longer going to be tenable, especially since the jury was going to find out that Linda's fingerprints were all over the Coleman fuel cans and that John's weren't. In fact, assistant attorneys general Sherwin and Powell had actually taken the precaution of charging Knapp with murder not only as a principal but also *as an accessory* — allowing them to argue, if need be, that perhaps he had aided and abetted Linda to murder the children. (There was still insufficient evidence, however, to charge Linda herself with the crime. In addition, Linda was still absolutely immune from prosecution, assuming Judge Hardy had been empowered, as he thought he was, to grant her transactional immunity during the first trial in 1974.)

In addition, the prosecution would approach Knapp's confession in a very different way in 1991 than it had in 1974. The theory of Hyder's case in 1974 was simplicity itself: the crime had occurred exactly the way Knapp said it had in his confession. Knapp had literally poured a gallon of Coleman fuel in the bedroom using the can from the hall closet. Hyder had even argued that one of the ways jurors could tell that Knapp's confession was true was that Knapp had said he used the can from the hall closet — the very can deputy fire marshal Dale thought had most likely been used.

In 1991, however, White would take a different tack. The confession was true only in an impressionistic sense. *The details of the confession might not be right.* Knapp may *not* have actually used the can from the hall closet. This adjustment accommodated the fact that the 1991 jury, unlike the 1974 juries, was going to find out that the can in the closet had lots of identifiable fingerprints on it and that none of them were John's (except for one that was underneath one of

---

* One study, for instance, involving the fire department for the city of Rochester, New York, found that from 1985 to 1991, firefighters responded to 270 fires that were later determined to have been set by children four years old or younger. Of those fires that had been set with *matches*, 27 were set by three-year-olds; 14 by two-year-olds; and one by a one-year-old.

When the study began, researchers would go to a fire scene only if the firefighters reported back to them that children appeared to have been involved. But as the study progressed the researchers began to realize that whenever an alarm went off in the early morning hours, it was so likely set by preschool-age children that they would just go along with the firefighters from the outset. The morning hours before work or school began appeared to be a time when preschoolers were often up before their parents and unsupervised.

Linda's). The 1991 jury was also going to find out that, two weeks after the fire, Linda told detective Malone that the can in the closet had been empty long *before* the fire.

Accordingly, White was going to have to be very vague about precisely which can *was* the murder weapon. The can from the bookshelf — which was about half full when recovered — was a possibility, although it could not have contributed a full gallon of fuel, and it suffered the same problem as the can from the closet: none of the fingerprints on it were John's.

The can on the floor could not have been the weapon, since it had been full or nearly so when it was recovered.

In fact, in 1991 White was going to be so pressed for murder weapons that he would conscript into service two possibilities that had never even been mentioned in 1974: the two cans lying outside in the yard, one of which was not a Coleman can, but a gasoline can. The original investigators had never even taken these two cans into evidence. Those investigators had either somehow overlooked the possibility that one of these cans could have been the murder weapon, or they had ruled out those cans for reasons they had not recorded at the time. In 1991 fire inspector James McDaniel would testify that it had been obvious to him — from dirt, cobwebs, or rust — that those cans in the yard had been empty for a long time. Still, there was room for White to *take the position* that maybe one of those cans lying outside had been the murder weapon.

At the same time, White in 1991 would also depart from the words of Knapp's confession by suggesting that Knapp may not have actually used a full gallon of fuel after all. This adjustment accommodated the fact that the state's new expert, DeHaan, conceded that the window in the Knapp children's bedroom had not broken out for "some many minutes" into the fire and that DeHaan himself had had trouble setting off any quantity of Coleman fuel in a closed compartment without immediately blowing the window out.

Tall, commanding, confident, and dressed in a light gray suit, White began his opening statement with an introduction that prosecutors often use in murder trials.

"We read you a long list of names the first day you were in here," he said, referring to the witness lists that were read to the prospective jurors, to make sure the jurors did not know any of them. "I lost count after about ninety-four, ninety-five. . . . There were some names we didn't read you from that list: Iona Knapp and Little Linda Knapp. . . . Little Linda is three and a half years old. Iona is the smaller one, two and a half years old, and they're not going to be with us.

"They are not going to be witnesses because on November 16, 1973, they were burned to death in their own bedroom here in Maricopa County in Mesa."

White took a few steps back from the jury box and toward the defense table.

"This trial is an account of how they died," White continued, "and the person who murdered them."

Now White wheeled and pointed right into Knapp's face.

"That person is this man right here, John Henry Knapp."

Hammond thought that Knapp might be rattled by having White do this to him.

"I remember putting my hand on John's forearm," Hammond recalled later, "and thinking that I would feel some tension or that I might need to calm him down or restrain him. But it was like I had touched a dead man. He just wasn't reacting."

Juror Dolores, the young accounts receivable clerk, was watching Knapp intently at the time.

"I mean David White points the finger at [him] — and he showed no emotion," Dolores remembered a little over a year later. "[Knapp] wasn't even intimidated by the prosecuting attorney," she said. She began to think that maybe Knapp had too strong a personality to have been bullied into confessing falsely.

White then began to describe to the jurors Knapp's behavior on the day of the fire.

"[Two neighbors] were crawling down that hallway, fighting the smoke and the fire and the heat to get those little babies out of that room. What was John Knapp, the defendant, doing? Standing outside that house, drinking a cup of coffee, smoking a cigarette while other people tried to save his babies. . . .

"You are also going to hear that he was callous, one witness will testify, like a host at a cocktail party. Jovial, as his babies burned to death."

White briefly summarized the confession with acceptable adversarial distortion, telling it as if Knapp had spontaneously narrated the whole thing without any prompting from Malone.

White's approach to Linda Knapp was agnostic. At this stage he did not know whether the defense would pursue the Linda-did-it theory, so he did not yet know whether he would have to pursue the maybe-they-both-did-it theory.

"Was Linda Knapp involved? . . . Well, she was interrogated . . . [and] she never confessed. . . . You are going to hear evidence [however] that's going to make you believe she covered for this defendant. . . . . So maybe she was involved, too. I will let you decide that."

To conclude, White returned to more solid ground.

"Memories dim. There is one memory that has not dimmed. The people of the Capri neighborhood . . . have not forgotten that while other people were risking their lives to save those babies, while other people were frightened and upset and nervous, this defendant was calm and clean and composed and callous. That's because he wasn't in shock. He was satisfied. Because he set that fire."

Although everyone hopes that a lawyer's personal appearance, skill, and personality play no role in determining the outcome of any court case, let alone a capital murder case, such factors obviously do matter. If they did not, there would be no such thing as a standout trial lawyer. In those states that have a death penalty, the personal appeal and skill of the prosecutor may determine whether a given defendant walks home or is strapped into a chair and electrocuted, suffocated, or intravenously poisoned.

"Charismatic, I would think," said Jadean, a thirty-three-year-old postal clerk on the jury, trying to describe White's manner in an interview in 1993. "He knew how to throw a look. I don't know, maybe it was flirtatious or maybe it was —," she said, unable to find the precise word. "He could've been a televangelist because he *played* to the jury. The man is good at what he does."

In addition, White's effective use of sarcasm, together with his intonation and body language, invited the jurors to see their vote about Knapp's innocence or guilt as something akin to a statement about their own personal politics. Were the jurors the kinds of gullible, hand-wringing liberals who overanalyzed the obvious and fell for the junk science and psychobabble these high-priced defense lawyers were about to lay on them? Or would they cut through all the nonsense, use their God-given common sense, and convict?

Through such means he effectively diverted the trial from a search for truth into a political referendum. Doing so is not unethical; it's skillful.

Henze delivered the defense opening in a light-colored poplin suit, a blue button-down shirt, and a conservative red tie. His opening, like the defense case in general, was less emotional than White's, more professorial in tone, and about twice as long.

For precisely the same reason that White needed to distance himself from the details of Knapp's confession — which were improbable at best and scientifically impossible at worst — Henze wanted to "marry" the state to the confession, as the members of the defense team put it.

"You have to analyze the words of this confession," he told the jury. "We think that when you do this . . . you will find that this confession is not reliable and it's not true. . . . It is not reliable because of the tactics that a police officer, Bob Malone, used to secure the confession. And it's not true . . . because it doesn't square with the scientific evidence that you are going to hear in this case.

"[And] that confession that they took — that's the theory of the state's case. It always has been and it always will be, because that's what they got John Knapp to confess to."

But Henze was whistling in the graveyard. The state's theory could be anything David White said it was.

Twenty-seven

Nobody asks: Is a knife true? The question is: Is it sharp? Can I use it? Litigators evaluate evidence and testimony the same way: Can I use it? Prosecutor White illustrated the principle on the fifth day of the trial, when he called Melba Burr to testify about Knapp's alleged confession to her on the afternoon of November 16, 1973 — the confession that she had never mentioned at either of the 1974 trials or in any of her four interviews that year with Hyder or his investigator.

White was asked in 1993 why he called a witness as seemingly incredible as Melba Burr. His answer was totally pragmatic — and totally unrelated to the truth or falsity of what Burr was saying.

"The question you always ask yourself is: Is this witness going to hurt me more than help me?" he said. Though White could see that Burr "clearly . . . had some problems," he did not see how she could hurt him. "Let's assume that ten of the jurors didn't believe her, but two did. Now there's two more votin' guilty."

As the September 1991 trial had approached, lawyers for each side had interviewed Burr and asked her to explain why she had never told Hyder or Elardo about Knapp's confession in 1973 or 1974, and why she had never testified about it. Over time, she offered three main responses.

The first — the one she gave to prosecutor Sherwin and investigator Schwartz in early 1990, a defense investigator in late 1990, and defense lawyers again in June 1991 — was that she *did* tell Hyder or his investigator about the confession, but that Hyder had, for unknown reasons, chosen not to ask her about it at trial.

But Hyder and Elardo vehemently denied this version, which was, in any event, inherently preposterous.

At the trial in September, Burr offered a second and a third theory. The second was that two men, one of whom was "real good-looking," met with Burr early in 1974 and told her the confession was inadmissible hearsay and "it wouldn't do me any good to tell anybody." The two men had something to do with Knapp's defense, Burr said, but she did not know if they were attorneys.

This story, too, was virtually inconceivable. A tape recording existed of prosecutor Hyder interviewing Burr over the phone on August 1, 1974, just a week before the first trial began. Burr told Hyder then that she had met the defense lawyers, did not trust them, and that if they tried to interview her she was going to tape the interview and play the tape for Hyder. Burr had also told Hyder in that conversation that she could not believe that either John or Linda could have set the fire, although she felt that both should be prosecuted for neglect.

Could anyone seriously believe that this same woman had, in fact, already heard Knapp confess and that she was keeping the confession secret from Hyder because some "good-looking man" associated with the defense team told her it was hearsay?

Burr's third theory was that, in late 1973 or early 1974, Burr's then-husband Bob had told her not to mention the confession to anybody.

"I listened to what Bob told me," Burr testified. "He was beating on me [at the] time; I was afraid of him."

But this theory was also flawed. In a taped interview three months earlier, Burr had said that her ex-husband Bob, on being told of the confession, had responded, "You've got to go to court and . . . see to it that [Knapp] pays for what he's done."

Rather than cut his losses and abandon Burr's improbable recollections, White tried to bolster them. He called Louise Ramsey for the task. But it soon became apparent that Louise's credibility was at least as suspect as Burr's.

In early 1991, as the trial had approached, Burr had phoned Louise Ramsey and asked her if she did not remember Burr telling her back in 1973 that Knapp had confessed to her. Louise told her that she did not, Burr had admitted at a taped pretrial interview in June.

But by the time she testified at trial, three months later, Louise said she *did* recall that Burr had told her about the confession back in 1973! Louise had not taken Burr's statement seriously at the time, she now testified, because she thought "Melba was just being Melba, and joking." And that's why Louise had never told Hyder or Elardo or either jury about it in 1974.

Twelve of the sixteen jurors and alternates who sat in the case agreed to be interviewed for this book in 1993. None appeared to have credited Burr's testimony about the confession, and several singled her out as a witness who brought discredit on the prosecution.

"Who was the one who lied all the time — the wild one?" Jim had asked, unable at first to recall Melba's name.

Prosecutor White had spent almost two full days of a capital murder trial trying to sell the jury on a confession that everyone in the courtroom knew had never occurred.

Or almost everyone.

Prosecutor White was asked in 1993 if he really believed that Knapp told Burr on November 16, 1973, "I killed my babies for nothing."

"I don't think she's lying about that," White responded. "That doesn't mean it — I can't guarantee that it happened. Melba may now remember things that didn't happen."

White's point was that Burr was not committing perjury, and that White was not knowingly using perjured testimony.

He was then asked again whether he believed, more likely than not, that Knapp confessed to Burr.

He paused briefly.

"Yeah, I think that happened," he said. White said he thinks a "good-looking man" — whom White believes was defense lawyer Chuck Diettrich — *did* speak to Burr. In fact, in a breathtaking feat of bootstrapping — relying on one hallucination to rescue another — White speculates that Diettrich was so worried about Burr mentioning the confession that he wanted her off the witness stand at any cost, and that's why he decided not to ask her about having seen Little Linda light matches even though he knew all about that statement!*

Holding a trial eighteen years after the fact was, inevitably, a bizarre spectacle. Witnesses could not possibly insulate their original memories from erosion, distortion, or, indeed, *augmentation* by everything they had read or heard or said or thought about the case in the eighteen intervening years. Officer Chernko, for instance, the first deputy sheriff on the scene, now remembered that Knapp

---

* See Source Notes for more discussion.

had been sipping a cup of coffee when he arrived — a detail he had never mentioned in his notes taken the day of the fire, in his testimony at the 1973 inquest, or in his testimony at either of the 1974 trials. Similarly, in 1991 Louise Ramsey remembered John having laughed and joked with neighbors immediately after the fire, something she did not appear to have ever mentioned in any context in 1973 or 1974. In a sense, the most reliable witnesses were the dead ones, since they were incapable of revising or supplementing their earlier testimony, which would be read to the jury just as it had stood in 1974.

Having been saddled with this massive, complex case at the last minute — after attorney general Woods inadvertently disqualified his whole office — prosecutor White was litigating at a frantic pace and in a perpetual state of emergency. Even assuming he could have brought any objectivity to the case, which is doubtful, he simply had no time to pore over conflicting records and testimony and try to figure out which version might possibly be true. There was only time to determine what was *useful*. What would help him more than it hurt him.

When there were mistakes in the records, it was exceedingly difficult to correct them now. For example, White impugned Knapp's credibility by constructing an effective argument based upon one such apparent mistake. When Knapp was hospitalized after suffering a severe headache in August 1973, his neurologist, Donald Urrea, had asked Knapp to undergo a "lumbar puncture," or spinal tap, to make sure he was not suffering from intracranial hemorrhaging. When the admitting physician, Talmadge Shill, visited Knapp at about 7:30 in the evening on August 16, 1973, Knapp was balking — as many patients do — at undergoing the painful and dangerous procedure.

A year later, when Shill recounted his treatment of Knapp at a pretrial hearing — without the benefit of the medical records — and, later, in a short, written report as well, he mentioned his recollection that Knapp had refused to undergo the spinal tap.

But overwhelming evidence showed that Shill was mistaken. About two hours after Shill visited Knapp, at 9:40 P.M. on August 16, 1973, Knapp *had* signed the necessary consent form, which was timed and dated and among the medical records. At least four notations in the medical records showed that the neurologist Urrea had then *performed* the "L.P." — lumbar puncture. Neurologist Urrea had testified without rebuttal at each of the two 1974 trials that he had, in fact, performed the spinal tap. And the medical records even recorded the *results* of the tap: *the fluid was "clear and colorless" and had a pressure reading of "110 mm. [of] CSF [cerebrospinal fluid]."*

But White, coming across Shill's mistaken recollections in the record, now forcefully argued that Knapp had refused the spinal tap. Therefore, he reasoned, Knapp could not have been genuinely concerned about his headaches and must have been faking them all along. Though Hammond rebutted White's claim using the seemingly incontrovertible medical records themselves, juror Dolores said in 1993 that she credited White's version: that Knapp had refused to undergo the spinal tap.

The longer the Knapp case was litigated, the farther it receded from reality and the deeper it voyaged into the realm of pure litigation craft and wordplay.

The triumph of litigation craft over the search for truth may have reached its apogee with White's examination of the original gas chromatographer, Jack Strong.

By this time Strong had joined the long list of those whose careers or health had been adversely affected by the John Knapp case — Diettrich, Basham, Hyder, Dale, McDaniel.

From about the time of the 1986 hearings, when defense chemist Canfield had accused Strong of having committed perjury at the 1974 trials, Strong had been suffering from a deteriorating mental and emotional condition. In 1988 he became "medically retired" from the Department of Public Safety. He told his employer at the time that the stress of the hearing in the John Knapp case seemed to coincide with the onset of his problems and may have contributed to them. In 1991 Strong asked to be excused from testifying at Knapp's trial due to mental incompetence, but Martone, after a hearing, denied the request.

Strong's testimony became a paradigm of White's and Hammond's differing approaches to the case.

White's presentation was short, crisp, and simple for every juror to grasp.

Hammond's was complex, time-consuming, and a challenge for jurors to follow.

The only thing that Hammond's examination had to recommend it was that, unlike White's, it shed light on the issue of guilt or innocence.

In his brief direct examination, White showed Strong a list of the scientific conclusions he had reached in 1973 — not the actual chromatograms.

"Is there any doubt in your mind," White asked Strong, "that in 1973 you found . . . vapors similar to Coleman fuel?"

"No, there is no doubt in my mind."

Hammond's cross-examination took most of the day. It was methodical and arduous. He educated the jurors about how the gas chromatograph machine worked. He showed sample chromatograms on an overhead projector. He eventually arrived at the point where he hoped the jurors had the background necessary to understand the meat of the examination.

He asked Strong if he did not agree that a sample of Coleman fuel that had been through an intense fire ought to look *different* from a sample of "unweathered" Coleman fuel — that is, fuel that had never been through a fire.

Strong agreed.

Then he asked Strong if he did not agree that a sample of fire debris containing both solvent (methylene chloride) and Coleman fuel that had been through an intense fire ought to look *very different* from a sample containing just pure, unweathered Coleman fuel.

Strong agreed.

Finally, Hammond asked Strong to go the extra mile and admit that his own graphs, which purported to show a nearly perfect match between samples of precisely those disparate descriptions, were therefore impossible.

"I am almost in a state of total confusion," Strong said. "I cannot really concentrate at this point."

Judge Martone called a brief recess, to allow Strong to collect himself. Then, after the break, Hammond asked Strong if he did not agree that if tests were properly performed on samples like the ones Strong had tested, results like those he got simply "can't happen"?

"That's correct."

"[And if those are the results] we know that something is wrong?"

"We would have some suspicions."

". . . And our suspicions might be either that the jars . . . or the graphs have been mislabeled and aren't what we thought they were?"

"Right."

It had been a tortuous path, but if the jury understood, it had been a devastating result.

How would White ever rehabilitate this witness? What would his explanation be for why Strong's graphs for the solvent samples matched perfectly, now that Strong himself agreed that, under the circumstances, *they shouldn't.*

But White stood up for redirect with the same self-confidence he projected at every moment in the trial.

White suggested to the jurors that Strong must have known what he was doing back in 1974, even if he seemed to be having trouble explaining some things today. He stressed, for instance, that Strong had possessed, back in 1974, his original notes and chromatograms, which would have made the job of interpreting them easier. (In fact, of course, Strong had *never* been able to explain the key anomalies in his results — not in August 1974, when defense chemist Parsons had asked him to do so in their taped telephone conversation, and not in 1986, when defense lawyer Colin Campbell had asked him to do so at Knapp's fifth post-conviction relief hearing.)

Finally, White turned to the crux of Hammond's cross-examination — that Strong's results were simply impossible. His entire redirect on that issue was as follows:

"Has anything that Mr. Hammond has said to you today made you doubt the opinion you reached, sir, in 1973?"

"No, sir."

"Thank you. That's all I have."

Of the twelve jurors and alternates interviewed in 1993, only two mentioned Strong's gas chromatograms as having figured prominently in their weighing of the evidence, and both weighed them in the state's favor.

"Some of that stuff got a little deep for any of us," Gladys, the court clerk, said.*

---

* See Source Notes for more discussion.

Twenty-eight

Prosecutor White called thirty witnesses in his case, which consumed a grueling month of trial.

During this period Tom Henze would visit his own office only on Fridays — when Judge Martone adjourned the trial to devote time to his other cases. Henze spent the rest of the week either in court or camped out in 20 South, the small conference room in Meyer, Hendricks's offices.

Making no money.

Shortly after the trial began, Judge Martone had partially relented on his refusal to appoint a second counsel and agreed to allow one lump-sum payment of $20,000 to Henze and another $20,000 payment to Meyer, Hendricks for Jon Sands's work on the case.

Yet that sum, while welcome, barely covered six weeks of Henze's overhead. He was going to spend, in all, close to six months on the Knapp case. To get him through the squeeze, his commercial landlord allowed Henze to postpone portions of his rent payments.

At times Jon Sands was logging in more than 100 hours per week on the Knapp case. At night his infant, Madeline, was depriving him of whatever sleep he might have hoped to wedge into his schedule.

Each morning before court Sands would take a fresh shirt, tie, and pair of pants to the holding cell at the court, so that Knapp would be able to appear before the jury in civilian clothes. (Sands had decided that a suit or sports jacket would look too artificial on Knapp.) Unless Sands brought him new clothes each morning and collected them each evening, the jail would store Knapp's civilian clothes in a plastic garbage bag, where they would wrinkle and mildew.

Sands, who had been responsible for finding clothes for Knapp, gave Deb Heller and Zig Popko veto power over matters of taste. But Knapp did not always care for their decisions. One day Knapp had, under circumstances Sands found suspicious, somehow ripped a pair of gray trousers that he had previously complained about, causing a delay in the start of court while Sands found him another pair. On another occasion Knapp balked at wearing one of Sands's own ties.

"A man is on trial for his life," Sands recalled. "The lawyers are tired. Nerves are frayed. And you're having a discussion with John about why he doesn't want to wear a tie which you picked out."

Knapp gave in and wore the tie. But at the end of the day he urged Sands, — Let's find a different one. —

Sands missed most of the testimony because he was usually interviewing future witnesses. Since each side usually did so in the presence of a member of the opposing camp, Sands spent a good deal of time with Charles "Bud" Miltenberger, the retired detective who was prosecutor White's investigator. Sands came to admire Miltenberger professionally and personally.

Together, Miltenberger and Sands interviewed many of the witnesses who remembered the filth of the Knapp home, John and Linda's neglect of their children, and John's strange conduct after the fire. Often Miltenberger and Sands would get a cup of coffee after an interview.

— You still really think he's innocent? — Miltenberger would ask.

"I feel in my gut that John is innocent," Sands recalled in 1993. "But to be honest, there were times during the case when you just stopped and wondered.

"And when Maddie was born I'm thinking — and it's so easy to think I would have done this — I would've dived into the fire [to save her] rather than do what John did, which was try and get a hose, and whatnot."

Sands sometimes felt a selfish anger toward John, he admitted in 1993, arising from the sacrifices he and others were making to handle the case. If only John had asked for a lawyer when Malone offered him one, Sands would think, then the whole case would not even exist!

These were thoughts that Sands could share with Henze, Popko, and Heller. But not with Hammond. As much as Sands and the others revered Hammond, they also saw him as a True Believer. They did not utter blasphemies in his presence.

Hammond, who, as an obsessive jogger, was rail thin to start with, lost fifteen to twenty pounds during the trial. His wife, Frances, and his children saw little of him.

"Sometimes he might be there in bed, but he wasn't asleep," Frances later recalled. "Sometimes he would get up very early and either go out to his little outside office [in the garage] or just go back to work early, before anybody had gotten there."

"I had a hard time with the idea of sleep," Hammond acknowledged. "There was something about sleeping more than I absolutely had to that just wasn't right."

Hammond never felt satisfied by any aspect of the trial. Even the best days left him thinking that he had still come up a hair short.

"I think as a lawyer to be able to say I did a death case right — I think I could quit at that point," he said later. "I would really feel like that was as great an accomplishment as I could hope to achieve.

"I don't think I had a single day that I felt that way."

Though prosecutor White's case had had its ragged moments, his performance on October 9 was masterful. So was that of his witness: fire expert John DeHaan.

As always, DeHaan's posture was that of the neutral scientist. His diction was precise, his credentials impeccable, his experience vast.

"Over the past 16 years," he told the jury, "I have set or at least taken part in the setting of some 200 to 250 structure fires all across the country, and, in fact, some in Australia as well."

In the morning session DeHaan explained the multiple foundations for his conclusion. He discussed the flammability of fabrics, gas chromatography, toxicology, pathology, and child psychology. Although DeHaan was not an expert in all these fields, and was often merely relying on his memory and understanding of things he had read or been told by true experts in those fields, the jurors did not know that. As a result, DeHaan appeared to them to possess a breathtaking amount of knowledge.

As he testified, it gradually became clear that in 1991 the state was focusing special attention on two aspects of the fire damage that had spawned only minor discussion at the 1974 trials.

The first was the triangular area formed behind the entry door to the children's room, when that door was opened as far as it would go — striking up against the corner of the dresser. DeHaan found the damage in this area to be suspiciously severe.

"That's one of the most unusual features of this pattern," DeHaan told the jury. "And in the fire experiments that I have conducted, it's very difficult to get fire behind a door if it's standing in such a position."

Another area to which DeHaan drew attention was the area immediately *in front of* that door, where the carpet had burned down to the nap, but had not been completely consumed. Here DeHaan found the damage to be suspiciously *light.*

"Let me make sure I understand," White said, simplifying for the jury. "What you're saying is, if this were a normal fire, the carpet in front of this door would be more . . . heavily damaged?"

"I would expect this to be one of the most heavily damaged areas in the room, because of the ventilation factor. . . . In the fires that I have set that have gone to the flashover stage, one typically sees . . . an area right inside the door that's most heavily damaged because of [the added ventilation from the door]."

Hammond, as he listened, still did not yet understand why DeHaan was focusing so intently on these two areas — especially the area *in front of* the door. Ascribing significance to the relative lack of burning in front of the door — which DeHaan had also done at the preliminary hearing in 1990 — was something new to the case since DeHaan's involvement. In fact, in 1974 deputy fire marshal David Dale had considered that area so *severely* burned that he had opined that flammable liquid must have been poured there.

But what Hammond did not understand was that his Weyerhaeuser tests had not produced *all* the kinds of damage in the Knapp children's bedroom that DeHaan had thought, in 1989 and 1990, were indicative of an arson fire. While those tests had produced *most* of those types of damage, including several that DeHaan had thought could *only* be produced by flammable liquids, they had *not* duplicated two types of damage — the burning in front of and behind the door — that DeHaan had *also* thought were suspicious. Accordingly, these two areas had now become the focus of the case.

When the trial broke for lunch Hammond was in good spirits. DeHaan had given him some great opportunities for impeachment, he thought.

But just before the afternoon session resumed, Debbie Heller had noticed something.

— He's going to use our tape, — she told Hammond. — He's got it on his desk. — David White had taken Hammond's own Weyerhaeuser test video-tapes from the table where the exhibits were stored and had placed them on the corner of the prosecution's counsel table. Hammond's full-scale tests, the tests that had cost more than $100,000 to perform, were about to become a state's exhibit.

— No, no. — Hammond said, shrugging her off. — He's not going to do anything with them. —

But a few moments later, Heller's prediction played out. And with a sly, bril-liant twist. Not only would White use Hammond's tests, *he would not show the jury any of DeHaan's.*

"Did you yourself do any full-scale duplication of the Knapp room?" White asked DeHaan.

"In terms of precise duplication, no, I didn't."

Actually, DeHaan had once described the seven full-scale tests he had per-formed in Phoenix and Jefferson Parish as almost exactly the sort of test he was now claiming never to have performed. In a draft of an article he had once planned to publish about those tests, he had described them as "a series of full-scale reconstructions duplicating a particular fire scene with variations only in the presence or absence of an accelerant."

Strategically, however, it was no longer wise to characterize them that way. That would invite comparison between DeHaan's very casual tests and the de-fense expert Custer's exceedingly meticulous work.

Though White himself held DeHaan in the highest esteem and would never have characterized DeHaan's tests in a pejorative way, he also knew that Ham-mond was prepared to mount a punishing assault on DeHaan's tests. It was wis-est not to get bogged down with them.

"Are you aware that some of those kinds of tests [i.e., meticulous tests] *were* done?" White asked DeHaan.

"Yes, I am."

Then White asked Judge Martone for permission to play for the jury Ham-mond's Weyerhaeuser tests, which White was now going to have DeHaan use as *his* evidence.

Hammond objected, but there was little basis for doing so, and Martone overruled him.

"There was some civil war general," White commented later, "that said, 'The guy that wins is the guy that gets there the firstest with the mostest.' I think that's true in trials as well. If you've got a great piece of evidence, why wait for somebody else to present it in their own perspective? Might as well present it in your own perspective."

The tactic leveled Hammond.

"[Hammond] looked white," Debbie Heller recalled. "It was almost like he was dying. I can't remember there being a lower point than that. Because that was his baby and somebody else stole it."

"There were some moments of that trial that we really enjoyed," White later remembered. "One of them was Larry Hammond's discomfort at us using that tape. . . . Certain physiological changes occurred in my body that you experience in great moments of pleasure."

If, by not introducing DeHaan's tests, White had hoped to avoid unflattering comparisons between DeHaan's scientific slovenliness and the meticulousness of the defense experts, the maneuver succeeded beyond his wildest dreams.

When Cheryl, the quality supervisor at an aerospace company, was interviewed for this book fourteen months after deliberations ended, she said that DeHaan's tests had been far more carefully performed and better documented than those of the defense experts. In fact, that was the chief reason, she said, she had been so much more impressed with DeHaan than with the defense experts.

"The key thing for me," she recalled, "was DeHaan's credibility, his expertise, the tests he had run, how he had run 'em, how he had documented them, how he had generated the same like situations, and documented those situations as he went through the experiments. . . . I suppose I look at it more analytically, because that's what I do for a living. . . . You must document those situations and keep them as closely alike as you possibly can. And [the defense] failed to do that."

In fact, Cheryl knew next to nothing about any of DeHaan's experiments,* and she knew literally nothing about their methodology and documentation. That was so because prosecutor White *chose not to introduce DeHaan's tests into evidence.* In concluding that DeHaan was a meticulous scientist, Cheryl can only have been responding to his aura, presentation, and impressive credentials. (It is even possible, though Cheryl denied it, that she may have gotten confused and come to believe that the Weyerhaeuser tests, introduced during DeHaan's testimony, were DeHaan's own tests.)

---

*As will be explained later, the jurors did eventually see brief snippets from two of DeHaan's tests for limited purposes. But they learned nothing about their methodology or documentation at that time.

For whatever reason, Cheryl became DeHaan's greatest champion in the jury box.

After prosecutor White showed the jurors the Weyerhaeuser tests, Hammond found out why White, during the morning session, had been focusing on the damage to the carpeting in front of and behind the entry door.

"In the Knapp household, sir, there was some damage behind that door, is that correct?"

"Yes, there is."

"In the full-scale test . . . did that same severe damage, did that occur to the carpet and pad behind the door?"

"No, it did not."

DeHaan was right. In each of the two Weyerhaueser tests, that triangular area behind the door was not as severely burned as it was in the Knapp children's bedroom.

DeHaan told the jurors that the difference was powerfully incriminating.

"This test confirms a number of tests that I have conducted under a variety of conditions," DeHaan testified, "and the only way I have been able to produce the damage behind the door is have a significant fuel load behind the door in the form of flammable liquid or some other fuel."

The other key area in which the carpet in the Weyerhaeuser test looked different from the carpet in the Knapp bedroom was the area *in front of* the door. In each of the Weyerhaeuser tests, portions of that area had been entirely burned away, while in the Knapp children's bedroom, the carpet there had been less severely burned.

"Why wasn't it burned away in the Knapp house?"

"Because in the Knapp house, the process of flames coming out that door opening as a result of flashover conditions inside the room was much shorter, less intense than you saw in that test."

The fires in the Weyerhaeuser tests had gone only a little over one minute past flashover before they were extinguished. So DeHaan appeared to be saying that the fire in the Knapp house must have lasted a much briefer period past flashover, since the carpet in front of the door in the Knapp bedroom was less burned than the carpet there in the Weyerhaeuser tests. If the Knapp fire had lasted such a short time past flashover, DeHaan seemed to be saying, then flashover conditions could not account for the burn damage in the Knapp bedroom, and only flammable liquids could.

Though DeHaan's precise reasoning was exceedingly subtle, the message was crystal clear. The country's foremost expert on fire investigation was telling the jury: Look, the carpet was burned severely in the doorway of the defense tests, but not in the actual fire. That proves that the Knapp fire was set with flammable liquid!

Late that afternoon, Jon Sands happened to be on his way out of Meyer, Hendricks's office building when Hammond and Heller were returning from court. Heller had already phoned Sands to tell him what had happened.

— Bad day, huh? — Sands said to Hammond

— Oh, I think they gave us some good material to work with, — Hammond responded, with the earnest optimism the other lawyers came to mock him for.

But a step behind Hammond was Heller. Her eyes were wide, her expression was urgent, and she was silently and vigorously shaking her head in the negative.

Though Hammond had interviewed DeHaan just two weeks before the trial began, DeHaan had told him then that he still had not analyzed the Weyerhaeuser tests. So Hammond had not foreseen that he would be focusing in this way on the areas in front of the door and behind it.

Late that evening Hammond leaned back in the wood, swivel armchair in his office, looked out the window into the night, and spoke by telephone to his fire expert, Custer, in Worcester, Massachusetts.

"I remember him telling me," Hammond recalled later, "that the behind-the-door issue was, to him, offensive. Ridiculous."

— We *did* get burning behind the door, — Custer reminded Hammond.

In fact, the carpet there had begun to melt and char, and a portion near the door hinge had been burned severely. While the test fires had not produced *as much* burning behind the door as the Knapp fire had, the test fires had not been allowed to burn nearly *as long* as the Knapp fire. The test fires were allowed to burn just three and a half to four minutes, while the Knapp fire had burned for at least ten minutes and possibly as long as twenty-five.

Custer pointed out that what protected the space behind the door was, obviously, the *door*. The door in the brief test fires had only had time to burn part way down to the floor when those fires were extinguished, so it still afforded some protection to that space. The door in the Knapp room, in contrast, had burned away completely — down to the rail! The door was not protecting that space anymore, because the door was gone!

Hammond felt pretty secure about the burn damage behind the door.

But what about the area *in front of* it?

That was more complicated.

— That's the type of thing that happens when you burn a room in isolation under a hood, — Custer told him, — as opposed to a room as part of a building system, with other rooms and halls and doorways. When you have a hallway, a lot of the smoke that's produced gets recirculated, and gets drawn back into the room. Well, that smoke is deficient in oxygen, and it tends to slow down the burning rate in the room, which means you don't get as much flame out the door as you would if you were in a test facility with fresh air coming in at the bottom and all of the nasty stuff going up the hood. —

Custer's explanation was complex. In the end, the jury was just going to have to weigh Custer's black-box experience against DeHaan's on this point.

As Custer spoke to him late that night, Hammond began to realize that, even though the case had now been litigated for eighteen years, and his own law firm had spent millions of dollars pursuing it, he still kept encountering totally uncharted terrain. In the search for truth, even the meticulous, exorbitant Weyerhaeuser tests were just crude, primitive tools. The hallway outside the children's bedroom would make a difference. The hood at the test site would make a difference. The unique ventilation patterns inside the Knapp house would make a difference. The direction and velocity of the wind in East Mesa, Arizona, on November 16, 1973, at 8:10 A.M. would make a difference.

"I was constantly finding throughout the trial," Hammond later recalled, "that no matter how much work we had done, there were still things that we hadn't focused on — that we hadn't thought of. I remember sitting there at my desk very late at night and talking to [Custer] on the phone and thinking to myself, 'Well, how could I be such an idiot? How could we be this far along in this case and not have considered that.'"

"Do you remember giving those answers at the time of the preliminary hearing?" Hammond asked DeHaan, early in his cross-examination.

He was referring to DeHaan's statement, less than a year earlier, that an accidental fire in the Knapp children's bedroom would have taken at least thirty minutes to an hour to build to flashover.

"Yes I do."

"And do they then fairly reflect your opinion at that time?"

"Yes, they do."

"Do they fairly reflect your opinion today?"

"No, they do not."

This sequence of questions became the central refrain of Hammond's cross-examination, repeated over and over, as he acquainted the jury with all the beliefs that the nation's leading fire expert had so confidently expressed a year earlier, on the basis of the 200 to 250 structure fire tests he had allegedly performed over the past sixteen years — but which had then been disproven by two carefully performed tests at the Weyerhaeuser facility in March 1991.

DeHaan no longer believed that it would take a half hour to an hour for an accidental fire to reach flashover; each of the two Weyerhaeuser tests had flashed over in less than two and a half minutes.

He no longer believed that a polyurethane mattress would be required to make such a room flash over in less than a half hour; each Weyerhaeuser test had involved only cotton mattresses.

He no longer believed that only flammable liquid could burn holes through nylon carpet and butyl rubber pad. Flashover alone had burned such holes in the carpets at Weyerhaeuser.

He no longer believed that nylon carpet could not contribute significantly to a fire; he now conceded that, under the right conditions, it could contribute to and, indeed, drive such a fire.

He no longer doubted that the Knapp room had gone to flashover. Instead, he conceded that it probably *had* gone to flashover and, indeed, that the exceedingly intense post-flashover conditions may have lasted for as long as "possibly three or four minutes" or more, as he testified.

He had been wrong about burning inside the perimeter of the dresser and wrong about burning in corners — areas which he had declared a year earlier, based on the 200 to 250 structure fire tests he had performed, could have been caused only by flammable liquid.

By exposing the dramatic shifts in DeHaan's opinions during his brief involvement in the case, Hammond hoped to damage DeHaan's aura of neutrality and omniscience. But Hammond's examination covered unavoidably difficult, technical terrain. And it took time, lasting two days. Would jurors have the attention span to follow what Hammond was saying?

At midday on October 16, 1991, DeHaan finished, and the state rested its case. The determination of whether Knapp would live or die now hinged primarily on conflicting interpretations of burn damage to a carpet in front of and behind a door that had burned down to its rail eighteen years earlier.

* * *

Precisely what DeHaan found so incriminating about the condition of the carpet *in front of* the door is elusive. In his direct testimony he seemed to be saying that the Knapp fire must have lasted a "much shorter" period past flashover than the Weyerhaeuser tests and that intense post-flashover burning, therefore, could not have accounted for the burn damage seen in the Knapp bedroom. That is what the jurors understood him to be saying. Cheryl — DeHaan's most devoted disciple inside the jury room — had concluded, in fact, that the Knapp fire must not have gone to flashover at all, based on what DeHaan was saying.

But that was not, in fact, DeHaan's claim. He actually now conceded that the Knapp fire *had* gone to flashover and that it may well have burned three or four minutes past flashover — *much longer past flashover than either of the two Weyerhaeuser tests.*

Which meant that *DeHaan* could not explain the relative lack of burning in front of the door in the Knapp room *either.*

DeHaan was asked in 1994[*] how *he* accounted for the relative lack of burning in the Knapp doorway, since he conceded that post-flashover conditions in the Knapp room may have actually lasted *longer* than they had in the Weyerhaeuser tests, where that area of the carpet had been much more severely damaged.

He then said almost exactly what Custer had explained to Hammond: the amount of burning in the doorway would depend on the intensity of the flames coming out the door, which, in turn, would depend on the different ventilation conditions outside that door.

In other words — just as Custer said — the presence of the hallway could make all the difference!

"And because we weren't there, watching in the Knapp room when the fire occurred," DeHaan said, "we don't know how energetic that [flame] plume was [coming out the door]. So it's all approximations. I mean, to be able to compare one test against another is very difficult at this point. . . . I hesitate to call it guesswork, but it's an estimate."

And there was a second oddity inherent in DeHaan's analysis.

The Weyerhaeuser tests, which DeHaan had agreed were good attempts to replicate the Knapp room, showed that a fire in that environment, set with a

---

[*]When interviewed in 1994, DeHaan was invited to take time to refresh his recollection, and he was offered copies of any materials he might need to review. DeHaan declined the offer, maintaining that he had recently reviewed the materials for a different reason and remembered the situation.

match and two pieces of crumpled newspaper, could go to flashover in just 140 seconds.

One might have thought, then, that if that same room had been ignited with a quart to a gallon of Coleman fuel (rather than just two pieces of crumpled newspaper) that it might have reached flashover in an even shorter period of time.

Yet DeHaan was predicting just the opposite. He was claiming that the Coleman fuel fire would have progressed much more *slowly* than the crumpled newspaper fire, only finally just beginning to reach flashover after about fifteen minutes — the length of time DeHaan estimated the fire had lasted — and therefore causing less burning to the carpet in front of the doorway.

But wouldn't an accelerated fire reach flashover more *quickly* than an unaccelerated fire? In short, wouldn't accelerant accelerate a fire?

"No," DeHaan explained to the author in late 1994. "A number of the tests I've done over the years [have shown me] that using an accelerant is not a guarantee that you're going to have a faster fire. It's all part of the balance, of the fuel and the ventilation and the heat and time. . . .

"I mean if I'm going to be a professional fire setter, I'm not going to use a flammable liquid," DeHaan said, "because you end up pushing the balance the wrong way far too often. You're much better off using a crumpled newspaper under some combustibles to get a good, sustained fire going."

So John Knapp had come full circle. In 1974 the state's fire expert, David Dale, thought the fire in the Knapp children's bedroom had developed too quickly to have been anything but a flammable liquid fire.

In 1991 the state's fire expert, John DeHaan, thought it had developed too *slowly* to have been anything but a flammable liquid fire!

Twenty-nine

After much strategizing in the war room at 20 South, the defense team decided to call their lead fire expert, Richard Custer, as their *last* witness. That way they hoped to end the defense case on a strong note.

Though they had considered calling Custer first — since the lead-off witness makes a big impression — it made more sense, they decided, to call mechanical engineer Marshall Smyth first. The gentlemanly, gray-haired sixty-nine-year-old Smyth would lay the foundation for Custer and all the other defense experts, since Smyth had actually inspected the fire scene in 1974.

They also decided to call very early, as their third witness, the only eyewitness other than John who was actually in the house when the fire started: Linda Knapp. They anticipated — correctly — that the jury would be dying to hear from her. And her account, if she was telling the truth, was exceedingly difficult to square with an arson fire.

Linda was now thirty-nine, squat and heavy, with a ruddy complexion and straight strawberry blond hair that fell a little past the shoulders. She wore a light blue collarless blouse, dark blue slacks, and sandals. (She had, coincidentally, moved back to Phoenix in 1989 — in part, she later explained, to get away from an environment in which she had developed a cocaine addiction.) Neither John nor Linda showed any emotion on seeing each other again.

When Tom Henze asked her to describe the fire, Linda closed her eyes and told the same story she had at the 1974 trials. Her demeanor was distant and matter of fact. She did not cry or display any sense of loss, regret, or terror. She showed no obvious vindictiveness toward John or affection for him.

Toward the end of her direct testimony, Henze elicited from Linda, without elaboration, her prophetic dream or vision two days before the fatal fire, in which she saw the two children holding hands and enveloped in flame. He also had Linda describe the earlier fire in Pomona and her three subsequent fires in Utah, although Henze never directly suggested that she had been responsible for any of them.

Henze was following the strategy the defense team had mapped out in January. Though they would never accuse Linda of setting the fire, they would acquaint the jurors with some of the evidence implicating her, and allow them to make of it what they would. (They never used the testimony of any of three unreliable witnesses — whom Sands referred to as "our Melba Burrs" — who claimed that Linda had, in some fashion or another, confessed to them.)

White's cross-examination was confusing. Like Hyder, White sometimes used Linda as his own witness, eliciting the most awful things she had ever said about Knapp's character, while at other times he suggested that Linda was lying to protect John. (The latter claim was particularly strained at this point, since Linda had refused even to speak to Knapp's lawyers before trial. She was testifying under a subpoena.) The thrust of White's cross-examination was that Linda was lying, although White never explained precisely what he thought she was lying about, or why.

At about 4:30, at the end of the day's testimony, Jon Sands alerted David White, in accordance with a pact they had made, to the next day's witnesses. In a surprise move, Sands told him that the next witness would be John Knapp.

Usually, if a defendant testifies at all, he will be the last witness. But placing Knapp in such a prominent spot would be too risky, the defense team had decided.

"Let's face it," Henze commented later. "Some people are just more verbal and more expressive than others."

And Knapp's personality, which was already raising eyebrows in 1973, was now crusted over with the experiences that a man gathers during fourteen years of maximum security incarceration, including twelve on death row.

"John Knapp lived in a different world than the rest of us for the seventeen years preceding his trial," Henze later recounted. "It's incredible to me that anybody could expect any person to somehow sit in a courtroom after all that and just be normal — whatever normal is."

For many days preceding his testimony Sands and Henze had been spending time with Knapp in the evenings, preparing. Sands had asked Knapp to get some sun in the exercise yard, so that he could put a dent in his deathly inmate's pallor. But his entire pod had been temporarily transferred to Level Two, to make room for some juveniles, and that level's exercise yard was essentially indoors, open to the air only through the metal louvered vents in the walls.

"When I saw him on the day that the examination was to begin," Hammond recounted, "he just looked awful. His face just lost all color."

He was also almost paralyzed with fear.

"I was frankly afraid that he was not going to be able to function," Hammond recalled. "We would ask him a question, and we would get either no answer or kind of a 'Huh?'"

John Knapp took the stand at 2:00 in the afternoon, wearing blue slacks, a white button-down shirt, and a subdued, maroon tie.

Henze started him out with easy personal history questions that seemed to calm him down. His direct examination then went relatively smoothly.

Knapp showed little emotion except when he recounted the one memory that, through the years, always seemed to get to him: receiving on November 25, 1973, the photographic portraits of his children that had been made only a few weeks before their death. Knapp's voice broke as he described the moment.

His direct examination carried over into the next morning. At 10:15 A.M., Henze turned Knapp over to White.

"Mr. Knapp, you will lie if you think it helps you, won't you?" White asked, right off the bat.

"No, sir," Knapp responded.

But then White forced Knapp to admit that he had, for instance, lied to the police when he confessed — or at least so he claimed.

"[So] you'll lie, if you think you have a good reason, won't you?" White demanded.

"To protect my wife, yes."

As Hammond had feared, the theme of White's cross-examination would be Knapp-the-liar.

Inevitably, when two people have a conversation or see an event, each person's honest memory of it will vary, due to innocent mistakes in seeing, speaking, and hearing, differences in interpretation and assumption, and flaws in memory. When it comes to recounting conversations, the unreliability of human memory is so well established that witnesses are generally barred from describing out-of-court statements — hearsay — in court.

But accounts of a *defendant's* out-of-court statements are admissible under a broad exception to the hearsay rule. As a result, whenever Knapp's memory of a conversation differed from that of a police officer, or a neighbor, an insurance agent, a dentist, a co-worker, or a store clerk, White was free to argue that the discrepancy arose from the fact that Knapp was lying.

On a flip chart set up on an easel between the jury box and Knapp, White listed nine instances in which a witness's memory of a remark or of an event differed from Knapp's.

Thus, White argued, if a neighbor remembered Knapp saying, "If that doesn't kill them, nothing will," and Knapp could not recall saying it, then Knapp was lying.

If a bank employee remembered Knapp telephoning him sometime during the morning after the fire, and Knapp remembered telephoning him in the afternoon, then Knapp was lying.

If a witness claimed that Knapp was "clean-shaven" on the morning of the fire, and Knapp said he had not shaved that morning, Knapp was lying.

If a co-worker remembered giving Knapp a lift home from work the day before the fire, but Knapp remembered taking a cab home that day, Knapp was lying.

White was sometimes careless in his zeal. He drew on strong and weak arguments in almost equal measure, indiscriminately. White's mind saw sinister and incriminating meanings so readily that he seemed incapable of distinguishing the weighty from the piddling — or even the fantastic.

White was on reasonably solid ground when he pointed out, for instance, that Knapp had apparently inflated his salary on the credit application he signed when he bought his carpet in 1973.

But shortly thereafter, one of White's wilder theories backfired. White was in the process of mocking Knapp for not caring enough about his family's welfare to manage the simple task of getting both the electricity and the gas turned on in one day — a reasonably strong point. But when White got sidetracked onto a discussion about some "double-knit" clothing Knapp had said he bought for his children that day, White made a strange claim.

"You knew that synthetic clothes were important in terms of fire, didn't you?"

"No, sir. I don't believe I did."

White was suggesting that Knapp had realized in 1974 that synthetic fabrics would burn more quickly than natural fibers.

For Sunny, one of the jurors, White's remark was too much. She audibly gasped in the jury box, for which she was later chastised by the bailiff.

"That just tipped me all the way back in my chair," Sunny recalled in 1993. "I could not believe that that came out of that man. I mean, that's what they had on the market at that point in time! . . . And Mr. White pops up and says, 'Oh, and you bought all these polyester clothes that you knew would burn quickly.' "*

After the midmorning break, however, White recovered and made headway trying to suggest that John Knapp never really suffered from severe headaches. It was unquestionably suspicious that John Knapp's headaches were far more severe during the second half of 1973 than they were at any other stage in his life.

White pointed out that when Knapp filled out a medical questionnaire to get into the army in 1965, he had not checked the box for "frequent or severe headaches" at all.

Had he been lying? White asked.

"I guess you would say it was a lie," Knapp admitted, suggesting that he had wanted to make sure he was accepted into the army at that time.

But then White showed him the similar questionnaire he had filled out in 1969, when he *left* the army. Again, he had not checked the box for headaches.

"Was that a lie, Mr. Knapp?"

"Not at that time, sir. When I went into the service, I did have headaches that I personally considered severe. . . . And while in the service I was stationed at the medical center where I learned the difference." Knapp said he had discussed his headaches with a doctor there, who told him that his headaches did not sound severe to him.

"I thought he was more qualified than I was," Knapp testified.

It was a terrible answer. It sounded like Knapp was lying then and there — in front of the jurors.

Hammond was furious. Knapp did not seem familiar with the questionnaires, and Hammond thought that Sands had failed to prepare him adequately.

"I have said to people in this law firm for years," Hammond remarked in 1993, "that if you put your client on the stand in any case, and there is a piece of

---

*White was not, as Sunny thought, suggesting that Knapp had bought flammable clothing in order to make sure his children would burn to death.

He *was* suggesting, however, something at least as improbable. Shortly before the first 1974 trial, defense expert Smyth had asked Knapp to write down a list of everything he remembered having been in the children's room at the time of the fire. In describing the children's clothing, Knapp had written: "double knits." White was now suggesting that by "double knits" Knapp was implying specifically *synthetic* double knits and that, further, Knapp may have been lying in doing so because he understood that synthetics would burn more readily than natural fibers.

paper [with his name on it] that you haven't put in front of your client to look at before cross-examination, you're committing malpractice. Truthful people who haven't thought about a subject are going to seem evasive unless they are well prepared."

When they broke for lunch, Hammond cornered Sands outside Knapp's presence.

— Are there any other documents with John Knapp's name on them that you didn't bother to show the client? — Hammond demanded.

Sands thought Hammond just did not appreciate how unpredictable Knapp was. Preparation could achieve only so much.

"Given the amount of work Sands and Henze had put into preparing Knapp, it was not appropriate for me," Hammond acknowledged later.

At the noon break, while Knapp was taken back into a holding cell, Knapp's lawyers had a bag lunch at counsel's table and tried to do some strategizing. But Hammond was still smoldering over the incident concerning the military records. He pressed Sands again about how that had happened.

Finally Henze cut Hammond off.

— Larry, — he said philosophically, — there are good witnesses. There are bad witnesses. And then there's John Knapp. —

White closed his cross-examination by focusing on his list of nine witnesses who had voiced recollections that differed from Knapp's.

"Mr. Knapp, of the people on that list . . . how many have admitted that they'd lie if they had a reason? . . ."

"I did make that statement. . . ."

". . . There's only one person on that list who will lie if they have a good enough reason, and that's you, isn't it?"

"Uh — basically, yes."

"I enjoyed that," White recalled later.

His young intern, Reagen Kulseth, thought Knapp's admission that he would lie to help himself was one of the high points of the state's case.

Hammond was initially glum about how the cross-examination had gone.

"The John-the-liar line was one that I feared," he later recounted. "Even though we believed that John had not lied about anything that was on the David White list of lies, nobody is attentive enough to go through and debunk each one of 'em. It just takes too much time."

Hammond's outlook gradually lightened, however, as the defense team hashed everything over in 20 South that evening, over soft drinks, pretzels, and beer. Henze, Sands, Popko, and Heller were all quite relieved with Knapp's testimony, on balance. The defense had "taken some water," as Sands put it, but, knowing how peculiar Knapp was, and how skillful White was, they felt it could have gone much worse.

— I'd give it a C, — Sands told the group.

On the Monday after Knapp's testimony, Hammond called a psychology professor to testify about interrogation techniques, and about the fact that they can, in fact, sometimes lead innocent people to confess to crimes they didn't do. It's hard to judge what impact the professor's testimony might have had in isolation, because, in a freak coincidence, on the morning after he testified, a spectacular display of false confessions began to unfold right in Phoenix.

The stage had been set in August 1991, the month before Knapp's trial began, when nine people — including six monks and a nun — had been shot to death at a Thai Buddhist temple thirty miles west of Phoenix. It was the worst mass slaying in Arizona history.

During the first week of Knapp's trial, four suspects were picked up in Tucson for the temple murders. They were driven to Phoenix, given their Miranda warnings, and then subjected to lengthy, separate interrogations. Each suspect ultimately confessed, implicating himself and each of the other three. None of the four — who ranged from nineteen to twenty-eight — ever claimed afterward that the confessions were obtained through physical force or threats. While one of the four had a history of mental illness, the other three didn't.

All four men were arrested and charged with first-degree murder, and the state served notice of its intent to seek the death penalty in each case. But on October 26, 1991, a high school boy who lived near the temple, Alessandro Garcia, confessed to having committed the nine temple slayings with a classmate. Garcia led investigators to the murder weapons. He and the confederate were then arrested (and later convicted).

Garcia's arrest for the temple murders was disclosed in Arizona newspapers on October 29, the morning after the psychology professor testified in Knapp's case. The Tucson Four were released in late November, while the Knapp jury was deliberating. By that time it had become apparent that all four had falsely confessed without the use of physical force.*

---

*In January 1993, when Alessandro Garcia pleaded guilty to the temple murders, he also admitted having committed an unrelated murder in a Phoenix campground in October 1991, and, again, led

Though the Knapp jurors were told to avoid media accounts of the Knapp case, they were not barred from reading about *other* cases. Jim, the juror who was a marketing consultant, later recalled thinking at the time, "If the police could coerce four false confessions from innocent people today, twenty years ago the police could coerce all types of confessions out of people."

Hammond called forty witnesses for the defense. Hammond felt he could not take anything for granted or leave any prosecution claim unrebutted.

"When it's a death case," he said later, "everything gets magnified. Because everything could be the one thing that a jury latches onto that saves your client's life, or that becomes the rallying cry for twelve people to do something insane."

But the length of the trial was taking a toll on the jurors.

"I don't think it's necessary to pick up every pebble and show them what's under it," Martone told Hammond with exasperation, in early November.

And as long as the trial stretched, there was one type of evidence in John Knapp's favor that the jury would never hear, though the defense lawyers knew that such evidence existed.

As a strategic matter, the defense had little choice but to refrain from introducing the evidence that would have portrayed Knapp as a good or caring father. The jury would not be told, for instance, of Knapp taking the children to the circus, or Disneyland, or Knott's Berry Farm, or the zoo. They would not be told of a neighbor's recollection of seeing the children run to John Knapp when he came home from work and seeing him scoop them up in his arms and hug them.

Hammond could not afford to present such evidence, because he was fearful of *opening the door* to allowing the state to rebut that evidence by portraying Knapp as a child beater, wife beater, and a sex pervert.

At the outset of the trial Judge Martone had agreed to exclude those allegations from trial. But they could all come roaring back into the case if Henze or Hammond opened the door, by allowing a witness to imply that Knapp was a loving father or husband.

The necessary omission took a toll. Since Melba Burr, Louise Ramsey, and

---

investigators to the murder weapon. It turned out that another innocent man, George Peterson, had already falsely confessed to *that* murder during an interrogation by Maricopa County deputy sheriffs on October 22, 1991. Peterson had been in custody for 14 months facing murder charges, and the state had already served notice of its intent to seek his death as well. He was released within days of Garcia's confession to the campground murder.

Linda were all portraying Knapp as uncaring of the children, and jealous of the way the children allegedly distracted Linda's attention from him, the absence of countervailing evidence lent credence to their claims.

"If I had found something throughout that trial somewhere," juror Cheryl said later, "[showing me] that he was a caring father, that he spent time with his kids at all, or that he held his kids at all, or that they just crawled up in his lap, and he hugged 'em or read stories to 'em or anything, I would have found it impossible to believe that he would have done something like that."

Amid the inevitable jokes about the defense's "last stand," the defense called fire expert Richard Custer as its last witness late on Monday, November 12, two months after the trial began.

Custer's aura was very different from DeHaan's. It was not hard to imagine the burly, white-bearded Custer as the firefighter he once was, "dragging hose" and wearing red suspenders. Though his experiments were infinitely more meticulous than DeHaan's, his speech and phraseology were less well turned, his enunciation less clipped, his vocabulary less technical, his manner less polished.

"So we now know," he testified at one point, for instance — referring to the results of his mattress experiments at Weyerhaeuser — "that when fire gets underneath a piece of furniture or, that normally wouldn't by itself, tested out in the open, produce much heat, and if there is a carpet or something combustible underneath it, that it's going to burn vigorously."

Custer showed the jurors each of the Weyerhaeuser tests, and the damage that had resulted, including almost every form of damage that either David Dale in 1974 or John DeHaan in 1990 had testified could be produced only by flammable liquids.

Then Custer addressed the two areas of burn damage that, in 1991, had become the Achilles' heel of the defense case: the burning behind and in front of the door.

Custer showed the jurors how portions of the area behind the door *had* burned away in the Weyerhaeuser test, and how other areas had already begun melting or charring when the fire had been extinguished, after just four minutes. Over White's objection Hammond had Custer cut off a piece of carpet and give it to the jurors to pass around, so that they could see and feel the extent to which it had already started burning.

"Had this [test] fire continued another minute or two," Custer said, "that bedroom door . . . would have been burned all the way down to the floor level

... and that would expose this entire area behind the door to the intense radiation from the hot gas layer in the room."

As for the area *in front of* the door, Custer explained how and why he believed the burning out the door of the Knapp bedroom, which opened onto a narrow, low-ceilinged* hallway, would be different from the burning out the door of the test room, which opened straight into the open air under an exhaust hood.

During his cross-examination of Custer, White attempted to protect his own Achilles' heel: DeHaan's contention that Knapp could have set off a sizable quantity of Coleman fuel in the children's tiny room without breaking the window out until "some many minutes" into the fire.

White asked Custer to concede that it was possible to ignite Coleman fuel in the children's room without blowing the window out.

Custer was doubtful.

Then, over Hammond's objection, White won from Judge Martone the right to show Custer and the jury — *for impeachment purposes only* — DeHaan's first Coleman fuel test in Phoenix.

Judge Martone gave the jury an abstract, legalistic instruction about the limited purposes for which they could consider this test, apologizing even as he delivered it for the manifest absurdity of what he was asking them to do.

"You can use it," he explained, "to test this witness's opinions. We're not showing you the tape to prove any of the matters asserted within the tape itself. And I know that's kind of a . . . metaphysical distinction. . . . But . . . use the tape to evaluate this witness's opinion. Do not use the tape for its independent significance with respect to fire tests."

Hammond was sinking into despair. Since White was introducing DeHaan's test *for impeachment purposes only,* it was being introduced without any foundation; that is, the jury would learn nothing about DeHaan's casual methodology and his slapdash documentation for this and all his other tests.

DeHaan's first Coleman fuel test was the one in which DeHaan had, indeed, succeeded in igniting Coleman fuel in a small room without blowing the window out — by artificially propping the door open with a block of wood. DeHaan had put the wood there precisely to keep the overpressure situation from slamming the door shut and then *blowing the window out and otherwise*

---

*To make space for the conduits from the evaporative cooler, which sat on the roof, the hallway ceilings were only seven feet high, though the rooms themselves had eight-foot ceilings.

damaging the structure. In fact, at the time, DeHaan had feared that, without the block of wood, the Coleman fuel might have actually blown down the walls.

But White did not tell Custer or the jury about the block of wood!

"And you saw tests, sir," White asked Custer, "where they spread three quarts of Coleman fuel, and they left the door open only a couple inches and ignited it and the window did not break out, isn't that true, sir?"

But DeHaan had not *"left"* the door open, he had *propped* it open — precisely to prevent the overpressure situation from damaging the structure.

But Custer could not remember the conditions under which DeHaan's test had been run.

"Just opening that door just an inch apparently makes a big difference, at least in those tests?" White asked him, again telling neither Custer nor the jury about the block of wood *propping* the door open.

Custer fumbled about, unable to provide a convincing response.

"And if the door is left open, then you wouldn't necessarily get the window blowing out?" White misleadingly asked for yet a third time.

"If the door is fully open the whole time, no, might not."*

In his redirect examination, Hammond showed the jury DeHaan's other two Coleman fuel tests, in which igniting a half gallon or even a quart of Coleman fuel had instantly blown the glass out, with shards landing thirty feet away.

He also tried to set the record straight about how DeHaan had actually performed his Phoenix test, the one in which the window had *not* broken out. But, in truth, Hammond himself had never fully appreciated the role of the block of wood in the Phoenix test. He had always assumed that the window had not blown out in the Phoenix test for a *different* and simpler reason. That window was *open* by four or five inches, Hammond thought. The gases created by the overpressure situation had just vented out the open window, he thought.

Hammond thought the window was open because that was what DeHaan had written in his notes. That was what DeHaan had written in a draft of an article he had prepared concerning those tests. And that was what DeHaan had said in *testimony* at the preliminary hearing in 1990.

---

*White told the author in 1995 that he did not consider his cross-examination misleading, because, in accordance with DeHaan's theory, he was assuming that the door in the Knapp room could not have slammed shut — either because it had been wide open when Knapp set the fire, or because Knapp had propped it open with his own body when he set the fire.

But neither White nor DeHaan ever told the jury that this was their theory of how the fire was set.

But now, on the last day of this capital murder trial, Hammond learned for the first time that DeHaan had changed his mind! He had gone back, reviewed his videotape, and had realized that the window had actually been closed. (Judging from the videotape, the window does appear to be closed.) DeHaan's notes, article, and prior testimony had all been wrong.

It was a mess. On the very last day of a ten-week trial, the jurors were suddenly exposed to a flurry of confusing new fire tests, about which they were being given conflicting and misleading information, and which they were being told to use for only a narrow, unintelligible purpose.

When Sands, Hammond, and Henze had mapped out their strategy in 20 South weeks earlier, they had envisioned Custer's presentation as the grand finale.

But the plan had proved a terrible mistake.

When Hammond contrasted DeHaan and Custer in his mind, he compared DeHaan's sloppy work to Custer's painstaking work. But the jurors had not seen most of DeHaan's work and had not analyzed any of it. They compared DeHaan's speech patterns to Custer's speech patterns. And John DeHaan spoke more like a scientist than Custer did.

More important, the defense case had dragged on too long. DeHaan had made a powerful impact, and a month was too long for some jurors to wait for a rebuttal. Since Marshall Smyth had been the first expert called for the defense, and he had come immediately after DeHaan, most jurors assumed that Smyth was the key defense expert. Rather than comparing DeHaan to Custer, as Hammond had intended, they compared DeHaan to Smyth — which had not been the goal at all.

While all twelve jurors and alternates who were interviewed in 1993 remembered DeHaan and Smyth vividly, only four remembered who Custer was.

Thirty

On Tuesday, November 19, the jurors heard five hours of closing argument and about fifteen minutes of jury instructions.

The most important instruction was that the state was required to prove its case beyond a reasonable doubt.

Judge Martone read them one of the standard definitions of "reasonable doubt," which is brief, circular, and enigmatic:

> The term "reasonable doubt" means doubt based upon reason. This does not mean an imaginary or possible doubt. It is a doubt which may arise in your minds after a careful and impartial consideration of all the evidence or from the lack of evidence.

Had the state proven Knapp guilty beyond a reasonable doubt? What *is* proof beyond a reasonable doubt?

Those legal abstractions that are interpreted by *judges* gradually gain meaning over the years by being applied in specific, concrete situations. A judge trying to understand what, for instance, "probable cause" means, can look up published cases in which other judges have grappled with that question, and can find out what fact patterns other judges have considered sufficient or insufficient to constitute "probable cause" over the centuries.

But those legal abstractions, like "reasonable doubt," which are left for *juries* to interpret never gain such clarifying glosses. Jurors struggling with what "reasonable doubt" means cannot look in a book somewhere and find out what other juries have done in similar circumstances.

Perhaps a jury's interpretation of the "reasonable doubt" requirement — like a jury's interpretation of the civil "negligence" standard — is supposed to be an expression of the community's judgment about a somewhat nebulous and yet, nonetheless, meaningful concept. But, if so, what exactly are criminal juries expressing the community's judgment *about*? Is the jury saying, in effect, we believe the community ought to require *this degree of proof* before imposing the sort of punishments that a conviction may entail? That sounds plausible — except that juries are usually *also* instructed that they are *not supposed to take punishment into account* when determining whether or not the "reasonable doubt" standard has been met.

Though there may be law professors who think they know what "reasonable doubt" means, they are not typically permitted to serve on juries.

The meaning of the phrase is, in reality, reinvented every time twelve people retire to the jury room to deliberate. The only content the phrase ever possesses is improvised anew by each new group, and that jury's unique standard vanishes forever once that jury disbands.

And no matter how tortuous a jury may find its task — no matter how many days a jury agonizes before reaching a decision, no matter how many juries must deliberate before one finally reaches a unanimous verdict — once a defendant is convicted, the line that that particular jury has improvised becomes definitive and objective in the eyes of the law. All ambiguities vanish, and, in death-penalty states, the convict may now be put to death.

Proof beyond a reasonable doubt is the elusive enigma at the core of our criminal justice system.

After the instructions were read aloud in the jury's presence, four of the sixteen jurors, whose names were picked from a basket, were excused. Two were then leaning toward acquittal, and two were then leaning toward conviction.

The remaining twelve jurors were excused for the evening and told to return the next morning, Wednesday, November 20, at 9:30 A.M. to begin deliberations. (The jury was not sequestered.)

The jury had, until this point, impressed Judge Martone and the lawyers as the most collegial they had ever seen, with members often bringing in cookies, salsa and chips, and other homemade treats for the whole group.

"In the history of the courthouse, no jury has ever produced more food than this jury," Judge Martone remarked a week before the jury began deliberating.

But within hours after it did, all camaraderie vanished.

Law students spend three years learning to discuss legal issues in a constructive way: trying to sieve out ad hominem, emotional attacks; learning to compartmentalize their thoughts; distinguishing related, but distinct arguments, and trying to address each separately, thoroughly, and methodically. But the Knapp jurors were thrown into a room with no preparation and asked to decide whether a man should live or die. It became a wild free-for-all.

As the twelve jurors seated themselves in plastic molded chairs around a rectangular table on Friday morning, November 20, Tim, a home improvement store salesman, leaned over to Jim and commented, — Well, I don't care what's said in here. I think he's guilty and that's how I'm going to see it. —

— How can you say that, — Jim responded, — when we haven't even started to deliberate yet? —

Tim stood up and walked to the other end of the table, placing as much distance as possible between himself and Jim.

The group then selected Cheryl, the quality supervisor at an aerospace concern, as foreperson, because of her previous experience serving on three other juries. She held an initial vote, by secret ballot, to see where people stood.

The vote was perfectly split: four for acquittal, four for conviction, and four undecided.* Then Cheryl went around the table having each person explain his or her preliminary thinking.

The very fact of disagreement had come as a great surprise to some jurors, who had underestimated how differently other people would see the same evidence.

"I was shocked that [the vote] was even," Jim recalled later. "To me the evidence was: He was not guilty. This is really pretty easy. [But after the vote,] my first reaction was, 'My God. There are [four] people in here who have just voted guilty.' "

Cheryl was strongly for conviction, largely because of her extremely high opinion of DeHaan.

"His basic knowledge of fire and reactions to fire were overwhelming," she said in 1993. She stressed, in particular, the fact that the carpet in front of the door to the Knapp bedroom had not burned away, the way it had in the Weyer-

---

*Jurors' memories differ. Newspaper accounts reported the first vote as five for acquittal, four for conviction, three undecided.

haeuser tests, which she took to mean that flashover could not have occurred in the Knapp bedroom at all.

Also strongly in the conviction camp were Tim (the home improvement store salesman), Elsa (known jocularly as Iris, an acronym for her employer, the Internal Revenue Service), and Dolores (the young mother). Most of these jurors were impressed with DeHaan's testimony, with the confession, and with the neighbors' testimony about Knapp's suspicious behavior on the morning of the fire.

Favoring acquittal were Gladys* (the court clerk), Sunny (the divorcée who had audibly gasped during White's cross-examination of Knapp), Jim (the self-employed marketing consultant), and Charlie (a fifty-three-year-old aerospace maintenance electrician who had kept aloof from the other jurors throughout the trial). Charlie had been working the swing shift at his job after court each day, which was running him ragged. During lunch breaks he had sometimes napped in the jury room.

Charlie's vote surprised all the other jurors, who had had no inkling of which way he was leaning. Based on personal experiences setting flammable liquid fires while in the military, Charlie thought Knapp couldn't have set off a large quantity of Coleman fuel in that little room without blowing the windows out and, perhaps, injuring himself as well.

Still undecided as of the first vote were Gary (an airline ramp supervisor), Jadean (the postal clerk), Kirti (a research technician on a federal agricultural project), and Rick (an engineer for an aerospace company). Soon, however, Jadean peeled off into the acquittal camp, and Rick into the conviction group, making it five to five, with Gary and Kirti unaligned.

Most of those favoring acquittal were convinced that the fire could not have occurred the way John had confessed to doing it. The Knapps' incredible fire trap of a home seemed to them like an accident waiting to happen. Hammond had successfully damaged DeHaan's credibility with these jurors, and they were terribly impressed with the rapidity with which comparable rooms had gone up in flames in the Weyerhaeuser tests.

"If you never had respect for a fire before," Gladys later remarked in an interview, "you sure do after [seeing] those tapes [of the Weyerhaeuser tests].

---

*Hammond had guessed exactly right about Gladys, the grandmother who had taken her grandchild away from her own daughter for the child's protection. "I put myself in [Mary Knapp's] position," she said later, "because the hardest call I ever made was to [the child protective services] over my grandson, okay. And she did the same thing. And I have a problem with Linda's mother."

When you watch that clock and see how many seconds [it takes] and whoosh, it's gone — it takes your breath away."

In addition, three of these jurors — Sunny, Gladys, and Jim — felt that even if DeHaan was right about the fire being set with flammable liquids, Linda could just as easily have set it as John. In this respect, Henze's strategy of telling the jury about some of the evidence implicating Linda, while never overtly accusing her, was an enormous success.

Although every juror who agreed to be interviewed for the book cited what the author considered reasonable arguments based on the evidence they had heard, many members of each camp caricatured and derided the opinions of the opposing camp as irrational, speculative, or foolish.

"She would take over the discussion," Cheryl said about one juror in the acquittal camp, "but she had nothing to say based on evidence. Everything she had to say was pure opinion. . . . It was real difficult for us that were leaning toward guilty to get any substantial information from those that were voting not guilty, because they . . . couldn't come up with coherent reasons of rebuttal for those things that concerned us."

"There was no substance to her arguments," Sunny said of a woman in the guilty camp. "She would just ramble on and on and on and say literally nothing. She couldn't even back up her own feelings."

Jadean, the postal clerk, thought that both sides were probably suffering from symmetrical forms of tunnel vision.

"What seems logical and reasonable to one person must not be reasonable to somebody else," she observed in early 1993. "[Maybe] it's just human nature for you to hear as much as you want to hear and then dismiss the rest. It still puzzles me. I still think about it."

There were literally hundreds of disputed issues in the case, most of which were logically independent of one another. Yet, once a juror joined one or the other camp, he or she seemed to settle all those disputes in a single direction. With the stakes so high, each juror's mind appeared to be insulating itself from the possibility of error, by resolving every controversy in a manner that bolstered that juror's ultimate decision.

Most pro-conviction jurors, for instance, not only doubted that Knapp's headaches could have played any role in his having falsely confessed, they believed he had not really suffered from headaches that night and that, indeed, he had probably never really suffered from headaches ever.

Those who favored acquittal believed that the destruction and loss of evidence was intentional; those who favored conviction did not. Those who favored acquittal thought Knapp was a "wimpy" man who was easily pushed around and who was pathetically in love with Linda. The pro-conviction jurors saw him as smart, forceful, calculating, and eager to pin the blame on Linda to save himself.

Since there was great confusion about where to begin, Gladys, the court clerk, made a suggestion.

— The law says you're innocent till proven guilty, — she said. — If you think he's guilty, prove it to me. —

But her suggestion aggravated several of those who favored conviction; they thought it was unfair to force them to do the job of a professional prosecutor.

The jury turned instead to Judge Martone's jury instructions as a sensible place to begin. They read them to themselves and then read them aloud. Eventually, they focused on the very heart of the matter: What did "reasonable doubt" mean? They wanted more guidance than the brief, cryptic phrase Martone had read. They sent a note to Judge Martone asking for a definition of reasonable doubt.

He responded by referring them back to the one he had already given them.

The jurors then focused on another key instruction, the one concerning "missing evidence." The jurors who favored acquittal, plus Gary and Kirti, who were undecided, and even Dolores, who was in the guilty camp, were upset that the jars containing the fire residue from the room had been destroyed by the clerk's office in 1982. DeHaan had acknowledged that if those jars still existed, it might still have been possible, using scientific techniques available today, to identify what substances had been in there.

"I know that if I was on trial," Jim said later, "I would want every piece of evidence there, to prove my case, if it was a murder case."

The pro-acquittal jurors argued that the lost evidence could be a grounds for reasonable doubt under Martone's instructions.

But Martone's instruction about the missing evidence was confusing. The pro-conviction faction interpreted the instruction differently, and thought they could *not* find reasonable doubt merely from the fact that the fire residue samples had been destroyed. To settle the dispute, Cheryl, the foreperson, sent Judge Martone a note seeking clarification.

In his response, Judge Martone effectively confirmed the pro-acquittal group's interpretation.

About two hours later Cheryl sent Martone another note protesting that his new instruction seemed to be a "direct contradiction" of his original one.

Judge Martone, without specifically addressing the accusation, advised the jury again that they could find reasonable doubt "from the lack of any evidence."

Though the acquittal faction felt vindicated, Martone's decision had no impact on the conviction faction.

The whole group then turned to several new avenues of attack. They passed around photographs of the Knapps' burn-damaged and filthy East Capri home. These became known, with black humor, as the Knapp family album. Though jurors from both sides could agree that the filth was astounding, they could not agree on what inferences to draw. Knapp was not on trial for keeping a filthy home, the acquittal camp felt. But the filth showed his depraved lack of concern for the children, according to the conviction camp.

Personal problems surfaced. Foreperson Cheryl's habit of standing up and leading the discussion irritated Sunny — the most outspoken, polarizing, and combative member of the acquittal faction. She and other members of the acquittal faction began to mock Cheryl by standing themselves.

Each faction began belittling the motives of members of the opposing faction. Pro-acquittal jurors speculated that certain pro-conviction jurors had been charmed by prosecutor White's personal charisma.

Pro-conviction jurors, on the other hand, dismissed Sunny as biased, because of her early, undisguised distaste for White. They speculated that her forceful personality had effectively overborne the independence of Jim and Gladys, and they dismissed those two jurors as if they were mere satellites of Sunny.

Gladys, the court clerk, also mentioned to the jurors things she had read about the Knapp case in newspapers — references to the Meyer, Hendricks firm's enormous pro bono commitment to the case and to the misconduct allegations against the original prosecutor, Hyder. These were unquestionably improper topics for discussion, and the pro-conviction jurors were infuriated by this breach of the rules.

"I remember a lot of us saying emphatically, 'Shut your mouth' — literally," Gary recounted. " 'We can't be talking about those kinds of things.' "

In fact, the transgression solidified the pro-conviction camp's confidence in their own position, since it tainted the pro-acquittal faction as corrupt and immoral.

On the other hand, Cheryl, on the conviction side of the aisle, also brought up an unquestionably improper topic at one point, according to two jurors. She had allegedly mentioned in passing that during one of her previous experiences as a juror she had voted to convict in a robbery case, but the jury had deadlocked. After a mistrial was declared she found out that there was additional proof that the defendant was guilty that had been kept out of evidence. Two pro-acquittal jurors remember feeling that, in electing Cheryl foreperson because of her previous jury experience, they had unwittingly chosen someone with a chip on her shoulder.

Cheryl confirmed having had that earlier jury experience — learning about additional evidence of a defendant's guilt after a hung jury was declared — but she denied having brought the incident up during deliberations.

The emerging factions largely coincided with previously defined social cliques. One car pool that drove in from the north — Sunny, Jim, and Gladys — was solidly for acquittal; the car's fourth occupant, an alternate, had also been leaning for acquittal when she was excused.

The other car pool, which came in from the East Valley communities of Tempe and Mesa, included Dolores and Rick, who were for conviction, and Kirti and Gary, who were currently uncommitted.

Although the jurors were not supposed to discuss the case except when all twelve were present and in the jury room, one member of each car pool conceded that there were inevitable breaches.

"It's human nature," said a member of one car pool.

"I think that was basically an outlet, to relieve some of the tension," said a member of the other.

Deliberations swiftly became quite nasty. An acquittal juror told a conviction juror to shut up, and she told him to fuck himself. A conviction juror mocked Hammond's stutter. An acquittal juror questioned the virility of a state witness.

The jurors, who had once given impromptu potluck parties for each other, now began to dread seeing each other from the moment they awoke. Their stomachs tightened and churned as they drove to court.

"That was like the most stressful time in my whole entire life," Jadean remembered. "If there had been windows, we probably would have thrown each other out." Gary, Dolores, Kirti, and Cheryl all cried at times.

At some point the acquittal faction suggested that the group go through the confession, point by point — as the defense lawyers had invited them to do —

to see whether people really believed that Knapp could have committed the crime this way. They asked for, and got permission to look at, a chart Henze had used, listing ten improbable details of Knapp's confession. Had Knapp really crawled in and out of bed without waking Linda? Had he really used the can in the hall closet without leaving fingerprints? (Regardless of White's and Hyder's protestations that fingerprints were "meaningless," Jadean, Jim, Sunny, and Gladys all thought the absence of John's fingerprints on that can — except for one that was underneath one of Linda's — obviously cast doubt on the confession.)

The jury spent almost a day on this exercise. Jim and Jadean emerged with the impression that they had won unanimous agreement that the crime could not have really occurred the way Knapp said it had in his confession.

But, if so, they had merely proved something that never bothered the pro-conviction camp, whose members accepted White's view that it was the mere fact of the confession that mattered, not its precise content.

"That's where I found my biggest frustration," Jadean later remembered. "They're basing his guilt on a confession that nobody believes."

After three full days of deliberation, the jurors broke for the weekend, and then returned on Monday, November 25. By this time, Sunny's forceful personality was alienating and angering the pro-conviction jurors.

"I think it was always unanimous that we all wanted to string Sunny up," said one member of the pro-conviction camp.

— Well, by God, you're going to have to make up your mind one of these days, — Sunny yelled at Kirti during the second week of deliberations. — He's either guilty or he isn't. —

— All right, then, — Kirti responded. — Guilty! —

Kirti had been persuaded by DeHaan's testimony about the burn damage to the carpeting on each side of the door.

Cheryl took another vote. Now it was six to six. Gary, the ramp supervisor, had moved from the undecided column to acquittal, partly because he thought igniting flammable liquid would have blown out the window. He had also begun to think that the group was so divided that acquittal was the only way out of the impasse.

Cheryl then sent a note to Martone advising him of a "deadlock."

Taking a cue from a judicial seminar, Judge Martone offered to have the lawyers deliver supplemental closing arguments focused on the issues that were giving them trouble. (This was a very unusual procedure. Neither side could find any precedent for it, and the defense team objected to it. But Martone felt he had nothing to lose at this point.)

So the jurors spent the next day discussing which points they wanted re-argued, while they continued debating as well.

Sometime that day, a juror excused herself to go to the bathroom, causing discussion to momentarily cease. The jury had a general rule, enforced by foreperson Cheryl, that they would not deliberate without the full contingent of twelve present.

When that juror, who was pro-conviction, came out of the restroom, Gladys, who was pro-acquittal, went in. But this time discussion resumed while Gladys was out of the room.

"I came unglued," Sunny later admitted.

— By God, — she shouted at Cheryl, — if you don't want to foreman this place and do it properly and do it even, sit the hell down and we'll get somebody else that can do this job. —

— That's it, — Cheryl said, breaking into tears. — I resign. —

"She accused me of being opinionated and biased in running the deliberations," Cheryl said, "and at that point, I said, 'You take it. It's yours.' . . . I couldn't deal with the emotions of going through the whole process — and her mouth."

Nobody wanted to take Cheryl's place. By then the deliberations were nasty, personal, and out of control.

"Somebody would say something," Gary recalled, "and the other person would disagree and just jump all over 'em and ridicule 'em and . . . it was destructive, instead of constructive."

"There were all these minds racing," Jadean remembered, "and people wouldn't slow down long enough to hear the one thing you were trying to say."

Someone suggested that Gary take over as foreperson. He had maintained his calm throughout the deliberations and was not entrenched in either camp.

— I will do it, — Gary said, — but, if so, we're gonna do it my way. I don't want to offend anyone, but I'm going to have complete control over this crowd here. We're going to be like a classroom. —

Seeing the need for structure, the jurors agreed to Gary's terms. Deliberations resumed with people raising their hands when they wished to speak, and Gary calling on them.

*　　*　　*

At the close of business on Wednesday, November 27 — after six full days of deliberation — the jurors were still discussing amongst themselves which issues they wanted to hear more argument about. Since the long Thanksgiving weekend was upon them, Judge Martone adjourned court until Monday, December 2.

At about 11:00 A.M. on the morning of the jury's return, Gary sent Judge Martone a note listing the issues they wanted argued.

It amounted to a laundry list of every major issue in the case, including the "flashover concept," "the confession," "missing evidence," "John's character," and so forth. In addition, Gary asked the lawyers to address a central dispute that was dividing the jury: "If you believe the confession, must you believe all of it? Is the confession the state's case?"

The lawyers delivered their supplemental arguments that afternoon.

Prosecutor White sought to assure the jurors that they could have plenty of questions about the case and still convict. To help illustrate his point, he displayed a large jigsaw puzzle he had made for the occasion from a poster of the Statue of Liberty. He showed how, *even with most of the puzzle pieces missing*, it was still obvious that it was the Statue of Liberty.

"I was never good at puzzles," White quipped, "but I figured this one out okay. Just because you have a question doesn't mean you have a reasonable doubt."

"That's when I felt comfortable about my vote," remembered one pro-conviction juror. "I felt that I could say 'guilty' with a clear conscience after that."

But Jim still seemed genuinely surprised and confused by White's argument when interviewed a year later.

"That was something I guess I didn't know about the law," he said. "You don't need everything to convict somebody."

And the argument won no converts from the acquittal camp. In fact, Jadean found White's argument appalling.

"He's got the few pieces in, and says, 'Well, you can tell that this is the Statue of Liberty, so I really don't need to put the rest of the pieces in here.' That sort of portrayed the attitude to me: 'I really don't have to go the extra mile and prove this to you.' . . . It just bothered me that the system is winning cases, and not what's right."

Jadean's impression was reinforced by White's further argument that the jurors should convict even if they thought Knapp's confession was completely wrong.

"You don't have to believe each part of the confession," White told them. "You don't have to believe all of it *or any of it* to find this defendant guilty."

In fact, White invited the jurors to come up with their own theories of how Knapp did it.

"You have to be unanimous that he caused the fire, all right? You do not have to be unanimous about whether it was this way or this way. . . . Did he do it with a gallon of Coleman fuel or a pint? *Did he use . . . the charcoal lighter [fluid] that was there on the kitchen counter?* You don't have to be unanimous about that."

There was, in fact, a quart-size container of charcoal lighter fluid visible in photographs of the Knapps' kitchen. No investigator had ever theorized that Knapp had used it to start the fire; no one had ever fingerprinted it, or taken it into evidence, or checked to see whether it was empty or full, or seen what its gas chromatogram would have looked like.

White was telling the jury: just convict; everything else is negotiable.

Hammond, the great believer in fixed targets, was stunned. All his and Henze's efforts to "marry" the state to the confession were now a mockery.

Hammond was so stunned, in fact, that he did not object until the next morning. But, by then, Judge Martone declined to decide whether or not the argument was proper, since the objection had come too late.

That morning, December 3, when the jury resumed deliberations, foreperson Gary changed his vote to guilty. He had decided that his belief that a flammable liquid fire would have blown the window out was not a true "reasonable doubt" but rather just "an assumption" on his part.

"Smyth, and the defense experts," Gary explained in an interview, "did not prove this out to me. And I think if they had proved this out to me, I might have changed my mind."

Gary appears to have reversed the burden of proof, demanding that the defense prove that the window would have blown out, rather than demanding that the state prove that it could have stayed in. Although Judge Martone had correctly instructed the jurors about the burden of proof, Martone had also permitted prosecutor White repeatedly to stress, sometimes over defense objection, that the defense experts had not *proved* that the fire was innocent — which was an accurate statement about the state of evidence. Understandably, Gary was confused by the paper-thin distinctions.

— Hey folks, — Gary said after a half day of deliberation, — We're just gonna have to take a vote and I'm gonna have to give him the numbers, because we're not getting anywhere. —

The car pool from the north voted solidly for acquittal (three votes), while the car pool from the east voted solidly for conviction (four votes). The remaining five split, three to two for conviction.

The final tally was seven to five for conviction — exactly the same result as had occurred at the first trial in 1974.

At 1:35 P.M. on December 3, Gary notified Judge Martone that the jury had reached a "major impasse."

Judge Martone declared a mistrial.

The only jury that ever convicted John Henry Knapp was the second one convened in 1974, the one that prosecutor Hyder had — lawfully — prevented from seeing Marshall Smyth's fire tests. Those jurors therefore never learned that the peculiar system created by the cotton-sisal crib mattress propped up at an angle over the thick nylon carpet in the Knapp children's bedroom would burn like a Roman candle if a match fell in the right spot and that the resulting conflagration could leave many of the "hallmarks" of a flammable liquid fire.

That same jury, for reasons that are less well understood, was also given materially false information about the state of the fingerprints on the critical can of Coleman fuel; never learned about a state fire test that was apparently videotaped in April 1974; never learned that a tape recording existed of the defendant explaining why he had falsely confessed within twenty-four hours after he had done so; and never learned that a prominent prosecution witness claimed to have seen Little Linda set an entire book of matches on fire on "four or five" occasions before the fatal fire.

Thirty-one

Arizona's third attempt to put John Henry Knapp to death had cost Maricopa County at least $450,255.05 in defense-related fees and expenses. The largest chunks were $256,426.27 for Hammond and paralegal Deb Heller; $20,000 each for Henze and Sands; $42,900.34 for two investigators; and $46,196.95 for transcripts.

The taxpayer funds expended on the various prosecution agencies that had brought the case and on the judges who presided over it are harder to estimate, but no less substantial.

Though the reimbursements that Meyer, Hendricks received for Hammond's, Heller's, and Sands's time were enormous from the perspective of Maricopa County's budget for indigent defense, they were confiscatory from the perspective of the firm. Defending Knapp in 1991 alone represented a donation by the firm of about $1,554,000 in attorney fees alone, or about $44,400 for each of its 35 partners. (That number excludes five months of intense work in 1990, as well as all the hours the firm donated from 1981 to 1987 pursuing Knapp's second, third, fourth, and fifth post-conviction relief proceedings.)

"All the lawyers involved in the case — certainly those in the past and to some extent those in the present — have become personally consumed by the case," Judge Martone lectured Hammond and White in a telephone status conference two days after declaring the mistrial. "Counsel for both sides . . . have invested so much personal energy and identification into it that it has almost crossed the bounds of professional advocacy into . . . some sort of cause — on both sides."

After reviewing with the lawyers some of the cost estimates he had been given over the past two days, Judge Martone seemed to be begging the lawyers not to force the county to throw away more time and money on this case.

Having completed his pitch, Judge Martone popped the question.

"Has the process of [making] policy choices in the executive branch begun?" Martone asked White.

"They have begun and they have concluded," White answered. "And the answer is that the state is going to proceed with another trial."

Since White wanted to spend some time with his family over the holidays, he consented to Knapp's release pending retrial in exchange for the defense team's agreement to put off the fourth trial until the following year.

Knapp strode out the side door of the concrete jail on the afternoon of December 6 in a more business-like fashion than he had in 1987. Wearing khaki pants, white shirt, and a tie, and carrying a dark red accordion file under his arm, he followed Hammond's advice and declined comment to the waiting swarm of reporters. With Sands leading him by the arm, he briskly made his way to Hammond's pickup truck, which once again whisked him off to the firm.

Knapp had spent 1 year and 134 days in pretrial detention since his rearrest on July 25, 1990. He had spent 14 years and 159 days in custody since the fire, including 12 years and 52 days on death row.

At the firm Sands got him a soft drink from the firm's four-spout dispenser — which impressed Knapp, since it did not require coins to operate — and then Sands introduced him to various Meyer, Hendricks attorneys, paralegals, and staff.

While criminal lawyers often consider a hung jury a victory — and many around town called Hammond to congratulate him — Hammond did not see it that way, and neither did most of his colleagues at the firm, who did not seem sure what to say.

Sands gave Knapp some possessions they had been storing for him, including a science encyclopedia, a Bible, and a ball of string (useful for passing notes to other inmates). Sands would mail Knapp a few bulkier possessions, including a 19-inch television and a clock-radio, once Knapp got settled elsewhere.

He and the other members of the defense team took Knapp out for dinner that evening at Durant's, an old-fashioned, pink stucco steakhouse a few blocks from the firm, where Diettrich and Basham had taken Knapp for dinner to celebrate his first hung jury in September 1974. Knapp ordered a ground steak, but the others eventually cajoled him into ordering something more expensive.

After putting Knapp up at a hotel for the night, Hammond and Sands took him to the airport the next morning. They gave him $500 to get started with — Knapp did not even own a coat — and he took off.

Knapp took up residence in a rooming house near Pittsburgh.

Judge Martone desperately wanted the attorneys to resolve the case. Realizing that the prospect of winning the death penalty might be what was keeping this case from ever ending, he told the lawyers that such a penalty might not be realistic at this stage, even if Knapp were ever convicted.

"In each case that the defendant was allowed to have expert testimony," Judge Martone explained in 1993, "the jury was hung. So it struck me, because of the . . . reasonable doubt that many jurors concluded existed in the case, [the lawyers] better consider whether that in itself would be a mitigating factor in connection with anybody's decision to impose the death sentence."

Henze and Sands were willing to enter plea negotiations. Though John Knapp could never plead guilty, he might be willing to plead "no contest" — a resolution in which the defendant admits no wrongdoing, but allows the state to record a conviction. If the state were willing to let Knapp plead no contest to some reduced charge in exchange for "time served" — a sentence to a term of years he had already completed — then it would be awfully difficult not to recommend that Knapp take such an offer.

A fourth trial would be a mammoth waste of time and expense and would most likely end in another hung jury, both Sands and Henze thought. The confession was always going to be a tremendous obstacle to outright acquittal.

And Sands greatly feared and respected prosecutor White's skill. At a second trial White had won a conviction and death sentence for inmate John Serna — who may well be innocent — so he might be able to win a conviction of Knapp, too.

Hammond, on the other hand, was already planning trial four. When Sands spoke to Hammond about looking into a plea, Hammond resisted. Once he even lashed out at Sands. — You don't represent innocent people! This case is different. —

But later Hammond relented. He knew the confession would always be a great hurdle to outright acquittal.

"On the one hand," he recounted, "I really wanted to do it again, so that we could do it right. And on the other hand, the idea of going through that experience again was unimaginable."

Hammond also knew that his partners dreaded the costs of a fourth trial, though, stoically, they never exerted overt pressure.

In January Hammond and Henze drove to Tucson to meet with White. They told him they thought Knapp might consider a no contest plea to an involuntary manslaughter charge in exchange for time served, since Knapp acknowledged responsibility for having helped create the firetrap that killed his children.

"Any kind of homicide's fine — I don't care what the label is," White later remembered thinking. "I just want him behind the wall."

White demanded that Knapp serve at least five more years in prison.

Hammond and Henze thought that if they could talk White down to a year or eighteen months, that would be something they would have to take to Knapp and discuss.

In late January, Hammond flew to Pittsburgh to discuss the options with Knapp at his home. Knapp was living on the second floor of a rooming house, with windows overlooking a barber shop, a funeral parlor, and a bridge over a stream. He had joined a local Presbyterian congregation, and his Bible and biblical concordance were prominent features in his room.

Though Knapp was paying the rent, he was having a hard time. During his 1990–1991 incarceration, the engine block in his car had cracked during a freeze. The lack of transportation made every other task difficult. And because of the outstanding charges he could not land a good job.

He had, therefore, begun working as a "thumper," unloading trucks at a warehouse. The truck drivers would pay him $50 to $100 cash per truck. He could sometimes make $150 a day, but the work was irregular and strenuous. The bus ride, with connections, took about an hour and a half each way.

On the second day of Hammond's visit, the lawyers held a conference call to discuss plea possibilities. Hammond was with Knapp at a law office near Knapp's home, while Sands and Henze participated from Henze's office, and Popko listened in from Meyer, Hendricks.

"It's always difficult," Henze said later about broaching the topic of a plea agreement with a client. "It was difficult here."

Hammond wanted no concerted pitch. Each lawyer should just give Knapp his candid, personal opinions, he thought, so Knapp could hear different perspectives.

Sands ended up as "the designated heavy," Sands later recalled, stressing the dangers of going to trial. Sands felt it would be better if he were the one to do so, so that Knapp would not think that his trial lawyers, Henze and Hammond, had lost faith.

And Sands was also, in fact, the lawyer who was most fearful that Knapp could still be convicted and executed. There was no guarantee that Martone would still be the judge if a fourth trial took place. Although Arizona still had not used its gas chamber since 1963, it was now readying the device to asphyxiate Donald Eugene Harding, a convicted triple murderer, who was scheduled to die on April 6, 1992.

The discussions became heated. Though a no contest plea would not be an admission of guilt, the way a guilty plea would, it would still be a conviction — a judicial determination of guilt.

Knapp's brother Bob had been urging Knapp to tell the prosecutors to shove any offer up their asses. Though Knapp wanted to get the ordeal over with, he also agreed with his brother — or wanted to.

And Knapp was adamant that he would not agree to serve another day.

Sands got angry with Knapp's intransigence at one point. He felt Knapp was not being realistic about the dangers of a fourth jury trial.

— Plop, plop, fizz, fizz, John, — he shouted. — How long can you hold your breath once the pellets drop? —

But Knapp held firm. Not another day.

A week later Judge Martone was appointed to the Arizona supreme court, and in early March David White asked that the case be transferred back to the Maricopa County attorney's office, which no longer had the conflict of interest that had forced it off the case in 1987. White had been appointed Pima County's chief criminal deputy in January, and his boss wanted him to devote time to his Pima County duties.

Maricopa County attorney Richard Romley then reassigned the case to deputy county attorney Susan Sherwin — who, of course, had the greatest familiarity with it — along with Cleve Lynch and Paul Ahler.

To adequately prepare, the new prosecutors wanted to get the transcripts of the third trial, which would take months and cost the county at least $20,000.

Henze began negotiating with Lynch and Ahler.

"It was very hard," Henze recalled, "because Ahler and Lynch were not founded in the facts at all, and that left them in the hands of Susan [Sherwin]. We didn't like that because we believed she had an [emotional] attachment to the case, and a predisposition to want to try it again."

Ahler and Lynch reevaluated the case but, after doing so, decided to press forward. According to Hammond, the prosecutors emphasized that the state's fire expert, John DeHaan, was far superior to the defense fire experts.

Ahler, Lynch, and Sherwin declined interviews.

In March, in an interview with the *Arizona Republic*, Attorney General Grant Woods spoke out in favor of the death penalty, arguing that the John Knapp case illustrated why the death penalty must be carried out quickly.

"Knapp should have been executed a long time ago," Woods said. "Why put someone in prison for life if, decades from now, we think that science may give us a new theory? We do the best we can with what we have today."

On April 6, 1992, Donald Harding was placed in Arizona's gas chamber, in the dark blue stucco "death house" at the Central Unit of the Arizona State Prison Complex at Florence.

The clunky gray contraption resembles an eight-sided bathosphere. Five of the six side walls are fitted with thick windows — each secured in its frame by forty rivets — while the sixth wall houses a door that can be hermetically sealed into the vaseline-coated, rubber-lined doorframe by turning a large metal wheel on its exterior. The black, perforated-steel chair inside had recently been fitted with black nylon straps to replace the decaying leather restraints that, it was feared, might not have been strong enough to bind Harding's arms, legs, and torso.

The chamber is set midway through a cinderblock wall, so that three of its windowed gray sides project into a narrow adjoining room. There the invited witnesses can stand and observe. The inmate's chair faces away from the visitors.

Harding died eleven minutes after the gas started to fill his chamber. For the first six minutes he gasped, convulsed, and struggled against his restraints. Newspaper reporters in the observers' room were shaken by the spectacle, as was attorney general Grant Woods himself, who later admitted revulsion at the sight.

As a result of the gruesome event, the Arizona legislature decided that executing people in the gas chamber was a poor way to demonstrate Arizona's reverence for the sanctity of life.

Accordingly, it adopted lethal injection as the mode of execution for subsequent death sentences.

*　　*　　*

John Knapp telephoned Hammond or Zig Popko twice a month, as Judge Martone had ordered (to ensure that the lawyers kept track of their client's whereabouts).

During a call in late April, John read Hammond a list of his conditions for any plea.

— Time served. No contest. No probation. Involuntary manslaughter, — he said. — But if [Maricopa County Attorney] Romley says no, then we're back to square one. —

— Well, if we get to the point that the county refuses this proposal, — Hammond said, — we'll want to talk further about what we do next. —

— If they refuse this deal, the only thing we will have to talk about is a trial date. —

— John, we need to take this one step at a time. —

Before a May 6 status conference the new prosecutors responded to Knapp's offer with a counterproposal. They demanded ten more years in prison.

"We are light-years apart," Henze told Judge Reinstein, the county's presiding criminal judge, who had been handling the case since Judge Martone's elevation to the state supreme court.

Reinstein beseeched the lawyers to keep talking and said that three superior court judges, all of whom were former prosecutors, had shared with him their belief that the case, if tried, could never end in either an acquittal or a conviction.

Hammond assumed they were going to trial again. The firm began to prepare a motion, for which there was really little legal basis, asking the court to dismiss the case in the interests of justice. Hammond entitled it, candidly, the "Enough Is Enough" motion.

Hammond visited John again in Pittsburgh, flew him to Phoenix once, and regularly spoke with him by phone. Knapp was having a hard time. Given his age and weight, unloading trucks was arduous, and his ankles would swell up and give him trouble. He kept to himself and confided, it seemed to Hammond, in no one. He had bouts of apparent depression, when he would not get out of bed for days.

Although Knapp had interests, his enthusiasm for them was short-lived. He would lose some weight, but gain it back. He went to church, then stopped, then started again. He spoke about getting his car fixed, but it never happened. He spoke often about going fishing, but never got around to it.

Knapp was as bad at handling money as he had ever been. He had even gone to Atlantic City to gamble once.

— I was up $500 at one point, but I lost it all, — he told one of his lawyers in a telephone call. — Lost my concentration. —

In late September an inmate who had briefly been Knapp's cellmate in jail in July 1991 began claiming that Knapp had confessed to him. Prosecutors initially showed some excitement about the new witness, even mentioning his existence at a court hearing, resulting in newspaper coverage.

But he fizzled. Steven Bazin (among other names) was a career con man, with convictions for burglary, credit card fraud, fraudulent schemes, forgery, and theft. He had claimed to have heard confessions from several inmates over the years. The Knapp team's investigator, Mary Durand, happened to have interviewed Bazin for another case in January 1992. Bazin had told Durand then that Knapp never spoke to anyone about his case and that everyone in the pod "knew [Knapp] was innocent."

After Bazin failed a lie detector test, prosecutor Lynch told Hammond he did not plan to use him as a witness.

In late October or early November Michael Berch, the A.S.U. law professor who had assisted the Meyer, Hendricks lawyers on the Knapp case during the pretrial stage, happened to be chatting with county attorney Richard Romley, a former student of his, when Romley expressed surprise that they had been unable to resolve the Knapp case.

Berch passed the information along to Hammond, suggesting that he write Romley after the upcoming election. (On November 3, Romley easily won reelection.) Hammond did, and a few days later Romley called Berch to say he would offer a no contest plea to second-degree murder in exchange for time served. Suddenly the demand that Knapp serve five to ten years of additional time had vanished.

Hammond still has no idea what caused the change.

"I don't know if it had been just a tremendous series of miscommunications, or whether there was a war going on there between the [line] deputies and Romley or whether it was the cost estimate for transcripts. I just don't know what caused it."

(Romley declined to be interviewed.)

The defense lawyers flew Knapp to Phoenix to discuss the proposed plea. This meeting was more sedate than the telephone conference months earlier.

— Look, — one defense lawyer said. — The state wants a murder conviction. They don't want involuntary. You want no time served, you want this thing ended, and you want to be able to go in there with your head held high and say, 'I didn't do it.' Under this agreement, you could do all of those things. —

(Since the plea would be "no contest," Knapp would not have to admit guilt, as is required of people who plead guilty.)

Knapp agreed that it sounded acceptable.

Still, it would be a great humiliation. He never told his brother Robert or sister Marilyn how the case had been finally resolved. (In 1994, when they asked, the author told them.)

By November 16, 1992, the nineteenth anniversary of the fire, the defense lawyers had worked out a written agreement with the prosecutors.

"I know that Larry called me one morning," Sands said, "to tell me that the offer's been accepted. Larry sounded very tired and dispirited. . . . You live with a case. You are [primed] for the big moment — guilt or innocence — and then, as Eliot says, we don't end with a bang, we end with a whimper."

When Hammond was asked what he thought about the plea, he just shook his head back and forth.

In exchange for letting the state score the Knapp prosecution as a conviction, the state agreed to stop trying to kill John Knapp and to leave him in peace. It was a bizarre resolution for a capital case.*

At the change-of-plea proceeding, Judge Daniel Nastro, who had been assigned the case a couple months earlier, asked each side to state on the record why it was agreeing to the no contest plea.

---

* But not unprecedented. John Serna's case had been resolved in a similar fashion when he went from death row to freedom in December 1994.

Professors Bedau and Radelet, in compiling their list of probably innocent people who have been sentenced to death, found several cases in which inmates ultimately pleaded guilty or no contest in exchange for time served, after having won new trials on the basis of exonerating evidence. Since such cases — including Knapp's — formally end in conviction, the professors did not count any of them among the 416 "miscarriages of justice" they reported. See also, David Von Drehle, *Among the Lowest of the Dead*, pp. 327–357 (the case of Earnest Lee Miller and William Riley Jent)(1995).

A no contest or guilty plea saves face for state officials and affords some protection from civil liability.

Knapp read a prepared statement.

"I could never plead guilty to a charge that I killed my daughters," he said, "since I am innocent. . . . I did not murder my daughters, period. . . . This plea allows me to have my freedom and to walk out of this courtroom through the same door I walked in this afternoon. . . . This plea allows me to put an end to an ordeal that has lasted for nineteen years."

When Judge Nastro asked deputy county attorney Lynch why the plea was in the interests of the public, Lynch said that the state was accepting this lenient outcome only because, after nineteen years, the loss of evidence and the disappearance of witnesses had weakened the state's case.

But Lynch made one additional observation.

"For years now," Lynch said, "there's been comments by various people that this is an innocent man on death row. I think this plea today will end those comments. We know this was not an innocent man that was on death row."

Lynch's statement was the closest anyone ever came to offering a credible explanation for why prosecutors had, in 1987, resurrected the then fourteen-year-old case and litigated it for another five years. They were trying to prove to themselves, if to no one else, that innocent men do not really wind up on death row! Now, in exchange for letting Knapp go scot-free, they could *take the position* that Knapp was guilty!

"You know he took a plea?" prosecutor White asked the author in late 1992 when White was first contacted in connection with this book.

In her letter threatening to sue, prosecutor Sherwin emphasized that Knapp "has been convicted of those murders on his own plea."

In his letter threatening to sue, prosecutor Hyder's lawyer Kraig Marton wrote — falsely — that Knapp had "pleaded guilty."

After the no contest plea, Hammond and Henze brought Knapp back to the firm for a last subdued celebration.

Hammond toasted Knapp.

Then Knapp, dressed in a white shirt and tie and a gray sweater vest, toasted the firm.

— I want to thank this firm for giving me my life back. There is no way I will ever be able to repay you. —

The next morning, before heading to the airport, Knapp asked Popko to drive him to the cemetery in Mesa where Iona Marie and Linda Louise were buried. The girls' grave had no headstone or marker, so Popko got a map from the superintendent to try to find the girls' plot of land. Using other gravestones as landmarks, they found the vicinity of the children's shared casket. Knapp believed he could pinpoint their grave site as well, though Popko was not so sure. Knapp placed flowers on the grass there. The girls would have been twenty-one and twenty-two years old.

Popko then drifted away and gave Knapp some time alone with his children and his conscience.

Epilogue

In 1976 Justice Lewis Powell Jr. — the justice for whom Larry Hammond clerked in 1972 — helped forge the judicial compromise that effectively restored capital punishment in this country. Until his retirement in 1991 Powell went on to shape the constitutional law governing capital punishment more than any other justice, according to his biographer, Professor John Jeffries Jr.[*]

In 1993, however, Justice Powell told Jeffries that he had changed his mind about capital punishment. He would now vote to hold it unconstitutional in all circumstances, he said. The penalty served no useful purpose and simply could not be imposed fairly, reliably, and expeditiously.

In 1994 David Basham, Knapp's public defender at his first trial, began practicing law again in Tucson, after a sixteen-year layoff. He handles mainly civil cases while continuing to pilot a jet for a private company on an on-call basis.

Knapp's other lawyer at his 1974 trials, Charles Diettrich, is a repeat felony offender, serving a three-and-a-half-year term in the Arizona state prison. (He was convicted in 1992 of possessing a crack pipe; in 1994 of possessing a small quantity of crack cocaine; and again, in September 1995, of possessing small quantities of methamphetamine and crack cocaine.)

John Knapp's original prosecutor, Charles Hyder, is a federal prosecutor in

---

[*]John C. Jeffries Jr., *Justice Lewis F. Powell Jr.*, 1994.

Phoenix. In late 1993 or early 1994, a secret decision maker at the state bar of Arizona, after viewing sealed written submissions from Hyder, his counsel, and other invited parties — only one of which was ever shown to Hammond for comment — decided that there was "no probable cause" to believe that Hyder had engaged in any unethical conduct during the Knapp trials in 1974, and that it was therefore unnecessary to hold evidentiary hearings on that question. In accordance with applicable rules, the secret decision maker issued no explanation of any kind.

Linda Knapp was divorced, unemployed, and living with a new boyfriend in Utah when I visited her in June 1993. Although Linda was adamant that John was certainly capable of killing the two children, she could not decide whether she thought he had really done so. Everything she heard about flashover during the 1991 trial sounded "totally believable" to her, she said, judging from what she saw of the actual fire.

In addition, she still did not see how Knapp *could* have committed the crime.

"He would've had to crawl over top of me to do it," she said. "That's hard to do — to get in and out of a bed with me in it, without waking me up. I'm an extremely light sleeper."

In September 1993 John Knapp lived alone in a rooming house near Pittsburgh.

Knapp declined to be interviewed. "I'm not interested in any book," he said. "I'm just trying to start my life over again. It's rough as it is."

In 1981, when John Knapp was still on death row, Steven Twist, chief assistant Arizona attorney general, published an article in *Phoenix Magazine* articulating arguments in favor of the death penalty.

Twist argued that to understand great moral issues like capital punishment, it was useful to focus on the concrete images presented by particular cases. One case he recommended looking at was that of John Henry Knapp. People could learn much from their "visceral reaction" to the Knapp case, he wrote, and could judge from it "the morality of executing deadly criminals."

The reader is now equipped to do just that.

Source Notes

Those who want to preserve a sense of suspense as they read this book should be warned that reading the notes will, in places, foreshadow future events.

This book is based primarily on official transcripts, court orders, motions, and other records contained in court files; police, fire, and social services department reports; and witness statements to prosecutors, defense lawyers, and investigators. The defense lawyers' time sheets have also been used to help establish the chronology of events from 1983 to 1987 and from mid-1990 to late 1991.

That basic skeleton has been fleshed out with information from more than 200 interviews the author conducted with about 150 people from 1993 to 1995. (About 65 hours of those interviews were taped.)

Quotations that are not attributed to any other source are drawn from interviews with the author. Some quotations have been edited for clarity and brevity.

Conversations that are punctuated using dashes (—) rather than quotation marks represent statements that were neither recorded nor transcribed at the time they were made. They have been reconstructed from the memories of one or more persons who either participated in the conversation or overheard it.

(Where the "Ramseys," "Arthur Holiday," or "Patricia Jensen" were sources, the notes continue to refer to them by those pseudonyms.)

The following abbreviations are used in the notes:

RT officially reported court transcript
SP statement to a police officer (or deputy sheriff or state investigator)
SE statement to Michael Elardo, a county attorney's office investigator
TI taped or transcribed interview

AI   author interview
VT   videotaped testimony

Chapter 1

4 *David Contreras's account:* RT, August 14, 1974, pp. 64–75.

4 *Shirley Grenko's account:* RT, August 14, 1974, pp. 75–82; also SP, November 20, 1973, and March 1, 1974.

4 *Three other neighbors also said they saw Knapp break out the window with the hose:* Guenodine Sheets (RT, August 21, 1974, p. 31); Ernest Paredes (RT, August 21, 1974, p. 47); and Shirley Grenko's husband, Alvin. Because Alvin Grenko died before the 1974 trials, he never testified. But a police officer who interviewed him wrote in a report dated four days after the fire, "Mr. Grenko said that when Mr. Knapp broke the window there was an explosion of some kind and flames shot out of the room."

4 *Garrison's account:* RT, August 13, 1974, pp. 78–86; October 23, 1974 (A.M.), pp. 81–92. Also, SP, November 17, 1973 (report dated November 20, 1973); SP, March 1, 1974 (report dated March 13, 1974). The neighbor who alerted him was Susan Webb; she placed the time at RT, August 14, 1974, p. 93.

5 *Two neighbors . . . said he was carrying his shoes:* Susan House, SE, May 17, 1974, and RT, August 14, 1974, p. 59; Leonora Ybarra, SE, May 20, 1974.

5 *The firemen's accounts:* From the contemporaneous reports and/or later testimony of firefighters and other fire department officials, including Geary Roberts, Monty Brow, John Wilson, Roy Skowron, Gary Hopkins, John Mayhall, Ronald Butler, James McDaniel, and Stephen Hermann. All of the firefighters worked for the Rural/Metro Fire Dept., Inc., a private company that served, by subscription, unincorporated communities including East Mesa. It also served nearby Scottsdale, where it operated under the name Scottsdale Fire Department.

6 *— There's two little girls trapped inside, — :* Monty Brow's and John Wilson's reports, November 28, 1973; Brow, RT, August 13, 1974, pp. 29–30; Wilson, RT, August 13, 1974, p. 68.

6 *— My two daughters are in there . . .— :* Same.

6 *— Throw the damn cat in the garbage, —:* John Wilson's report and testimony.

6 *— They're not in the attic . . . —:* Gary Hopkins's report, November 23, 1973; Hopkins, RT, August 13, 1974, p. 47.

7 *— and if you don't do something I'll knock your damn head off. —:* E.g., Geary Roberts, RT, August 13, 1974, p. 107; Monty Brow, RT, same, p. 33; Roy Skowron, RT, same, p. 52; John Knapp, RT, August 27, 1974 (P.M.), p. 36.

8 *— Are you sure they're in the house? —:* Susan Fratini, SE, May 16, 1974; RT, August 14, 1974, pp. 34–36, 38.

8 *By 8:55 two deputy sheriffs had arrived:* Deputy John Chernko and Sergeant Lamont Skousen. Skousen described the positions of the children's bodies in his report (November 16, 1973) and deposition (August 2, 1974). Chernko and Skousen were members of the police agency that was known, from 1973 to 1976, as the Maricopa

County Sheriff's Department. Throughout all of its history before 1973 and since 1976, however, that agency has been known as the Maricopa County Sheriff's Office. In this book, it is referred to by its current name, the sheriff's office.

8 — *You might as well forget it* —*:* Molly Cameron, RT, August 14, 1974, p. 84.

8 — *If that don't kill them . . ."* — Same.

8 *"It's hard to explain exactly":* James Garrison, RT, October 23, 1974, p. 84.

10 *As the smoke cleared:* Descriptions of the house come from the reports and later testimony of the previously listed fire officials and deputy sheriffs, plus chief deputy state fire marshal David Dale and deputy sheriff Leon Stratton.

11 *Five neighbors later remembered that Linda . . . showed no emotion until her mother arrived:* Susan Webb, SP, March 1, 1974 (dated March 13, 1974); Kathleen Schulte, SE, May 16, 1974; Leonore Ybarra, SE, May 20, 1974; Loren and Grace Elsworth, SE, May 16, 1974. Webb and Schulte remembered the ensuing conversation. Two others — Ybarra and Sandra Rosales, SE, May 16, 1974 — also remembered portions of it.

11 *Linda's mother, Louise, later told a state investigator:* Louise Ramsey, SE, April 17, 1974.

11 *The Carolyn Goodman incident:* Carolyn Goodman's testimony of August 28, 1974, and November 15, 1974.

13 *about 9,000 fires:* RT, September 26, 1991, pp. 15, 75, 134.

14 *He had the firefighters clean the floor with squeegees and dry it with rags:* McDaniel, RT, October 28, 1974, p. 105.

14 — *My wife's the world's worst housekeeper,* —*:* Monty Brow's report, November 28, 1973.

14 *Edward Beyer's role:* Beyer, RT, November 15, 1974, pp. 49–55.

15 *Kenneth Templeton incident:* Templeton's SE, September 19, 1974; Templeton, RT, November 15, 1974, pp. 5–9.

15 *David Dale's observations:* Dale's report, November 23, 1973; Dale, RT, August 16, 1974, pp. 93–119, and August 19, 1974, pp. 2–10, 16–24, 33–35, 73–82.

16 *Knapp's errands with Melba Burr:* Melba Burr, SE, July 22, 1974, RT, August 14, 1974, pp. 44–57, and TI by Charles Hyder, August 1, 1974; George Bryant (the doctor who prescribed sedatives), SE, September 19, 1974; William Gibbons (the dentist), SE, September 19, 1974, and RT, November 15, 1974, pp. 14–18; Edward Moore (insurance agent), SE, July 23, 1974.

17 *Lila Johnson incident:* Lila Johnson, SE, September 25, 1974.

17 *Auto accident:* James Keller (the police officer), accident report, November 17, 1973; SP, December 5, 1973; and RT, August 15, 1974, pp. 21–23.

Chapter 2

19 *The children were "well nourished":* Karnitschnig's medical examination reports for each child, November 17, 1973.

19 *Carboxyhemoglobin levels:* Laboratory reports of Ramon Moreno (November 16, 1973).

20 *They heard more horror stories:* Assorted neighbors' SP, November 17, 1973.

20 *fly-covered chicken:* Linda Crumpton, SP, November 17, 1973; RT, August 15, 1974, p. 119 (reading from her deposition of July 23, 1974).

20 *Knapp's first interrogation:* Events leading up to the interrogation, and the general nature of its content, are drawn from Stratton, report of November 21, 1973, and RT, August 19, 1974, pp. 116–137, August 20, 1974, pp. 2–17; Dale, report of November 23, 1973, and RT, August 19, 1974, pp. 25–31, 94–99.

20 *John Knapp's account:* Quoted portions are drawn from John Knapp, RT, August 27, 1974, pp. 20–23, 26–27, 30–40; RT, November 15, 1974, p. 108. They have been edited for clarity and brevity and in order to convert question-and-answer colloquy and direct and cross-examinations into a single narrative. Paraphrased portions come from Stratton's report of Knapp's statements on November 19, 1973.

24 *Linda Knapp's account:* Quoted portions are drawn from Linda Knapp, RT, August 26, 1974, pp. 20–23, 29–33; RT, November 13, 1974, pp. 39–40, 44, 64, 75, 81–82, 93; and VT, October 22, 1991 (1:42–1:45), supplemented with information from Stratton's report of Linda's statements on November 19, 1973, and SE, April 18, 1974. Linda's statements have been edited in the same manner as John's.

26 *Then Dale explained what he had learned from the fire damage:* Dale, RT, August 19, 1974, pp. 94–95, 97; Stratton, RT, October 31, 1974, p. 59.

27 *Incident in which Melba Burr takes Linda to rendezvous with her natural father:* Melba Burr, RT, August 14, 1974, pp. 49–50; Linda Knapp, RT, August 26, 1974, p. 38; Louise Ramsey, RT, August 21, 1974, p. 95, and November 12, 1974, p. 114; John Knapp, RT, August 27, 1974 (P.M.), pp. 48–50.

28 *Subpoena incident:* Robert Malone, RT, August 6, 1974, 50–51, 75–76; John Knapp, RT, August 27, 1974, p. 50.

30 *sitting at the Ramseys' kitchen table, weeping:* Louise Ramsey, RT, November 12, 1974, p. 128, and TI by defense, August 26, 1991, pp. 44–45; Melba Burr, SE, July 22, 1974, and TI by Hyder, August 1, 1974, pp. 4–5.

30 *The polygraph incident:* Charles Fuchs's report, November 26, 1973.

31 *Events after polygraph:* Ashford, RT, August 7, 1974, p. 71; RT, November 6, 1974, p. 86; Knapp, RT, August 7, 1974, pp. 56–57, 63.

Chapter 3

32 *Incident at the Circle K:* Louise Edwards, SP, November 29, 1973; RT, August 14, 1974, p. 143 (reading deposition testimony, July 8, 1974).

32 *The inquest:* From inquest transcripts, November 27, 1973.

33 *"I recall just telling him":* Hugo Zettler, TI by defense, March 7, 1991, p. 28.

33 *"Mr. Knapp asked me to appoint a public defender":* Leo Coombs, RT, August 6, 1974, p. 98.

34 *picking up a third detective:* Memories vary about whether the third detective, Robert Barrett, was with Ashford and Malone from the start, was picked up on the way to the East Capri house, or joined the others at the East Capri house.

34 — *But Judge Coombs told me I couldn't have a lawyer* —: Malone and Ashford's report, November 28, 1973; Malone, RT, August 6, 1974, p. 11; Ashford, RT, August 6, 1974, p. 119; Knapp, RT, August 7, 1974, p. 38.

34 — *Well, I'll answer questions, but only those questions I have direct knowledge of* —: Malone, RT, August 6, 1974, p. 11; Malone and Ashford's report, November 28, 1973 ("he would only answer questions he had full knowledge of"); Ashford, RT, August 7, 1974, p. 7; Knapp, RT, August 7, 1974, p. 41 ("I told them I could only answer . . . what I knew what I had done, and anything pertaining to my wife on that particular morning, what she had done, I would not be able to answer . . . any questions because I didn't know what she had done that morning at all. I wasn't too sure.").

35 *Other incidents at the East Capri house:* Malone, RT, October 31, 1974, pp. 118–120; Ashford, RT, August 7, 1974, pp. 73–76, and August 21, 1974, p. 66; Knapp, RT, August 7, 1974, p. 60, and August 27, 1974, pp. 52–54, 79.

36 *had never taped any of the roughly 1,000 interrogations:* Malone, RT, August 20, 1974, p. 53; RT, October 8, 1991, pp. 13, 62.

38 *Knapp's account of the confession:* Knapp, RT, August 27, 1974, pp. 14–17, 56–60; RT, August 7, 1974, pp. 50–52; RT, November 13, 1974, p. 128.

40 *"You might as well have hit me with a Mack truck":* Louise Ramsey, TI by defense, August 26, 1991, pp. 46–47.

40 — *Well, you really tore your ass now,* —: Kenneth Ramsey, SE, April 18, 1974.

40 *'Well, you really messed up this time':* Kenneth Ramsey, RT, November 12, 1974, p. 56. The descriptions of Knapp as "a little defiant like" and "angry" come from Ramsey, RT, August 7, 1974, p. 6.

40 *'Well, I want you to believe that I didn't do it':* RT, November 12, 1974, p. 56. Some prosecutors, reading this language very literally, later refused to acknowledge that this statement amounted to a recantation of Knapp's confession. But Ken Ramsey never doubted that John was telling him that he was innocent, and his account of Knapp's words was, on earlier occasions, less ambiguous. E.g., RT, August 7, 1974, p. 6 ("He said, well I didn't do that"); SE, April 19, 1974.

41 *"I can't actually say":* Knapp, RT, August 27, 1974, p. 93.

Chapter 4

42 *"The employer gave the officers a letter":* Report of K. Lines, dated November 29, 1973, concerning November 28, 1973, interviews.

43 *Dale protested:* Dale's supplementary report, dated December 3, 1973.

43 — *Here's a little case I think would be good for you* —: AI. Many of Basham's recollections about the Knapp case have been either corroborated or supplemented by his testimony from January 6, 1975; May 14, 1979; March 23, 1984; June 26, 1991.

44 *Furman v. Georgia:* 408 U.S. 232 (1972). This case struck down all laws that permitted juries or judges unfettered discretion in deciding whether to impose the death penalty. A few states — including Arizona — also had *mandatory* death-penalty

411

laws for certain crimes, which were unaffected by *Furman*. However, the Arizona law authorizing the death sentence for murder was struck down.

44 *Arizona's new law:* Arizona Revised Statute, ∫13-454 (1973). See Crane McClennen, "Capital Punishment in Arizona: Past, Present, and Future," *Arizona Attorney* (October 1992).

44 *Description of jail:* Author's visit on September 20, 1994; also, Maricopa County Sheriff's Office, Custody Bureaus, Jail Information Booklet.

45 *Interrogation of Linda Knapp:* Drawn from transcripts of three surviving tape recordings of the interview; Malone and Ashford's report of December 4, 1973; and later testimony of Malone and Linda Knapp. (Also, defense investigator's report concerning his in-person interview of Arthur Holiday on May 30, 1991, and defense memorandum summarizing defense interview of Arthur Holiday on June 5, 1991.)

45 *roughly six hours:* According to the police report. The exact length later became a subject of dispute.

47 *"If I can't have you and the kids":* Transcript of interrogation prepared by defense lawyers in 1991, using electronically enhanced tape, p. 38.

47 *confirm only that this was the* detectives' theory: Same, p. 29.

47 *"He never really liked kids":* Same, p. 83.

47 *"He denied it, but I'd seen him":* Same, p. 21.

48 *"I can't see how he could have did this":* Same, p. 70.

48 *"This was an empty or full one?":* Same, p. 19.

49 *Iona "had on a yellow nylon top":* Same, p. 61.

49 *"You never suspected him?":* Same, p. 27.

49 *"I just wanted to go away":* Same, p. 29.

49 *"I knocked the candle off the sink":* Same, pp. 35–36.

49 *Malone's attempts to get confession from Linda:* Same, pp. 99–102.

50 *John had no insurance on the children:* RT, November 15, 1974, p. 60 (where the prosecution and defense stipulated that "the complete investigation by the County Attorney's office in this case since the date of the fire has shown that Mr. Knapp had no insurance on his children's lives").

51 *Footnote: "He knew I wrote it":* Defense-prepared transcript of surviving tapes of Linda Knapp interrogation, p. 39.

51 *Footnote: "I gave it to him to mail":* Linda Knapp, RT, November 13, 1974, p. 74.

51 *Footnote: "She gave it to me to mail":* John Knapp, RT, August 27, 1974, p. 69.

52 *"I believe we should shoot for the death penalty. . . . Get the S.O.B.":* Zettler's entry in the prosecution case log for December 4, 1973. Though lawfully withheld from the defense as confidential work product, an unexpurgated page from the case log was provided to the author by Kraig Marton, a lawyer for Charles Hyder, in October 1994.

Chapter 5

53 *Charles Hyder:* Hyder provided limited cooperation with this book. He declined to be interviewed, although he did respond to certain select questions from among a larger number posed to him in writing.

Nevertheless, Hyder testified about the outlines of his career and about many aspects of his handling of this case on July 10, 11, 17, and 18, 1991, and his attorney, Kraig Marton, set forth Hyder's perspectives on many of these matters in letters to the author dated October 11, 1994, and November 3, 1995. Descriptions of Hyder's reputation are based on the author's interviews with two investigators and eleven lawyers who, as prosecutors or defense lawyers, either practiced with Hyder or against him or both. Some background information about Hyder also comes from Pamela Manson, "Lawyers Clashed, Lives Diverged in Knapp Case," *Arizona Republic*, August 4, 1991, p. A1; Tom Fitzpatrick, "The Fire This Time," *New Times*, July 3–9, 1991, p. 5; Tom Fitzpatrick, "The Prints on the Can," *New Times*, July 17–23, 1991, p. 6; and Steven Brill, "Innocent Man on Death Row," *The American Lawyer*, December 1983, p. 1.

54 *Retention of Charles Diettrich:* Diettrich, RT (pretrial hearing), February 15, 1974, pp. 22–25; Affidavit of Mary Knapp, April 10, 1974; Affidavit of Diettrich, April 9, 1974; Diettrich, AI; Basham, AI.

56 *Diettrich's supervisors were becoming less convinced:* Stanley Patchell, RT, July 17, 1991, pp. 33–34.

57 *he or a younger colleague returned about half a dozen times:* Basham, RT, May 14, 1979; Donald Sims (the "younger colleague"), RT, May 14, 1979; Diettrich, RT, April 20, 1979; defense memorandum concerning defense interview of Jack Richmond on December 7, 1990.

57 *The most important thing investigators were looking for was evidence that either child was capable of lighting a match:* Diettrich, RT, April 20, 1979, pp. 40–45; AI with Diettrich and Basham.

57 *An early police report:* Jim Garrison's SP, November 17, 1973 (dated November 20, 1973).

57 *— One time we saw the little girls . . . —:* Sandra Rosales, SE, May 16, 1974; Tony Rosales, RT, August 21, 1974, pp. 23–27, and November 6, 1974, pp. 38–39.

57 *"Ernest Paredes said":* Paredes, SP, April 5, 1974, and RT, August 21, 1974, pp. 46–55, and November 6, 1974, pp. 47–52.

57 *Richmond's interview with Louise Ramsey:* defense memorandum concerning interview of Jack Richmond on December 7, 1990. The circumstances under which California authorities gave the Ramseys custody of the girls are discussed in the Pomona (California) Police Department report of officer B. J. Miller, dated March 21, 1972. When Malone asked Linda Knapp about this situation in Fremont, Nebraska, on December 1, 1973, she said the California authorities told Louise Ramsey that Louise "couldn't give [the girls] back to me until I seen a psychiatrist. And I didn't see one." (Defense-prepared transcript of surviving tapes of Linda's interrogation, p. 56.)

58 *The dream incident:* Linda Knapp's, Louise Ramsey's, and Kenneth Ramsey's joint SE, April 18, 1974; Linda Knapp, SE, September 20, 1974; Richmond's notes of his interview, December 2, 1973; defense memorandum concerning interview of Jack Richmond, December 7, 1990.

58 *told psychiatrists he still loved her:* Reports of Harrison Baker, M.D., February 11, 1974; Maier Tuchler, M.D., February 1, 1974; M.B. Ruland, M.D., February 4, 1974.

60 *"procedurally, morally, and ethically improper":* State's motion for determination of counsel, February 6, 1974. Also, RT, February 6, 1974, p. 17.

60 *"Is it this big a problem really?"* RT, February 6, 1974, p. 17.

60 *Marshall Smyth:* Smyth, AI, and Smyth's contemporaneous notes and diaries. The criminal case arising from the Pioneer International Hotel fire was *State v. Taylor*, 112 Ariz. 68, 537 P.2d 938 (1975).

62 *Strangely, . . . Hyder was still not satisfied:* Same, pp. 38–41.

62 *The house inspection:* Based on notes of Smyth, February 16, 1974; report of Corporal C. L. Carnes, who videotaped the inspection, February 19, 1974; Ashford's report, February 16, 1974; Dale's report, February 19, 1974; the videotape footage itself; Smyth, RT, August 23, 1974; Dale, RT, August 28–29, 1974; and AI with Diettrich, Basham, and Smyth.

63 *a major embarrassment to the state investigators:* Compare, for instance, fireman Roy Skowron, RT, August 13, 1974, pp. 60–61; McDaniel, RT, August 15, 1974; Smyth, August 23, 1974, pp. 17, 19, 20–26; McDaniel, RT, October 23, 1974; McDaniel, RT, September 26, 1991, pp. 62, 136, 141; Smyth, video, October 16, 1991 (2:13 P.M.); Smyth, VT, October 17, 1991 (3:58); Smyth, VT, October 21, 1991 (11:18, 11:34); RT, Richard Custer, November 13, 1991, pp. 120–122.

64 *"accomplished with my assistance," etc.:* Dale's report to Hyder, February 22, 1974.

65 *"On 4-2-74 at 1300 hrs":* Report of Carnes, April 2, 1974.

65 *Carnes referred . . . in the second document:* Sheriff's office property custodian's form, signed by Carnes on April 2, 1974.

65 *The discovery rules required:* Rule 15.1(a)(3) of the Arizona Rules of Criminal Procedure (1973).

65 *Footnote: Hyder later explicitly took the untenable position:* RT, August 22, 1974, p. 22. When Diettrich protested that he had been provided no discovery concerning David Dale's fire experiments, Hyder responded, "I believe the rule says we must yield what we intend to introduce in our case in chief."

65 *Hyder and Carnes would each say that he had no recollection:* RT, Carnes, June 26, 1991, pp. 44, 79, 86; RT, Hyder, July 11, 1991, pp. 60–84; letter of Hyder's lawyer Kraig Marton to author, October 11, 1995, p. 17.

66 *Deputy fire marshal Dale, on the other hand, would state that he had a dim memory:* RT, July 2, 1991, pp. 153, 154, 172.

66 *And indeed, many years later, Dale would vaguely recall that there may have been, in fact, two separate days of tests:* RT, July 2, 1991, pp. 143, 147, 149, 192–193.

66 *Hyder later subscribed to a variant of this theory:* RT, July 11, 1991, p. 64.

67 *Footnote: the alleged November 27, 1973, fire test:* Dale, RT, August 19, 1974, pp. 31–32, 49. Dale's report, ostensibly dated February 20, 1974.

69 *not to "the full paraphernalia of a defense":* State v. Crose, 88 Ariz. 389, 357 P.2d 136 (1960).

69 *"The state . . . has conducted tests . . . and the defense has been privy to all the material":* State's response to defendant's motion for appointment of expert, p. 5 (April 11, 1974).

69 *Today, the courts do recognize:* Ake v. Oklahoma, 470 U.S. 68 (1985).

69 *seen the girls walking alone along Broadway:* Leonore Ybarra, SE, May 20, 1974.

69 *seeing Iona, two, all alone in the middle of that highway:* Mary Sevits, SE, May 17, 1974.

70 *There was a persistent rumor:* Linda Crumpton, SP, November 17, 1973 (report dated November 20, 1973). Compare Tony Rosales, SE, May 16, 1974, to Contreras, RT, August 13, 1974; compare Grace Ellsworth, original SE, May 16, 1974, to its later amendment; compare Molly Cameron, SP, November 17, 1974, to Cameron, RT, August 14, 1974.

70 *Later that same day . . . another neighbor:* Mary Sevits.

70 *Three days later, another neighbor:* Leonore Ybarra.

71 *one neighbor . . . thought she had smelled "gas or fuel":* Guenodine Sheets, SP (report dated March 13, 1974).

71 *And in May, when Elardo began asking them:* See House, RT, October 24, 1974, p. 18.

71 *two more said . . . they remembered smelling something like gasoline:* Susan House and Leonore Ybarra.

Chapter 6

Although Knapp's lawyers, with Knapp's consent, cooperated with the author in the writing of this book, Knapp himself declined to be interviewed for it. (The author had previously interviewed Knapp in April 1991, while writing an article for *The American Lawyer* magazine about the case.)

Much of the information about John Knapp's early years comes from the notes of a defense psychologist, Camille Wortman, who interviewed Knapp in the spring of 1991. (Her notes were eventually provided to the prosecution pursuant to discovery rules and, at that point, were no longer protected by the attorney-client privilege.)

These notes have been corroborated and amplified, where possible, by interviews with two of Knapp's siblings: Robert and "Marilyn" — a pseudonym.

They have also been corroborated and amplified with reports of various social workers and mental health care professionals — including the three state psychiatrists who examined Knapp in early 1974 to determine his competency to stand trial, the probation officer who interviewed him upon his conviction, and a psychological intern who evaluated him in prison on November 3, 1983, for the use of the Arizona Board of Pardons and Parole — as well as school, military, medical, and employment records that both prosecutors and defense lawyers eventually obtained for use in the case. In some instances, information about Knapp comes from defense lawyers who spoke with him, or from internal defense memoranda recording Knapp's comments to his lawyers.

Inevitably, there are some passages of this chapter that rely on Knapp's memory and word alone. However, no evidence has ever come to light contradicting those passages.

74 *One of John Knapp's first memories:* As told to psychologist Wortman, among others.

74 *"He attempted to burn his baby sister to death"*: RT, November 12, 1974, pp. 87–88. See also, RT, August 21, 1974, p. 115.

74 *Footnote: "[John] remembers setting [his sister Iona's] playpen on fire when he was about five"*: Defense-prepared transcript of surviving tapes of the Linda Knapp interrogation, p. 83.

75 *Footnote: when Basham asked her about it in 1974:* RT, August 21, 1974, p. 116.

76 *John does not remember his father kissing him or hugging him ever:* Wortman's notes, p. 23. *tears streamed down his face:* Same, pp. 14–15.

78 *Linda remembers John telling her fondly of the children he treated there:* Linda Knapp, AI.

78 *"pretty in her way"*: Knapp, AI (for magazine article), April 22, 1991.

79 *Linda's mother, Louise, was born:* Biographical facts about Linda's upbringing come from Louise and Kenneth Ramsey, TI by defense, August 26, 1991; Louise and Kenneth Ramsey, AI; and Linda Knapp, AI.

80 *She was always very, very hard-headed"*: This sentence and the remainder of the paragraph come from Kenneth Ramsey, TI by defense, pp. 14–15. Previous portion of the sentence comes from Kenneth Ramsey, AI, March 31, 1993.

84 *"Linda left medicine lying around the house"*: Mary Knapp, RT, November 13, 1974, p. 24.

84 *The incident in which the Pomona police take the children away from Linda:* Drawn primarily from the contemporaneous Pomona police department reports and photographs; Mary Knapp, SP, November 21, 1973; Mary Knapp, RT, August 21, 1974, pp. 113–114, and November 13, 1974, pp. 24–25.

85 *"Iona's eyes were glassed over"*: John Knapp, VT, October 23, 1991 (3:36).

85 *"John Knapp was very concerned"*: Davis, VT, September 24, 1991 (4:17).

86 *— They are cute little girls, —:* Linda Caldwell, SE, October 13, 1974.

87 *"a little Sherman tank"*: All of Linda's memories about the children and John's interactions with them are from her AI.

87 *"John was always speaking highly of his family"*: Deposition by Cunningham, December 29, 1983.

87 *"probably the only woman he could get"*: Beckley, notes of defense interview, July 8, 1991.

88 *"She ruled the roost"*: Beckley, TI by prosecution, August 13, 1991.

88 *Continental Can was an obvious bright spot:* Knapp's experiences at Continental Can are based on accounts of Thomas Cunningham (RT, August 6, 1974, August 27, 1974, and November 6, 1974; deposition testimony from December 29, 1983; TI by prosecution, August 29, 1991; notes of interview with defense lawyers, February 22, 1991; and AI), James Beckley (VT, October 29, 1991; TI by prosecution, August 13, 1991; notes of telephone conversation with defense lawyers, February 6, 1984), Joe Karowski (VT, October 29, 1991; AI), and notes of interviews with five other co-workers conducted by state investigator Malcolm MacMillan and defense investigator Richard Todd in November 1977.

88 *"John pretty much kept to himself"*: Cunningham, deposition, December 29, 1983.

The next two sentences come from notes of a defense interview of Cunningham, February 22, 1991.

90 *"crawling all over the floor, like he was going berserk":* Burr, TI by Hyder, August 1, 1974, p. 19.

90 *"They called me at home":* Cunningham, VT, October 28, 1991 (9:49).

90 *"Linda came in to pick John up":* Same (10:00).

90 *"I told John if he could get his house in order":* Same (9:58).

91 *At other times, however, she said John did give her money:* RT, November 13, 1974, p. 70.

91 *Linda was* giving away *food:* Nancy Hardin, SP, February 17, 1978; AI.

91 *one of these big, oversized glass kerosene lamps":* Knapp, RT, August 27, 1974, p. 18.

92 *"I never followed through":* Goodman, RT, August 28, 1974, p. 15.

92 *Footnote: One prosecutor (not Hyder) even theorized:* Prosecutor Susan Sherwin wrote in a court filing on August 17, 1990: "Rather than pay the bills to resume [utility] service, [Knapp] brought Coleman appliances and fuel into his home and left them and matches within easy reach of his toddler daughters. When no fire occurred accidentally, he lost patience and took action."

93 *"I did get a little upset":* Knapp, RT, August 27, 1974, p. 69.

93 *"So I gave them a call":* Same, p. 27.

Chapter 7

94 *"unseemly":* Knapp v. Hardy, 111 Ariz. 107, 112, 523 P.2d 1308, 1313 (1974), quoting *State v. Madrid,* 104 Ariz. 534, 535, 468 P.2d 561, 562 (1970).

94 *In the ensuing months Hyder would, indeed,* take the position: RT, August 22, 1974 (A.M.), p. 22.

95 *Brady v. Maryland:* 373 U.S. 83 (1963).

96 *an aggressive prosecutor might* even take the position: Hyder actually made this very argument later. RT, July 17, 1991, pp. 205–206 ("I don't think that was exculpatory"). The deputy county attorney handling that proceeding, David White, made the same argument.

97 *"The only person at the scene of the fire":* RT, July 9, 1974 hearing, pp. 87, 91.

97 *Hyder demanded that defense expert Smyth be barred from testifying:* Same, pp. 17–19.

98 *Judge Hardy refused both requests:* Same, pp. 22–24.

98 *Hyder took the position that he had to provide only those statements that he planned to use in his "case in chief" [and colloquy that follows]:* Same, pp. 72–74.

99 *Judge Hardy then ordered the state not to destroy any tape recordings:* Same, p. 75, and written order of July 10, 1974.

99 *Discussion of the autopsy photos:* RT, July 9, 1974, pp. 35–37, 66–67; state's memorandum in support of allowing photographs into evidence.

99 *On the afternoon of July 22:* Burr, SE, July 22, 1974.

101 *Footnote: In testimony many years later:* RT, July 10, 1991, pp. 182–183.

102 *Smyth's tests:* From Smyth, RT, August 22, 23, 24, and 26, 1974; the tapes and still photos of those tests; RT, October 16, 17, and 21, 1991; and AI.

104 *But a police chemist's gas chromatograms . . . were simply not attorney work product:* The advisory comments to the September 1973 edition of the Arizona Rules of Criminal Procedure specified: "The work product exception . . . does not apply to the opinions, theories and conclusions of experts contained in reports to be disclosed under [Rule 15.1(a)(3)]." That rule, in turn, required the prosecutor to turn over "the results of physical examinations and of scientific tests, experiments or comparisons" performed by "experts who have personally examined . . . any evidence in the particular case." 17 Ariz. Rev. Stat. Anno. 241 (1973).

104 *"Not work product . . . Just reports."* Hyder, in TI of Strong, August 2, 1974, p. 13.

104 *"The problem is":* Same, p. 14.

105 *"Hell no. . . . Underline that":* Same, p. 62.

105 *"Mr. Knapp started making statements pertaining to spots" [and quotations that follow]:* Malone, RT, August 6, 1974, pp. 18–22 , 25, 27.

107 *"When you offered him aspirin":* Same, pp. 65–66.

108 *He asked, once again, that Smyth be barred from testifying:* RT, August 8, 1974, pp. 8–9.

108 *The defense lawyers offered Hyder a postponement:* Same, p. 18.

108 *Alternatively, again, he asked that the court suspend:* Same, p. 16. In fact, early in the hearing, Hyder appears to have believed, incorrectly, that Judge Hardy had already granted him this suspension at the July 9, 1974, hearing. Same, p. 7.

109 *"I would like to have the court rule":* Same, pp. 21–22.

Chapter 8

110 *On Monday, August 12:* E.g., RT, August 14, 1974, pp. 112–113.

111 *Hyder's opening statement:* RT, August 13, 1974, pp. 20–22, 26.

112 *Because Judge Hardy had, by this time, ruled twice:* RT, July 9, 1974, pp. 36–37; Judge Hardy's written order (after reconsideration) of July 16, 1974.

112 *five of his earliest witnesses:* Monty Brow, RT, August 13, 1974, p. 32; Roy Skowron, same, p. 52; John Wilson, same, p. 70; Geary Roberts, same, p. 106; Heinz Karnitschnig, August 14, 1974, pp. 15–18.

112 *"The skull had split open":* Brow, RT, August 13, 1974, p. 32.

112 *"removed his glasses, buried his face in his hands":* Jack Swanson, "Fatal Fire," *Arizona Republic,* August 14, 1974, p. B1.

112 *"As firemen fought a blaze":* Same.

112 *"after we got done removing the [children's] bodies":* Brow, RT, August 13, 1974, p. 35.

112 *The only person who had implied:* RT, August 13, 1974, p. 21 ("during that fire . . . he was . . . drinking coffee, smoking cigarettes"); RT, same, p. 41 ("Is it unusual to see a father whose children are burning up sit out there and drink coffee . . . ?").

Although there were neighbors who had told Hyder's investigator Elardo before the trial that they had seen Knapp smoking cigarettes "during the fire," many of these same neighbors also later acknowledged that they had not even arrived on the scene until well after the firemen had put out the fire. It is apparent that these neighbors were understanding the phrase "during the fire" to mean "during the several-hour period when the fire trucks and firefighters were on the scene and dominating the neighborhood's activities."

112 *one neighbor did substantiate Hyder's version:* Nancy Hardin, RT, August 21, 1974, p. 21.

113 *Iona had suffered "fire decapitation":* RT, August 14, 1974, p. 17.

113 *"aids me in making the determination":* Same, pp. 18–20.

113 *"acted like he was at a cocktail party":* Same, p. 60.

113 *a theme became apparent:* Garrison, RT, August 13, 1974, p. 81; Contreras, RT, August 14, 1974, p. 67; Webb, same, p. 92; Crumpton, same, p. 120.

114 *it appears that the interview never actually took place:* In a taped telephone interview with Hyder on Thursday, August 1, 1974, Burr says that the defense lawyers plan to interview her that coming Sunday, and that if they do, she will tape it and play it for Hyder. There is no evidence that the planned interview ever took place. (Hyder's taped telephone interview with Burr, which should have been turned over to defense lawyers in 1974, also appears to have been withheld. When it came to light many years later, Hyder testified that he did not know if he had turned it over. RT, July 11, 1991, p. 17.)

114 *But the lawyers hoped they could persuade Judge Hardy:* They eventually made this argument on the record and, in fact, Judge Hardy ruled in their favor. RT, August 14, 1974, pp. 54–55.

114 *Discussion between Diettrich, Hyder, and Judge Hardy about Melba Burr's testimony and her prior statements:* Same, pp. 39–42.

116 *by means of a court order:* RT, August 22, 1974 (P.M. session), pp. 50–51.

116 *So while Strong was on the stand:* RT, August 15, 1974, p. 21.

116 *"In other words":* RT, August 16, 1974, p. 14.

117 *"Aren't you assuming":* Same, p. 25.

117 *"It's rather obvious":* Same, p. 80.

117 *Diettrich also exposed another curious theory:* Same, pp. 16–18.

118 *Michael Parsons:* This discussion is drawn primarily from TI of Parsons by Elardo on August 16, 1974, and August 21, 1974; Parsons's testimony of August 27, 1974, and November 6, 1974; and from surviving photocopies of the gas chromatograms.

118 *Strong's poor record keeping would have been unacceptable:* TI, August 16, 1974, p. 18.

118 *really impossible to say what those substances were:* Same, pp. 14–19, and trial testimony.

118 *did not appear to match:* RT, November 6, 1974, p. 113.

119 *The graphs of the extracts matched . . . too well:* TI, August 16, 1974, pp. 7–9.

119 *Their dominant feature should have been a huge single peak:* Same, p. 12.

119 *the methylene chloride . . . seemed to have been very impure:* Same, pp. 6, 9, 11–12.

119 *Elardo secretly tape-recorded their conversation:* Elardo, TI, May 30, 1991, p. 61.

120 *"I am not convinced":* Same, p. 6.

120 *"This is between you and I":* Same, p. 7.

Source Notes

120 *Parsons explained that the lighter compounds:* Same, p. 8.

120 *"It does resemble Coleman fuel?":* Same, pp. 14–16.

120 *"This isn't the only piece of evidence":* Same, pp. 17–20.

121 *"Dr. Parsons agreed":* Elardo's report, dated August 19, 1974.

121 *"I think probably I was leaning":* Dale, RT, August 19, 1974, p. 33.

121 *"flammable liquid runs" on her left cheek:* Same, pp. 11–16, 37–48.

122 *Smyth's additional tests:* From Smyth, RT, August 22, 23, 24, and 26, 1974, and October 16, 17, and 21, 1991.

123 *He had meant to say that Knapp was feigning irrationality:* Malone, RT, August 20, 1974, pp. 28, 56–57, 62, 79, 87.

123 *never actually* screamed: Same, pp. 57, 79, 81, 89.

123 *headache . . . might have come* after *the confession":* Same, pp. 28, 65.

124 *Malone testified that Knapp made the statement* after *making his spot-related confession:* Same, p. 25.

124 *But after the lunch recess, Malone changed his mind:* Same, pp. 54, 58–60, 65.

Chapter 9

125 *Excerpts from Basham's opening:* RT, August 21, 1974, pp. 2–8.

127 *And he had already begun bombarding Judge Hardy:* See, e.g., RT, July 9, 1974, pp. 55, 64–66.

127 *Mary Knapp's testimony:* RT, August 21, 1974, pp. 104–106, 110, 112.

128 *But, again, there was a theme:* RT, August 21, 1974, pp. 15, 25, 34, 53.

128 *"I have some matters I want to take up":* Same, p. 119.

129 *"I would like also to say":* Same, pp. 41–42.

129 *Elardo's telephone interview of Parsons, with Jack Strong on the line:* TI, August 21, 1974; quotations from pp. 8, 9, 13.

131 *inadmissible because they were conducted* at night: RT, August 22, 1974 (A.M.), pp. 66–68, III; (P.M.) p. 27.

131 *inadmissible because they contained ten-second gaps when Smyth was reloading the film magazine:* Same (P.M.), pp. 32–33.

131 *"As I understand him":* Same (A.M.), pp. 107–108.

131 *Then Judge Hardy ruled for the defense again:* Same, pp. 115–116.

132 *"filibustering":* Same (P.M.), p. 31.

132 *"barbecue pit," an "oven," and "a little bomb":* Same, pp. 26–27.

132 *"I will say":* Same, p. 38.

133 *From electronic evidence:* Anthony Pellicano, RT, June 18, 1991, p. 109; June 19, 1991, pp. 9–11, 25, 89–94.

133 *the jury was excused yet again:* August 23, 1974, p. 38.

133 *Judge Hardy agreed with Diettrich:* Same, pp. 46–47, 55–56.

133 *Accordingly, Judge Hardy allowed:* Same, pp. 44, 47.

133 *Hyder argued with that ruling for another fifteen or twenty minutes":* Same, pp. 47–57.

134 *Hyder changed strategy:* Same (3:30 P.M. session), p. 4.

134 *Strategizing regarding Linda Knapp:* Drawn from lawyer colloquy, RT, August 22, 1974, pp. 39–51; Linda Knapp, RT, August 26, 1974; AI with Basham and Diettrich.

134 *Linda Knapp's testimony:* RT, August 26, 1974, pp. 24–28.

135 *Dale . . . had testified at the suppression hearing:* RT, August 7, 1974, p. 81.

136 *"There would be substances left":* Parsons, RT, August 27, 1974, p. 56.

137 *"Did you bother to videotape":* RT, August 29, 1974, p. 8.

137 *Jury votes:* RT, September 2, 1974, p. 20, and Edythe Jensen, "Knapp Fire Case Ends In Mistrial," *Phoenix Gazette,* September 3, 1974, p. A1.

138 *"Hyder was outraged":* Judge Charles Hardy, AI.

139 *"I was hoping they'd decide":* Edythe Jensen, "Knapp Fire Case Ends In Mistrial," *Phoenix Gazette,* September 3, 1974, p. A1; Tom Kuhn, "Mistrial Ruled In Fire Deaths Of Knapp Girls," *Arizona Republic,* September 3, 1974, p. A1.

Chapter 10

140 *just going to reaffirm:* RT, October 7, 1974, pp. 4–5, 7.

140 *they held no true expert opinions:* RT, October 15, 1974, pp. 18–40.

140 *"You can't put a man on the stand" and following quotations:* Same, pp. 24–25, 26, 30, 36.

141 *Diettrich did offer a serious response":* Same, p. 28.

141 *But Judge Hardy ultimately ruled that doing so would be too expensive:* RT, November 7, 1974, pp. 108–109.

141 *Judge Hardy said he would reserve decision:* RT, October 15, 1974, p. 41.

141 *But there are several broad exceptions:* See *United States v. Perez,* 9 Wheaton (22 U.S.) 579 (1824).

142 *More surprisingly, however, each now denied:* McDaniel, RT, October 28, 1974, pp. 54–62. Dale had undergone the same transformation earlier, at the first trial, when, after Smyth testified, Dale returned to testify on rebuttal: RT, August 28, 1974, pp. 9–20.

142 *Instead, he was adamant that some damage:* E.g., McDaniel, October 28, 1974, pp. 35–38. See also, Dale, October 30, 1974, pp. 42–49.

142 *At the second trial Dale now remembered having been much cagier:* Compare, RT, August 19, 1974, pp. 97–98, to RT, October 30, 1974, p. 59, and RT, November 15, 1974, pp. 31–33.

143 *he now testified that he believed she had played no role in it:* RT, October 30, 1974, p. 72. In 1991, however, Dale admitted that it always was and "still is" his opinion that Linda was involved in the fire. RT, July 2, 1991, p. 201.

143 *"Do you have an opinion what the black peninsular-like mark is":* RT, October 30, 1974, p. 118.

143 *"That's the doctor's testimony":* RT, November 18, 1974, pp. 160–161.

143 *Hyder's cross-examination of Parsons:* RT, November 6, 1974, pp. 111–112.

144 *Elardo's testimony about Parsons:* RT, November 15, 1974, pp. 21–23.

145 *Malone testified this time:* RT, October 31, 1974, p. 84.

145 *Molly Cameron also now remembered:* RT, October 23, 1974, pp. 100–101.

145 *"had on dress clothes":* Susan Fratini, RT, October 24, 1974, p. 7.

145 *"about the way he is now":* Susan Webb, RT, October 23, 1974, pp. 94–95.

146 *The jury was excused:* RT, November 7, 1974, pp. 87–88.

146 *"This time . . . I think Mr. Hyder's argument is well taken":* Same, p. 97.

146 *"I'd like the record to reflect":* Same, pp. 108–109.

147 *The most conservative estimates:* See, e.g., Ronald J. Tabak and J. Mark Lane, "The Execution of Injustice: A Cost and Lack-of-Benefit Analysis of the Death Penalty," 23 *Loyola (Los Angeles) Law Review* 59, 70 n. 63 (1989), citing John Conyers, Jr., "The Death Penalty Lottery," *New York Times*, p. A15, col. 1; AI with Robert Spangenberg, president, The Spangenberg Group and Stephen Bright, director, The Southern Center for Human Rights, and J. Skelly Wright Fellow and Visiting Lecturer in Law, Yale Law School. See generally, Stephen B. Bright, "Counsel For the Poor: The Death Sentence Not for the Worst Crime but for the Worst Lawyer," 103 *Yale Law Journal* 1835 (1994).

148 *Diettrich had decided to be more direct:* RT, November 12, 1974, p. 65.

148 *"he cannot call a witness to the stand with the intention of blaming them":* RT, November 6, 1974, pp. 134–136.

148 *Judge Hardy himself finally thought of a more plausible:* RT, November 12, 1974, pp. 65–85 (especially 81), 103–110.

149 *Once again, Hyder asked at least seven witnesses:* Jim Garrison, RT, October 23, 1974, p. 85; Susan Webb, same, p. 95; Molly Cameron, same, p. 99; Tony Rosales, RT, November 6, 1974, p. 39; Ernest Paredes, same, p. 52; Linda Knapp, RT, November 13, 1974, p. 94; John Knapp, RT, November 14, 1974, p. 26.

149 *Hyder had never turned over a Dictaphone tape:* RT, November 14, 1974, p. 18.

149 *"We don't have to reveal rebuttal evidence":* Same, pp. 19–20.

149 *"If the court will recall":* RT, November 14, 1974, p. 21.

149 *Quotations from the first half of Hyder's closing argument:* RT, November 18, 1974, pp. 18–19, 35, 37, 50, 67, 73–75.

150 *Quotations from Diettrich's closing argument:* Same, pp. 136–137, 155.

151 *Hyder's reply closing:* Same, pp. 156–157.

152 *Quotations from the sentencing:* RT, January 6, 1975, pp. 167–168.

Chapter 11

157 *The preparation of Knapp's appeal:* This account is drawn from Diettrich, RT, March 22, 1985; Catherine Hughes, RT, March 22, 1985; H. Allen Gerhardt Jr., RT, March 22, 1985; and from AI with Diettrich, Hughes (July 15, 1994), and Gerhardt (July 18, 1994). Diettrich's quotations are from his testimony; Hughes's are from her AI.

160 *a 1970 case: Bowen v. Eyman*, 324 F. Supp. 339 (D. Ariz. 1970).

162 *the U.S. Supreme Court heard oral argument in five capital cases:* On March 30 and 31, 1976, it heard argument in *Gregg v. Georgia*, 428 U.S. 153 (1976); *Proffitt v. Florida*, 428 U.S. 242 (1976); *Jurek v. Texas*, 428 U.S. 262 (1976); *Woodson v. North Carolina*,

428 U.S. 280 (1976); *Roberts v. Louisiana*, 428 U.S. 325 (1976). The discussion is also based on information from Hugo Adam Bedau, *supra*, pp. 247–293.

162 *about 460 new inmates: Gregg v. Georgia*, 428 U.S., at 182.

163 *"The defense theory then was merely an alternative": State v. Knapp*, 114 Ariz. 531, 540, 562 P.2d 704, 713 (1977).

163 *Diettrich was still in the hospital when:* This account is drawn from contemporaneous court filings, including an affidavit from Diettrich, filed May 11, 1977.

164 *From the time the United States won its independence:* Hugo Adam Bedau, *supra*, especially pp. 15–16; William J. Bowers, *Legal Homicide: Death as Punishment in America*, especially pp. 12–13 (1982).

164 *At 7:00 A.M.:* According to Diettrich's taped radio interviews, and a dictated letter to Knapp, taped that same day.

165 *The lead had arrived the same morning as the stay:* Drawn from contemporaneous court filings; testimony of Diettrich (April 20, 1979) and his secretary, Angela Smallidge (May 14, 1979); written reports by Richard Todd (November 23, 1977, and January 5, 1978); statements from Continental Can workers obtained by Todd and state investigator Malcolm MacMillan during November 1977; AI with Diettrich and Richard Todd.

165 *a low reputation among some law enforcement officials:* E.g., memorandum from state investigator MacMillan to Hyder, November 29, 1977.

165 *"while many inconsistencies . . . are apparent": State v. Brazil*, 18 Ariz. App. 545, 546, 504 P.2d 76, 77 (1972).

166 *Gregory remembered:* Todd's report, January 5, 1978; Gregory's statement to MacMillan, February 20, 1978; Gregory's testimony, May 24, 1979.

166 *From late 1977 through early 1978, five clients:* From records obtained from the State Bar of Arizona and the Supreme Court of Arizona.

167 *diagnosed him as a manic-depressive:* Letter of Robert H. Barnes, M.D., dated March 30, 1978; appended to defendant's motion for rehearing on petition to vacate the verdict and sentence, filed March 30, 1978.

169 *an updated version of their list:* Michael L. Radelet, Hugo Adam Bedau, and Constance E. Putnam, *In Spite of Innocence* (1992). The original list was published in Hugo Adam Bedau and Michael L. Radelet, "Miscarriages of Justice in Potentially Capital Cases," 40 *Stanford Law Review* 21 (1987). For a critique of that article and a rebuttal, see Stephen J. Markman and Paul G. Cassell, "Protecting the Innocent: A Response to the Bedau-Radelet Study," 41 *Stanford Law Review* 121 (1988), and Hugo Adam Bedau and Michael L. Radelet, "The Myth of Infallibility: A Reply to Markman and Cassell," 41 *Stanford Law Review* 161 (1988).

170 *Nineteen days before Knapp's second scheduled execution:* Injunction Pendente Lite in *Knapp v. Cardwell*, Civ. 78–385 (PHX), signed by Judge Carl A. Muecke, May 12, 1978, relying on *Richmond v. Cardwell*, 450 F. Supp. 519 (D. Ariz. April 21, 1978).

170 *the U.S. Supreme Court struck down an Ohio capital-punishment law": Lockett v. Ohio*, 438 U.S. 586 (July 3, 1978).

170 *the Arizona Supreme Court tried to fix the problem: State v. Watson*, 120 Ariz. 441, 586 P.2d 1253 (1978), *cert. denied*, 440 U.S. 924 (1979).

170 *The stay lasted four years: Knapp v. Cardwell*, 459 U.S. 1055 (November 29, 1982), declining to review 667 F.2d 1253 (9th 1982).

170 *two more defense lawyers:* Deputy public defender Garth Smith and appointed counsel James Hamilton Kemper.

171 *"They were just babes":* RT, May 25, 1979, p. 66.

171 *both affirmed by September 1980: State v. Knapp*, 125 Ariz. 503, 611 P.2d 90 (1979) and 127 Ariz. 65, 618 P.2d 253 (1980).

171 *Description of prison life:* Drawn from prison records; author's visit to the Florence Complex (September 21, 1994); interviews with corrections officers and with Michael Arra, public information officer for the Arizona Department of Corrections; John Knapp, AI, April 22, 1991; and Knapp's recollections as later remembered by defense lawyers or recorded in defense memoranda.

Chapter 12

179 *"Although their statements were not inconsistent": State v. Knapp*, 114 Ariz. 531, 534, 562 P.2d 704, 707.

180 *In early 1982 the federal appellate court: Knapp v. Cardwell*, 667 F.2d 1253 (9th 1982), *cert. denied*, 459 U.S. 1055 (1982).

181 *They were set to proceed at a rate of one per week:* Crane McClennen, "Capital Punishment in Arizona: Past, Present, and Future," *Arizona Attorney*, October 1992, p. 9.

186 *one justice dissenting:* Justice Stanley Feldman.

Chapter 13

The general chronology of Linda's history from 1975 is based primarily on police reports and files concerning Linda Knapp from the Division of Family Services of Utah's Department of Social Services, which includes caseworker logs, correspondence, requests for child-neglect petitions, and juvenile court records. These files were eventually obtained by lawyers for both sides in the Knapp case.

189 *Detective John Panter was staggered:* Panter, police report, August 4, 1977, and Utah juvenile court "minutes" (a summary, not a transcript) of August 23, 1977, hearing.

190 *— You can't take him! —:* AI with Patricia Jensen, corroborated by juvenile court minutes from August 23, 1977.

192 *At about 9:00 P.M. on January 12, 1983:* This account comes from police reports; Officer Roger Van Cleave, RT, April 13, 1984; and AI with Linda Knapp and Daniel's uncle, whose name is being withheld to protect Daniel's identity.

195 *On November 2, Steven Brill . . . visited Linda:* Brill, affidavit, March 9, 1984; Steven Brill, "Innocent Man on Death Row," *American Lawyer* (December 1983); and AI with Brill.

197 *But the next day she got a call from Clifford Hilton:* Based on notations in caseworker Brady's log; Phillip Esplin, RT, May 4, 1984 (about his conversations with Hilton); and AI with Hilton.

200 *"Naturally, our office is loath" and quotations that follow:* RT, November 28, 1983, pp. 16–17.

200 *"Just stop right there" and quotations that follow:* From a tape of the argument provided by the Supreme Court of Arizona. Again, since there is no transcript, it is difficult to identify the justices' voices with certainty. The voice is presumably that of either Chief Justice William Holohan or Justice Jack Hays, since they are the two who ultimately voted to deny the stay.

200 *"With one justice absent, the court split two to two":* Justice James Duke Cameron was absent. Vice Chief Justice Stanley Feldman and Justice Frank Gordon voted for the stay; Chief Justice Holohan and Justice Hays voted against.

200 *"What do you suggest" [and quotations that follow]:* RT, December 2, 1983, pp. 3 and 8.

Chapter 14

203 *Esplin told him that:* Esplin, RT, May 4, 1984, especially pp. 34–41; AI with Campbell and Esplin. Quotations are from Esplin's testimony.

203 *In April 1984, Judge Hendrix heard evidence:* Primarily from transcripts of hearing on April 13, 1984, supplemented by AI with Scarboro, Campbell, Judge Hendrix.

204 *Let's put E. T. over on the desk" [and the quotations and summaries of testimony that follow]:* RT, April 13, 1984, pp. 26, 36, 44, 47, 51.

204 *one justice dissenting:* Justice Stanley Feldman.

204 *Linda had her next fire:* The account of this fire and subsequent events comes, again, from Division of Family Services records, supplemented by Mary Martinez, RT, November 5, 1991, pp. 9–23; and AI with Patricia Jensen.

205 *ninth fire-related incident:* The kitchen fire in Pomona; Iona and Little Linda knocking a candle onto the living room carpet in East Mesa; adult Linda dropping a candle in the bathroom in East Mesa; the fatal fire in East Mesa; the January 1983 fire that burned Daniel in Ogden; the September 1983 mattress fire in Linda's backyard; Daniel singeing his hair playing with matches in September 1983; Lisa's allegedly pouring lamp oil on her bed on November 14, 1983; Daniel's setting the drapes and rug on fire in late June 1984.

Chapter 15

212 *had not had a drink in eighteen months, [etc.]:* Diettrich, RT, March 22, 1985, pp. 96–107.

214 *one justice dissenting:* Justice Stanley Feldman.

215 *Account of the hearing before Judge Belloni:* RT, September 30, 1985, supplemented by

AI with Campbell, Hammond, McClennen, and Smyth. Quotations from the hearing are from pp. 68–71, 89.

Chapter 16

Background information on fire research comes from the testimony of various experts and the articles and videotapes they allude to in their testimony, including defense experts Richard Bright (September 24–25, 1986, and November 5–6, 1991); William Lowry (December 5, 1986, and October 21–22, 1991); Dennis Canfield (October 1, 1986); Richard Custer (November 12–14, 1991); and prosecution expert John DeHaan (August 29, 1990; September 12, 14, 17, 19, 28, 1990; and October 9–10, 15–16, 1991).

223 *That was especially so . . . in a room composed of Sheetrock walls and ceilings:* B.T. Lee, "Effect of Wall and Room Surfaces on the Rates of Heat, Smoke and Carbon Monoxide Production in a Park Lodging Bedroom Fire," February 1985, Report No. NBSIR 85–2998.

223 *In a 1977 test, a single mattress:* Vytenis Babrauskas, "Combustion of Mattresses Exposed to Flaming Ignition Sources," September 1977, Report No. NBSIR 77–1290.

225 *There was also now more documentation:* E.g., Michael J. Karter, Jr., "Patterns of Fire Deaths Among the Elderly and Children in the Home," *Fire Journal* (February 1986), p. 19; Rita Fahy, "Fatal Fires and Unsupervised Children," *Fire Journal* (January 1986), p. 19.

225 *Fire battalion chief Geary Roberts and a deputy sheriff:* Geary Roberts, RT, November 27, 1973 (inquest), p. 93; Lamont Skousen (police report of November 16, 1973), and deposition of August 2, 1974.

228 *it, too, had somehow lost or destroyed its only copies of the Knapp chromatograms:* Jack Strong, RT, October 7, 1986, pp. 43–45.

228 *— . . . couldn't distinguish Coleman fuel from bug spray —:* Based on Canfield's testimony, RT, October 1, 1986, pp. 63–64.

229 *— This is a negative, —:* Same, p. 69, and Canfield affidavit of October 1, 1986.

229 *In his opinion, Strong had perjured himself:* Canfield affidavit of October 1, 1986.

229 *"I would not make a determination" [and quotations that follow]:* Strong, RT, October 7, 1986, pp. 43, 52–53.

230 *Footnote: Prosecutor Hyder opposed any retesting by the defense, just as he had . . . since 1974:* E.g., RT, October 15, 1974, pp. 41–42; RT, June 2, 1978, hearing on defense motion for scientific analysis; Hyder's memorandum "in opposition to defendant's motion to allow scientific analysis of evidence" of September 8, 1978; Judge Hardy's memorandum order of December 8, 1978; Hyder's motion for rehearing of January 4, 1979; Judge Hardy's memorandum order of January 10, 1979.

230 *Footnote: Defense expert Parsons then testified . . . that he could draw no conclusions:* Parsons, RT, May 25, 1979, pp. 30, 33–34, 35.

230 *Footnote: If, however, one were to hypothesize:* Same, pp. 7–11, 20, 25, 28, 30, 32, 35.

230 *But, when asked directly, state experts would concede that what did remain of that chro-*

matogram was not a match: See, e.g., John DeHaan, RT, August 29, 1990, p. 83; RT, October 9, 1991 (P.M.), pp. 41–42; RT, October 15, 1991, pp. 110–111.

231   *Chief Roberts's testimony:* RT, October 2, 1986, pp. 48, 85, 122–123. (Compare RT, October 24, 1974, p. 118.)

231   *Deputy fire marshal Dale . . . now claimed to have understood . . . But he could not account:* RT, September 30, 1986, p. 56; October 6, 1986, pp. 30–41, 66–67.

231   *Dale's voluble memory:* Compare RT, October 6, 1986, pp. 125–126 (and RT, September 30, 1986, p. 69) with RT, August 28, 1974, pp. 2–4.

232   *Medical examiner Heinz Karnitschnig was adamant:* Karnitschnig, RT, October 2, 1986, pp. 19–20.

232   *"It's very nice to have these":* Same, p. 35.

Chapter 17

242   *"There was never a period":* Twist, AI.

242   *Ray Girdler's case: State v. Girdler,* 138 Ariz. 482, 675 P.2d 1301 (1983).

243   *the Knapp children may have been* beaten unconscious: Dale, RT, in *State v. Girdler,* July 2, 1982, pp. 67–68, as quoted in Knapp's second motion to amend petition for post-conviction relief, filed on February 16, 1984, and in the state's response to that motion, filed on March 15, 1984. See also Dale's affidavit, May 22, 1984.

245   *The evidence against Girdler:* Relying on J. W. Casserly, "An Innocent Man?" *New Times,* August 22–28, 1990, p. 22; and the September 20, 1991, report of John J. Lentini, an expert appointed by and for the court in *State v. Girdler.*

247   *In fact, he could identify only one: State of New Jersey v. Loretta Ruvolo,* Superior Court of New Jersey, Ocean County, Indictment No. 57-1-85, testimony of October 22, 1986.

248   *An innocent, unaccelerated fire would have taken far too long . . . probably from a half-hour to an hour:* RT, September 28, 1990, pp. 47–49.

248   *the room may have never reached flashover conditions at all:* RT, September 12, 1990, pp. 28, 64; September 19, 1990, p. 57.

249   *neither the nylon carpet nor the butyl rubber pad could have . . . contributed significantly to the fire:* RT, September 12, 1990, p. 26; September 14, 1990, p. 11; September 28, 1990, pp. 53–54. Also, DeHaan's draft Physical Evidence Examination Report of June 26, 1991, p. 9.

249   *that a number of types of burn damage . . . could have been produced only by flammable liquids:* E.g., RT, September 12, 1990, pp. 52, 54, 98, 111–114; September 14, 1990, p. 11; September 19, 1990, p. 59.

249   *After spending thirty-eight hours:* RT, September 17, 1990, p. 71.

249   *Susan Sherwin:* Sherwin declined to be interviewed but did respond to a few questions posed to her in writing; biographical information about her comes primarily from her testimony of July 9, 1991, and AI with DeHaan and Powell.

250   *Footnote: a July 1991 magazine article:* Roger Parloff, "They Still Want to Kill Him," *American Lawyer,* July-August 1991, p. 80.

251 *polyurethane foam "saw virtually no use" in upholstered materials until about 1973:* De-Haan, RT, August 29, 1990, p. 111.

251 *"Polyurethane foam started to be used commercially . . . to any extent . . . from* approximately the mid-1960s": Damant, TI by defense, August 30, 1991, p. 5. While polyurethane was being used in mattresses from the mid-1960s, if not earlier, its use greatly expanded in the early 1970s, when the state of California and, later, the federal government began requiring that mattresses meet minimum standards of resistance to smoldering cigarettes — the most common cause of mattress fires. Since polyurethane pads resisted *smoldering* ignition, most manufacturers began to use it at that point. Ironically, however, polyurethane is highly flammable when touched with an open flame (Damant, AI).

251 *"There may well have been polyurethane":* Dale, RT, August 29, 1974, p. 46.

252 *In a scathing report:* Lentini's "Evaluation of Evidence and Proceedings Prepared for the Court," September 20, 1991; quotations from pp. 9, 18–19.

254 *Footnote: were in fact "well nourished":* Karnitschnig's Postmortem Examination and Reports for Linda Louise Knapp and Iona Marie Knapp, November 1973 (page 2 in each report).

254 *"some many minutes":* DeHaan, RT, September 12, 1990, p. 68.

256 *"[Knapp] advised":* Malone, RT, August 6, 1974, p. 21.

257 *And what the burn patterns showed, DeHaan had testified in 1990 and 1991, was that the door had been* closed *or* nearly closed *during the early stages of the fire:* E.g, RT, September 12, 1990, p. 119; September 28, 1990, pp. 25–27; October 9, 1991, pp. 62–63.

Chapter 18

Information about Knapp's life in freedom comes from Knapp, AI, April 22, 1991; 1994 AI with Knapp's brother Bob and sister "Marilyn"; his employment records (which were subpoenaed by defense lawyers); and AI with five co-workers.

261 *"As you have previously requested, I will advise you":* Letter from Susan M. Sherwin to Larry Hammond, February 20, 1990.

266 *In Alabama, for instance:* From Stephen B. Bright, *supra*, 103 *Yale Law Journal*, at 1853, and footnote 103.

Chapter 19

271 *"While it is not the defendant's fault":* RT, August 30, 1990, p. 18.

272 *"Nylon doesn't burn all that well":* DeHaan, RT, September 14, 1990, p. 12.

273 *"The only kind of localized fuel":* Same, September 17, 1990, p. 129.

273 *DeHaan saw many burn patterns in the room that could* only *have been caused by flammable liquids:* E.g., same, September 12, 1990, p. 122; September 14, 1990, pp. 8–9; September 17, 1990, pp. 20–21, 34; September 19, 1990, p. 59.

273 *"Well, anywhere from, say, three ounces to as much as a gallon"*: Same, September 17, 1990, pp. 13–14.

275 *"I conducted a visual comparison"*: September 28, 1990, p. 117.

276 *DeHaan had . . . never measured . . . precisely how much Coleman fuel he used in his accelerated tests:* Same, pp. 123–124, 145–146.

276 *DeHaan did not know whether there had been any burn patterns left on the floor after his first Coleman fuel test:* Same, p. 142.

277 *DeHaan testified that he "noted a good correlation":* Same, p. 177.

277 *"You took out the carpet and the pad" and quotations that follow:* Same, pp. 177–179.

278 *"Was the floor examined" and DeHaan's response:* Same, p. 199.

Chapter 20

280 *Linda had remembered this conversation only sketchily:* RT, August 7, 1974, pp. 17–19; August 26, 1974, pp. 39–40; November 13, 1974, p. 56.

280 *He stressed that Knapp never told . . . Ken Ramsey either of those reasons:* Kenneth Ramsey, RT, August 7, 1974, pp. 8–9, 12; August 21, 1974, pp. 89–91, 94; November 12, 1974, pp. 58–60; Hyder's cross-examination of John Knapp, RT, August 7, 1974, p. 63; August 27, 1974, pp. 92–94; November 14, 1974, pp. 68–70; Hyder's closing argument, RT, November 18, 1974, pp. 63–64. See also, state's response (by Hyder) to defendant's petition to vacate the conviction, March 3, 1978 (making this argument at length).

281 *the first "friendly face":* RT, November 18, 1974, pp. 63–64.

281 *The Arizona Supreme Court had expressly cited that argument:* State v. Knapp, 114 Ariz. 531, 538–539, 562 P. 2d, at 711–712.

282 *— It seems like they might have taped over it at some point, — :* According to an internal defense memorandum by Hammond on December 7, 1990, documenting a conversation with Sherwin on December 6, 1990.

282 *From electronic analysis . . . Hammond learned:* Anthony Pellicano, RT, June 18, 1991, pp. 51–75, 94.

283 *by Hyder's assistants:* That is, Detective Ashford on one occasion; Corporal Carnes — the deputy assigned to assist Hyder with videotaping on the Knapp case — on all other occasions.

283 *Then, at 7:50 P.M.:* Anthony Pellicano, RT, June 19, 1991 (A.M.), pp. 14–25.

Chapter 21

287 *The meeting on January 8, 1991:* Drawn from AI with Hammond, Sands, Henze, Heller, and Popko.

291 *"I'm going to try cases myself":* John Winters, "ENSCO Changes Sought by Woods," *Arizona Republic*, January 8, 1991, p. B1.

291 *he fired eleven attorneys and an investigator:* John Winters, "Woods Ousts 12 from Office, Including Bolles Prosecutor," *Arizona Republic,* January 9, 1991, p. B2.

292 *"I was approached regarding going to work":* Letter from Susan Sherwin to the author, dated May 12, 1994.

293 *"I . . . completely turned over the Knapp file":* Same.

293 *Footnote:* DeHaan also believed that he could tell, by examining photographs of the fire scene, that the eyewitnesses at that scene (battalion chief Geary Roberts and deputy sheriff Lamont Skousen) had been mistaken in thinking that Little Linda had crawled under the mattress for protection. DeHaan proposed that when the fire began Little Linda had been lying on the mattress or on the floor next to the bed — but not underneath it. He then proposed that the mattress had slid off the bed when two of the bed's legs collapsed and had wound up on top of Little Linda. (E.g., RT, September 12, 1990, pp. 63, 130.) However, Chief Roberts had testified that Little Linda's body was not only under the mattress, but under the *"entire bed."* Roberts, RT, November 27, 1973 (inquest), p. 93.

297 *The meeting at the attorney general's office:* Based on AI with Hammond, Sands, Henze, and Powell.

Chapter 22

300 *The Weyerhaeuser tests:* This account is based on the written reports, photographs, and videotapes generated by the Weyerhaeuser Fire Technology Laboratory; trial testimony of Marshall Smyth and Richard Custer; the author's visit to the Weyerhaeuser facility; and AI with Hammond, Smyth, Custer, Jim White, and three other members of the Weyerhaeuser crew.

307 *They burned one cotton-sisal crib mattress alone:* This account is a simplification, with the sequence changed for clarity. Four mattress tests were conducted in the following order: two cotton-sisal mattresses with carpeting beneath them; one cotton-sisal mattress alone; and one polyurethane mattress alone.

310 *One by one he checked off Dale's hallmarks:* After the test, on videotape, Custer walked through the fire residue and pointed out such damage. See also, Custer, RT, November 13, 1991, e.g., pp. 50–63, 85–88, 104.

311 *DeHaan's predictions had also been savaged:* Same, pp. 50–53, 59, 62, 65, 67–68, 71–72, 75, 77, 99, 100–103, 105.

Chapter 23

317 *Knapp's "hand print stayed with that child for two weeks":* Louise Ramsey, SE, September 24, 1974.

320 *As soon as Judge Campbell read it, he saw it as his ethical obligation to file a bar complaint against Hyder, and did:* AI with Hammond, who said he infers that Campbell filed it from Campbell's comments to him. Campbell declined comment.

320 *Hyder hired a prominent civil lawyer, Donald Daughton:* Brent Whiting, "Legal Help Requested for Ex-Prosecutor," *Arizona Republic*, May 10, 1991, p. B2; Mike Padgett, "Ex-Prosecutor's Defense Fund Boosted," *Phoenix Gazette*, October 6, 1992, p. A4.

Chapter 24

322 *"camp lantern fuel had been doused on the rug":* "Father Held in Daughters' Fire Death," *Arizona Republic*, November 29, 1973, p. A1.

323 *"To the best of my recollection":* Hyder, TI, March 8, 1991, p. 109.

324 *"Chuck Diettrich . . . is a convicted felon":* RT, July 18, 1991 (P.M.), pp. 42–44.

324 *Hyder said at first . . . that he vividly recalled turning over the copy to Diettrich:* Same, pp. 32–34.

324 *At that point Hyder testified that he recalled having handed the tape over to* Basham: RT, July 10, 1991, pp. 123, 134–138.

324 *Footnote: He repeatedly took this position:* RT, July 9, 1974, pp. 72–74; November 14, 1974, pp. 19–20.

324 *(The chief investigator in the case, detective Malone, testified . . . that he never knew about the tape):* Malone, RT, June 19, 1991, pp. 95–98, 106–107.

324 *Footnote: "He took this position":* RT, August 22, 1974 (A.M.), p. 22.

325 *Footnote: "My recollection is that the statement was mailed":* RT, July 11, 1991, p. 31.

326 *(There were no signs that either can had been handled by cloth or gloves.):* AI with William Watling. Watling said that cloth often leaves impressions; it was standard procedure to note such impressions if observed, and none were noted on either report.

326 *investigators took his* palm *prints — which was not routine:* Watling, RT, July 17, 1991, pp. 48–49.

327 *There were serious flaws in Zettler's logic, however, and it was at least as likely that the reports were never turned over due to simple administrative oversight:* The two fingerprint analyses that turned up identifiable prints — unlike the one performed on the *full* can, which really *did* have smudged prints — were performed by the state Department of Public Safety at the request of inspector McDaniel of the Scottsdale Fire Department. (The full can had, by contrast, been analyzed by the sheriff's office itself.) Accordingly, when the Department of Public Safety finished its analyses, it would have sent the reports back to the fire department, not to the sheriff's office or to the county attorney. (Zettler, TI, March 7, 1991, pp. 47–48.)

While most of the police reports generated by the sheriff's office appear to have been provided promptly to the prosecutor — who could, then, turn them over to the defense lawyers — many photographs and reports generated by the fire department were not provided to the prosecutor until many months later — if at all. (E.g., RT, August 8, 1974, pp. 12–16; August 22, 1974 [A.M.], pp. 22–23.) Similarly, the reports of firefighters Monty Brow, Gary Hopkins, Roy Skowron, and John Wilson — though written in November 1973 — do not appear to have been turned over to the defense as of April 1974, since their names do not appear on a list of the state's prospective witnesses that was filed at that point, and Basham protested during the trial that those firemen's reports had never been turned over at all. (RT, August 14, 1974, p. 41.)

In addition, the critical disputed fingerprint reports — the ones that were sent to DPS by the fire department — were located in a different part of the prosecution's files from the one fingerprint report performed by the sheriff's office. When investigator Debora Schwartz, of the state attorney general's office, first began looking for all the fingerprint reports in early 1990, she readily found the one performed by the sheriff's office among the police reports in the prosecution's files. (Schwartz, RT, July 9, 1991, pp. 142–145.) She could *not*, however, locate either of the now disputed DPS fingerprint reports in those files. Instead, she had to obtain copies of those reports from DPS itself. Later, copies of those two reports *were* found in Hyder's personal trial folders within the prosecution's files.

In March 1991 Hammond interviewed former justice court prosecutor Hugo Zettler, who was still a deputy county attorney. At that time Zettler said that procedures at the justice court in the early 1970s were not as "efficient" as they were today and that fingerprint reports were not always sent directly to the prosecutor. Even though he knew he had elicited hearsay testimony about the fingerprints from fire inspector McDaniel at the inquest on November 27, 1973 — to establish that there were no children's prints found on the cans — Zettler told Hammond that he could not say whether or not he had ever possessed the fingerprint reports himself during the period that he handled the case. (Zettler, TI, March 7, 1991, pp. 13, 47–50.)

By the time he testified at the misconduct hearings, however, Zettler had refreshed his recollection during two evening preparation sessions at his friend Hyder's home. By that time he had examined more documents and had come to feel certain, he said, that he turned over the fingerprint reports at a court appearance on December 4, 1973. He could deduce that fact, he testified, from seeing that he had included the fingerprint experts' names among a list of prospective witnesses he had provided to the defense at that time. Based on office policy, Zettler said, he was certain that he would have listed their names only if he had had their reports; and if he had had them, he would have turned them over.

Another long-time friend of Hyder's and Zettler's, Rodger Golston, provided further support for their position. Golston, who had been the administrative deputy county attorney in late 1973, executed an affidavit in 1991 stating that he, too, believed, based on office policy, that the fingerprint reports must have been turned over.

But office policy may not have been so dispositive as Hyder, Zettler, and Golston maintained. In an interview with the author Golston acknowledged that the office policy was merely to list the witnesses that the prosecutor knew he would be calling. There was, therefore, no reason not to list fingerprint analysts whom the prosecutor knew would be witnesses, even if he had not yet physically received copies of their reports.

Hyder and his allies also focused on a document known as a "filing summary checklist" filled out by detective Robert Barrett before the original complaint against Knapp was filed on November 30, 1973. In that document Barrett had checked the box indicating that all laboratory reports were "complete." Hyder, his lawyers, and allies argued that the document proved that the fingerprint reports must have already been in the prosecutor's file on December 4, 1973, when Zettler turned over many of those documents to Basham.

The checklist, however, is not much to go on. Many of its other assertions are unquestionably false. The checklist also indicates, for instance, that "all DRs" — i.e., police reports — were completed, when, in fact, they were not. (Zettler wrote in the case log four days later, "I did not have all DRs when I filed," and, "[Defense] had copies of our DR — not all, only ones I had on this date.") Barrett also checked boxes indicating that all witnesses had been interviewed and that no supplementary police reports were contemplated — statements that were clearly wrong. Finally, the checklist indicated that there had been no "electronic surveillance of defendant's conversations," when in fact Knapp's telephone conversation with Linda had been secretly taped.

Detective Barrett, who filled out the checklist, was only briefly and peripherally involved in the case. He dismissed the checklist as a document of no consequence when Hammond interviewed him about it in late February 1991, and said he doubted he did any investigation of the case before filling it out.

328 *"There are no fingerprints on the cans other than adult prints":* RT, August 6, 1974, p. 88.

328 *"Mr. Diettrich's theory of the case . . . and his appreciation of the evidence is much different than mine":* Same, p. 89.

328 *At the 1991 misconduct hearings Hyder conceded that he had known that Diettrich was telling the judge incorrect information, but he claimed that his own response had set Judge Hardy straight:* RT, July 10, 1991, pp. 17, 20, 28–31.

328 *"And you found no fingerprints on the can you could identify?":* Watling, RT, August 15, 1974, p. 38.

328 *he claimed to see nothing wrong with Watling's answer:* Hyder, RT, July 10, 1991, pp. 35–36.

328 *Hyder and Diettrich entered into a* stipulation: RT, October 31, 1974, pp. 172–174.

329 *In 1974 in Arizona, to commit or suborn perjury:* A.R.S. ʃ13–572. See also Crane McClennen, "Capital Punishment in Arizona," *supra,* pp. 3–5.

329 *The fingerprint experts must have mistakenly told him:* Hyder, TI, March 8, 1991, pp. 47–52.

330 *"I'm not sure exactly what happened":* Hyder, RT, July 10, 1991, pp. 42–43; see also, pp. 17 and 20.

330 *Martone sought an answer from the state's witnesses:* Hyder, RT, July 17, 1991, pp. 184–188; Joseph Howe, pp. 141–150.

331 *"Do you have an opinion as to why":* Howe, RT, July 17, 1991, p. 146.

331 *That truth was finally volunteered:* Testimony of John Jolly and Carey Chapman, June 27, 1991.

331 *Though prosecutor Susan Sherwin had known about this information:* Sherwin, RT, July 9, 1991, pp. 120–125.

Chapter 25

335 *"What level of detail":* RT, June 17, 1991, p. 156.

335 *What had gone wrong was that:* Judge Martone, AI.

336 *Sands's visits with John Knapp:* This account is drawn from defense memorandums Sands and other defense lawyers drew up shortly after their visits with Knapp; AI with Knapp in jail (with Sands present), April 22, 1991; from AI with Sands in 1993; and the author's visit to the jail in September 1994. Conversations between Sands and Knapp are drawn from defense memorandums.

341 *Roger Coleman's case: Coleman v. Thompson,* 501 U.S. 722 (1991).

342 *In 1968 the U.S. Supreme Court expressed concern: Witherspoon v. Illinois,* 391 U.S. 510 (1968).

343 *In 1986, after such studies had been performed: Lockhart v. McCree,* 476 U.S. 162 (1986); Welsh S. White, *The Death Penalty in the Nineties,* Chapter 9 (1991).

Chapter 26

345 *Footnote: One study, for instance:* Paul Schwartzman, RT, November 12, 1991, pp. 61–75.

345 *The theory of Hyder's case in 1974:* E.g., RT (Malone's testimony), October 31, 1974, pp. 165–167 ("no doubt in my mind that John Knapp done exactly what he said he done," etc.).

345 *Hyder had even argued that one of the ways:* RT (Hyder's argument), November 18, 1974, pp. 62–63, 174–175; RT (Malone's testimony), October 31, 1974, pp. 156–159, 165–167; RT (Dale's testimony), November 15, 1974, pp. 26–30, 33.

346 *In 1991 fire inspector James McDaniel:* RT, September 26, 1991, pp. 67–69.

346 *"We read you a long list of names" [and following quotations]:* RT, September 12, 1991 (state's opening), pp. 3–4, 7–8, 21–22, 25, 27.

349 *"You have to analyze the words" [and following quotations]:* RT, September 12, 1991 (defendant's opening), pp. 4, 52.

Chapter 27

Portions of the 1991 trial were videotaped by the Courtroom Television Network (Court TV). Citations to those tapes refer to the approximate time of day when the testimony occurred, according to Court TV's timecoded videotape.

350 *The first . . . was that she did tell Hyder or his investigator:* Summary of Interviews

for Prosecution Evaluation, Debora Schwartz, July 20, 1990, p. 16 (told Hyder or Elardo); Burr, TI with defense investigator Mary Durand, September 18, 1990 (told "Hyder and Elardo both").

351 *But Hyder and Elardo vehemently denied this version:* Elardo, TI, May 30, 1991, pp. 44–46; Hyder, RT, July 18, 1991, p. 62.

351 *The second was that two men . . . told her the confession was inadmissible hearsay:* RT, September 24, 1991, pp. 74–87.

351 *Burr's third theory:* Same, pp. 87–88.

351 *"You've got to go to court":* TI, June 5, 1991, p. 62.

351 *Louise told her that she did not:* Same, p. 61.

352 *"Melba was just being Melba, and joking":* RT, September 25, 1991, p. 43.

352 *that is why he decided not to ask her about having seen Little Linda light matches even though he knew all about that statement!:* White's theory is that Diettrich was so eager to get Burr off the stand that he did not ask questions on cross-examination, fearful that they would give Hyder an opportunity to do a redirect examination, during which the confession might come out. But the theory makes no sense, since Diettrich *did* ask questions on cross-examination — at both the first and second trials — and Hyder *did* in fact do redirect examinations of Burr at each trial.

In fact, at one point during the second trial, when Diettrich became frustrated with Burr's having testified to something she had not mentioned at the first, Diettrich asked her sarcastically, "Anything else new this time you can think of that you want to throw in?" (RT, October 29, 1974, p. 60.) It is not the sort of question Diettrich would be expected to ask if Burr had once told him that Knapp had confessed to her.

352 *Officer Chernko . . . now remembered:* VT, October 2, 1991 (2:42).

353 *Similarly, in 1991 Louise Ramsey remembered John having laughed:* RT, September 25, 1991, p. 23; TI, August 26, 1991, p. 28.

353 *And neurologist Urrea had testified without rebuttal:* RT, August 21, 1974, p. 75; RT, November 6, 1974, p. 119.

354 *"medically retired":* RT (Strong), October 1, 1991, p. 4.

354 *He told his employer at the time:* RT, September 5, 1991, pp. 111–116.

354 *"Is there any doubt in your mind":* RT, October 1, 1991, p. 29.

355 *that a sample of Coleman fuel that had been through an intense fire ought to look* different *from a sample of "unweathered" Coleman fuel:* Same, pp. 71–72, 97.

355 *sample of fire debris containing both solvent (methylene chloride) and Coleman fuel that had been through an intense fire ought to look* very different *from a sample containing just pure, unweathered Coleman fuel:* Same, pp. 74, 83, 85, 96–98.

355 *I am almost in a state of total confusion":* Same, p. 99.

355 *"can't happen":* Same, p. 109.

356 *"Has anything Mr. Hammond has said to you today made you doubt":* Same, pp. 148–149.

356 *Footnote:* The state's fire expert, DeHaan, also vouched in a general way for two of Strong's chromatograms, stating that, based on his memory, they resembled the

sorts of chromatograms he was getting during that period for light petroleum distillates that he had analyzed using similar techniques. (He could not produce any chromatograms he had made during that period using similar techniques, however.)

DeHaan did not address at trial either of the problems with Strong's chromatograms that made them, in the context of the case, seemingly impossible: the fact that the residues appearing in the chromatograms showed no evidence of having been through a fire, and the fact that the chromatograms showed no trace of the methylene chloride solvent used to extract the residues.

Chapter 28

359 *"Over the past 16 years":* RT, October 9, 1991, p. 7.

360 *"That's one of the most unusual features":* Same, p. 28.

360 *"Let me make sure I understand":* Same, pp. 47–48.

360 *Deputy fire marshal David Dale had considered that area so severely burned:* RT, August 16, 1974, pp. 103–104; August 19, 1974, p. 25; August 29, 1974, p. 29; October 29, 1974, p. 95.

361 *"Did you yourself do any full-scale duplication":* RT, October 9, 1991, p. 40.

361 *"Are you aware that some of those kinds of tests":* Same.

363 *"In the Knapp household, sir, there was some damage":* Same, pp. 63–64.

363 *"This test confirms a number of tests that I have conducted":* Same, p. 65.

363 *"Why wasn't it burned away":* Same, p. 67.

364 *"the Knapp fire had burned for at least ten minutes and possibly as long as twenty-five":* One neighbor, who said she had looked at a clock, said it was 8:10 when she first noticed the fire. (Susan Webb, RT, August 14, 1974, p. 93.) Fire department records show that firefighters received the alarm at 8:28, arrived at the Knapp residence at 8:30, and put the fire out by 8:34.

    Based on the fire damage, expert John DeHaan estimated that the fire had lasted about fifteen minutes, plus or minus five minutes. RT, September 17, 1990, p. 121; RT, September 28, 1990, pp. 40–41.

365 *"Do you remember giving those answers":* RT, October 10, 1991, p. 10.

366 *He no longer believed:* E.g., same, pp. 10, 19, 45, 58, 60, 63, 66; VT, October 15, 1991 (9:40–10:00 A.M.).

366 *"possibly three or four minutes" or more:* RT, October 10, 1991, p. 97.

Chapter 29

371 *"Mr. Knapp, you will lie if you think it helps you":* VT, October 24, 1991 (10:15).

372 *"You knew that synthetic clothes":* Same (10:44).

373 *"I guess you would say it was a lie" [and following quotations]:* Same (11:14–11:30).

374 *"Mr. Knapp, of the people on that list"*: Same (2:31).

375 *The Thai Buddhist temple incident*: See, for instance, Roger Parloff, "False Confessions," *American Lawyer*, May 1993, p. 58.

376 *a neighbor's recollection of seeing the children run to John Knapp*: Valerie Rowley, TI by prosecution, September 5, 1991, p. 15; AI.

377 *"Had this [test] fire continued another minute or two"*: RT, November 13, 1991, p. 76.

378 *As for the area in front of the door"*: Same, pp. 78–85.

378 *"You can use it . . . to test this witness's opinions"*: RT, November 14, 1991, p. 36.

379 *"And you saw tests, sir"*: Same, pp. 29–30.

379 *"Just opening that door just an inch"*: Same, p. 43.

379 *"And if the door is left open"*: Same, p. 45.

Chapter 30

383 *"In the history of the courthouse"*: RT, November 13, 1991, p. 54.

383 *As the twelve jurors seated themselves*: The account of jury deliberations is drawn from interviews with eight of the twelve deliberating jurors: Cheryl, Dolores, Gary, Gladys, Jadean, Jim, Sunny, and one juror who requested anonymity. (The four alternates were also interviewed.)

Since the jurors were interviewed in early 1993, thirteen to fifteen months after deliberations ended, their memories were imperfect, and the sequence of events presented is approximate. The only reliable mileposts for much of it were the notes that the jurors sent out to the judge, which were timed and dated.

391 *"I was never good at puzzles"*: RT, December 2, 1991, p. 34.

392 *"You don't have to believe each part of the confession"*: Same, p. 32.

392 *"You have to be unanimous that he caused the fire"*: Same.

Chapter 31

394 *Defending Knapp in 1991 alone*: According to the firm's administrator, Richard Zwemke.

394 *"All the lawyers involved in the case" [and quotations that follow]*: RT, December 5, 1991, pp. 1–6.

395 *He had spent 14 years and 159 days in custody*: These numbers are 28 days higher than those contained in a stipulation between defense lawyers and prosecutors entered on November 18, 1992. The stipulation appears to have omitted 12 days Knapp spent in custody in 1987 (after his release was ordered by the superior court but before it took effect) and 16 days he spent in custody in Pittsburgh in 1990 (between his July 25 arrest and his arrival in Arizona on August 10).

399 *"Knapp should have been executed a long time ago"*: Pamela Manson, "Woods Fought Death Penalty as a Lawyer, Now Backs It," *Arizona Republic*, March 17, 1992, p. B3.

400 *— Time served. No contest. No probation . . . —*: From a defense memorandum.

Source Notes

400 *"We are light-years apart" and information contained in the following paragraph:* "Talks Fail in Plea Bid for Knapp," *Arizona Republic*, May 7, 1992, p. B4.

401 *— I was up $500 at one point, but I lost it all, — :* From a defense memorandum.

402 *Footnote: Professors Bedau and Radelet, in compiling:* Hugo Adam Bedau and Michael L. Radelet, *supra*, 40 *Stanford Law Review*, at 55.

403 *"I could never plead guilty to a charge":* VT (press pool), November 19, 1992.

ACKNOWLEDGMENTS

This book could not have been written without the assistance of many people.

Steven Brill, the editor in chief of *The American Lawyer* magazine, enabled me to write this book by permitting me to remain on staff at that magazine on various makeshift schedules for the better part of three years. Steve, who is not best known for flexibility or patience, was a model of both in this instance. I also thank Steve for his editorial suggestions on the manuscript and, indeed, for introducing me to the Knapp case in the first place, by assigning me, in 1990 and 1991, to look into the then-breaking developments in it. (As discussed in the book, Steve's own 1983 *American Lawyer* article about the Knapp case altered the way lawyers on both sides viewed the case ever after.)

While I am indebted to everyone who agreed to be interviewed, Larry Hammond and Jon Sands are owed special thanks. They were especially generous with their time, and their cooperation was essential. I also owe special thanks to those prosecutors who cooperated with me — Crane McClennen, David Powell, and David White.

All members of the Phoenix law firm then known as Meyer, Hendricks, Victor, Osborn & Maledon deserve thanks, since the firm permitted me to do a great deal of research at their offices. While that firm broke up in May 1995, most of its members remain at one of two successor firms: Osborn Maledon or Meyer, Hendricks, Victor, Ruffner & Bivens. (Larry Hammond and Deborah Heller are now with Osborn Maledon; Jon Sands and Sigmund Popko are with the federal public defender's office in Phoenix.) I am especially grateful to firm administrator Richard Zwemke (now with the new Meyer, Hendricks) and to the paralegals and secretaries who assisted me in finding what I needed, especially Debbie Heller, Joann Jacobs, Sarah Molinsky, and Terri Gniewkowski. (To enable me to use its photocopying machines, the firm assigned me a client number, and I then reimbursed the firm at its ordinary rates.)

In the process of paring this book down to manageable size, I have omitted mention of many people who played very important roles in the Knapp case. Among them are defense investigators Mary Durand and Eloi Ysasi, who were crucial members of the defense team from 1990 to 1991, and Randall Nelson (now of Osborn Maledon), who chaired Meyer, Hendrick's pro bono committee during much of the Knapp case. I would like to thank them in advance for graciously tolerating my failure adequately to acknowledge their contributions in the text.

I owe great thanks to my editors, Jim Silberman and Catherine Crawford, for their excellent advice, to copyeditors Faith Hanson and Betty Power for their time and care with the manuscript, and to my agent, Jane Gelfman, for her assistance and thoughts at every stage.

Eric M. Freedman, a death-penalty specialist and professor at Hofstra University School of Law, kindly agreed to read the manuscript in an effort to help me avoid legal errors, and wound up offering very good editorial suggestions while he was at it. My mother, Gloria, gave the manuscript a thorough copyediting, and both she and my father, Morris, made very helpful, more global suggestions as well.

Caroline Bowyer, the art director at *The American Lawyer*, deserves thanks for her volunteer work preparing the handsome diagrams of the Knapp house and the children's bedroom.

While in Phoenix, I received great moral and logistical support from my friends Linda Vance; Sharon and Michael White and their children, Lexi, Kelsey, and Tres; Jon Sands, his wife, Joyce Grossman, and their daughter Madeline. Back in New York I was the beneficiary of like support from my brother Mike, my sister-in-law, In-Mo, and my nephew Eugene; my friends Mark and Suzi Kaminsky; Stephen O'Donnell and Maria Pope; and Ellen Joan Pollock.